Lecture Notes in Computer Science 8555

Commenced Publication in 1973
Founding and Former Series Editors:
Gerhard Goos, Juris Hartmanis, and Jan van Leeuwen

T0236541

Emiliano De Cristofaro   Steven J. Murdoch (Eds.)

Privacy Enhancing Technologies

14th International Symposium, PETS 2014
Amsterdam, The Netherlands, July 16-18, 2014
Proceedings

Springer

Volume Editors

Emiliano De Cristofaro
University College London, Department of Computer Science
Gower Street, London WC1E 6BT, UK
E-mail: e.decristofaro@ucl.ac.uk

Steven J. Murdoch
University of Cambridge, Computer Laboratory
15 JJ Thomson Avenue, Cambridge CB3 0FD, UK
E-mail: steven.murdoch@cl.cam.ac.uk

ISSN 0302-9743   e-ISSN 1611-3349
ISBN 978-3-319-08505-0   e-ISBN 978-3-319-08506-7
DOI 10.1007/978-3-319-08506-7
Springer Cham Heidelberg New York Dordrecht London

Library of Congress Control Number: 2014941760

LNCS Sublibrary: SL 4 – Security and Cryptology

Typesetting: Camera-ready by author, data conversion by Scientific Publishing Services, Chennai, India

Printed on acid-free paper

Springer is part of Springer Science+Business Media (www.springer.com)

Preface

Either through a deliberate desire for surveillance or an accidental consequence of design, there are a growing number of systems and applications that record and process sensitive information. As a result, the role of privacy-enhancing technologies becomes increasingly crucial, whether adopted by individuals to avoid intrusion in their private life, or by system designers to offer protection to their users.

The 14th Privacy Enhancing Technologies Symposium (PETS 2014) addressed the need for better privacy by bringing together experts in privacy and systems research, cryptography, censorship resistance, and data protection, facilitating the collaboration needed to tackle the challenges faced in designing and deploying privacy technologies.

There were 86 papers submitted to PETS 2014, which were all assigned to be reviewed by at least four members of the Program Committee (PC). Following intensive discussion among the reviewers, other PC members, and external experts, 16 papers were accepted for presentation, one of which was the result of two merged submissions. Topics addressed by the papers published in these proceedings include study of privacy erosion, designs of privacy-preserving systems, censorship resistance, social networks, and location privacy. PETS continues to widen its scope by appointing PC members with more diverse areas of expertise and encouraging the submission of high-quality papers outside of the topics traditionally forming the PETS program.

We also continue to host the one-day Workshop on Hot Topics on Privacy Enhancing Technologies (HotPETs), now in its seventh year. This venue encourages the lively discussion of exciting but possibly preliminary ideas. The HotPETS keynote was given by William Binney, a prominent whistleblower and advocate for privacy, previously employed by the US National Security Agency. As with previous years there are no published proceedings for HotPETs, allowing authors to refine their work based on feedback received and subsequently publish it at a future PETS or elsewhere.

PETS also included a keynote by Martin Ortlieb (a social anthropologist and senior user experience researcher at Google), a panel discussing surveillance, and a rump session with brief presentations on a variety of topics. This year, PETS was co-located with the First Workshop on Genome Privacy, which set out to explore the privacy challenges faced by advances in genomics.

We would like to thank all the PETS and HotPETs authors, especially those who presented their work that was selected for the program, as well as the rump session presenters, keynote speakers, and panelists. We are very grateful to the PC members and additional reviewers, who contributed to editorial decisions with thorough reviews and actively participated in the PC discussions, ensuring a high quality of all accepted papers. We owe special thanks to the following

PC members and reviewers who volunteered to shepherd some of the accepted papers: Kelly Caine, Claude Castelluccia, Roberto Di Pietro, Claudia Diaz, Paolo Gasti, Amir Houmansadr, Rob Jansen, Negar Kiyavash, Micah Sherr, and Reza Shokri.

We gratefully acknowledge the outstanding contributions of the PETS 2014 general chair, Hinde ten Berge, and publicity chair, Carmela Troncoso, as well as the PETS webmaster of eight years, Jeremy Clark. Moreover, our gratitude goes to the HotPETs 2014 chairs, Kelly Caine, Prateek Mittal, and Reza Shokri who put together an excellent program. Last but not least, we would like to thank our sponsors, Google, Silent Circle, and the Privacy & Identity Lab, for their generous support, as well as Microsoft for its continued sponsorship of the PET award and travel stipends.

May 2014
Emiliano De Cristofaro
Steven J. Murdoch

Organization

Program Committee

Alessandro Acquisti	Carnegie Mellon University, USA
Erman Ayday	EPFL, Switzerland
Kelly Caine	Clemson University, USA
Jan Camenisch	IBM Research – Zurich, Switzerland
Srdjan Capkun	ETH Zurich, Switzerland
Claude Castelluccia	Inria Rhone-Alpes, France
Kostas Chatzikokolakis	CNRS, LIX, Ecole Polytechnique, France
Graham Cormode	University of Warwick, UK
Emiliano De Cristofaro	University College London, UK
Roberto Di Pietro	Università di Roma Tre, Italy
Claudia Diaz	KU Leuven, Belgium
Cynthia Dwork	Microsoft Research, USA
Zekeriya Erkin	Delft University of Technology, The Netherlands
Paul Francis	MPI-SWS, Germany
Paolo Gasti	New York Institute of Technology, USA
Ian Goldberg	University of Waterloo, Canada
Rachel Greenstadt	Drexel University, USA
Amir Herzberg	Bar-Ilan University, Israel
Nicholas Hopper	University of Minnesota, USA
Amir Houmansadr	University of Texas at Austin, USA
Rob Jansen	U.S. Naval Research Laboratory, USA
Mohamed Ali Kaafar	NICTA, Australia
Apu Kapadia	Indiana University, USA
Stefan Katzenbeisser	TU Darmstadt, Germany
Negar Kiyavash	University of Illinois, Urbana Champaign, USA
Markulf Kohlweiss	Microsoft Research, USA
Adam J. Lee	University of Pittsburgh, USA
Brian N. Levine	University of Massachusetts Amherst, USA
Marc Liberatore	University of Massachusetts Amherst, USA
Benjamin Livshits	Microsoft Research
Nick Mathewson	The Tor Project, USA
Prateek Mittal	Princeton University, USA
Steven Murdoch	University of Cambridge, UK
Arvind Narayanan	Princeton, USA
Claudio Orlandi	Aarhus University, Denamrk
Micah Sherr	Georgetown University, USA

Reza Shokri   ETH Zurich, Switzerland
Radu Sion   Stony Brook University, USA
Paul Syverson   U.S. Naval Research Laboratory, USA
Gene Tsudik   University of California, Irvine, USA
Eugene Vasserman   Kansas State University, USA
Matthew Wright   University of Texas at Arlington, USA

Additional Reviewers

Abdelberi, Chaabane   Haque, S.M. Taiabul
Acar, Gunes   Harvey, Sarah
Achara, Jagdish   Hoyle, Roberto
Acs, Gergely   Jagdish, Achara
Afroz, Sadia   Johnson, Aaron
Almishari, Mishari   Kaizer, Andrew
Balsa, Ero   Knijnenburg, Bart
Bordenabe, Nicolas   Kostiainen, Kari
Caliskan-Islam, Aylin   Krol, Kat
Chaabane, Abdelberi   Nguyen, Lan
Chan, T-H. Hubert   Nilizadeh, Shirin
Chen, Rafi   Norcie, Greg
Cunche, Mathieu   Oguz, Ekin
de Hoogh, Sebastiaan   Ohrimenko, Olga
Elahi, Tariq   Orlov, Ilan
Faber, Sky   Papillon, Serge
Farnan, Nicholas   Procopiuc, Cecilia
Freudiger, Julien   Qiao, Yechen
Gambs, Sebastien   Sedenka, Jaroslav
Garg, Vaibhav   Seneviratne, Suranga
Garrison III, William C   Shen, Entong
Gelernter, Nethanel   Tan, Zhi Da Henry
Ghali, Cesar   Veugen, Thijs
Gilad, Yossi   Washington, Gloria
Gong, Xun   Yu, Ge
Gurses, Seda   Zeilemaker, Niels

Table of Contents

CloudTransport:
Using Cloud Storage
for Censorship-Resistant Networking

Chad Brubaker[1,2], Amir Houmansadr[2], and Vitaly Shmatikov[2]

[1] Google, USA
[2] The University of Texas at Austin, USA

Abstract. Censorship circumvention systems such as Tor are highly
vulnerable to network-level filtering. Because the traffic generated by
these systems is disjoint from normal network traffic, it is easy to recognize and block, and once the censors identify network servers (e.g., Tor
bridges) assisting in circumvention, they can locate all of their users.

CloudTransport is a new censorship-resistant communication system
that hides users' network traffic by tunneling it through a cloud storage
service such as Amazon S3. The goal of CloudTransport is to increase the
censors' economic and social costs by forcing them to use more expensive forms of network filtering, such as large-scale traffic analysis, or else
risk disrupting normal cloud-based services and thus causing collateral
damage even to the users who are not engaging in circumvention. Cloud-
Transport's novel passive-rendezvous protocol ensures that there are no
direct connections between a CloudTransport client and a CloudTransport bridge. Therefore, even if the censors identify a CloudTransport
connection or the IP address of a CloudTransport bridge, this does not
help them block the bridge or identify other connections.

CloudTransport can be used as a standalone service, a gateway to
an anonymity network like Tor, or a pluggable transport for Tor. It does
not require any modifications to the existing cloud storage, is compatible
with multiple cloud providers, and hides the user's Internet destinations
even if the provider is compromised.

1 Introduction

Internet censorship is typically practiced by governments [3,45,53] to, first, block
citizens' access to certain Internet destinations and services; second, to disrupt
tools such as Tor that help users circumvent censorship; and, third, to identify
users engaging in circumvention. There is a wide variety of censorship technologies [30]. Most of them exploit the fact that circumvention traffic is easy to
recognize and block at the network level. Traffic filtering is cheap, effective, and
has little impact on other network services and thus on the vast majority of
users in the censorship region who are not engaging in circumvention. Another
problem with the existing censorship circumvention systems is that they cannot
survive partial compromise. For example, a censor who learns the location of

E. De Cristofaro and S.J. Murdoch (Eds.): PETS 2014, LNCS 8555, pp. 1–20, 2014.

a Tor bridge [6] can easily discover the locations of all of its users simply by enumerating the IP addresses that connect to the bridge.

While there is no comprehensive, accurate data on the technical capabilities of real-world censors, empirical evidence suggests that they typically perform only line-speed or close-to-line-speed analysis of Internet traffic. In particular, they neither store huge Internet traces for a long time, nor carry out resource-intensive statistical analysis of all observed flows. Furthermore, many state-level censors appear unwilling to annoy regular users, who are not engaged in circumvention, by significantly disrupting popular services—even if the latter employ encrypted communications. This is especially true of services used by businesses. For example, Chinese censors are not blocking GitHub because of its popularity among Chinese users and the gigantic volume of traffic they generate [17], nor are they blocking some of Google's encrypted services [19].

Some censors are willing to risk popular discontent by taking more drastic measures. Ethiopia has been reported to block Skype [13] (denied by the Ethiopian government [14]), Iran occasionally blocks SSL [26], and the Egyptian government cut the country off the Internet entirely during an uprising [12]. We focus on the more common scenario where, instead of blocking all encrypted communications, the censors aim to distinguish censorship circumvention traffic from "benign" encrypted traffic and block only the former.

Our contributions. We design, implement, and evaluate CloudTransport, a new system for censorship-resistant communications. CloudTransport is based on the observation that public cloud storage systems such as Amazon S3 provide a very popular encrypted medium accessible from both inside and outside the censor-controlled networks. For example, Amazon's cloud services are already used to host mirrors of websites that are censored in China, yet Chinese censors are not blocking Amazon because doing so would disrupt "thousands of services in China" with significant economic consequences [20].

CloudTransport is a general-purpose networking system that uses cloud storage accounts as passive rendezvous points in order to hide network traffic from censors. Since censors in economically developed countries like China are not willing to impose blanket bans on encrypted cloud services—even if these services are known to be used for censorship circumvention [20]—they must rely on network filters to recognize and selectively block circumvention traffic. Cloud-Transport uses exactly the same cloud-client libraries, protocols, and network servers as any other application based on a given cloud storage (we refer to this property as *entanglement*). Consequently, simple line-speed tests that recognize non-standard network protocols are not effective against CloudTransport.

CloudTransport's passive-rendezvous protocol helps survive partial compromise. Because CloudTransport clients never connect to a CloudTransport bridge directly, a censor who discovers a CloudTransport connection or learns the IP address of a bridge can neither block this bridge, nor identify its other users. The bridge can also transparently move to a different IP address without any disruption to its clients (e.g., if it experiences a denial of service attack). Our rendezvous protocol may be useful to other censorship resistance systems, too.

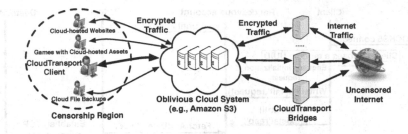

Fig. 1. High-level architecture of CloudTransport

CloudTransport is versatile and lets the user select a trusted cloud storage provider in a jurisdiction of the user's choice. On the user's machine, it presents a universal socket abstraction that can be used as a standalone communication system, a gateway for accessing proxies or Tor, or a pluggable transport for Tor.

The goal of CloudTransport is to raise the economic and social costs of censorship by forcing the censors to use statistical traffic analysis and other computationally intensive techniques. False positives of statistical traffic classification may cause the censors to disrupt other cloud-backed services such as enterprise applications, games, file backups, document sharing, etc. This will result in collateral damage, make censorship tangible to users who are not engaging in circumvention, and increase their discontent.

We analyze the properties provided by CloudTransport against ISP-level censors, cloud providers, and compromised bridges. We also show that its performance is close to Tor pluggable transports on tasks such as Web browsing, watching videos, and uploading content.

2   Protocol Design

The overall architecture of CloudTransport is shown in Fig. 1. The user installs CloudTransport client software on her machine and creates a *rendezvous account* with a cloud storage provider such as Amazon S3 in a jurisdiction of her choice outside the censor's control. The user must also choose a CloudTransport bridge and send the rendezvous account's access credentials to the bridge via the bootstrapping protocol described in Section 3. We envision CloudTransport bridges being run by volunteers in uncensored ISPs. A natural place to install CloudTransport bridges is on the existing Tor bridges [6], so that CloudTransport users benefit from Tor's anonymity properties in addition to the censorship circumvention properties provided by CloudTransport.

On the user's machine, the CloudTransport client presents a socket that can be used by any application for censorship-resistant networking. For example, the user may run a Web browser or a conventional Tor client over CloudTransport. The CloudTransport client uses the cloud storage provider's standard client library to upload application-generated network packets to the rendezvous account; the bridge collects and delivers them to and from their destinations.

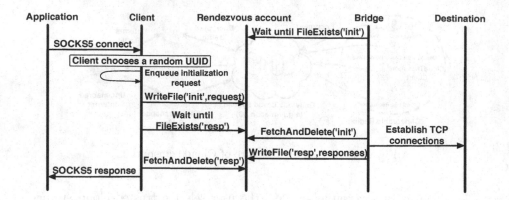

Fig. 2. Cirriform: connection initialization

CloudTransport uses existing cloud storage services "as is," without any modifications. This is a challenge because cloud-storage APIs are designed for occasional file uploads with many downloads, not for fast sharing of data between two parties. They do not typically support file locking or quick notification of file changes. CloudTransport clients and bridges, on the other hand, write to cloud storage often and must learn as quickly as possible when the other party has uploaded data to the shared account. To solve this challenge, each file used by CloudTransport is written by only one connection and read by only one connection. Writes happen only if the file does not already exist and all reads delete the file, to signal that it is safe to create the file anew and write into it.

We designed and implemented two variants of CloudTransport, Cirriform and Cumuliform. The protocol flow is the same, the only difference is how often they write into the cloud-based rendezvous account and poll for updates.

Cirriform. Cirriform uses one file in the rendezvous account per connection per direction, plus one file per direction for connection setup.

Figure 2 shows the protocol for setting up a new Cirriform connection. Connection requests and responses are queued and uploaded in batches. The client and the bridge periodically check the rendezvous account for pending messages. Once the connection is established, Figures 3 and 4 show how data is transferred from the application and the destination, respectively.

Typical cloud-storage API does not support pushing storage updates to customers, thus the client and the bridge must poll the rendezvous account. In our prototype, the polling rate for initialization requests and responses is set randomly and independently by each client, with the expected value of once per 0.5 seconds. For maximum performance, polling for data connections starts at once per 0.1 seconds, halves after every 20 failed checks, and resets to once per 0.1 seconds after every successful check. To avoid generating a regular signal, random jitter is added or subtracted to the interval after each poll.

Cumuliform. Applications such as Web browsing create many parallel connections, and polling cloud storage on all of them can incur a non-trivial cost

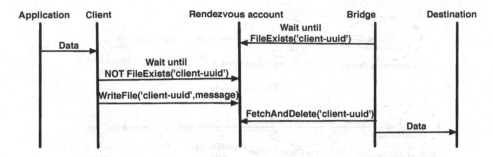

Fig. 3. Cirriform: client sending data

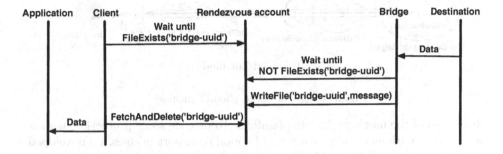

Fig. 4. Cirriform: destination sending data

Table 1. Prices charged by cloud storage providers (2013)

Provider	Bandwidth cost	Storage cost	Operation cost
Amazon S3	$0.12/GB after first GB	$0.0950/GB	$0.004/10000 GET $0.005/1000 PUT
Rackspace CloudFiles	$0.12/GB after first GB	$0.1000/GB	None
Google Cloud Storage	$0.12/GB (USA/Europe) $0.21/GB (Asia/Pacific)	$0.0865/GB	$0.01/10000 GET $0.01/1000 PUT

if the provider charges per operation (see Table 1). To reduce the polling cost, Cumuliform uses one file per direction rather than per connection. All requests are enqueued; the client and the bridge check 5 times a second for pending requests. Unlike Cirriform, which uploads data as soon as it is ready, Cumuliform uploads in batches, which can add extra delays.

Usage modes. CloudTransport can be used directly to send and receive network packets. We refer to this as the *transport mode*. The transport mode does not provide any privacy against the cloud storage provider since the provider can

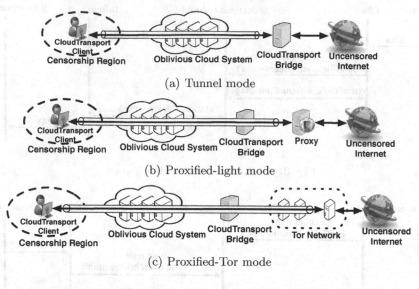

(a) Tunnel mode

(b) Proxified-light mode

(c) Proxified-Tor mode

Fig. 5. Usage modes of CloudTransport

observe all of the user's packets in plaintext. To provide some protection against malicious or curious cloud providers and CloudTransport bridges, we developed three usage modes illustrated in Figure 5. These modes represent different points in the tradeoff space between performance and censorship resistance.

The *tunnel mode* of CloudTransport hides the user's Internet destinations—but not the fact that she is using CloudTransport —from the cloud provider. In this mode, the user uses a CloudTransport bridge as a gateway to censored destinations. The traffic between the user's CloudTransport client and the bridge is encrypted, preventing the cloud provider from observing traffic contents. The bridge runs an OpenSSH server and authenticates the client using the temporary public key from the client's bootstrapping ticket (see Section 3.2). The client connects to this server via the rendezvous account, as described in Section 2, and tunnels all of its traffic over SSH.

In the *proxified-light mode*, the client uses CloudTransport to access a one-step proxy, e.g., Anonymizer [2]. The user's activities are thus hidden from the bridge if the traffic between the client and the proxy is encrypted end-to-end.

For strongest privacy, the client can use a system that aims to provide protection against itself, e.g., the Tor anonymity network in conjunction with Cloud-Transport. In the *proxified-Tor mode*, the client either runs a conventional Tor client and forwards Tor traffic over CloudTransport, or else uses CloudTransport as a pluggable transport [39] for Tor.

3   Bootstrapping

Bootstrapping is a critical part of any circumvention system. Many systems [4,7, 25,35,37,39,51] must send their clients some secret information—for example, IP addresses of circumvention servers or bridges, URLs of websites covertly serving censored content, etc.—and hope that this information does not fall into the censors' hands. As shown in [33, 34], censors can easily obtain these secrets by pretending to be genuine users and then block the system. Existing, trusted clients can help bootstrap new clients [49, 50], but this limits the growth of the system, especially in the early stages. Another way for the clients to discover circumvention servers is by probing the Internet [23, 54].

By contrast, bootstrapping in CloudTransport is initiated by users and performed "upstream": clients send information to the bridges without needing to obtain any secrets first. Therefore, insider attacks cannot be used to block CloudTransport bridges or discover other users.

3.1   Selecting a Cloud Provider and a Bridge

To start using CloudTransport, the user must set up a rendezvous account with a cloud storage provider. The user should select a cloud storage provider which is (1) outside the censor's jurisdiction, (2) already used by many diverse applications unrelated to censorship circumvention, and (3) unlikely to cooperate with the censor. We believe that using a cloud storage account for CloudTransport does not violate the typical terms of service, e.g., Amazon S3's "Conditions of Use" [1] or Dropbox's "Acceptable Use Policy" [9], since CloudTransport does not cause harm to other users or the provider itself.

Global providers such as Amazon S3 let customers specify a region for their data, e.g., "US West (Oregon)", "Asia Pacific (Tokyo)", etc. To evade flow correlation attacks discussed in Section 4.4, a CloudTransport bridge should access its clients' rendezvous accounts through the cloud provider's servers located outside the censorship region.

Due to the distributed nature of cloud storage, there is a delay between uploading a file and this file becoming visible for download, as well as other temporary inconsistencies between customers' views of the same account. This is typically a non-issue for conventional uses of cloud storage, but the primary source of delays for CloudTransport. Delays are much smaller and consistency achieved much faster by services such as Amazon S3 that charge per storage operation, as opposed to services such as Google Drive that simply charge per amount of storage regardless of how frequently this storage is accessed.

The monetary costs of using cloud storage is another consideration (see Table 1). We hope that some providers would be willing to donate their storage services (e.g., in the form of free accounts) to support censorship resistance.

The user must also select a CloudTransport bridge. Unlike Tor bridges [6], which must remain hidden from the censors, the list of CloudTransport bridges, along with other information needed for their usage, can be publicly advertised. It can be hosted on a directory server similar to the directory server of Tor relays [48]. For each CloudTransport bridge, this public directory should contain (1) a certificate with the bridge's public key, and (2) the URL of the bridge's *dead drop*, whose purpose is explained in Section 3.3.

We distinguish between the *login credentials* (e.g., username and password) and *access credentials* (e.g., API Key and Access Key in Amazon S3) for the rendezvous account. Access credentials allow reading and writing files, but do not give access to management data such as the billing information, IP addresses from which the account was accessed, etc. Only the access credentials for the rendezvous account should be sent to the bridge. The user can do this via one of the methods described in Section 3.3.

3.2   Creating a Bootstrapping Ticket

To use a bridge, a CloudTransport client first obtains the bridge's public key K_B from CloudTransport's directory server. The client then creates a *bootstrapping ticket* with (1) the name of the cloud provider chosen by the user, (2) the access credentials for the rendezvous account (API Key and Access Key in the case of Amazon S3), and (3) optionally, the client's temporary public key, which is used in the tunnel mode (Section 2) to authenticate the client. The ticket is encrypted using K_B as an S/MIME [42] message in the `EnvelopedData` format.

3.3   Delivering the Ticket to the Bridge

Dead drop. A bridge can set up its own cloud storage account, create a "dead drop" in it as a world-readable and -writable file directory, and advertise its URL in the bridge directory. Clients will write their tickets into the dead drop as files with arbitrary names and the bridge will periodically collect them.

To protect tickets in network transit from tampering, the dead drop should be accessible via HTTPS only (most cloud storage services use HTTPS by default). Unlike rendezvous accounts used for actual networking, bootstrapping is not latency-sensitive, thus free services like Dropbox, SkypeDrive, or Google Drive can be used to set up the dead drop.

Out-of-band channels. Since latency is not critical for bootstrapping, a user can deliver her bootstrapping ticket to the bridge by asking a trusted friend who is already using CloudTransport, or by posting the ticket to an anonymous chat room, social network, or public forum.

4   Analysis

Table 2 shows what information CloudTransport aims to hide from, respectively, the censoring ISP, cloud storage provider, and CloudTransport bridges. The cloud storage provider is trusted not to reveal to the censors the identities and network locations of its customers who are using CloudTransport. The bridges are trusted not to perform flow correlation (see Section 4.4). In the tunnel mode, the bridges must also be trusted not to reveal the contents and destinations of CloudTransport traffic; this assumption is not required in the proxified modes.

In the rest of this section, we discuss how CloudTransport resists different types of attacks that may violate these properties.

Table 2. Intended properties of CloudTransport

	Users' ISP	Cloud storage provider	CloudTransport bridge
Network locations of CloudTransport users	Hidden	Known	Hidden
Destinations of Cloud-Transport traffic	Hidden	Hidden	Known (tunnel mode) Hidden (proxified modes)
Content of Cloud-Transport traffic	Hidden	Hidden	Known (tunnel mode) Hidden (proxified modes)

4.1   Recognizing CloudTransport Network Traffic

CloudTransport aims to increase the technological complexity of censorship and, in particular, to force censors into using computationally expensive techniques such as statistical traffic analysis [10] as opposed to simple network-level tests.

Protocol discrepancies. CloudTransport's encrypted tunnels use exactly the same clients, same protocols, and same network servers as any other application based on a given cloud storage API. Due to this "entanglement" property, CloudTransport is immune to attacks that find discrepancies [21, 47] between genuine protocols like SSL and Skype and the imitations used by systems such as Tor and SkypeMorph [35]. This significantly raises the burden on the censors because simple line-speed tests based on tell-tale differences in protocol headers, public keys, etc. cannot be used to recognize CloudTransport. Also, CloudTransport's reaction to active perturbations such as dropping and delaying packets is similar to any other application based on the same cloud API.

The network servers used by Tor, SkypeMorph, Obfsproxy [37] and similar systems are disjoint from those used by other services. Once these servers are discovered, censors can block them without zero impact on non-circumvention users and their traffic. By contrast, blocking the network servers used by Cloud-Transport would effectively disable all uses of a given cloud provider, causing economic damage to users and businesses in the censorship region [20].

Statistical analysis. We do not claim that no statistical classification algorithm can distinguish CloudTransport traffic from the traffic generated by other cloud applications. We believe, however, that it will be technically challenging for the censors to develop an algorithm that simultaneously achieves low false negatives (to detect a significant fraction of CloudTransport traffic) and low false positives (to avoid disrupting non-CloudTransport cloud services).

First, note an important difference between the encrypted cloud traffic and the encrypted traffic generated by Skype and other standalone applications. All of Skype traffic is generated by copies of the same client or, at most, a few variations of the same client. Therefore, censors can whitelist typical Skype patterns and block all traffic that deviates from these patterns (this includes traffic generated by Skype imitators such as SkypeMorph or Stegotorus [21]).

By contrast, encrypted traffic to the cloud provider's servers is generated by thousands of diverse applications. This makes it difficult to create an accurate whitelist of traffic patterns and block all deviations without disrupting permitted services. Instead, censors must rely on blacklisting and use statistical analysis to positively recognize traffic patterns characteristic of CloudTransport. Furthermore, this analysis must be performed on every cloud connection, increasing the censors' computational burden.

Detailed analysis of traffic patterns generated by CloudTransport vs. all the diverse uses of cloud storage is beyond the scope of this paper. The main challenge for accurate statistical recognition of CloudTransport traffic is that CloudTransport is unlikely to account for more than a tiny fraction of all monitored connections. Due to the base-rate fallacy inherent in detecting statistically rare events, we expect that even an accurate classifier will either fail to detect many CloudTransport connections, or occasionally confuse CloudTransport with another cloud service. In the former case, some CloudTransport traffic will escape detection. In the latter case, censorship will cause collateral damage to at least some non-CloudTransport cloud applications. This will make censorship visible to non-circumvention users and potentially disrupt cloud-based business services, thus increasing the economic and social costs of censorship.

4.2 Abusing the CloudTransport Bootstrapping Protocol

The dead-drop variant of the CloudTransport bootstrapping protocol described in Section 3.3 can be potentially abused by censors to deny service to bona fide CloudTransport users. Since bridges publicly advertise their dead drops, censors can read and write them like any other user.

Even though reading other users' tickets does not reveal who these users are because the tickets are encrypted under the bridge's public key, censors may delete or tamper with them in order to deny service to genuine users. Fortunately, many cloud storage providers store all versions of each file (e.g., a free Dropbox account keeps all file versions for 30 days[1]). Therefore, the bridge should collect the first version of every file in the dead drop.

Censors may also stuff the dead drop with tickets that contain credentials for non-existing rendezvous accounts or real rendezvous accounts that are never used. The bridge will be forced to repeatedly poll these accounts, potentially exhausting its resources. To partially mitigate these attacks, the bridge backs off on polling if the account remains inactive (see Section 2). If the rate at which the censors can stuff the dead drop with fake tickets is significantly higher than the rate at which the bridge can check and discard them, this attack may hinder the bootstrapping process.

---

[1] https://www.dropbox.com/help/11/en

4.3   Attacking a CloudTransport Bridge

It is relatively easy for the censors to discover the IP addresses of CloudTransport bridges. For example, a censor can pretend to be genuinely interested in circumvention, pick a bridge, set up a rendezvous account, and find out the bridge's IP address from the account's access logs.

CloudTransport clients do not connect to bridges directly. Therefore, the censors cannot discover CloudTransport clients by simply enumerating all IP addresses inside the censorship region that connect to the bridges' addresses. For the same reason, blacklisting the addresses of known bridges has no effect on CloudTransport if these addresses are outside the censorship region. Unless the censors take over a bridge, they cannot observe or disrupt the connections between this bridge and the cloud provider because these connections take place entirely outside the censorship region (see Fig. 1 and Section 3.1).

Censors may stage a denial-of-service attack by flooding the IP address of a known bridge with traffic. In addition to standard defenses against network denial of service, some operators may be able to move their bridges to another IP address. This change is completely transparent to the users: as long as the bridge is hosted at an address from which it can access the cloud storage, CloudTransport remains operational even if the users don't know this address. Censors may also pose as genuine clients and send large volumes of requests via CloudTransport, but this involves heavy use of rendezvous accounts and will incur significant monetary costs. Furthermore, a bridge can throttle individual clients.

A denial-of-service attack on the bridge may cause a correlated drop in traffic on CloudTransport connections utilizing that bridge, and thus help the censors recognize CloudTransport connections by finding these correlations. This attack requires large-scale traffic analysis, which will be more expensive for the censors than simply enumerating all clients connecting to a bridge.

Finally, the censors may create their own bridge or take over an existing bridge. In either case, they gain full visibility into the traffic passing through this bridge, including the access credentials for the rendezvous accounts of all CloudTransport users communicating through the bridge. These credentials do not directly reveal these users' identities or network locations. Furthermore, the proxified modes of CloudTransport (see Section 2) encrypt traffic end-to-end between the client and the apparent destination: either a proxy, or a Tor entry node. Consequently, the censors in control of a bridge do not learn the true destinations or contents of CloudTransport traffic.

By controlling the bridge, the censors gain the ability to perform flow correlation attacks—see Section 4.4. Furthermore, the censors in control of a bridge can write content into rendezvous accounts that is legally prohibited in the cloud provider's jurisdiction. They can then use the presence of such content to shut down the accounts and/or convince the cloud provider to ban CloudTransport.

4.4   Performing Large-scale Flow Correlation

A censor who observes all traffic to and from the cloud storage provider may attempt to identify flows that belong to the same CloudTransport connection by correlating packet timings and sizes [8,22] In particular, the censor may look for flows between a user and the cloud provider that are correlated with the flows between the provider and a known or suspected CloudTransport bridge. A precondition for this attack is the ability to observe the traffic between the provider and the bridge. As explained in Section 3.1, we assume that the bridge is connecting to the provider through a server located outside the censorship region. That said, flow correlation can be feasible if the censors set up their own bridges or compromise an existing bridge.

Flow correlation is resource-intensive. Passive correlation attacks [8] require recording hundreds of packets from each flow and cross-correlating them across all flows. Active correlation [22] requires fine-grained perturbations and delays to be applied to all suspected flows. Furthermore, correlation must be done separately and independently for each flow reaching a given bridge.

The censor may attempt a side-channel attack such as website fingerprinting [5, 38, 44] to infer websites being browsed over CloudTransport. This attack exploits patterns in object sizes which are preserved by encryption. Random padding used by some SSH[2] [43] (respectively, TLS) implementations greatly complicates this attack against CloudTransport's tunnel (respectively, proxified-light) mode. Tor's use of equal-sized cells mitigates this attack in the proxified-Tor mode, but may not completely prevent it [5, 38]. To address this, Tor pluggable transports use traffic morphing [28], replaying old traffic traces [35, 51], and format-transforming encryption [11]. A CloudTransport client, too, can deploy these countermeasures, which can be hosted on users' machines [31, 32] or network proxies [31, 41], at the cost of additional bandwidth overhead.

5   Performance

We evaluated CloudTransport on four use cases: browsing the front pages of the Alexa Top 30 websites, uploading 300 KB images via SCP to a remote server, watching 5 minutes of 480p streaming video from Vimeo, and uploading a 10MB video to YouTube. All experiments involved a single client and a single bridge. The client was running on a machine with 16 Mb down- and 4 Mb up-bandwidth, while the bridge was running in a datacenter 2,400 kilometers (1,500 miles) away. Evaluating the performance of CloudTransport in a realistic, large-scale deployment is a topic of future work.

Table 3. *Browsing*, per-page costs

Provider	Cirriform	Cumuliform	Cirriform Profixied	Cumuliform Profixied
S3	0.00240¢	0.00100¢	0.00300¢	0.00430¢
CloudFiles	0	0	0	0
Cloud Storage	0.00570¢	0.00234¢	0.00600¢	0.00900¢

---

[2] http://www.gnutls.org/manual/gnutls.html#On-Record-Padding

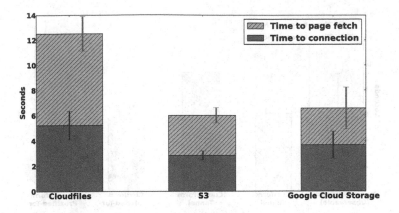

Fig. 6. *Browsing* (different providers)

Fig. 6 compares different cloud storage providers with CloudTransport operating in the tunnel mode. Table 3 shows the corresponding costs. Amazon S3 and Google Cloud Storage have similar performance and costs; S3 is slightly cheaper and quicker to propagate changes. RackSpace CloudFiles does not charge per operation and is thus much cheaper, but also significantly slower.

All of the following experiments were performed with a rendezvous account hosted on Amazon S3.

Performance. Fig. 7 shows that the performance of Cirriform in tunnel and profixied-Tor modes is similar to Tor with Obfsproxy [37]. Note that in the proxified-Tor mode, CloudTransport traffic enters the Tor network after passing through the bridge and is therefore subject to the same performance bottlenecks as any other Tor traffic. Unlike CloudTransport, Tor+Obfsproxy is easily recognizable at the network level and thus marked "(observable)" in the charts.

Cumuliform is noticeably slower because it buffers messages for all connections (as many as 30 when browsing). The variance for CloudTransport is much lower than for Tor+Obfsproxy, mainly because delays in CloudTransport are due to waiting for data to become available in the rendezvous account and S3 has fairly consistent delays in propagating small files used by CloudTransport.

Uploading files involves a lot of back-and-forth communication to set up the SCP connection. This puts CloudTransport at a disadvantage because of its per-message overheads, but Fig. 8 shows that it still outperforms Tor+Obfsproxy in all modes but one. Uploading a video to Youtube has similar issues to uploading small images, but with larger data sizes and more back-and-forth communication. Fig. 9 shows that CloudTransport still outperforms Tor+Obfsproxy in all Cirriform modes. Cumuliform in tunnel and proxified-Tor modes is, respectively, similar to and slower than Tor+Obfsproxy.

CloudTransport in all modes consistently plays streaming videos without pause after some initial buffering. Tor+Obfsproxy starts playing earlier but often buffers again later in the clip. Fig. 10 shows the average time spent buffering.

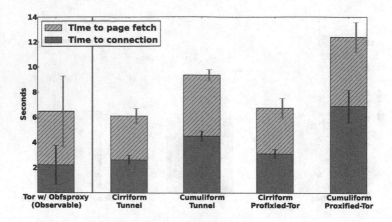

Fig. 7. *Browsing* (different usage modes)

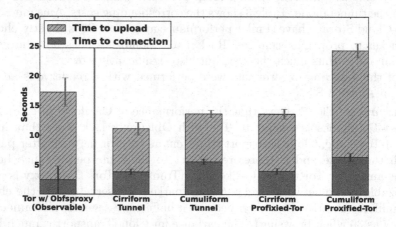

Fig. 8. *Image uploading*

Bandwidth. CloudTransport connections have minimal bandwidth overhead per message: 350-400 bytes for S3, 700-800 for CloudFiles, and 375-450 for Google Cloud Storage. HTTPS uploads and downloads have extra 2-3% overhead. When Cirriform polls an S3 account 3 times per second and 5 times per second per connection, its total overhead is 1.2KB + 2KB/connection per second.

Costs. Cirriform's performance is consistently superior to Cumuliform in all modes, but Cumuliform uses many fewer operations and is thus almost half as cheap when using providers who charge per operation (Table 3). In profixied modes, connections are re-used, thus Cumuliform no longer enjoys the cost advantage. Cirriform's polling costs are higher because it takes longer to run.

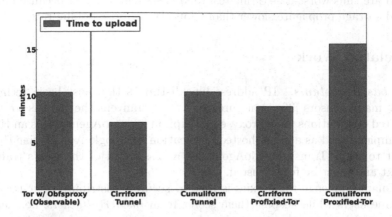

Fig. 9. *Youtube Uploading*

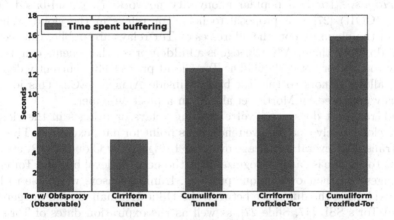

Fig. 10. *Streaming Video*

Table 4. Idle-polling costs

Provider	Cirriform	Cumuliform
S3	$0.185/day + $0.34/day/connection	$0.34/day
CloudFiles	0	0
Cloud Storage	$0.215/day + $0.86/day/connection	$0.86/day

The costs of idle-polling the rendezvous account regardless of whether communication is taking place are shown in Fig. 4. These assume one write per every poll and are thus worst-case estimates. Real costs will be lower because uploads to cloud storage propagate slower than CloudTransport's polling rate.

6   Related Work

Proxy-based systems. IP address blacklisting is the most basic technique used by many censors [30]. A natural way to circumvent the filter is to access blacklisted destinations via a proxy, e.g., Psiphon [40]. GoAgent [18] is an HTTP proxy implemented as a cloud-hosted application in Google App Engine [16]. In contrast to CloudTransport, GoAgent has access to all of the user's traffic in plaintext and must be fully trusted.

The main challenge for proxies is how to securely distribute their locations to genuine users while keeping them secret from *insider attackers*, i.e., censors pretending to be genuine users [33,50]. As soon as the censor learns the proxy's location, he can blacklist it, identify past users from network traces, or even leave the proxy accessible in order to identify and punish its future users [34].

Tor bridges. Tor is a popular anonymity network [7]. Cloud-based Onion Routing (COR) [27] is a proposal to host Tor relays in the cloud. Whether hosted in the cloud or not, the addresses of Tor relays are public, thus censors can and do block them. A Tor bridge is a hidden proxy that clients can use as a gateway to the Tor network [6]. The Tor Cloud project [46], currently deployed by Tor, allows donors to run Tor bridges inside Amazon EC2. This idea was previously proposed by Mortier et al. [36] in a position paper.

CloudTransport does not involve running relays or bridges in the cloud; it uses the cloud solely as a passive rendezvous point for data exchange. This gives CloudTransport several advantage over Tor bridges, Tor Cloud, COR, etc.

First, Tor traffic is easily recognizable at the network level because Tor clients and bridges run their own unique protocol. Iranian censors were able to block Tor by exploiting the difference between the Diffie-Hellman moduli in "genuine" SSL and Tor's SSL [47, Slide 27], as well as the expiration dates of Tor's SSL certificates [47, Slide 38]. By contrast, CloudTransport uses exactly the same protocol, cloud-client library, and network servers as any other application based on a given cloud storage service.

Second, blacklisting the IP address of a Tor bridge completely disables this bridge with zero impact on other network services. By contrast, blacklisting the IP addresses of CloudTransport bridges has no effect on CloudTransport, while blacklisting the IP addresses of cloud servers used by CloudTransport disrupts other cloud-based applications using the same servers.

Third, a censor who discover the IP address of a Tor bridge (e.g., via a probe [52, 53] or insider attack [33, 34, 50]) can easily enumerate the network locations of clients who connect to this bridge. By contrast, even a censor in complete control of a CloudTransport bridge does not learn the locations of its clients without computationally intensive flow correlation analysis.

Fourth, when a Tor bridge changes its IP address (e.g., when it is attacked or blacklisted), all of its clients must be securely notified about the new address.

By contrast, when a CloudTransport bridge changes its IP address, this change is completely transparent to its clients.

Fifth, bootstrapping Tor bridges is challenging because their addresses must be distributed only to genuine users but not to censors pretending to be users. By contrast, bootstrapping in CloudTransport is initiated by clients. Even if a censor pretends to be a user, he cannot discover who the other users are.

CloudTransport's reliance on rendezvous accounts hosted by cloud storage providers has some disadvantages, too. Unlike Tor clients, which only require Internet access, CloudTransport clients require every user to set up a cloud storage account outside her region. This may negatively impact usability, impose financial costs, generate a pseudonymous profile, and disclose the user's identity and the fact that she is using CloudTransport to the cloud storage provider, as well as the financial institutions processing her payments.

Imitation systems. To remove characteristic patterns from Tor traffic, Tor deployed *pluggable transports* [39]. For example, Obfsproxy [37] re-encrypts Tor packets to remove content identifiers. Systems such as SkypeMorph [35], Stego-Torus [51], and CensorSpoofer [49] proposed pluggable transports that aim to imitate popular network protocols like Skype and HTTP. A recent study showed multiple flaws in the entire approach of unobservability-by-imitation [21].

Hide-within systems. A promising alternative to imitation is to actually run a popular protocol and hide circumvention traffic within its network channels, thus entangling circumvention and non-circumvention traffic. This ensures that the circumvention system is "bug-compatible" with a particular implementation of the chosen protocol and therefore immune to tests that find discrepancies between actual protocol implementations and partial imitations [21].

We call such systems *hide-within*. CloudTransport is a hide-within system that tunnels circumvention traffic through cloud storage protocols. Other hide-within designs include FreeWave [24], which encodes circumvention traffic into acoustic signals sent over VoIP connections, and SWEET [25], which tunnels circumvention traffic inside email messages.

Steganography-based systems. In Infranet [15], the client pretends to browse an unblocked website that has secretly volunteered to serve censored content. Requests for censored content are encoded in HTTP requests, the responses are encoded in images returned by the site. By contrast, CloudTransport uses cloud storage obliviously, without any changes to the existing services.

Collage [4] hides censored content in user-generated photos, tweets, etc. on public, oblivious websites. It does not support interactive communications such as Web browsing.

In decoy routing [23, 29, 54], ISPs voluntarily help circumvention by having their routers recognize covert, steganographically marked traffic generated by users from the censorship region and deflect it to the blocked destinations specified by the senders. Unlike CloudTransport, decoy routing is not deployable without cooperation from at least some ISPs in the middle of the Internet.

7   Conclusions

We presented the design and implementation of CloudTransport, a new system for censorship-resistant communications. CloudTransport hides network traffic from censors by reading and writing it into rendezvous accounts on popular cloud-storage services. It can be used as a standalone networking medium or as a pluggable transport for Tor, enhancing Tor's censorship resistance properties.

Unlike Tor, SkypeMorph, and other systems utilizing network bridges to assist in circumvention, CloudTransport can survive the compromise of one or more of its bridges because its rendezvous protocol does not reveal the locations and identities of CloudTransport users even to the bridge.

CloudTransport aims to increase the economic and social costs of censorship. Empirical evidence shows that censors in relatively developed countries like China are not willing to impose a blanket ban on encrypted cloud services even when these services are used for censorship circumvention [20]. Because CloudTransport uses exactly the same network tunnels and servers as the existing cloud-based applications, censors can no longer rely on simple line-speed tests of protocol-level discrepancies to recognize and selectively block Cloud-Transport connections. Instead, they must perform statistical classification of every cloud connection. In contrast to systems like Tor, which can be recognized and blocked with zero impact on the vast majority of users, any false positives in the censors' recognition algorithms for CloudTransport will disrupt popular and business-critical cloud services. This will make censorship visible and increase discontent among the users who are not engaging in censorship circumvention.

Acknowledgements. This research was supported by the Defense Advanced Research Projects Agency (DARPA) and SPAWAR Systems Center Pacific, Contract No. N66001-11-C-4018, NSF grant CNS-0746888, and a Google research award.

References

1. Amazon: Conditions of Use, http://www.amazon.com/gp/help/customer/display.html?ie=UTF8&nodeId=508088
2. Anonymizer, https://www.anonymizer.com/
3. Joining China and Iran, Australia to Filter Internet, http://www.foxnews.com/scitech/2009/12/15/like-china-iran-australia-filter-internet
4. Burnett, S., Feamster, N., Vempala, S.: Chipping Away at Censorship Firewalls with User-Generated Content. In: USENIX Security (2010)
5. Cai, X., Zhang, X., Joshi, B., Johnson, R.: Touching from a Distance: Website Fingerprinting Attacks and Defenses. In: CCS (2012)
6. Dingledine, R., Mathewson, N.: Design of a Blocking-Resistant Anonymity System, https://svn.torproject.org/svn/projects/design-paper/blocking.html
7. Dingledine, R., Mathewson, N., Syverson, P.: Tor: The Second-generation Onion Router. In: USENIX Security (2004)

8. Donoho, D.L., Flesia, A.G., Shankar, U., Paxson, V., Coit, J., Staniford, S.: Multiscale Stepping-Stone Detection: Detecting Pairs of Jittered Interactive Streams by Exploiting Maximum Tolerable Delay. In: Wespi, A., Vigna, G., Deri, L. (eds.) RAID 2002. LNCS, vol. 2516, pp. 17–35. Springer, Heidelberg (2002)
9. Dropbox: Acceptable Use Policy,
   https://www.dropbox.com/terms#acceptable_use
10. Dusi, M., Crotti, M., Gringoli, F., Salgarelli, L.: Tunnel Hunter: Detecting Application-layer Tunnels with Statistical Fingerprinting. Computer Networks 53(1), 81–97 (2009)
11. Dyer, K., Coull, S., Ristenpart, T., Shrimpton, T.: Protocol Misidentification Made Easy with Format-transforming Encryption. In: CCS (2013)
12. Egypt Leaves the Internet,
   http://www.renesys.com/blog/2011/01/egypt-leaves-the-internet.shtml
13. Ethiopia Bans Skype, Other VoIP Services,
   http://www.sudantribune.com/spip.php?article42946
14. Ethiopia: Govt Denies Banning Skype and Other Internet Communication Services,
   http://allafrica.com/stories/201206250202.html
15. Feamster, N., Balazinska, M., Harfst, G., Balakrishnan, H., Karger, D.: Infranet: Circumventing Web Censorship and Surveillance. In: USENIX Security (2002)
16. Google App Engine, https://developers.google.com/appengine/
17. China's GitHub Censorship Dilemma, http://mobile.informationweek.com/
   80269/show/72e30386728f45f56b343ddfd0fdb119/
18. GoAgent proxy, https://code.google.com/p/goagent/
19. Google Transparency Report,
   http://www.google.com/transparencyreport/traffic/
20. Activists Say They Have Found Way Round Chinese Internet Censorship,
   http://www.theguardian.com/world/2013/nov/18/
   activists-chinese-internet-censorship-mirror-sites
21. Houmansadr, A., Brubaker, C., Shmatikov, V.: The Parrot Is Dead: Observing Unobservable Network Communications. In: S&P (2013)
22. Houmansadr, A., Kiyavash, N., Borisov, N.: RAINBOW: A Robust and Invisible Non-Blind Watermark for Network Flows. In: NDSS (2009)
23. Houmansadr, A., Nguyen, G., Caesar, M., Borisov, N.: Cirripede: Circumvention Infrastructure Using Router Redirection with Plausible Deniability. In: CCS (2011)
24. Houmansadr, A., Riedl, T., Borisov, N., Singer, A.: I Want My Voice to Be Heard: IP over Voice-over-IP for Unobservable Censorship Circumvention. In: NDSS (2013)
25. Houmansadr, A., Zhou, W., Caesar, M., Borisov, N.: SWEET: Serving the Web by Exploiting Email Tunnels. In: PETS (2013)
26. Iran Reportedly Blocking Encrypted Internet Traffic, http://arstechnica.com/
   tech-policy/2012/02/iran-reportedly-blocking-encrypted-internet-traffic
27. Jones, N., Arye, M., Cesareo, J., Freedman, M.: Hiding Amongst the Clouds: A Proposal for Cloud-based Onion Routing. In: FOCI (2011)
28. Kadianakis, G.: Packet Size Pluggable Transport and Traffic Morphing. Tor Tech Report 2012-03-004 (2012)
29. Karlin, J., Ellard, D., Jackson, A., Jones, C., Lauer, G., Mankins, D., Strayer, W.: Decoy Routing: Toward Unblockable Internet Communication. In: FOCI (2011)
30. Leberknight, C., Chiang, M., Poor, H., Wong, F.: A Taxonomy of Internet Censorship and Anti-censorship (2010),
   http://www.princeton.edu/~chiangm/anticensorship.pdf

31. Li, Z., Yi, T., Cao, Y., Rastogi, V., Chen, Y., Liu, B., Sbisa, C.: WebShield: Enabling Various Web Defense Techniques without Client Side Modifications. In: NDSS (2011)
32. Luo, X., Zhou, P., Chan, E., Lee, W., Chang, R., Perdisci, R.: HTTPOS: Sealing Information Leaks with Browser-side Obfuscation of Encrypted Flows. In: NDSS (2011)
33. McCoy, D., Morales, J.A., Levchenko, K.: Proximax: Measurement-Driven Proxy Dissemination (Short Paper). In: Danezis, G. (ed.) FC 2011. LNCS, vol. 7035, pp. 260–267. Springer, Heidelberg (2012)
34. McLachlan, J., Hopper, N.: On the Risks of Serving Whenever You Surf: Vulnerabilities in Tor's Blocking Resistance Design. In: WPES (2009)
35. Moghaddam, H., Li, B., Derakhshani, M., Goldberg, I.: SkypeMorph: Protocol Obfuscation for Tor Bridges. In: CCS (2012)
36. Mortier, R., Madhavapeddy, A., Hong, T., Murray, D., Schwarzkopf, M.: Using Dust Clouds to Enhance Anonymous Communication. In: IWSP (2010)
37. A Simple Obfuscating Proxy,
    https://www.torproject.org/projects/obfsproxy.html.en
38. Panchenko, A., Niessen, L., Zinnen, A., Engel, T.: Website Fingerprinting in Onion Routing Based Anonymization Networks. In: WPES (2011)
39. Tor: Pluggable Transports,
    https://www.torproject.org/docs/pluggable-transports.html.en
40. Psiphon, http://psiphon.ca/
41. Reis, C., Dunagan, J., Wang, H., Dubrovsky, O., Esmeir, S.: BrowserShield: Vulnerability-Driven Filtering of Dynamic HTML. TWEB 1(3), 11 (2007)
42. Secure/Multipurpose Internet Mail Extensions (S/MIME) Version 3.1 Message Specification (2004), http://www.ietf.org/rfc/rfc3851.txt
43. The Secure Shell (SSH) Transport Layer Encryption Modes (2006),
    http://www.ietf.org/rfc/rfc4344.txt
44. Sun, Q., Simon, D.R., Wang, Y., Russell, W., Padmanabhan, V., Qiu, L.: Statistical Identification of Encrypted Web Browsing Traffic. In: S&P (2002)
45. Syria Tightens Control over Internet, http://www.thenational.ae/
    news/world/middle-east/syria-tightens-control-over-internet
46. The Tor Cloud Project, https://cloud.torproject.org/
47. How Governments Have Tried to Block Tor,
    https://svn.torproject.org/svn/projects/presentations/slides-28c3.pdf
48. Tor Directory Servers and Their URLs,
    https://silvertunnel.org/doc/tor-directory-server-urls.html
49. Wang, Q., Gong, X., Nguyen, G., Houmansadr, A., Borisov, N.: CensorSpoofer: Asymmetric Communication Using IP Spoofing for Censorship-Resistant Web Browsing. In: CCS (2012)
50. Wang, Q., Lin, Z., Borisov, N., Hopper, N.: rBridge: User Reputation Based Tor Bridge Distribution with Privacy Preservation. In: NDSS (2013)
51. Weinberg, Z., Wang, J., Yegneswaran, V., Briesemeister, L., Cheung, S., Wang, F., Boneh, D.: StegoTorus: A Camouflage Proxy for the Tor Anonymity System. In: CCS (2012)
52. Wilde, T.: Knock Knock Knockin' on Bridges' Doors (2012),
    https://blog.torproject.org/blog/knock-knock-knockin-bridges-doors
53. Winter, P., Lindskog, S.: How the Great Firewall of China Is Blocking Tor. In: FOCI (2012)
54. Wustrow, E., Wolchok, S., Goldberg, I., Halderman, J.: Telex: Anticensorship in the Network Infrastructure. In: USENIX Security (2011)

A Predictive Differentially-Private Mechanism
for Mobility Traces

Konstantinos Chatzikokolakis, Catuscia Palamidessi, and Marco Stronati

CNRS, INRIA, LIX Ecole Polytechnique, France

Abstract. With the increasing popularity of GPS-enabled handheld devices, location based applications and services have access to accurate and real-time location information, raising serious privacy concerns for their millions of users.
Trying to address these issues, the notion of *geo-indistinguishability* was recently
introduced, adapting the well-known concept of Differential Privacy to the area
of location-based systems. A Laplace-based obfuscation mechanism satisfying
this privacy notion works well in the case of a *sporadic* use; Under repeated use,
however, *independently* applying noise leads to a quick loss of privacy due to the
correlation between the location in the trace.

In this paper we show that correlations in the trace can be in fact exploited in
terms of a *prediction function* that tries to guess the new location based on the
previously reported locations. The proposed mechanism tests the quality of the
predicted location using a private test; in case of success the prediction is reported
otherwise the location is sanitized with new noise. If there is considerable correlation in the input trace, the extra cost of the test is small compared to the savings
in budget, leading to a more efficient mechanism.

We evaluate the mechanism in the case of a user accessing a location-based
service while moving around in a city. Using a simple prediction function and
two budget spending strategies, optimizing either the utility or the budget consumption rate, we show that the predictive mechanism can offer substantial improvements over the independently applied noise.

1 Introduction

In recent years, the popularity of devices capable of providing an individual's position with a range of accuracies (e.g. wifi-hotspots, GPS, etc) has led to a growing use
of "location-based systems" that record and process location data. A typical example
of such systems are Location Based Services (LBSs) – such as mapping applications,
Points of Interest retrieval, coupon providers, GPS navigation, and location-aware social
networks – providing a service related to the user's location. Although users are often
willing to disclose their location in order to obtain a service, there are serious concerns
about the privacy implications of the constant disclosure of location information.

In this paper we consider the problem of a user accessing a LBS while wishing to
hide his location from the service provider. We should emphasize that, in contrast to
several works in the literature [1,2], we are interested not in hiding the user's *identity*,
but instead his *location*. In fact, the user might be actually authenticated to the provider,
in order to obtain a personalized service (personalized recommendations, friend information from a social network, etc); still he wishes to keep his location hidden.

E. De Cristofaro and S.J. Murdoch (Eds.): PETS 2014, LNCS 8555, pp. 21–41, 2014.

Several techniques to address this problem have been proposed in the literature, satisfying a variety of location privacy definitions. A widely-used such notion is k-anonymity (often called l-diversity in this context), requiring that the user's location is indistinguishable among a set of k points. This could be achieved either by adding *dummy locations* to the query [3,4], or by creating a *cloaking region* including k locations with some semantic property, and querying the service provider for that cloaking region [5,6,7]. A different approach is to report an *obfuscated* location z to the service provider, typically obtained by adding random noise to the real one. Shokri et al. [8] propose a method to construct an obfuscation mechanism of optimal privacy for a given quality loss constraint, where privacy is measured as the expected error of a Bayesian adversary trying to guess the user's location [9].

The main drawback of the aforementioned location privacy definitions is that they depend on the adversary's background knowledge, typically modeled as a prior distribution on the set of possible locations. If the adversary can rule out some locations based on his prior knowledge, then k-anonymity will be trivially violated. Similarly, the adversary's expected error directly depends on his prior. As a consequence, these definitions give no precise guarantees in the case when the adversary's prior is different.

Differential privacy [10] was introduced for statistical databases exactly to cope with the issue of prior knowledge. The goal in this context is to answer aggregate queries about a group of individuals without disclosing any individual's value. This is achieved by adding random noise to the query, and requiring that, when executed on two databases x, x' differing on a single individual, a mechanism should produce the same answer z with similar probabilities. Differential privacy has been successfully used in the context of location-based systems [11,12,13] when *aggregate* location information about a large number of individuals is published. However, in the case of a single individual accessing an LBS, this property is too strong, as it would require the information sent to the provider to be independent from the user's location.

Our work is based on "*geo-indistinguishability*", a variant of differential privacy adapted to location-based systems, introduced recently in [14]. Based on the idea that the user should enjoy strong privacy within a small radius, and weaker as we move away from his real location, geo-indistinguishability requires that the closer (geographically) two locations are, the more indistinguishable they should be. This means that when locations x, x' are close they should produce the same reported location z with similar probabilities; however the probabilities can become substantially different as the distance between x and x' increases. This property can be achieved by adding noise to the user's location drawn from a 2-dimensional Laplace distribution.

In practice, however, a user rarely performs a *single* location-based query. As a motivating example, we consider a user in a city performing different activities throughout the day: for instance he might have lunch, do some shopping, visit friends, etc. During these activities, the user performs several queries: searching for restaurants, getting driving directions, finding friends nearby, and so on. For each query, a new obfuscated location needs to be reported to the service provider, which can be easily obtained by independently adding noise at the moment when each query is executed. We refer to independently applying noise to each location as the *independent mechanism*.

However, it is easy to see that privacy is degraded as the number of queries increases, due to the *correlation* between the locations. Intuitively, in the extreme case when the user never moves (i.e. there is perfect correlation), the reported locations are centered around the real one, completely revealing it as the number of queries increases. Technically, the independent mechanism applying ϵ-geo-indistinguishable noise (where ϵ is a privacy parameter) to n location can be shown to satisfy $n\epsilon$-geo-indistinguishability [14]. This is typical in the area of differential privacy, in which ϵ is thought as a privacy *budget*, consumed by each query; this linear increase makes the mechanism applicable only when the number of queries remains small. Note that any obfuscation mechanism is bound to cause privacy loss when used repeatedly; geo-indistinguishability has the advantage of directly quantifying this loss terms of the consumed budget.

The goal of this paper is to develop a *trace obfuscation* mechanism with a smaller *budget consumption rate* than applying independent noise. The main idea is to actually use the correlation between locations in the trace to our advantage. Due to this correlation, we can often *predict* a point close to the user's actual location from information previously revealed. For instance, when the user performs multiple different queries from the same location - e.g. first asking for shops and later for restaurants - we could intuitively use the same reported location in all of them, instead of generating a new one each time. However, this implicitly reveals that the user is not moving, which violates geo-indistinguishability (nearby locations produce completely different observations); hence the decision to report the same location needs to be done in a private way.

Our main contribution is a *predictive mechanism* with three components: a *prediction function* Ω, a *noise mechanism* N and a *test mechanism* Θ. The mechanism behaves as follows: first, the list of previously reported locations (i.e. information which is already public) are given to the prediction function, which outputs a predicted location $\tilde{z}$. Then, it tests whether $\tilde{z}$ is within some threshold l from the user's current location using the test mechanism. The test itself should be private: nearby locations should pass the test with similar probabilities. If the test succeeds then $\tilde{z}$ is reported, otherwise a new reported location is generated using the noise mechanism.

The advantage of the predictive mechanism is that the budget is consumed only when the test or noise mechanisms are used. Hence, if the prediction rate is high, then we will only need to pay for the test, which can be substantially cheaper in terms of budget. The configuration of N and Θ is done via a *budget manager* which decides at each step how much budget to spend on each mechanism. The budget manager is also allowed to completely skip the test and blindly accept or reject the prediction, thus saving the corresponding budget. The flexibility of the budget manager allows for a dynamic behavior, constantly adapted to the mechanism's previous performance. We examine in detail two possible budget manager strategies, one maximizing utility under a fixed budget consumption rate and one doing the exact opposite, and explain in detail how they can be configured.

Note that, although we exploit correlation for efficiency, the predictive mechanism is shown to be private independently from the prior distribution on the set of traces. If the prior presents correlation, and the prediction function takes advantage of it, the mechanism can achieve a good budget consumption rate, which translates either to better utility or to a greater number of reported points than the independent mechanism. If there is no correlation, or the prediction does not take advantage of it, then the budget consumption can be worse than the independent mechanism. Still, thanks to the arbitrary choice of the prediction function and the budget manager, the predictive mechanism is a powerful tool that can be adapted to a variety of practical scenarios.

We experimentally verify the effectiveness of the mechanism on our motivating example of a user performing various activities in a city, using two large data sets of GPS trajectories in the Beijing urban area ([15,16]). The results for both budget managers, with and without the skip strategy, show considerable improvements with respect to independently applied noise. More specifically, we are able to decrease average error up to 40% and budget consumption rate up to 64%. The improvements are significative enough to broaden the applicability of geo-indistinguishability to cases impossible before: in our experiments we cover 30 queries with reasonable error which is enough for a full day of usage; alternatively we can drive the error down from 5 km to 3 km, which make it acceptable for a variety of application.

Note that our mechanism can be efficiently implemented on the user's phone, and does not require any modification on the side of the provider, hence it can be seamlessly integrated with existing LBSs.

Contributions The paper's contributions are the following:
- We propose a predictive mechanism that exploits correlations on the input by means of a prediction function.
- We show that the proposed mechanism is private and provide a bound on its utility.
- We instantiate the predictive mechanism for location privacy, defining a prediction function and two budget managers, optimizing utility and budget consumption rate.
- We evaluate the mechanism on two large sets of GPS trajectories and confirm our design goals, showing substantial improvements compared to independent noise.

All proofs can be found in the report version of this paper [17].

2   Preliminaries

Differential Privacy and Geo-indistinguishability. The privacy definitions used in this paper are based on a generalized variant of differential privacy that can be defined on an arbitrary set of secrets $\mathcal{X}$ (not necessarily on databases), equipped with a metric $d_{\mathcal{X}}$ [18,19]. The distance $d_{\mathcal{X}}(x, x')$ expresses the *distinguishability level* between the secrets x and x', modeling the privacy notion that we want to achieve. A small value denotes that the secrets should remain indistinguishable, while a large value means that we allow the adversary to distinguish them.

Let $\mathcal{Z}$ be a set of *reported values* and let $\mathcal{P}(\mathcal{Z})$ denote the set of probability measures over $\mathcal{Z}$. The multiplicative distance $d_{\mathcal{P}}$ on $\mathcal{P}(\mathcal{Z})$ is defined as $d_{\mathcal{P}}(\mu_1, \mu_2) = \sup_{Z \subseteq \mathcal{Z}} |\ln \frac{\mu_1(Z)}{\mu_2(Z)}|$ with $|\ln \frac{\mu_1(Z)}{\mu_2(Z)}| = 0$ if both $\mu_1(Z), \mu_2(Z)$ are zero and ∞ if only one of them is zero. Intuitively $d_{\mathcal{P}}(\mu_1, \mu_2)$ is small if μ_1, μ_2 assign similar probabilities to each reported value.

A mechanism is a (probabilistic) function $K : \mathcal{X} \to \mathcal{P}(\mathcal{Z})$, assigning to each secret x a probability distribution $K(x)$ over the reported values. The generalized variant of differential privacy, called $d_{\mathcal{X}}$-privacy, is defined as follows:

Definition 1 $(d_{\mathcal{X}}$**-privacy**). *A mechanism* $K : \mathcal{X} \to \mathcal{P}(\mathcal{Z})$ *satisfies* $d_{\mathcal{X}}$*-privacy iff:*

$$d_{\mathcal{P}}(K(x), K(x')) \leq d_{\mathcal{X}}(x, x') \qquad \forall x, x' \in \mathcal{X}$$

or equivalently $K(x)(Z) \leq e^{d_{\mathcal{X}}(x,x')} K(x')(Z) \quad \forall x, x' \in \mathcal{X}, Z \subseteq \mathcal{Z}.$

Different choices of $d_{\mathcal{X}}$ give rise to different privacy notions; it is also common to scale our metric of interest by a privacy parameter ϵ (note that $\epsilon d_{\mathcal{X}}$ is itself a metric).

The most well-known case is when $\mathcal{X}$ is a set of databases with the hamming metric $d_h(x, x')$, defined as the number of rows in which x, x' differ. In this case ϵd_h-privacy is the same as ϵ-differential privacy, requiring that for adjacent x, x' (i.e. differing on a single row) $d_{\mathcal{P}}(K(x), K(x')) \leq \epsilon$. Moreover, various other privacy notions of interest can be captured by different metrics [19].

Geo-indistinguishability. In the case of location privacy, which is the main motivation of this paper, the secrets $\mathcal{X}$ as well as the reported values $\mathcal{Z}$ are sets of locations (i.e. subsets of $\mathbb{R}^2$), while K is an obfuscation mechanism. Using the Euclidean metric d_2, we obtain ϵd_2-privacy, a natural notion of location privacy called geo-indistinguishability in [14]. This privacy definition requires that the closer (geographically) two location are, the more similar the probability of producing the same reported location z should be. As a consequence, the service provider is not allowed to infer the user's location with accuracy, but he can get approximate information required to provide the service.

Seeing it from a slightly different viewpoint, this notion offers privacy *within any radius* r from the user, with a level of distinguishability ϵr, proportional to r. Hence, within a small radius the user enjoys strong privacy, while his privacy decreases as r gets larger. This gives us the flexibility to adjust the definition to a particular application: typically we start with a radius r^* for which we want strong privacy, which can range from a few meters to several kilometers (of course a larger radius will lead to more noise). For this radius we pick a relatively small ϵ^* (for instance in the range from $\ln 2$ to $\ln 10$), and set $\epsilon = \epsilon^*/r^*$. Moreover, we are also flexible in selecting a different metric between locations, for instance the Manhattan or a map-based distance.

Two characterization results are also given in [14], providing intuitive interpretations of geo-indistinguishability. Finally, it is shown that this notion can be achieved by adding noise from a 2-dimensional Laplace distribution.

Protecting Location Traces. Having established a privacy notion for single locations, it is natural to extend it to location *traces* (sometimes called *trajectories* in the literature). Although location privacy is our main interest, this can be done for traces having any secrets with a corresponding metric as elements. We denote by $\mathbf{x} = [x_1, \ldots, x_n]$ a trace, by $\mathbf{x}[i]$ the i-th element of $\mathbf{x}$, by $[\,]$ the empty trace and by $x :: \mathbf{x}$ the trace obtained by adding x to the head of $\mathbf{x}$. We also define $\mathtt{tail}(x :: \mathbf{x}) = \mathbf{x}$. To obtain a privacy notion, we need to define an appropriate metric between traces. A natural choice is the maximum metric $d_\infty(\mathbf{x}, \mathbf{x}') = \max_i d_{\mathcal{X}}(\mathbf{x}[i], \mathbf{x}'[i])$. This captures the idea that two traces are as distinguishable as their most distinguishable points. In terms of protection within a radius, if $\mathbf{x}$ is within a radius r from $\mathbf{x}'$ it means that $\mathbf{x}[i]$ is within a radius r

from $\mathbf{x}'[i]$. Hence, ϵd_∞-privacy ensures that all secrets are protected within a radius r with the same distinguishability level ϵr.

mechanism $\mathrm{IM}(\mathbf{x})$
$\mathbf{z} := [\,]$
for $i := 1$ to $|\mathbf{x}|$
$\quad z := N(\epsilon_N)(\mathbf{x}[i])$
$\quad \mathbf{z} := z :: \mathbf{z}$
return $\mathbf{z}$

Fig. 1. Independent Mechanism

In order to sanitize $\mathbf{x}$ we can simply apply a *noise mechanism* independently to each secret x_i. We assume that a family of noise mechanisms $N(\epsilon_N) : \mathcal{X} \rightarrow \mathcal{P}(\mathcal{Z})$ are available, parametrized by $\epsilon_N > 0$, where each mechanism $N(\epsilon_N)$ satisfies ϵ_N-privacy. The resulting mechanism, called the *independent mechanism* $\mathrm{IM} : \mathcal{X}^n \rightarrow \mathcal{P}(\mathcal{Z}^n)$, is shown in Figure 1. As explained in the introduction, the main issue with this approach is that IM is $n\epsilon d_\infty$-private, that is, the budget consumed increases linearly with n.

Utility. The goal of a privacy mechanism is not to hide completely the secret but to disclose enough information to be useful for some service while hiding the rest to protect the user's privacy. Typically these two requirements go in opposite directions: a stronger privacy level requires more noise which results in a lower utility.

Utility is a notion very dependent on the application we target; to measure utility we start by defining a notion of *error*, that is a distance d_{err} between a trace $\mathbf{x}$ and a sanitized trace $\mathbf{z}$. In the case of location-based systems we want to report locations as close as possible to the original ones, so a natural choice is to define the error as the average geographical distance between the locations in the trace:

$$d_{\mathrm{err}}(\mathbf{x}, \mathbf{z}) = \tfrac{1}{|\mathbf{x}|}\textstyle\sum_i d_2(\mathbf{x}[i], \mathbf{z}[i]) \tag{1}$$

We can then measure the utility of a trace obfuscation mechanism $K : \mathcal{X}^n \rightarrow \mathcal{P}(\mathcal{Z}^n)$ by the *average-case* error, defined as the expected value of d_{err}:

$$E[d_{\mathrm{err}}] = \textstyle\sum_{\mathbf{x}} \pi(\mathbf{x})\sum_{\mathbf{z}} K(\mathbf{x})(\mathbf{z})\, d_{\mathrm{err}}(\mathbf{x}, \mathbf{z})$$

where $\pi \in \mathcal{P}(\mathcal{X}^n)$ is a prior distribution on traces.

On the other hand, the worst-case error is usually unbounded, since typical noise mechanisms (for instance the Laplace one) can return values at arbitrary distance from the original one. Hence, we are usually interested in the p-th percentile of the error, commonly expressed in the form of $\alpha(\delta)$-*accuracy* [20]. A mechanism K is $\alpha(\delta)$-accurate iff for all δ: $Pr[d_{\mathrm{err}}(\mathbf{x}, \mathbf{z}) \leq \alpha(\delta)] \geq \delta$. In the rest of the paper we will refer to $\alpha(0.9)$ (or simply α) as the "worst-case" error.

Note that in general, both $E[d_{\mathrm{err}}]$ and $\alpha(\delta)$ depend on the prior distribution π on traces. However, due to the mechanism's symmetry, the utility of the Laplace mechanism is independent from the prior, and as a result, the utility of the independent mechanism (using the Laplace as the underlying noise mechanism) is also prior-independent. On the other hand, the utility of the predictive mechanism, described in the next section, will be highly dependent on the prior. As explained in the introduction, the mechanism takes advantage of the correlation between the points in the trace (a property of the prior), the higher the correlation the better utility it will provide.

3 A Predictive $d_{\mathcal{X}}$-private Mechanism

We are now ready to introduce our prediction-based mechanism. Although our main motivation is location privacy, the mechanism can work for traces of any secrets $\mathcal{X}$, equipped with a metric $d_{\mathcal{X}}$. The fundamental intuition of our work is that the presence of correlation on the secret can be exploited to the advantage of the mechanism. A simple way of doing this is to try to predict new secrets from past information; if the secret can be predicted with enough accuracy it is called *easy*; in this case the prediction can be reported without adding new noise. One the other hand, *hard* secrets, that is those that cannot be predicted, are sanitized with new noise. Note the difference with the independent mechanism where each secret is treated independently from the others.

Let $\mathcal{B} = \{0, 1\}$. A boolean $b \in \mathcal{B}$ denotes whether a point is easy (0) or hard (1). A sequence $\mathbf{r} = [z_1, b_1, \ldots, z_n, b_n]$ of reported values and booleans is called a *run*; the set of all runs is denoted by $\mathcal{R} = (\mathcal{Z} \times \mathcal{B})^*$. A run will be the output of our predictive mechanism; note that the booleans b_i are considered public and will be reported by the mechanism.

Main components. The predictive mechanism has three main components: first, the *prediction* is a deterministic function $\Omega : \mathcal{R} \to \mathcal{Z}$, taking as input the run reported up to this moment and trying to predict the next *reported value*. The output of the prediction function is denoted by $\tilde{z} = \Omega(\mathbf{r})$. Note that, although it is natural to think of Ω as trying to predict the secret, in fact what we are trying to predict is the reported value. In the case of location privacy, for instance, we want to predict a reported location at acceptable distance from the actual one. Thus, the possibility of a successful prediction should not be viewed as a privacy violation.

Second, a *test* is a family of mechanisms $\Theta(\epsilon_\theta, l, \tilde{z}) : \mathcal{X} \to \mathcal{P}(\mathcal{B})$, parametrized by $\epsilon_\theta, l, \tilde{z}$. The test takes as input the secret x and reports whether the prediction $\tilde{z}$ is acceptable or not for this secret. If the test is successful then the prediction will be used instead of generating new noise. The purpose of the test is to guarantee a certain level of utility: predictions that are farther than the threshold l should be rejected. Since the test is accessing the secret, it should be private itself, where ϵ_θ is the budget that is allowed to be spent for testing.

The test mechanism that will be used throughout the paper is the one below, which is based on adding Laplace noise to the threshold l:

$$\Theta(\epsilon_\theta, l, \tilde{z})(x) = \begin{cases} 0 \text{ if } d_{\mathcal{X}}(x, \tilde{z}) \le l + Lap(\epsilon_\theta) \\ 1 \text{ ow.} \end{cases} \tag{2}$$

The test is defined for all $\epsilon_\theta > 0, l \in [0, +\infty), \tilde{z} \in \mathcal{Z}$, and can be used for any metric $d_{\mathcal{X}}$, as long as the domain of reported values is the same as the one of the secrets (which is the case for location obfuscation) so that $d_{\mathcal{X}}(x, \tilde{z})$ is well defined.

Finally, a *noise mechanism* is a family of mechanisms $N(\epsilon_N) : \mathcal{X} \to \mathcal{P}(\mathcal{Z})$, parametrized by the available budget ϵ_N. The noise mechanism is used for hard secrets that cannot be predicted.

Budget management. The parameters of the mechanism's components need to be configured at each step. This can be done in a dynamic way using the concept of a *budget*

mechanism $\mathrm{PM}(\mathbf{x})$
$\quad \mathbf{r} := []$
$\quad \mathbf{for}\ i := 1\ \mathbf{to}\ |\mathbf{x}|$
$\quad\quad (z, b) := \mathrm{Step}(\mathbf{r})(\mathbf{x}[i])$
$\quad\quad \mathbf{r} := (z, b) :: \mathbf{r}$
$\quad \mathbf{return}\ \mathbf{r}$

mechanism $\mathrm{Step}(\mathbf{r})(x)$
$\quad (\epsilon_\theta, \epsilon_N, l) := \beta(\mathbf{r})$
$\quad \tilde{z} := \Omega(\mathbf{r})$
$\quad b := \Theta(\epsilon_\theta, l, \tilde{z})(x)$
$\quad \mathbf{if}\ b == 0\ \mathbf{then}\ z := \tilde{z}$
$\quad \mathbf{else}\ z := N(\epsilon_N)(x)$
$\quad \mathbf{return}\ (z, b)$

(a) Predictive Mechanism   (b) Single step of the Predictive Mechanism

manager. A budget manager β is a function that takes as input the run produced so far and returns the budget and the threshold to be used for the test at this step as well as the budget for the noise mechanism: $\beta(\mathbf{r}) = (\epsilon_\theta, \epsilon_N, l)$. We will also use β_θ and β_N as shorthands to get just the first or the second element of the result.

Of course the amount of budget used for the test should always be less than the amount devoted to the noise, otherwise it would be more convenient to just use the independent noise mechanism. Still, there is great flexibility in configuring the various parameters and several strategies can be implemented in terms of a budget manager.

The mechanism. We are now ready to fully describe our mechanism. A single step of the predictive mechanism, displayed in Figure 2b, is a family of mechanisms $\mathrm{Step}(\mathbf{r})$: $\mathcal{X} \to \mathcal{P}(\mathcal{Z} \times \mathcal{B})$, parametrized by the run $\mathbf{r}$ reported up to this point. The mechanism takes a secret x and returns a reported value z, as well as a boolean b denoting whether the secret was easy or hard. First, the mechanism obtains the various configuration parameters from the budget manager as well as a prediction $\tilde{z}$. Then the prediction is tested using the test mechanism. If the test is successful the prediction is returned, otherwise a new reported value is generated using the noise mechanism.

Finally, the predictive mechanism, displayed in Figure 2a, is a mechanism PM : $\mathcal{X}^n \to \mathcal{P}(\mathcal{R})$. It takes as input a trace $\mathbf{x}$, and applies $\mathrm{Step}(\mathbf{r})$ to each secret, while extending at each step the run $\mathbf{r}$ with the new reported values (z, b).

Note that an important advantage of the mechanism is that it is *online*, that is the sanitization of each secret does not depend on future secrets. This means that the user can query at any time during the life of the system, as opposed to *offline* mechanisms were all the queries need to be asked before the sanitization. Furthermore the mechanism is *dynamic*, in the sense that the secret can change over time (e.g. the position of the user) contrary to static mechanism where the secret is fixed (e.g. a static database).

It should be also noted that, when the user runs out of budget, he should in principle stop using the system. This is typical in the area of differential privacy where a database should not being queried after the budget is exhausted. In practice, of course, this is not realistic, and new queries can be allowed by resetting the budget, essentially assuming either that there is no correlation between the old and new data, or that the correlation is weak and cannot be exploited by the adversary. In the case of location privacy we could, for instance, reset the budget at the end of each day. We are currently investigating proper assumptions under which the budget can be reset while satisfying a formal privacy guarantee. The question of resetting the budget is open in the field of differential privacy and is orthogonal to our goal of making an efficient use of it.

The main innovation of this mechanism if the use of the prediction function, which allows to decouple the privacy mechanism from the correlation analysis, creating a family of modular mechanisms where by *plugging* in different predictions (or updating the existing) we are able to work in new domains. Moreover proving desirable security properties about the mechanism independently of the complex engineering aspects of the prediction is both easier and more reliable, as shown in the next sections.

3.1 Privacy

We now proceed to show that the predictive mechanism described in the previous section is $d_\mathcal{X}$-private. The privacy of the predictive mechanism depends on that of its components. In the following, we assume that each member of the families of test and noise mechanisms is $d_\mathcal{X}$-private for the corresponding privacy parameter:

$$\forall \epsilon_\theta, l, \tilde{z}. \ \Theta(\epsilon_\theta, l, \tilde{z}) \text{ is } \epsilon_\theta d_\mathcal{X}\text{-private} \tag{3}$$

$$\forall \epsilon_N. \quad N(\epsilon_N) \quad \text{ is } \epsilon_N d_\mathcal{X}\text{-private} \tag{4}$$

In the case of the test $\Theta(\epsilon_\theta, l, \tilde{z})$ defined in (2), we can show that it is indeed $d_\mathcal{X}$-private, independently of the metric or threshold used.

Fact 1 (Privacy of Test function) *The family of test mechanisms $\Theta(\epsilon_\theta, l, \tilde{z})$ defined by* (2) *satisfies assumption 3.*

The global budget for a certain run **r** using a budget manager β is defined as:

$$\epsilon_\beta(\mathbf{r}) = \begin{cases} 0 & \text{if } |\mathbf{r}| = 0 \\ \beta_\theta(\mathbf{r}) + b(\mathbf{r}) \times \beta_N(\mathbf{r}) + \epsilon_\beta(\texttt{tail}(\mathbf{r})) & o.w. \end{cases} \tag{5}$$

As already discussed, a hard step is more expensive than an easy step because of the cost of the noise mechanism.

Building on the privacy properties of its components, we first show that the predictive mechanism satisfies a property similar to $d_\mathcal{X}$-privacy, with a parameter ϵ that depends on the run.

Lemma 1. *Under the assumptions* (3),(4), *for the test and noise mechanisms, the predictive mechanism* PM, *using the budget manager β, satisfies*

$$\mathrm{PM}(\mathbf{x})(\mathbf{r}) \le e^{\epsilon_\beta(\mathbf{r}) \, d_\infty(\mathbf{x}, \mathbf{x}')} \mathrm{PM}(\mathbf{x}')(\mathbf{r}) \qquad \forall \mathbf{r}, \mathbf{x}, \mathbf{x}' \tag{6}$$

This results shows that there is a difference between the budget spent on a "good" run, where the input has a considerable correlation, the prediction performs well and the majority of steps are easy, and a run with uncorrelated secrets, where any prediction is useless and all the steps are hard. In the latter case it is clear that our mechanism wastes part of its budget on tests that always fail, performing worse than an independent mechanism.

Finally, the overall privacy of the mechanism will depend on the budget spent on the worst possible run.

Theorem 1 ($d_\mathcal{X}$-**privacy**). *Under the assumptions* (3),(4), *for the test and noise mechanisms, the predictive mechanism* PM, *using the budget manager* β, *satisfies* ϵd_∞-*privacy, with* $\epsilon = \sup_\mathbf{r} \epsilon_\beta(\mathbf{r})$.

Based on the above result, we will use ϵ-*bounded* budget managers, imposing an overall budget limit ϵ independently from the run. Such a budget manager provides a fixed privacy guarantee by sacrificing utility: in the case of a bad run it either needs to lower the budget spend per secret, leading to more noise, or to stop early, handling a smaller number of queries. In practice, however, using a prediction function tailored to a specific type of correlation we can achieve good efficiency.

3.2 Utility

We now turn our attention to the utility provided by the predictive mechanism. The property we want to prove is $\alpha(\delta)$-*accuracy*, introduced in Section 2. Similarly to the case of privacy, the accuracy of the predictive mechanism depends on that of its components, that is, on the accuracy of the noise mechanism, as well as the one of the Laplace mechanism employed by the test $\Theta(\epsilon_\theta, l, \tilde{z})$ (2). We can now state a result about the utility of a *single step* of the predictive mechanism.

Proposition 1 (accuracy). *Let* $\mathbf{r}$ *be a run,* β *a budget manager, let* $(\epsilon_\theta, \epsilon_N, l) = \beta(\mathbf{r})$ *and let* $\alpha_N(\delta)$, $\alpha_\theta(\delta)$ *be the accuracy of* $N(\epsilon_N)$, $Lap(\epsilon_\theta)$ *respectively. Then the accuracy of* $\mathrm{Step}(\mathbf{r})$ *is* $\alpha(\delta) = \max(\alpha_N(\delta), l + \alpha_\theta(\delta))$

This result provides a bound for the accuracy of the predictive mechanism at each step. The bound depends on the triplet used $(\epsilon_\theta, \epsilon_N, l)$ to configure the test and noise mechanisms which may vary at each step depending on the budget manager used, thus the bound is step-wise and may change during the use of the system.

It should be noted that the bound is independent from the prediction function used, and assumes that the prediction gives the worst possible accuracy allowed by the test. Hence, under a prediction that always fails the bound is tight; however, under an accurate prediction function, the mechanism can achieve much better utility, as shown in the evaluation of Section 5.

3.3 Skipping the Test

The amount of budget devoted to the test is still linear in the number of steps and can amount to a considerable fraction; for this reason, given some particular conditions, we may want to skip it altogether using directly the prediction or the noise mechanism. The test mechanism we use (2) is defined for all $\epsilon_\theta > 0, l \in [0, +\infty)$. We can extend it to the case $\epsilon_\theta = 0, l \in \{-\infty, +\infty\}$ with the convention that $\Theta(0, +\infty, \tilde{z})$ always returns 1 and $\Theta(0, -\infty, \tilde{z})$ always returns 0. The new test mechanisms are independent of the input x so they can be trivially shown to be private, with no budget being consumed.

Fact 2 (Privacy of Test function) *The test functions* $\Theta(0, +\infty, \tilde{z})$ *and* $\Theta(0, -\infty, \tilde{z})$ *satisfy assumption 3.*

Now if β returns $(0, \epsilon_N, -\infty)$ we always fallback to the noise mechanism $N(\epsilon_N)$; this is especially useful when we know the prediction is not in conditions to perform well and testing would be a waste of budget. For instance, consider a prediction function that needs at least a certain number n of previous observables to be able to predict with enough accuracy; in this case we can save some budget if we directly use the noise mechanism for those n steps without testing. Note that the bound on utility is preserved in this case, as we can rely on the $\alpha_N(\delta)$-accuracy of $N(\epsilon_N)$.

On the other hand, the budget manager can return $(0, 0, +\infty)$ which causes the prediction to be reported without spending any budget. This decision could be based on any public information that gives high confidence to the prediction. A good use of this case can be found in Section 5 where *timing information* is used to skip the test.

Note that the prediction is computed from public knowledge, so releasing it has no privacy cost. However in this case we loose any guarantee on the utility of the reported answer, at least in the general case; based on the criteria for skipping the test (as in the case of the user walking in the city), we could make assumptions about the quality of the prediction which would allow to restore the bound.

4 Predictive Mechanism for Location Privacy

The applicability of $d_\mathcal{X}$-privacy to location-based systems, called geo-indistinguishability in this context, was already discussed in Section 2. Having studied the general properties of our predictive mechanism, we are ready to apply it for location privacy.

As already described in the preliminaries the sets of secret and observables are sets of geographical coordinates, the metric used is the euclidean distance and we will use $\Theta(\epsilon_\theta, l, \tilde{z})$ (2) as test function. We start with the description of a simple prediction function, followed by the design of two budget managers and finally some heuristics used to skip the test.

Prediction Function. For the prediction function we use a simple strategy, the parrot prediction, that just returns the value of the last observable, which ultimately will be the last hard observable.

$$\texttt{parrot}((z, b) :: \mathbf{r}) = z \tag{7}$$

Despite its simplicity, this prediction gives excellent results in the case when the secrets are close to each other with respect to the utility required - e.g. suppose the user queries for restaurants and he is willing to accept reported points as far as 1 km from the secret point, if the next positions are tens of meters apart, then the same reported point will be a good prediction for several positions. Similarly, the prediction is quite effective when the user stays still for several queries, which is a typical case of a smartphone user accessing an LBS.

More concretely, we define the *step* of a trace as the average distance between its adjacent points $\sigma(\mathbf{x}) = \text{avg}_{0 \le i < |\mathbf{x}|}\, d(x_i, x_{i+1})$ and we compare it with the $\alpha_N(0.9)$-accuracy of the noise mechanism. The intuition is that the parrot prediction works well on a trace $\mathbf{x}$ if $\sigma(\mathbf{x})$ is smaller than $\alpha_N(0.9)$ or in the presence of clusters because once we release one hard point we can use it as a good enough prediction for several other secret points close to it.

Furthermore the parrot prediction can be trivially implemented on any system and it has the desirable property of being independent from the user; taking into account past traces of the user, for instance, would give a more effective prediction, but it would be restricted to that particular user.

Budget Managers. When configuring a mechanism we need to take into account 3 global parameters: the global privacy, the utility and the number of interactions, written (ϵ, α, n) for brevity. All three are interdependent and fixing one we obtain a relation between the other two. In our case we choose to be independent of the length of the traces; to do so we introduce the *privacy consumption rate* (or just rate) which is the amount of budget spent at each step on average: $\rho(\mathbf{r}) = \frac{\epsilon(\mathbf{r})}{|\mathbf{r}|}$. This measure represent the privacy usage of the mechanism or how *fast* we run out of budget and given this value we can easily retrieve how many points we can cover given a certain initial budget. As already done for d_{err}, we also introduce the average-case rate for the mechanism as the expected value of ρ, given a prior distribution $\pi \in \mathcal{P}(\mathcal{X}^n)$ on traces:

$$E[\rho] = \sum_{\mathbf{x}} \pi(\mathbf{x}) \sum_{\mathbf{r}} \mathrm{PM}(\mathbf{x})(\mathbf{r}) \, \rho(\mathbf{r})$$

Given that our main concern is privacy we restrict ourselves to ϵ-*bounded* budget managers, that guarantee that the total budget consumed by the mechanism will never exceed ϵ, and divide them in two categories:

Fixed Utility: In the independent mechanism if we want to guarantee a certain level of utility, we know that we need to use a certain amount of budget at each step, a fixed rate, thus being able to cover a certain number n of steps. However in our case, if the test is successful, we may save the cost of the noise and meet the fixed utility with a smaller rate per point; smaller rates translates in additional interactions possible after n. We fix the utility and minimize the rate.

Fixed Rate: Alternatively, if in the independent mechanism we want to cover just n steps, thus fixing the rate, we would obtain a certain fixed utility. On the contrary the predictive mechanism, in the steps where the test succeeds, spends less than the chosen rate, allowing the next steps to spend *more* than the rate. This alternance creates a positive behavior where hard points can use the saved budget to increase their accuracy that in turn makes predicting more accurate and likely to succeed, leading to more saving. Of course the average cost for all steps meets the expected rate. In this case we fix the rate and maximize the utility.

Configuration of the Mechanism. We now give an overview of the constraints that are present on the parameters of the predictive mechanism and a guideline to configure them to obtain the desired levels of privacy and utility. The only settings that the user needs to provide are ϵ and either α or ρ. The budget manager will define at each step the amount of budget devoted to the test ϵ_θ, the noise mechanism ϵ_N and the test threshold l, starting from the global settings.

Budget usage. First we define the *prediction rate PR* as the percentage points predicted successfully; this property will be used to configure and to verify how effective is the predictive mechanism. We can then introduce a first equation which relates ϵ_θ and ϵ_N to the budget consumption rate: $\rho = \epsilon_\theta + (1 - PR)\epsilon_N$. This formula is derived from

budget manager $\beta(r)$
  if $\epsilon(r) \geq \epsilon$ **then STOP**
  else

$$\epsilon_\theta := \eta \frac{c_\theta}{\alpha}(1 + \frac{1}{\gamma})$$

$$\epsilon_N := \frac{c_N}{\alpha}$$

$$l := \frac{c_\theta}{\gamma \epsilon_\theta}$$

  return $(\epsilon_\theta, \epsilon_N, l)$

budget manager $\beta(r)$
  if $\epsilon(r) \geq \epsilon$ **then STOP**
  else

$$\epsilon_N := \frac{\rho}{(1-PR) + \frac{c_\theta}{c_N}\eta(1+\frac{1}{\gamma})}$$

$$\epsilon_\theta := \epsilon_N \eta \frac{c_\theta}{c_N}(1 + \frac{1}{\gamma})$$

$$l := \frac{c_\theta}{\gamma \epsilon_\theta}$$

  return $(\epsilon_\theta, \epsilon_N, l)$

(a) Fixed Utility configured with ϵ and α (b) Fixed Rate configured with ϵ, ρ and PR

the budget usage of the mechanism (Lemma 1), with the two following approximations. First, ϵ_θ and ϵ_N in future steps are assumed constant. In practice they will be variable because this computation is re-done at each step with the actual remaining budget. Second, we assume the hard steps are evenly distributed along the run. This allows us to use PR, which is a global property of the trace, in a local computation.

Note that ρ is constant in the fixed rate case and is computed over the current run for the fixed utility case. We already knew that the budget available at each step had to be split between Θ and N, this result confirms the intuition that the more we manage to predict (higher PR) the less we'll need to spend for the noise generation (on average over the run).

Utility. From the utility result given by Proposition 1 we obtain an equation that relates all the parameters of the mechanism, ϵ_θ, ϵ_N and l. Given that the global utility will be the worst of the two, we decide to give both the noise and predictive components the same utility: $\alpha_N = l + \alpha_\theta$. Moreover, as discussed in the utility section, this result is a bound valid for every possible prediction function, even one that always fails, for this reason the bound may be too pessimistic for the practical cases where the prediction does work. In order to reduce the influence of the accuracy of the predictive component we introduce a parameter $0 \leq \eta \leq 1$ that can be set to 1 to retrieve the strict case or can safely go as low as 0.5 as shown in our experiments. Finally we obtain the following relation between the parameters: $\alpha = \alpha_N = \eta(l + \alpha_\theta)$.

Noise-threshold ratio. Now we have two equations for three parameters and to completely configure the mechanism we introduce an additional parameter $0 \leq \gamma \leq 1$ that is used to tune, in the predictive component, the ratio between the threshold l and the Laplacian noise added to it so that $\gamma = \frac{\alpha_\theta}{l}$. The intuition is that γ should not be bigger that 1, otherwise the noise could be more important than the threshold and we might as well use a random test. For our experiments we found good values of γ around 0.8.

Note that both η and γ are values that should be determined using a representative sample of the expected input, in a sort of tuning phase, and then fixed in the mechanism. The same goes for the expected prediction rate that is used to configure the budget managers, at least in the beginning this value is necessary to allocate some resource for Θ, after some iterations it is computed from the actual run.

Relation between accuracy and epsilon. The final simplification that we apply is when we compute the accuracy of the noisy components, for both the linear Laplacian and the polar Laplacian we can compute their maximum value up to a certain probability δ using their inverse cumulative probability distributions, that we denote $\mathtt{icll}$ and $\mathtt{icpl}$ respectively. Fixing δ to 0.9, both these functions can be expressed as the ratio of a constant and the epsilon used to scale the noise $\alpha_N(\delta) = \mathtt{icpl}(\epsilon_N, \delta) = \frac{c_N(\delta)}{\epsilon_N}$ and $\alpha_\theta(\delta) = \mathtt{icll}(\epsilon_\theta, \delta) = \frac{c_\theta(\delta)}{\epsilon_\theta}$.

Now that we have the equations that relate the various parameters, from the settings given by the user we can realize the two budget managers, shown in Figure 3a and 3b.

Furthermore we can compare the expected rate or accuracy of our mechanism with those of an independent mechanism and find the prediction rate that we need to meet to provide an improvement. We obtain in both cases a lower bound on the prediction rate: $PR \geq \eta \frac{c_\theta}{c_N}(1 + \frac{1}{\gamma})$. This gives an idea of the feasibility of a configuration before actually running it, for example using the parameters of our experiments we find that it is necessary to predict at least 46% of points to make up for the cost of the test.

5   Case Study

To evaluate our mechanism, we follow our motivating example stated in the introduction of a user performing several activities while moving around the city throughout a day, possibly using different means of transport. During these activities, the user performs queries to an LBS using his mobile device, while wishing to keep his location private.

We assume that the user queries the LBS only when being still or moving at a slow speed (less than 15 km/h); this reflect the semantic of a geo localized query: there is usually little value in asking information relative to one's current position if the position is changing quickly. We perform a comparison between the independent mechanism IM and our predictive mechanism PM, both using polar Laplace noise as the underlying noise mechanism. The mechanisms are evaluated on two data sets of real GPS trajectories, using both a fixed-utility and fixed-rate budget managers and a skip strategy.

Data sets. The first data set we tested our mechanism against, is the well known GeoLife [15] which collects 18.670 GPS trajectories from 182 users in Beijing during a period of over five years. In this set the users take a variety of means of transport, from walking and biking to car, train, metro, taxi and even airplane. Regarding the trajectories length we can roughly divide them on three equal groups, less than 5 km, between 5 and 20 km and more than 20 km. As for duration 58% are less than 1 hour, 26% between 1 and 6 hours and 16% more than 6 hours.

The second data set is Tdrive [16], a collections of about 9000 taxi trajectories, always in the city of Beijing. As opposed to the variety of Geolife in this set we have only cars movements and the trajectories tends to be longer in both time and distance. The interest of using this set, which does not exactly correspond to our target use case of a user walking in a city, is to test the flexibility of the mechanism.

In order to use this sets some preprocessing is needed in order to model our use case. GPS trajectories present the problem of having *all the movements* of the user, instead of just the points where the user actually *queried* the LBS, which is a small subset of the trajectory. For this reason we perform a probabilistic "sampling" of the trajectories that, based on the speed and type of user, produces a trace of query points. First, we select the part of the trace where the speed is less than 15 km/h, and in these segments we sample points depending on the type of user, as explained below.

Users are classified based on the frequency of their use of the LBS, from occasional to frequent users. This is achieved by defining two intervals in time, one brief and the other long (a *jump*), that could occur between two subsequent queries. Then each class of users is generated by sampling with a different *probability of jumping p*, that is the probability that the next query will be after a long interval in time. Each value of p gives rise to a different prior distribution π on the produced traces, hence affecting the performance of our mechanism.

The interval that we used in our experiments are 1 and 60 minutes, both with addition of a small Gaussian noise; frequent users will query almost every minute while occasional users around every hour. In our experiments we generated 11 such priors, with probability of jumping ranging from 0 to 1 at steps of 0.1, where each trace was sampled 10 times.

Configuration. In order to configure the geo-indistinguishable application, first the user defines a radius r^* where she wishes to be protected, that we assume is 100 meters, and then the application sets ϵ^*, the global level of privacy, to be ln 10. This means that taken two points on the radius of 100 meters their probability of being the observables of the same secret differ at most by 10, and even less the more we take them closer to the secret. We think this is a reasonable level of privacy in a dense urban environment. For what concerns the two budget managers, the fixed-rate was tested with a 3.3% rate, which corresponds to about 30 queries, which in a day seems a reasonable number even for an avid user. For the fixed-utility we set an accuracy limit 3 km, again reasonable if we consider a walking distance and that these are worst cases.

Skip-the-test strategy. While the aim of the mechanism is to hide the user's position, the timestamp of a point is observable, hence we can use the elapsed time from the last reported point to estimate the distance that the user may have traveled. If this distance is less than the accuracy required, we can report the predicted value without testing it, we know that the user can't be too far from his last reported position. The risk of this approach lies in the speed that we use to link elapsed time and traveled distance, if the user is faster that expected (maybe he took a metro) we would report an inaccurate point. To be on the safe side it should be set to the maximum speed we expect our users to travel at, however with lower values we'll be able to skip more, it is a matter of how much we care about accuracy or how much we know about our users. In our experiments we assumed this speed to be 0.5 km/h.

We would expect this approach to be more convenient in a context where accuracy is not the primary goal; indeed skipping the test will provide the greatest advantage for the fixed-utility case, where we just don't want to exceed a worst case limit.

Additionally we use another skip-the-test strategy to use directly with the noise mechanism when we are in the first step and thus there is no previous hard point for the parrot prediction to report. This is a trivial example of skip strategy, yet it can lead to some budget savings.

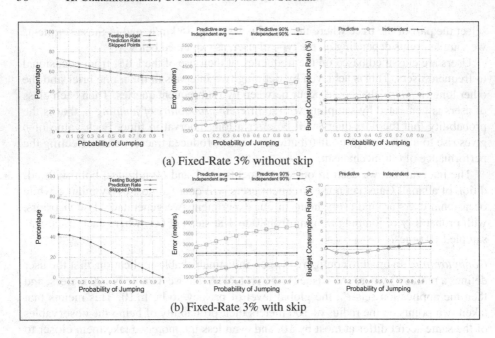

(a) Fixed-Rate 3% without skip

(b) Fixed-Rate 3% with skip

Fig. 4. General statistics, Average Error and Rate for Fixed-Rate budget manager

Results. It should be noted that both the preprocessing and the sanitization were performed with same configuration on both data sets. The results of running the mechanism on the samples traces from the Geolife data set, are reported in figures 4, 5, the graphs of Tdrive are omitted for reason of space as they show a very similar behavior to Geolife (they can be found in [17]). In the horizontal axis we have the probability p that was used during the sampling, to determine how often the user performs a *jump* in time: the smaller the value the more frequent the queries. For each budget manager we plot: In the first graph, some general statistics about the mechanism, such as the prediction rate achieved, the amount of budget devoted to Θ and the amount of skipped points; In the second column the average $(E[d_{\mathrm{err}}])$ and 90-th percentile $(\alpha(0.9))$ of the error; In the third the average budget consumption rate $E[\rho]$. Furthermore we run the experiments with and without the skip the test strategy, for the sake of comparison.

The graphs present a smooth behaviour, despite the use of real data, because of the sampling on each trace and the averaging over all traces of all users. As general remarks, we can see that the prediction rate degrades as the users become more occasional, thus less predictable, and the same goes for the number of skipped points. Notice that the testing budget adapts with the prediction rate which is a sign that the budget managers reconfigure dynamically.

Fixed-rate (Fig. 4): fixing the rate to 3.3% to cover 30 points, we can devote the budget saved to improve the accuracy. In the right most graph we see that indeed the rate is very stable even in the unpredictable cases, and very close to the rate of the independent mechanism. The graph in the center shows great improvements in the average error, 500 m in the worst case and 700 m in the best, and even more remarkable is the improvement for the maximum error, 1.3km up to 1.9km. With the skip strategy we see

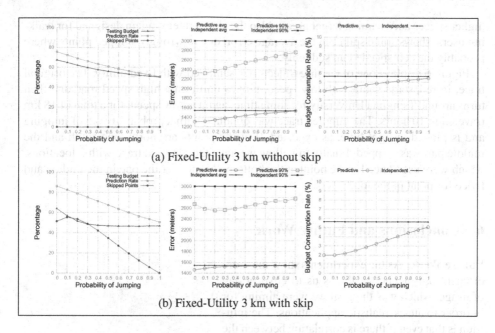

(a) Fixed-Utility 3 km without skip

(b) Fixed-Utility 3 km with skip

Fig. 5. General statistics, Average Error and Rate for Fixed-Utility budget manager

a small improvement for $p \leq 0.5$, again both in average and maximum error, which correspond to a decrease in the testing budget in the left most graph: the budget saved skipping the test is invested in more accurate noise.

Fixed-utility (Fig. 5): fixing the maximum utility (or in-accuracy) to 3 km, our mechanism manages to save up to 1.5% of budget rate. If we want to compare the number of points covered, the independent mechanism can do around 17 points while the predictive 24. As expected the average and max errors are below the independent mechanism corresponding values which confirms that the budget manager is working correctly keeping the utility above a certain level. Despite this they don't show a stable behavior like the rate in the fixed-rate case, this is due to the fact that while we can finely control the amount of budget that we spend, the error is less controllable, especially the one produced by the predictive component. With the skip strategy in this case we obtain a very noticeable improvement in this case, with rates as low as 2% in the best case which translates to 50 points covered. As already pointed out, in this case the skip strategy is more fruitful because we care less about accuracy.

Tdrive. This data set reports remarkably similar performance to Geolife when the probability of jumping p is less than 0.7. In this cases the predictive mechanism is consistently a better choice than the independent mechanism on both budget managers. On the contrary for higher values of p the independent mechanism performs better, it is interesting to notice that the prediction rate at $p = 0.7$ starts to be lower than 46%, as expected from Section 4. This difference between the best and worst case is more accentuated in Tdrive precisely because the prediction function was not designed for this scenario. The more sporadic users are even less predictable as they are moving at higher speeds and roaming larger areas. Also the skip strategy, again designed for walking users, shows some spikes in the average error, due to wrongly skipped points where probably the taxi speeded up suddenly.

Figure 6 displays one of Geolife trajectories sanitized with fixed utility. The original trace, in red, starts south with low speed, moves north on a high speed road and then turns around Tsinghua University for some time, again at low speed, for a total of 18 km traveled in 10 hours. The sampled trace was obtained with a probability 0.5 of jumping and is plotted in light blue: as expected, 9 of the points are north, one south and the middle part was skipped. Finally in yellow we have the reported trace with 3 locations, which were used once for the point at the bottom, 7 times for the one in the middle and twice for point in the top.

6   Conclusions and Future Work

Future Work. As the experiments show the more efficient use of budget allows us to cover a day of usage, which was the goal we were aiming for in order to attack realistic applications. The intuition is that even if there is correlation between the traces of the same user on several days (for example we go to work and home every day) still it is not enough to accurately locate the user at a precise moment in time (we might go to work later, or follow a different road). It is not clear though if one day is enough time to break the correlation and possibly reset the budget, we leave to future work to investigate in which cases it is indeed possible to reset the system and when on the contrary the epsilon keeps increasing.

One other possibility to prolong even further the use of the system is to improve the prediction. An extension we plan to develop consist in using the mobility traces of a user, or of a group of users, to designate locations where the next position is likely to be. In [21] the authors already developed inference attacks on the reported locations of users to discover points of interests and future locations, among other things; the idea is to use these attacks as a prediction.

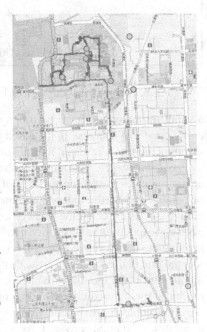

Fig. 6. Original trace (red), sampled trace (light blue) and reported trace (yellow)

We are also developing a *linearizing* prediction, that using past points tries to establish the next location using a linear regression method.

Alternatively we are considering the use of public geographic information to improve the prediction, which could simply translate to using already developed map-matching algorithms: typically in navigation systems an approximate location needs to be matched to an existing map, for example to place the user on a road. Map matching would make trivial predicting the direction of the user moving on a road for example, while in crossroads could be dealt with with the help of the mobility traces already discussed before: if on the left the is just countryside and on the right a mall, the user is more likely to turn right. Ultimately if more than one prediction function prove effective, we are interested in the possibility to merge them, for instance using multiplicative weights or related technique (e.g. Kalman filters).

Related Work. On the predictive mechanism side, our mechanism was mainly inspired by the median mechanism [20], a work on differential privacy for databases based on the idea of exploiting the correlation on the queries to improve the budget usage. The mechanism uses a concept similar to our *prediction* to determine the answer to the next query using only past answers. An analogous work is the multiplicative weights mechanism [22], again in the context of statistical databases. The mechanism keeps a parallel version of the database which is used to predict the next answer and in case of failure it is updated with a multiplicative weights technique.

A key difference from our context is that in the above works, several queries are performed against the *same database*. In our setting, however, the secret (the position of the user) is always changing, which requires to exploit correlations in the data. This scenario is explored also in [23] were the authors consider the case of an evolving secret and develop a differentially private counter.

Concerning location privacy, there are excellent works and surveys [24,25,26] that present the threats, methods, and guarantees. Like already discussed in the introduction the main trends in the field are those based on the expectation of distance error [9,8,27,28] and on the notion of k-anonymity [3,4,5,6,7], both dependents on the adversary's side information, as are some other works [29] and [30].

Notions that abstract from the attacker's knowledge based on differential privacy can be found in [11] and [12] although only for *aggregate* information.

The notion we based our work on, geo-indistinguishability [14], other than abstracting from the attacker's prior knowledge, and therefore being suitable for scenarios where the prior is unknown, or the same mechanism must be used for multiple users, can be used for single users. In addition, being the definition an instantiation of the more general notion of $d_\mathcal{X}$-privacy [19] we were able to generalize our mechanism as well, being the prediction the only domain specific component.

Conclusions. We designed a general framework for private predictive $d_\mathcal{X}$-private mechanisms able to manage the privacy budget more efficiently than the standard approach, in the cases where there is a considerable correlation on the data. The mechanism is modular and clearly separates the privacy protecting components from the predictive components, allowing ease of analysis and flexibility. We provide general configuration guidelines usable for any notion of $d_\mathcal{X}$-privacy and a detailed instantiation for geo indistinguishability. We tested the geo private mechanism obtained with two large sets of GPS trajectories and confirmed the goals set in the design phase. Experimental results show that the correlation naturally present in a user data is enough for our mechanism to outperform the independent mechanism in the majority of prior tested.

References

1. Gruteser, M., Grunwald, D.: Anonymous usage of location-based services through spatial and temporal cloaking. In: Proc. of MobiSys, USENIX (2003)
2. Mokbel, M.F., Chow, C.Y., Aref, W.G.: The new casper: Query processing for location services without compromising privacy. In: Proc. of VLDB, pp. 763–774. ACM (2006)
3. Kido, H., Yanagisawa, Y., Satoh, T.: Protection of location privacy using dummies for location-based services. In: Proc. of ICDE Workshops, p. 1248 (2005)
4. Shankar, P., Ganapathy, V., Iftode, L.: Privately querying location-based services with Sybil-Query. In: Proc. of UbiComp, pp. 31–40. ACM (2009)
5. Bamba, B., Liu, L., Pesti, P., Wang, T.: Supporting anonymous location queries in mobile environments with privacygrid. In: Proc. of WWW, pp. 237–246. ACM (2008)
6. Duckham, M., Kulik, L.: A formal model of obfuscation and negotiation for location privacy. In: Gellersen, H.-W., Want, R., Schmidt, A. (eds.) PERVASIVE 2005. LNCS, vol. 3468, pp. 152–170. Springer, Heidelberg (2005)
7. Xue, M., Kalnis, P., Pung, H.K.: Location diversity: Enhanced privacy protection in location based services. In: Choudhury, T., Quigley, A., Strang, T., Suginuma, K. (eds.) LoCA 2009. LNCS, vol. 5561, pp. 70–87. Springer, Heidelberg (2009)
8. Shokri, R., Theodorakopoulos, G., Troncoso, C., Hubaux, J.P., Boudec, J.Y.L.: Protecting location privacy: optimal strategy against localization attacks. In: Proc. of CCS, pp. 617–627. ACM (2012)
9. Shokri, R., Theodorakopoulos, G., Boudec, J.Y.L., Hubaux, J.P.: Quantifying location privacy. In: Proc. of S&P, pp. 247–262. IEEE (2011)
10. Dwork, C.: Differential privacy. In: Bugliesi, M., Preneel, B., Sassone, V., Wegener, I. (eds.) ICALP 2006. LNCS, vol. 4052, pp. 1–12. Springer, Heidelberg (2006)
11. Machanavajjhala, A., Kifer, D., Abowd, J.M., Gehrke, J., Vilhuber, L.: Privacy: Theory meets practice on the map. In: Proc. of ICDE, pp. 277–286. IEEE (2008)
12. Ho, S.S., Ruan, S.: Differential privacy for location pattern mining. In: Proc. of SPRINGL, pp. 17–24. ACM (2011)
13. Chen, R., Ács, G., Castelluccia, C.: Differentially private sequential data publication via variable-length n-grams. In: Proc. of CCS, pp. 638–649. ACM (2012)
14. Andrés, M.E., Bordenabe, N.E., Chatzikokolakis, K., Palamidessi, C.: Geo-indistinguishability: differential privacy for location-based systems. In: Proc. of CCS, pp. 901–914. ACM (2013)
15. Zheng, Y., Xie, X., Ma, W.Y.: Geolife: A collaborative social networking service among user, location and trajectory. IEEE Data Eng. Bull. 33(2), 32–39 (2010)
16. Yuan, J., Zheng, Y., Zhang, C., Xie, W., Xie, X., Sun, G., Huang, Y.: T-drive: driving directions based on taxi trajectories. In: GIS, pp. 99–108 (2010)
17. Chatzikokolakis, K., Palamidessi, C., Stronati, M.: A predictive differentially-private mechanism for mobility traces. CoRR abs/1311.4008 (2013)
18. Reed, J., Pierce, B.C.: Distance makes the types grow stronger: a calculus for differential privacy. In: Proc. of ICFP, pp. 157–168. ACM (2010)
19. Chatzikokolakis, K., Andrés, M.E., Bordenabe, N.E., Palamidessi, C.: Broadening the Scope of Differential Privacy using metrics. In: De Cristofaro, E., Wright, M. (eds.) PETS 2013. LNCS, vol. 7981, pp. 82–102. Springer, Heidelberg (2013)
20. Roth, A., Roughgarden, T.: Interactive privacy via the median mechanism. In: Proc. of STOC, pp. 765–774 (2010)
21. Gambs, S., Killijian, M.O., del Prado Cortez, M.N.: Show me how you move and i will tell you who you are. Trans. on Data Privacy 4(2), 103–126 (2011)

22. Hardt, M., Rothblum, G.N.: A multiplicative weights mechanism for privacy-preserving data analysis. In: FOCS, pp. 61–70. IEEE (2010)
23. Dwork, C., Naor, M., Pitassi, T., Rothblum, G.N.: Differential privacy under continual observation. In: STOC, pp. 715–724. ACM (2010)
24. Terrovitis, M.: Privacy preservation in the dissemination of location data. SIGKDD Explorations 13(1), 6–18 (2011)
25. Krumm, J.: A survey of computational location privacy. Personal and Ubiquitous Computing 13(6), 391–399 (2009)
26. Shin, K.G., Ju, X., Chen, Z., Hu, X.: Privacy protection for users of location-based services. IEEE Wireless Commun. 19(2), 30–39 (2012)
27. Hoh, B., Gruteser, M.: Protecting location privacy through path confusion. In: Proc. of SecureComm, pp. 194–205. IEEE (2005)
28. Dewri, R.: Local differential perturbations: Location privacy under approximate knowledge attackers. IEEE Trans. on Mobile Computing 99((PrePrints), 1 (2012)
29. Cheng, R., Zhang, Y., Bertino, E., Prabhakar, S.: Preserving user location privacy in mobile data management infrastructures. In: Danezis, G., Golle, P. (eds.) PET 2006. LNCS, vol. 4258, pp. 393–412. Springer, Heidelberg (2006)
30. Ardagna, C.A., Cremonini, M., Damiani, E., De Capitani di Vimercati, S., Samarati, P.: Location privacy protection through obfuscation-based techniques. In: Barker, S., Ahn, G.-J. (eds.) Data and Applications Security 2007. LNCS, vol. 4602, pp. 47–60. Springer, Heidelberg (2007)

On the Effectiveness of Obfuscation Techniques in Online Social Networks

Terence Chen[1,2], Roksana Boreli[1,2],
Mohamed-Ali Kaafar[1,2,3], and Arik Friedman[1,2]

[1] NICTA, Australia
[2] UNSW, Australia
[3] INRIA, France
firstname.lastname@nicta.com.au

Abstract. Data obfuscation is a well-known technique for protecting user privacy against inference attacks, and it was studied in diverse settings, including search queries, recommender systems, location-based services and Online Social Networks (OSNs). However, these studies typically take the point of view of a single user who applies obfuscation, and focus on protection of a single target attribute. Unfortunately, while narrowing the scope simplifies the problem, it overlooks some significant challenges that effective obfuscation would need to address in a more realistic setting. First, correlations between attributes imply that obfuscation conducted to protect a certain attribute, may influence inference attacks targeted at other attributes. In addition, when multiple users conduct obfuscation simultaneously, the combined effect of their obfuscations may be significant enough to affect the inference mechanism to their detriment. In this work we focus on the OSN setting and use a dataset of 1.9 million Facebook profiles to demonstrate the severity of these problems and explore possible solutions. For example, we show that an obfuscation policy that would limit the accuracy of inference to 45% when applied by a single user, would result in an inference accuracy of 75% when applied by 10% of the users. We show that a dynamic policy, which is continuously adjusted to the most recent data in the OSN, may mitigate this problem. Finally, we report the results of a user study, which indicates that users are more willing to obfuscate their profiles using popular and high quality items. Accordingly, we propose and evaluate an obfuscation strategy that satisfies both user needs and privacy protection.

1 Introduction

With the growing popularity of Online Social Networks (OSNs) in the past decade, users are sharing an increasing amount of personal information, ranging from their personal details and interests, to their habits and opinions. Access to some of this personal information can be restricted by configuring the OSNs' built-in privacy settings, but despite the OSN users' growing privacy awareness, a lot of this data is still considered harmless and made publicly accessible. This

E. De Cristofaro and S.J. Murdoch (Eds.): PETS 2014, LNCS 8555, pp. 42–62, 2014.

and other user-generated data is collected and mined by companies that provide personalized services, including recommendations and targeted advertising. Users' privacy can be compromised when the public information in their profiles is used to derive information they are not willing to reveal. Previous studies have shown that private attributes[1] can indeed be easily inferred based on information from others who revealed those attributes, either by utilizing social graph characteristics like social connections of the target user (the homophily principle) [8,11,13], or based on publicly shared items in common with other users, utilizing statistical inference/maximum likelihood approaches [3].

As users have full control of the publicly available OSN information, they can combat inference by obfuscating their public profiles, i.e., by adding or removing selected information, while still keeping their true purpose of information sharing. Obfuscation has been proposed to protect users' privacy against inference attacks in the context of search queries [14,18], movie ratings [17] and location-based services [1]. In the OSN domain, He and Chu [7] assumed that social relationships are publicly available, and proposed a protection method based on obfuscating (removing specific existing, or adding fake) social links. In this paper, we study generic statistical inference in OSNs, using a machine learning approach. We consider both the inference and the protection mechanisms, based on easily accessible interest items (activities, movies, music, etc.) from the OSN profiles. We assume that obfuscation is based on, e.g., an obfuscation application, that recommends a choice of items to users who wish to protect selected (one or more) attributes. These recommendations are based on a sample dataset collected from other OSN users. We show how obfuscation can be applied to protect user privacy and derive a practical (acceptable to users) and effective obfuscation strategy. We evaluate the practical aspects of obfuscation when users are protecting multiple attributes and in a system where there is a mix of privacy conscious users and users who do not share privacy concerns. Our contributions are as follows.

Using a dataset of close to 1.9 million Facebook profiles, we evaluate the effectiveness of different obfuscation strategies (to select items to be used for obfuscation) and obfuscation policies, including adding, removing or replacing selected items, with respect to a number of commonly used classifiers. We propose a novel obfuscation strategy, based on the χ^2 feature selection metric, which does not require knowledge of the classifier that the attacker is using (in general such knowledge is required for optimum obfuscation strategies). We show that this strategy can significantly reduce the inference accuracy, e.g., by 45% for the case when 40% of interest items are added to the user profile, compared to 60% reduction offered by the optimum strategy. The advantage of the optimum strategy decreases for the case when the same proportion of items are removed or replaced, or when a lower proportion of items are obfuscated.

This is the first work that evaluates the obfuscation of multiple attributes. We show that a strategy targeted towards protecting a single attribute can also offer

---

[1] We use the term "private attribute" to describe the information a user does not share publicly or, more generally, information that is not available online.

protection to other sensitive attributes. For example, our results show that while obfuscation targeting the *gender* attribute can reduce the inference accuracy by a factor of 3 (from 87% to 30%) when all users obfuscate 50% of their items, having a strategy targeting a different attribute, *relationship*, still results in an improvement factor of 1.3 for *gender*. A strategy targeting both attributes simultaneously can, for the same percentage of obfuscated items, increase this to 1.45. When attributes are correlated, however, a comparable protection level can be achieved while targeting both, e.g., for the case of *gender* and *interested in*, with a reduced inference accuracy of close to 30%.

We evaluate the effect of the obfuscation strategy that a group of users adopt on the privacy of all users, both in a static setting, and in a dynamic setting in which the strategy is adjusted based on the most recent OSN system data. We show that a static obfuscation strategy will not protect users in a system where other users share the same strategy. For example, with only 20% of users obfuscating their profiles by adding (or replacing) items, the accuracy of inference is increased from 45% when a single user obfuscates their profile, to 85%. Removing items results in a less significant, but still notable increase. Using a dynamic strategy can improve the resulting obfuscation gain for privacy conscious users, although a significant gain is only achieved for a small proportion of all users, indicating the need for further study of dynamic obfuscation strategies.

We evaluate the user preferences for various obfuscation strategies via a user study and show how the study results can be applied to derive a user-friendly obfuscation mechanism, which is both effective and practical. Our results indicate that quality and popularity are important factors in the choice of items for obfuscation and that having a mechanism that incorporates these factors is imperative for an effective solution.

The remainder of the paper is organized as follows. In Section 2, we discuss the background on inference techniques, we present the attack model and discuss the performance of different classifiers. Obfuscation is addressed in Section 3, including the obfuscation approaches and performance evaluation. Section 4 evaluates the performance of static and dynamic obfuscation techniques. The user preference study is presented in Section 5. We discuss the related work on inference and obfuscation techniques in Section 6 and conclude in Section 7.

2   Inferring Personal Information

In this section we evaluate the efficiency of private attribute inference attacks using machine learning in the context of OSNs. We first describe our attacker model, and then we introduce the feature selection process and the classifiers used in this study. Using a dataset consisting of 1.9 million Facebook profiles, we evaluate the performance of different classifiers on different types of background information.

2.1   Attack Model

The goal of the inference attack is to obtain the value of a user's private (not publicly accessible) attribute of their OSN profile, by analyzing publicly available background information using machine learning techniques. We assume the adversary is able to learn from a large set of static public profiles. We note that in this section we do not consider the impact of obfuscation on the performance of inference, this will be addressed in Section 4. We also note that, while finding the optimal inference attack model or inference algorithm is not the main focus of this study, our evaluations are based on state-of-the-art inference techniques that are used in the literature, e.g., in [17] and [9].

Assume an OSN profile comprises a total of k attributes (both public and private): $P = \{A_1, A_2, ..., A_k\}$. The attributes can have either a single value, e.g. for *age*, *gender*, and *relationship status*, or a list of values, e.g., for interest related items in *favourite movies*, *music*, *books*, etc. We define the target attribute of the attacker as $A_x \in P$, and the background attribute used for learning as $A_b \in P$. Throughout the paper, we use the terms "items" and "features" to refer to specific attribute values.

To infer the value of A_x based on A_b, we model the inference task as a document classification problem. We split the dataset into training and test groups of user profiles. First, from the training set and based on the background attribute A_b belonging to a set of users $N = \{1, 2, ..., n\}$ and a set of items (features) $M = \{1, 2, ..., m\}$, we construct a $n \times m$ binary matrix X_{train}. Matrix elements $x_{ij} \in \{0, 1\}$, where $i \in N$ and $j \in M$, represent the user-item relationship: $x_{ij} = 1$ indicates the item j is in user i's profile, and $x_{ij} = 0$ otherwise. Similarly, vector $Y_{train} = \{y_1, y_2, ..., y_n\}$, $y_i \in C$, represents the user-class relationship, with values of the target attribute A_x taken as classes $C = \{1, 2, .., c\}$. The classifier is trained with X_{train} and Y_{train}, resulting in a prediction function $F(\cdot)$. The test profiles are used to construct X_{test} and Y_{test} and the value A_x is then predicted by the trained classifier function $F(\cdot)$ as $Y'_{test} = F(X_{test})$, where the output Y'_{test} is the predicted value of A_x. The predicted results Y'_{test} are compared to the actual values in Y_{test} to evaluate the classifier performance, $E(Y'_{test}, Y_{test})$, where E denotes the performance metrics. For E, we use accuracy (the sum of all correct classifications divided by the total number of classifications) and Area Under Curve (AUC).

2.2   Feature Selection: χ^2

Feature selection is the process of selecting a subset of the terms occurring in the training set and using this subset as features in the classification task. This not only reduces the size of the training and test sets, but also increases the classification accuracy, by eliminating noise introduced by feature overfitting. Considering that wrapper and embedded feature selection methods are computationally expensive and specific to a prediction algorithm [6], we adopt the filter method [12], as it provides a fast pre-processing step while still retaining the utility of the feature set. Most importantly, the filter method is independent from the used prediction algorithm.

The filter method first computes a utility measure $S(t, c)$ for each term t and class c, and then selects k features that have the highest value of $S(t, c)$. In this study, we use the chi-square (χ^2) correlation coefficient, one of the most effective feature selection metrics for text classification [19], as the utility measure. The χ^2 score for term t to class c is computed by:

$$\chi^2(t, c) = \sum_{e_t \in \{0,1\}} \sum_{e_c \in \{0,1\}} \frac{(N_{e_t e_c} - E_{e_t e_c})^2}{E_{e_t e_c}} \tag{1}$$

Where e_t is an indication of the document containing the term t and e_c indicates whether the document is in class c. $N_{e_t e_c}$ is the observed frequency of t in the document with class c and $E_{e_t e_c}$ is the expected frequency, with $e_t \in \{0, 1\}$ and $e_c \in \{0, 1\}$. E.g., E_{11} is the expected frequency of the term $t = 1$ and class $c = 1$ occurring jointly in a document.

2.3   Selected Classifiers

A number of techniques can be used for document classification. After evaluating the performance of a number of state-of-the-art classifiers (including Naïve Bayes, Decision Tree, Random Forest, Support Vector Machines and Logistic Regression), we selected the top three performing classifiers for our experiments (we assume an attacker could easily perform a similar evaluation).

Bernoulli Naïve Bayes Classifier. Naïve Bayes classifier assumes the *independence* of features, in our case the presence of background attribute values in A_b, and that each of the features contributes independently to the probability that the prediction instance belongs to a class. We select the Bernoulli Naïve Bayes classifier because the features are binary values (corresponding to the presence of these features, or of interest related items, in a user profile). Maximum a posteriori (MAP) decision rule is used for class prediction, i.e., to select the most probable hypothesis. Given the background attribute contains m features, the predicted class label c is calculated below:

$$y' = \underset{c}{argmax}\; p(y = c) \prod_{i=1}^{m} p(A_i = a_i | y = c) \tag{2}$$

Logistic Regression Classifier. The logistic regression classification model is used for predicting the outcome of *dependent* features. Logistic Regression assumes a parametric form for the distribution $P(Y|X)$, then directly estimates its parameters $W = \{w_0, w_1, ..., w_m\}$ from the training data. The prediction is based on the following probability:

$$p(y = c | A) = \frac{1}{1 + exp(w_0 + \sum_{i=1}^{m} w_i A_i)} \tag{3}$$

Logistic regression is a binary classifier. For multi-class target attributes, we have used One-Versus-All strategy.[2]

Random Forest Classifier. Random Forest is an ensemble classification approach that combines a set of binary decision trees. At the learning stage, each tree is constructed using a portion of the training data and a subset of data features. Given a fixed set of features Φ that model the training data, $\log(\Phi)$ features and around 2/3 of the training data are randomly selected to construct each tree. Within the forest trees, each node uses for the decision making a single feature $f \in \Phi$, which is the best performing feature out of the selected subset of features. The class of an instance is determined by the majority voting of the terminal nodes reached when traversing the trees [2].

Table 1. Target attribute availability and their classes; total users: 249,847

Age: 13,308 users (5.3%)			Gender: 169,509 users (67.8%)		
classes	code	percentage	classes	code	percentage
13-17	0	35.59%	female	0	57.4%
18-24	1	42.85%	male	1	42.6%
25-34	2	13.49%			
35+	3	8.05%			
			Interested in : 70,476 users (28.2%)		
Relationship: 93,855 users (37.5%)			classes	code	percentage
classes	code	percentage	men	0	23.89%
in a relationship	0	62.2%	women	1	39.32%
single	1	37.8%	men and women	2	36.78%

2.4 The Performance of the Inference Attack

Dataset Used for Evaluation. We use a dataset of randomly sampled Facebook public profiles, comprising approximately 1.9 million profiles. We extract users' interest related items, i.e., activities, books, films, interests, movies, music, television, etc., and user personal information attributes, i.e., *age, gender, relationship* and *interested in*. The availability of target attributes in the used dataset is summarized in Table 1, and the distribution of the number of items per attribute and per user are summarized in Tables 2 and 3, respectively.

Table 2. Distribution of the number of items per attribute

attribute	# records	unique	avg # users	25%	50%	75%	95%
activities	918,525	11,405	80.54	15	27	66	277
books	371,142	5,125	72.42	13	21	45	240
films	313,679	3,577	87.69	15	28	66	303
interests	233,478	2,862	81.58	13	21	44	250
movies	975,105	6,693	145.69	15	30	89	555
music	2,055,576	16,313	126.01	13	22	53	375
television	1,362,780	6,462	210.89	14	26	72	658
all attributes	6,230,285	52,437	118.81	14	24	61	373

---

[2] http://scikit-learn.org/stable/modules/multiclass.html

Table 3. Distribution of the number of items per user

attribute	# users	avg # items	25%	50%	75%	95%
activities	95,779	9.59	2	3	7	28
books	134,219	2.77	1	2	4	6
films	50,547	6.21	2	4	7	18
interests	65,730	3.55	1	3	4	9
movies	174,119	5.6	3	5	5	15
music	236,653	8.69	3	5	8	29
television	233,893	5.83	3	5	6	15
all attributes	249,847	24.94	12	15	24	69

Inference Results. The inference attack on selected attributes is evaluated using the Facebook dataset, for *gender, age, relationship* and *interested in* (the actual values of classes are shown in Table 1), using the following shared interest attributes: *activities, books, films, interests, movies, music, television* and also *all attributes*, where we consider all possible public interest items from users' profiles as features. We use 10-fold cross validation and compute the average accuracy and AUC across all folds. For each combination of target attribute and interest type, we first extract all users who have revealed this target attribute and at least one item in the selected interest type, we then construct the user-item matrix based on this subset of users.

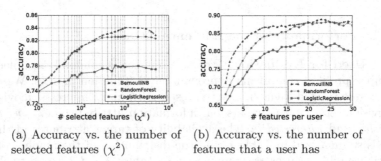

(a) Accuracy vs. the number of selected features (χ^2)

(b) Accuracy vs. the number of features that a user has

Fig. 1. Accuracy for inferring gender based on movie features, using different classifiers

To understand how the number of selected features affects the inference, we perform two preliminary measurements on (a) accuracy vs. the number k of features selected for inference, (b) accuracy vs. the number of features per user. As an example, Figure 1(a) shows the results for the accuracy of inferring *gender* using movie items. We observe that the accuracy improves as the number of selected features increases, for all classifiers, and becomes stable when k reaches 1000. Interestingly, we observe that by selecting only 10 features, all classifiers achieved an accuracy higher than 74%. Based on this observation, we use $k = 1000$ features for the remainder of this study.

Figure 1(b) shows the performance of gender inference when using movie features, and for a varying number of features that a user has (regardless of whether they were selected). We can again observe improved accuracy, in line with an increasing amount of available information. We note that the accuracy become stable when a user has more than 10 features.

Table 4. Performance of inferring **age, gender, relationship, interested in**, using different information and classifiers; ACC: accuracy, AUC: area under curve, NB: Naïve Bayes, LR: Logistic Regression, RF: Random Forest

Attribute	age inference						gender inference					
	NB		LR		RF		NB		LR		RF	
	ACC	AUC	ACC	AUC	ACC	AUC	ACC	AUC	ACC	AUC	ACC	AUC
activities	0.501	0.536	0.502	0.529	0.551	0.556	0.80	0.718	0.777	0.604	0.813	0.643
books	0.502	0.536	0.533	0.509	0.494	0.522	0.843	0.709	0.795	0.535	0.809	0.564
films	0.591	0.564	**0.616**	0.505	0.598	0.52	0.814	0.800	0.763	0.70	0.80	0.77
interests	0.444	0.500	0.456	0.496	0.452	0.509	0.841	0.649	**0.806**	0.548	0.823	0.604
movies	0.545	0.581	0.520	0.528	0.551	0.571	0.837	**0.824**	0.774	0.712	0.827	**0.785**
music	0.594	0.595	0.568	0.547	0.585	0.575	0.752	0.724	0.703	0.654	0.737	0.698
television	0.601	0.605	0.552	0.558	0.572	0.586	**0.85**	0.823	0.790	0.686	**0.834**	0.774
all attributes	**0.624**	**0.613**	0.568	**0.573**	**0.605**	**0.586**	0.822	0.808	0.736	**0.723**	0.796	0.778
Attribute	relationship inference						interested in inference					
	NB		LR		RF		NB		LR		RF	
	ACC	AUC	ACC	AUC	ACC	AUC	ACC	AUC	ACC	AUC	ACC	AUC
activities	0.629	0.620	**0.592**	**0.570**	0.589	0.563	0.526	0.474	0.476	0.510	0.518	0.508
books	0.593	0.591	0.561	0.539	0.577	0.567	0.47	0.549	0.456	0.488	0.456	0.523
films	0.591	0.591	0.556	0.553	0.567	0.567	0.485	0.473	0.518	0.497	0.541	0.604
interests	0.560	0.499	0.581	0.498	0.568	0.503	0.464	0.561	0.440	0.532	0.467	0.565
movies	0.610	0.609	0.561	0.560	0.578	0.577	**0.745**	**0.783**	**0.688**	**0.729**	**0.726**	**0.771**
music	0.604	0.607	0.549	0.546	0.565	0.562	0.529	0.508	0.463	0.510	0.480	0.511
television	0.614	0.608	0.572	0.557	0.578	0.570	0.542	0.573	0.472	0.584	0.495	0.559
all attributes	**0.640**	**0.632**	0.573	0.563	**0.602**	**0.591**	0.740	0.487	0.617	0.489	0.6876	0.465

Predictive Power of Interests. Table 4 shows the inference accuracy and AUC of predicting *age*, *gender*, *relationship* and *interested in* for all interest types and for the three selected classifiers. The values corresponding to the best performance are highlighted in each column. We observe that predicting *gender* is the least challenging target, with prediction accuracy of up to 85% using television (program) items. This is followed by *interested in*, where the classifier can predict as high as 74% of the cases correctly and with AUC of 78.36%. Inferring *age* is more difficult, as there are more classes and little difference between classes. Comparing the performance of different classifiers, we observe that Bernoulli Naïve Bayes classifier outperforms the other classifiers for this inference task. We can observe that the predictive power for different types of interests changes when inferring a different attribute, e.g., movie items are a good indicator of *interested in* and using television items results in the best performance when inferring *gender*. It is interesting to note that considering all available items from different interest categories does not always result in the best performance.

3   Obfuscating User Profiles

We assume that obfuscation of a user profile would be realized via an application, which would recommend changes to specific attribute values based on the knowledge of profiles of other users (contributed by users in, e.g., a crowdsourced scenario, and/or collected by the application back-end). The goal of obfuscation is to mitigate the inference attack on a selected (target) attribute, or a set of such attributes. We stress that in this work, we do not aim to provide provable privacy properties, but rather propose an empirical analysis of the state-of-the-art obfuscation techniques to protect users from inference attacks that leverage machine-learning approaches.

3.1   Obfuscating a Single Attribute: Strategies and Performance Evaluation

We first define the terms used to describe and evaluate the obfuscation approaches. For the sake of simplicity, we consider the case when a single attribute is targeted (and protected by obfuscation), although the following is also applicable to multiple target attributes. Obfuscation is accomplished by altering one or more background attributes A_b, so that the accuracy of inferring the class (value) of the target attribute A_x is minimized.

The attribute value (item) is chosen in the following way. In the initial step, all available items (from all users) are organized into classes, corresponding to the target attribute. Obfuscation is done using a selected item, from a class different from the one the target attribute belongs to. The user profile is modified according to a selected *obfuscation policy*, that can be: adding, removing or replacing an item. The item is chosen in line with a specific *obfuscation strategy*. The resulting improvement is measured as the reduction of the inference accuracy for the target attribute class, which can be perceived as *obfuscation gain*.

We consider a number of obfuscation strategies to choose the obfuscation items, based on rankings corresponding to selected metrics. For the purpose of obfuscation strategy evaluation, we first consider the optimal case of obfuscation, where the classifier used by the attacker is known to the (obfuscating) application. Therefore, we can choose the feature that achieves the highest *obfuscation gain*, based on the available data. To compute the *obfuscation gain* δ_k of a feature $k \in \{1, 2, ..., m\}$, we first set the kth element in each user's profile to 1, resulting in the test set $\hat{X}_{test}$. Then, we compute $\delta_k = E(F(X_{test}), Y_{test}) - E(F(\hat{X}_{test}), Y_{test})$, where $E(X, Y)$ represents accuracy.

Figure 3.1 shows the distribution of *obfuscation gain* for the *gender* attribute, and for three representative classifiers using all features. For all classifiers, the effect of adding a single feature to the profile has a limited effect on the prediction accuracy, as more than 90% of the features only result in a 10% accuracy reduction. The CDF curves indicate that Logistic Regression is most resilient to obfuscation using a single feature, while Naïve Bayes has the lowest level of resilience.

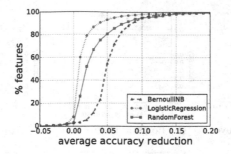

Fig. 2. Accuracy reduction distribution (CDF) for all features, using selected classifiers: Naïve Bayes, Logistic Regression and Random Forest

However, there are many possible classifiers an attacker may use and, in practice, the assumption of prior knowledge of the classifier is not realistic. We therefore consider the following classifier-independent *obfuscation strategies*:

- χ^2: Ranking the candidate obfuscation items based on the χ^2 feature selection metrics, defined in Section 2.3.
- **Popularity**: Ranking the candidate items based on the number of users who have these items.
- **Majority**: Ranking the items based on the proportion of users in a specific class who possess them.
- **Random**: Randomly selecting the obfuscation items from a specific class.

For the evaluation, the set of items from a user's profile A_b is transformed into a binary vector v, with elements corresponding to the presence of items in the profile. *Adding* an item to the profile is equivalent to changing the corresponding element from 0 to 1; *removing* an item is equivalent to reversing a 1 to 0; and *replacing* an item is the combination of *removing* one item and *adding* another. The performance of obfuscation is evaluated by comparing the accuracy of inference for the original profile v and the obfuscated profile $\hat{v}$. To simplify the evaluation, we use *movies* as the background attribute to infer the target attribute *gender*. The obfuscation framework can be easily applied to other attribute combinations.

Figure 3 shows the performance of different *obfuscation strategies* for selected classifiers, with inference accuracy computed for a varying level of obfuscated items in the user profiles. As expected, the classifier-optimized *obfuscation strategy* results in the best performance. However, as noted, this requires prior knowledge of the classifier and the metric is computationally expensive to generate. The *obfuscation policy* of replacing items results in the highest level of obfuscation. Comparing the classifiers, Random forest and Logistic regression are more resilient to random noise than the Bernoulli Naïve Bayes. Finally, the χ^2 *obfuscation strategy* is closest in performance to the optimal strategy for all classifiers, indicating that this would be a good choice for a practical and cost effective solution.

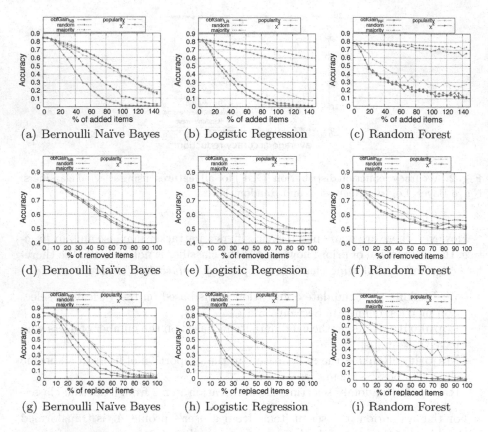

(a) Bernoulli Naïve Bayes   (b) Logistic Regression   (c) Random Forest

(d) Bernoulli Naïve Bayes   (e) Logistic Regression   (f) Random Forest

(g) Bernoulli Naïve Bayes   (h) Logistic Regression   (i) Random Forest

Fig. 3. Obfuscating *gender* inference by adding, removing and replacing movie items to user profiles using three selected classifiers: (a) - (c): Adding items; (d) - (f): Removing items; (g) - (i): Replacing items

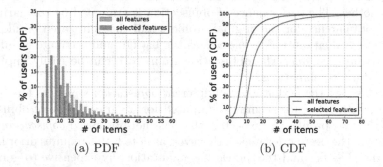

(a) PDF   (b) CDF

Fig. 4. Distribution of the number of (selected) movie items per user

To better understand the number of items that are needed to effectively obfuscate a user profile, Figure 4 shows the distribution of the number of items for all the users in our dataset, including the number of features before and after the χ^2 feature selection. Recall that for a meaningful inference, we filter out the users who have less than 10 items before the experiments, therefore the distribution starts with 10 items. The values shown in Figure 3 indicate that only 20-30% of added items are sufficient to obfuscate a profile (the resulting inference accuracy is below 50%). The CDF curve in Figure 4(b) indicates that over 60% of the users have less than 10 selected items, which suggests that they only need to add 2 to 3 items to obfuscate their profile.

3.2   Obfuscating Multiple Attributes

We now consider how obfuscating a selected attribute may impact the inference of a different attribute and how multiple attributes may be jointly obfuscated.

We study the problem using two example pairs of target attributes: *gender* and *relationship* status, and *gender* and *interested in*. We focus on the χ^2 feature selection metric, shown to be a successful *obfuscation strategy* for single attributes in Section 3.1. To understand how each feature may contribute to the obfuscation of both target attributes, we show the χ^2 score distribution of each movie item in a 2-dimensional Cartesian plane in Figure 5. As the χ^2 score only indicates the inference strength of an item, but does not indicate the class it belongs to, we represent one of the classes related to an attribute by negative χ^2 values. In the example on Figure 5, we define *gender* "female", *relationship* status "in a relationship" and *interested in* "female" as negative values.

We observe that χ^2 score values are distributed in all four quadrants for the *gender-relationship* pair shown in Figure 5(a), while the values for *gender-interested in* combination in Figure 5(b) are mainly distributed in quadrants II and IV, indicating that the latter two attributes are strongly correlated. We note that our dataset contained no features indicating a combination of "male" and "interested in male", and included only a few weak features indicating "female" and "interested in female."

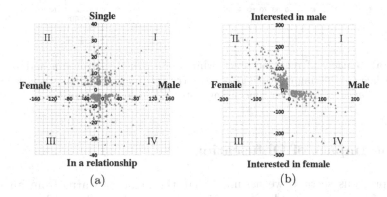

Fig. 5. χ^2 score of items for inferring pairs of attributes: (a) *gender* vs. *relationship*; (b) *gender* vs. *interested in*

We now evaluate the impact of obfuscating both single and multiple attributes on the inference of the selected attributes. Figures 6(a) and 6(b) show the inference accuracy for varying levels of obfuscation, for *gender* and for *relationship*, respectively, using the *obfuscation policy* of adding items, when either a single or multiple attribute classes are obfuscated. The *obfuscation strategy* is χ^2, modified for the case when both attribute classes are obfuscated. For this, we choose items from a quadrant (see Figure 5) determined by both attribute classes, e.g., if a user is protecting the "male" and "single" classes, obfuscating items are chosen from quadrant III ("female" and "in a relationship" classes). For the case of an attribute having multiple classes, or for multiple target attributes, a general rule would be to select items that are not in the target class, for all attributes that the user wishes to protect.

We observe from Figure 6(a) that, in line with Figure 5(b), *gender* and *interested in* are strongly correlated, and therefore obfuscating *interested in* also obfuscates *gender*, achieving a similar *obfuscation gain* as obfuscation based on *gender*. We can also observe that obfuscating based on *relationship* decreases the inference accuracy of *gender*, but by a much lower value, indicating that items introduced by obfuscating *relationship* are less relevant to *gender*. When considering multiple attributes, both *relationship-gender* and, in Figure 6(b), *relationship-gender* strategy, are very close, respectively, to the performance of obfuscation based on the *gender* and *relationship* attributes alone. However, when jointly targeting *interested-gender*, it is difficult to achieve a high obfuscation performance level.

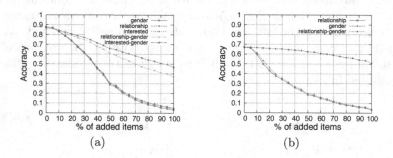

(a)   (b)

Fig. 6. (a) *Gender* inference accuracy while obfuscating *relationship* and *interested in*, and when considering multiple attributes. (b) *relationship* inference accuracy when obfuscating *gender*, and when considering both *gender* and *relationship*.

4   The Impact of Obfuscation

In the previous section, we assumed that the attacker learns from an initial version of user profiles, where no obfuscation was applied. As the number of obfuscating users increases, it is reasonable to assume that the attacker becomes aware of the obfuscation activity and adjusts the attack model. In this section, we examine how the obfuscation may affect the efficiency of the inference attacks, when the attacker re-learns constantly from the most up-to-date dataset (which includes obfuscated profiles). Then we discuss how the attacker may use the knowledge of the users' obfuscation strategy to further improve the attack.

For ease of presentation, we use the example of *gender* inference, however we note that very similar results and trends were observed for other attributes we tested. In the following, we observe the impact of attribute obfuscation on the inference accuracy of (i) regular users who do not take part in the obfuscation process (non-obfuscated), and as such keep their original public profiles unchanged; (ii) users who have adopted a specific obfuscation strategy; and (iii) all users in the system.

4.1 Static Obfuscation Strategy

We start by studying a static obfuscation strategy that relies on an initial (non-obfuscated) dataset, and always delivers a fixed set of items to users. We split the dataset into a training set, representing the background knowledge of the attacker, and a test set, representing the set of target users. Then, we "pollute" a portion of the training set using χ^2 obfuscation strategy we discussed in the previous section. We assume that the obfuscating users modify (add, remove or replace) 50% of their profile items (this achieves a reasonably low inference accuracy, as per Section 3).

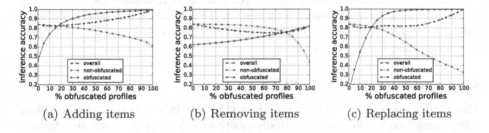

(a) Adding items   (b) Removing items   (c) Replacing items

Fig. 7. The impact of obfuscation on users' privacy: regular users, obfuscating users and overall users, with different portions of obfuscated profiles

The inference accuracy for different percentages of obfuscated profiles in the training set is shown in Figure 7, for the cases of adding, removing and replacing items from user's profiles. Our results show that the inference accuracy for obfuscated profiles increases as the proportion of other obfuscated profiles becomes higher. This suggests a paradox, where privacy loss increases as more users become privacy-conscious.

To better understand why the obfuscation fails as the obfuscating population increases, we analyze the new information that is injected into the system (as part of the training data) by the obfuscating users. A static obfuscation strategy always suggests the same set of items to achieve the best obfuscation. As a result,

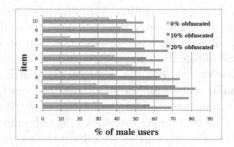

Fig. 8. The change in class bias for top 10 obfuscating features, as the percentage of obfuscated users increases

the suggested items establish strong correlation with the value that the user is trying to hide. For example, Figure 8 shows the percentage of *male* users who have one of the top-10 *female*-associated items (based on the χ^2 score) when there are 0%, 10% and 20% of obfuscated profiles. Initially all items are female dominant and hence have strong association with *female* during inference. As the number of *male* users who obfuscate their profiles by injecting these items increases, the *male/female* ratio changes and the *male* users become dominant at 10% and 20% obfuscated profiles in the system. Adding these (reversed) items to users' profiles hence becomes a strong indication for the class the users are attempting to hide.

Notably, the inference accuracy for regular users decreases as the number of users applying the obfuscation increases. This is again due to the attacker learning from a set of items consisting of more obfuscated items, which equates to adding noise to the "clean" profiles.

4.2   Dynamic Obfuscation Strategy

The main issue for the static strategy is that the injection of a similar set of false items into the system, eventually results in those items becoming indicative of the attributes users are attempting to keep private. We now investigate two obfuscation strategies that recommend items dynamically: first we revisit the experiment using a random obfuscation strategy; second, we assume the obfuscation engine refreshes the strategy based on the most up-to-date data.

Recall that the random strategy chooses items from a different class randomly, regardless of the obfuscation strength of the items. Although this approach has inferior performance compared to more optimal strategies, it introduces diversity, which increases the difficulty of identifying the obfuscated items. We perform the same experiment as in Section 4.1 using the random obfuscation strategy, and show the inference accuracy in Figure 9(a). We observe a similar result to what was achieved by the static χ^2 strategy (Figure 7(c)), which suggests that spreading the recommended items randomly does not resolve the issue.

We then consider two dynamic obfuscation scenarios: first, we assume there is a baseline of x% obfuscated profiles using the initial static strategy (static

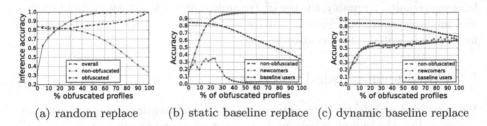

(a) random replace   (b) static baseline replace (c) dynamic baseline replace

Fig. 9. Impact of obfuscation on users' privacy using dynamic strategy, (a) random strategy is used by all users. (b) training set polluted using the baseline static strategy (c) training set polluted using the baseline dynamic strategy.

baseline). We evaluate the obfuscation gain for newcomers who obfuscate their profile based on up-to-date data; the results are shown in Figure 9(b). We observe that the early adopters (baseline users) of obfuscation face a high risk of successful inference. In contrast, newcomers who adopt the dynamic strategy, have well obfuscated profiles.

In the second scenario, we consider a realistic situation where obfuscation is adopted by users gradually over time; at each time period, we introduce 1% obfuscated profiles to the training dataset (dynamic baseline). We then show how the inference accuracy evolves as the portion of obfuscated profiles increases for both early obfuscation adopters (baseline users) and newcomers. The results are shown in Figure 9(c). We observe an increase in the inference accuracy for between 0% to 20% of the obfuscated profiles in the system, both for baseline users and newcomers. Unlike the previous scenarios, the inference accuracy becomes stable for both strategies. This observation suggests that using dynamic and the most up-to-date strategy is beneficial both for early adopters of obfuscation and for newcomers.

4.3   Limitations of the Obfuscation Strategies

In response to the obfuscation activities, the attacker can adopt stronger attack models that actively identify polluted items and detect obfuscated profiles and attributes. With such a capability, an attacker may use the knowledge of the obfuscating items as recommended by the obfuscation engine to filter out noisy items before launching the inference attacks. Likewise, an attacker may take advantage of detected obfuscation behavior to infer the private attribute that the user is trying to hide.

There are several ways to detect an obfuscated profile. Firstly, the attacker may access the obfuscation application in the same way as a legitimate user. This method is effective for static obfuscation strategies as the attacker can easily obtain a list of the most likely obfuscation items.

For the dynamic strategies, a powerful attacker may detect obfuscation by monitoring abrupt changes of profile items that are inconsistent with previous inference results. Arguably, the use of dynamic obfuscation strategy and progressive introduction of obfuscation items would benefit the users towards resisting more sophisticated inference attacks.

5   Considering User Preferences

We examined users' preferences for the choice of obfuscation items via a survey, performed on the online crowdsourcing survey platform CrowdFlower.[3]

Our survey first asked the respondents to rate the level of sensitivity of the personal information in their profiles on a scale of $1 - 5$. Then, the survey asked them to rate the preference for adding specific movies to their profile, in order to protect their *gender* and *relationship* information from being inferred by a third-party. The evaluation focused on three factors that may affect a user's decision to include an item in his/her profile: (1) *privacy protection level*: we included three levels, high, medium and low, corresponding to values of χ^2; (2) *popularity*: high or low, related to the number of users with this item in our dataset; and (3) *quality*: high or low, based on IMDb[4] movie ratings. The list of movies in the survey was carefully selected so that each item could be related to a combination of these factors. For different user groups, i.e., for different combinations of gender and relationship status, we provided a bespoke version of the survey. The full survey can be found in the technical report [4].

We received 254 responses, with 158 responses that we considered valid (we removed completed surveys that took less than 2 minutes to complete or that had identical responses to almost all questions). We restricted the survey to users from English speaking countries, with the respondents being from: US 36.7%, Canada 35.4%, UK 17.7%, Australia 6.3%, New Zealand 3.8%. The *gender-relationship status* distribution of the respondents was: male-single 17%, male-in a relationship 19.6%, female-single 12.6% and female-in a relationship 50.6%.

Based on the average rating for the level of sensitivity of their personal information, we classified users into two groups: privacy conscious users (rating above 3) and non-privacy aware users (rating below 3). The proportion of positive ratings (movies that were rated as acceptable for obfuscation) for the two groups is shown in Figure 10. We observe that the privacy conscious users have a higher likelihood of accepting movies that provide high protection, with a 17% difference between the high and low protection levels; the trend is less noticeable for non-privacy aware users, with only 7% difference between the two. Similarly, the respondents also prefer movies that are popular and of high quality.

In addition, we also sought participants' opinion about obfuscating OSN profiles in general. As this was an open question, we did not quantify the opinions, but based on the received comments the participants can be categorized to users who: (1) do not understand the inference attack; (2) do not wish to add any non-genuine content to their profiles; (3) would add any items to protect their privacy; (4) accept only items that are consistent with the image that they wish

---

[3] http://crowdflower.com/
[4] http://imdb.com/

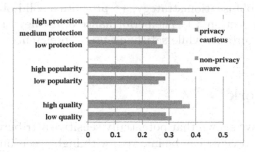

Fig. 10. User provided ratings for different criteria; privacy conscious user: average attribute sensitivity rating higher than 3; non-privacy aware user: average attribute sensitivity rating lower than 3

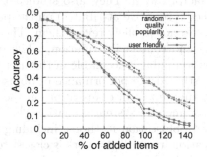

Fig. 11. Inference accuracy for gender using movie items

to present to others, i.e., items the users genuinely like. The last comment is representative of a non-negligible portion of users (12 out of 65 who answered this question) and motivates the design of a user-friendly obfuscation strategy.

5.1   User-friendly Obfuscation Strategy

We now consider the results of the user study, which indicate that *popularity* and *quality* of items need to be considered to have an acceptable obfuscation strategy. As shown in Figure 11, if we apply the obfuscation strategy solely based on these factors, the performance of the obfuscation is quite poor, i.e., similar to the random strategy.

We therefore propose a user-friendly obfuscation strategy that while taking into account both factors of *popularity* and *quality*, yields a significant improvement in obfuscation performance compared to the strategy that exclusively uses these factors. We first select items that are in the top n most popular and top n highest quality lists, where n is a variable that controls the size of the intersection between the popularity and quality sets. We heuristically choose $n = 100$, which results in a subset of 69 common items (that is sufficient for the majority of users to obfuscate their profiles). We then apply the χ^2 score metric to the set of items as the obfuscation strategy; χ^2 provides a solid obfuscation performance, as shown in Section 3.1. The performance of the new strategy is close to χ^2, as shown in Figure 11, while satisfying users' preferences for the choice of obfuscation items.

6 Related Work

Kosinski et al [9] have shown that potentially sensitive attributes like sexual orientation and political views can be inferred, with high precision, using Facebook likes. A number of other research works [8,13] address the inference of users' sensitive attributes from social links, and the protection mechanisms based on selective adding or removal of such links [7]. Ryu et al. [15] evaluated the performance of inferring sensitive attributes using a deterministic algorithm, logistic regression and matrix factorization. They also studied the impact of friends' privacy policies (for selected sensitive attributes) on the potential to infer these attributes for users who do not publicly reveal them. Their approach bases the inference on social links and contact information, while in this paper we only relied on on the information publicly available in the user's own profile.

Weinsberg et al. [17] studied the performance of obfuscation methods using different classifiers, and the impact of obfuscation on the utility of recommendations, in a movie recommender system scenario. They evaluated a number of classifiers and selected obfuscation methods, including greedy, sampled and random choice of obfuscation items. Their work is closest to the study presented in this paper, however their obfuscation approaches assume prior knowledge of the classifier used for the inference attack. Salman et al. [16] proposed a practical methodology to prevent statistical inference (relying on the theoretical framework of [5]); the proposed mechanism distorts the data before making it publicly available, while providing a guarantee of the data utility. Li at al. [10] also present a mechanism for preventing inference attacks (association rules) in a data publishing scenario. All these works considered, in a system setting, only the resulting loss of data utility for other system users and a static privacy mechanism. Our work evaluates the impact of obfuscation on the privacy of other users, and also considers a dynamic mechanism.

7 Conclusion

This paper investigated a set of practical problems related to the design of a usable obfuscation system, to mitigate inference attacks in OSNs. The user study indicates that a number of factors, not directly related to the performance of obfuscation mechanisms, need to be considered to progress towards a system that may be acceptable to privacy-conscious users. We believe that our user-friendly obfuscation strategy, which is designed to integrate the user preferences into an effective solution is a first step in the direction of user acceptability. However, there are a number of additional challenges. The proposed strategy needs to be verified in a real world setting, with development of such an application planned for future work. Then, although the dynamic obfuscation mechanism can provide improved performance compared to the static case, a level of coordination between users may be required in order to achieve an acceptable obfuscation performance in the long term.

References

1. Ardagna, C.A., Cremonini, M., Damiani, E., De Capitani di Vimercati, S., Samarati, P.: Location privacy protection through obfuscation-based techniques. In: Barker, S., Ahn, G.-J. (eds.) Data and Applications Security 2007. LNCS, vol. 4602, pp. 47–60. Springer, Heidelberg (2007)
2. Breiman, L.: Random forests. Machine Learning 45(1), 5–32 (2001)
3. Chaabane, A., Acs, G., Kaafar, M.A.: You are what you like! Information leakage through users' Interests. In: Proceedings of the 19th NDSS (2012)
4. Chen, T., Boreli, R., Kaafar, M.-A., Friedman, A.: On the effectiveness of obfuscation techniques in online social networks. Technical Report 1833-9646-8065, National ICT Australia (April 2014)
5. du Pin Calmon, F., Fawaz, N.: Privacy against statistical inference. In: Allerton Conference, pp. 1401–1408 (2012)
6. Guyon, I., Elisseeff, A.: An introduction to variable and feature selection. J. Mach. Learn. Res. 3, 1157–1182 (2003)
7. He, J., Chu, W.W.: Protecting private information in online social networks. In: Chen, H., Yang, C.C. (eds.) Intelligence and Security Informatics. SCI, vol. 135, pp. 249–273. Springer, Heidelberg (2008)
8. He, J., Chu, W.W., Liu, Z(V.): Inferring Privacy Information from Social Networks. In: Mehrotra, S., Zeng, D.D., Chen, H., Thuraisingham, B., Wang, F.-Y. (eds.) ISI 2006. LNCS, vol. 3975, pp. 154–165. Springer, Heidelberg (2006)
9. Kosinski, M., Stillwell, D., Graepel, T.: Private Traits and Attributes are Predictable from Digital Records of Human Behavior. PNAS 110(15) (2013)
10. Li, C., Shirani-Mehr, H., Yang, X.: Protecting individual information against inference attacks in data publishing. In: Kotagiri, R., Radha Krishna, P., Mohania, M., Nantajeewarawat, E. (eds.) DASFAA 2007. LNCS, vol. 4443, pp. 422–433. Springer, Heidelberg (2007)
11. Lindamood, J., Heatherly, R., Kantarcioglu, M., Thuraisingham, B.: Inferring Private Information Using Social Network Data. In: WWW (2009)
12. Manning, C.D., Raghavan, P., Schütze, H.: Introduction to Information Retrieval. Cambridge University Press, New York (2008)
13. Mislove, A., Viswanath, B., Gummadi, K.P., Druschel, P.: You Are Who You Know: Inferring User Profiles in Online Social Networks. In: WSDM (2010)
14. Peddinti, S.T., Saxena, N.: On the privacy of web search based on query obfuscation: A case study of trackMeNot. In: Atallah, M.J., Hopper, N.J. (eds.) PETS 2010. LNCS, vol. 6205, pp. 19–37. Springer, Heidelberg (2010)
15. Ryu, E., Rong, Y., Li, J., Machanavajjhala, A.: Curso: Protect yourself from Curse of Attribute Inference: a Social Network Privacy-analyzer. In: WDSN (2013)

16. Salamatian, S., Zhang, A., du Pin Calmon, F., Bhamidipati, S., Fawaz, N., Kveton, B., Oliveira, P., Taft, N.: How to Hide the Elephant or the Donkey in the Room: Practical Privacy Against Statistical Inference for Large Data. In: GlobalSIP (2013)
17. Weinsberg, U., Bhagat, S., Ioannidis, S., Taft, N.: Blurme: inferring and obfuscating user gender based on ratings. In: RecSys. ACM (2012)
18. Ye, S., Wu, F., Pandey, R., Chen, H.: Noise Injection for Search Privacy Protection. In: Conference on Computational Science and Engineering (2009)
19. Zheng, Z., Wu, X., Srihari, R.: Feature selection for text categorization on imbalanced data. SIGKDD Explor. Newsl. 6(1), 80–89 (2004)

The Best of Both Worlds:
Combining Information-Theoretic and Computational PIR for Communication Efficiency

Casey Devet and Ian Goldberg

University of Waterloo, ON, Canada
{cjdevet,iang}@cs.uwaterloo.ca

Abstract. The goal of *Private Information Retrieval* (PIR) is the ability to query a database successfully without the operator of the database server discovering which record(s) of the database the querier is interested in. There are two main classes of PIR protocols: those that provide privacy guarantees based on the computational limitations of servers (CPIR) and those that rely on multiple servers not colluding for privacy (IT-PIR). These two classes have different advantages and disadvantages that make them more or less attractive to designers of PIR-enabled privacy enhancing technologies.

We present a hybrid PIR protocol that combines two PIR protocols, one from each of these classes. Our protocol inherits many positive aspects of both classes and mitigates some of the negative aspects. For example, our hybrid protocol maintains partial privacy when the security assumptions of one of the component protocols is broken, mitigating the privacy loss in such an event. We have implemented our protocol as an extension of the Percy++ library so that it combines a PIR protocol by Aguilar Melchor and Gaborit with one by Goldberg. We show that our hybrid protocol uses less communication than either of these component protocols and that our scheme is particularly beneficial when the number of records in a database is large compared to the size of the records. This situation arises in applications such as TLS certificate verification, anonymous communications systems, private LDAP lookups, and others.

1 Introduction

One major goal of *privacy enhancing technologies* (PETs) is to give control over the dissemination of personal information to the users that the information pertains to. PETs rely on underlying primitives to provide a guarantee of privacy to users; these are generally primitives from fields such as cryptography and information theory. Many PETs protocols use the former, relying on assumptions about the infeasibility of solving a specific problem with a limited amount of computing resources. The advantage of the latter (information theory) approach, on the other hand, is that it provides the guarantee that no amount of computing resources will allow an adversary to discover the user's private information. However, using information-theoretic primitives instead of cryptographic ones requires some alternative assumption to support the protocol's privacy guarantees. An assumption used in many PETs, including mix networks [9], secret sharing [29], onion routing [13] and some voting protocols [5,25], is that no more than some threshold of agents are colluding against the user to discover the private information.

E. De Cristofaro and S.J. Murdoch (Eds.): PETS 2014, LNCS 8555, pp. 63–82, 2014.

1.1 Private Information Retrieval

Private Information Retrieval (PIR) is a PET that allows a user to query a database for some records without letting the operator of the database server learn anything about the query or the retrieved records. The most trivial form of PIR is for the client to download the entire database from the server and do the query herself. This is private because the user has not revealed any information about which record she is interested in, yet she still retrieves the record by finding it in the content of the entire database. In a 2007 study, Sion and Carbunar concluded that no single-server PIR protocol would likely outperform this trivial download PIR protocol [30]. However, more recent work has shown that there are indeed non-trivial PIR protocols that perform better than downloading the entire database [23]. PIR has applications in many privacy-sensitive applications, including patent databases [3], domain name registration [22], anonymous email [27], anonymous communication networks [21], and electronic commerce [17].

As a PET, a PIR protocol gets its privacy guarantees from its underlying primitives. One class of PIR protocols, called *computational PIR* (CPIR) encodes the query in such a way that the database server can serve records, while learning nothing about the queries or retrieved records. These privacy guarantees are based on the assumption that some problem is hard or impossible to solve given a limit on computational power. Olumofin and Goldberg [23] showed in 2011 that it is possible for a CPIR protocol to outperform the trivial download protocol. In particular, they showed using empirical results that the CPIR protocol by Aguilar Melchor and Gaborit [2] is faster than trivial download when using typical network connections. One advantage of many CPIR protocols is the ability to use *recursion* to reduce the communication costs. This technique is illustrated by Aguilar Melchor and Gaborit with their CPIR protocol [2].

The other class of PIR protocols, called *information-theoretic PIR* (IT-PIR) does not rely on the assumption that a cryptographic primitive is hard to solve with limited computing resources. In 1995, Chor et al. showed that non-trivial IT-PIR is impossible when there is only a single database server [8]. To combat this result, they designed a multi-server IT-PIR protocol that guarantees privacy as long as not all of the servers are colluding together against the user. Several IT-PIR protocols have since been proposed [4, 14, 16, 17] that use similar non-collusion assumptions. Olumofin and Goldberg [23] also showed that a number of these multi-server IT-PIR protocols perform better than the trivial download PIR.

There are five contributing factors to the speed of a PIR query for a particular protocol:

1. the time for the client to generate a private query;
2. the communication time required to send the query to the server(s);
3. the time for the server(s) to apply the query to the database;
4. the communication time required for the response from the server to the client; and
5. the time for the client to decode the response(s).

Over time, proposed PIR protocols have incrementally improved some or all of these time factors. This paper begins by comparing two PIR protocols, one from each of these two classes. We analyze the costs of the five factors listed above for these protocols in an attempt to improve their performance.

Our main contribution is a novel *hybrid* PIR protocol that incorporates aspects of both classes, including the recursive property of single-server CPIR and the low communication and computation costs of IT-PIR. Our protocol has lower costs, while incorporating the positive properties of both classes.

Our protocol is particularly well suited for databases that consist of a large number of relatively small records. As a practical example of where PIR over databases of this shape would be beneficial, consider the problem of determining the validity of TLS web server certificates. A web client, on receiving a TLS certificate from a server, must check to see whether the certificate is revoked, typically with the Online Certificate Status Protocol (OCSP) [26], or with the recently proposed Certificate Transparency (CT) Protocol [20]. However, doing these lookups will reveal the site the client is visiting to the OCSP or CT servers. PIR has been proposed [18] as a way for clients to privately determine the validity of these certificates. Other applications of PIR over databases of this shape could include sensor network data retrieval [31], private LDAP lookups [28], and efficient retrieval of network information in anonymous communications systems [21].

1.2 Notation

For clarity, we will use the following notation throughout the paper:

- D denotes the database.
- D_i denotes the ith record of the database D.
- n is the number of records in the database.
- s is the size of each record in bits.
- i_0 is the index of the database record that a client wants to retrieve.

Additional notation will be introduced in Sections 2.1, 3.1 and 4.1 to support the protocols presented in those sections.

2 Computational PIR

One class of PIR contains all protocols that assume that the server(s) are computationally bounded to make their privacy guarantees. These protocols generally show that breaking the security of their system would require an adversary to solve a problem that is believed to be hard. These types of assumptions are often used in cryptography, security and privacy; for example, the RSA public-key cryptosystem assumes that factoring large numbers is hard when an adversary has limited resources.

Computational PIR was first introduced by Chor and Gilboa in 1997 [7]. They showed that weakening the adversary to a computationally bounded entity improves the communication costs of PIR. Their work was soon followed by a protocol by Kushilevitz and Ostrovsky [19] that used the same computationally bounded adversary in their model, but did not require multiple servers as previous CPIR protocols did.

One advantage of single-server CPIR protocols is that they can be used recursively to improve the communication cost of PIR. This idea was introduced by Kushilevitz and Ostrovsky in addition to their new single-server CPIR protocol [19]. To do this, we evenly split our database into a set of virtual records, each one containing an equal number of the actual records. The client then queries the server for a particular virtual record, but instead of returning the result to the client, the server holds on to it. The result of the first query is treated as a virtual database containing smaller virtual records. The client then queries for one of the virtual records of this virtual database. The scheme continues in this fashion until we are left with the response for a single (actual) record, which is sent to the client. This idea will be further explored in the next section.

2.1 Aguilar Melchor and Gaborit's Protocol

Without being faster than the trivial download protocol for modest-sized databases, a PIR protocol is not very useful. The main problem with the CPIR protocols already discussed is that they do not generally perform queries faster than the trivial protocol. In 2007, Aguilar Melchor and Gaborit introduced a lattice-based single-server CPIR scheme with promising results [2]; we denote this protocol as AG07. In 2011, Olumofin and Goldberg [23] empirically showed that this protocol outperforms the trivial protocol, thus suggesting that CPIR may indeed be practical.

The idea behind their protocol is to add noise to the query in a way that the server cannot discover which record the client is interested in, but with the secret information that the client has, she can remove the noise from the server's response.

Notation: For this protocol we add the following notation:

- Each record in the database is encoded as an $L \times N$ matrix of w_{AG}-bit words, where N is a security parameter and $L = \left\lceil \frac{s}{w_{AG} \cdot N} \right\rceil$.
- $q \approx 2^{2 \cdot w_{AG}}$ is the *hard noise constant*.
- $p \approx 2^{3 \cdot w_{AG}}$ is the prime modulus of the field used for arithmetic. All matrices in the protocol are over $\mathbb{Z}_p$; the entries in the above database record matrices just happen to have relatively small values ($< 2^{w_{AG}}$) in $\mathbb{Z}_p$.

Aguilar Melchor and Gaborit [2] suggest the values $w_{AG} = 20$, $N = 50$, $q = 2^{40}$, and $p = 2^{60} + 325$ for the above parameters.

Protocol: A client wants to retrieve record i_0 from the database. For each database record, she generates two matrices, one that has been made noisy and one that has not. For the query matrices corresponding to record i_0 she adds hard noise (relatively large disturbances) and for the others she adds soft noise (small disturbances). The privacy guarantees for this protocol assume that the server can not distinguish between query matrices with hard noise and soft noise.

When the client sends the query to the server, the amount of communication (in bits) is $6N^2 w_{AG} \cdot n$.

To process the query, each record in the database is represented as an $L \times N$ matrix whose terms are words of size w_{AG} bits. When the server receives the query, it multiplies each database record D_i by the corresponding query matrix M_i and adds the results to get R.

The server sends the response R back to the client. The amount of communication (in bits) for this step is six times the size of each record, or $6s$.

Finally, when the client receives the response, she removes the soft noise to reveal the database record D_{i_0} that she requested.

For more details on this protocol, see the extended version of this paper [11, Appendix A].

The privacy of this protocol relies on the assumption that the *Hidden Lattice Problem* and the *Differential Hidden Lattice Problem* are hard to solve by computationally bounded adversaries [2]. Aguilar Melchor and Gaborit use related problems in coding theory to justify these assumptions.

Recursive AG07: As stated above, this CPIR protocol can be performed recursively to improve the communication cost of the scheme. We get optimal communication for a given recursive depth d if we split our database into $\sqrt[d]{n}$ virtual records at each iteration.

For example, if we have a database with 125 records and we are performing this recursive protocol with depth 3, in the first iteration we separate the database into $\sqrt[3]{125} = 5$ virtual records, each containing 25 actual records. This client will query the server for the virtual record that her wanted record belongs to, but instead of sending the result R_1 back to the client, the server will hold onto it. In the second iteration, we split up the result R_1 from the first iteration into 5 virtual records, each containing the encoding of 5 actual records. The client will query the server for the virtual record that contains her desired record and again the server holds onto the result R_2. Finally, for the last iteration, the server will split the result R_2 from the second iteration into 5 virtual records, each containing the encoding of one actual record. The client queries the server for the record that she is interested in and server sends the result R_3 of this last iteration to the client. The client must then perform the decoding algorithm 3 times, once for each iteration, to recover the database record.

In general, this improves the client-to-server communication cost to $6N^2 w_{AG} \cdot \sqrt[d]{n}$ bits. However, each iteration of the protocol increases the size of the result by a factor of 6. This makes the server-to-client communication cost $6^d s$ bits. Thus, it is important to find the appropriate recursive depth to balance out this decrease in client-to-server communication and the increase in server-to-client communication.

Advantages and Disadvantages: One advantage of this protocol is that it only requires a single server. As shown later in Section 3, multi-server protocols generally assume that some threshold of the servers are not colluding. CPIR protocols, however, remain secure even if all servers (or the one server in the single-server case) are trying to discover the client's private query.

The AG07 protocol also has the advantage that it can be used recursively, with a relatively low compounding overhead factor (6). As shown above, we can use this property to significantly improve the communication cost incurred by the protocol.

The main disadvantage of this scheme is that the security is based on lattice problems that are not well understood. Because of this, some clients may not completely trust the privacy of their queries. As stated by Aguilar Melchor et al. in a subsequent paper [1] and by Olumofin and Goldberg [23], the protocol resists known lattice-based attacks, but the protocol and its privacy assumptions are new and may not be secure.

Another disadvantage of the AG07 protocol is that it is considerably slower than many IT-PIR schemes [23]. This is due to the amount of computation involved in encoding the queries and because the server is performing a matrix-by-matrix multiplication (as compared to a vector-by-matrix multiplication used by some IT-PIR schemes).

3   Information-Theoretic PIR

The other class of PIR protocols, information-theoretic PIR (IT-PIR), includes all PIR schemes whose privacy guarantees hold no matter how computationally powerful and adversarial the server(s) may be. In 1995, Chor et al. [6] showed that any single-server IT-PIR scheme must have communication cost at least that of the trivial protocol. To avoid this problem, they developed IT-PIR protocols that used multiple servers. Since then, a variety of multiple-server IT-PIR schemes have been formulated [4, 14, 16, 17], making improvements on Chor et al.'s protocols. One of these improvements is *robustness*—the ability to retrieve the correct database records even when some of the servers are down or return incorrect or malicious responses.

An advantage to multiple-server IT-PIR is that it generally incurs smaller communication and computation costs. Like CPIR protocols, multiple-server IT-PIR protocols also need to make some assumptions to guarantee privacy; a commonly used assumption is that at most some threshold of the servers are colluding to discover the contents of a client's query.

3.1   Goldberg's Protocol

In 2007, Goldberg introduced a multiple-server IT-PIR protocol that was both efficient and provided for greater robustness than previous schemes. The idea is to use Shamir secret sharing [29] to split the client's query across multiple servers, and error-correcting codes to combine the responses. We denote this protocol by G07.

Notation: For this protocol we add the following notation:

- The database is laid out as an $n \times m$ matrix of w_G-bit words. Each record is one row of this matrix, and $m = \left\lceil \frac{s}{w_G} \right\rceil$.
- ℓ is the number of servers.
- k is the number of servers that respond to the query.
- t is the privacy level—no coalition of t or fewer servers can learn the query.
- v is the number of Byzantine servers—these are servers that may give incorrect responses.
- $\mathbb{F}$ is the field used for arithmetic ($|\mathbb{F}| \geq 2^{w_G}$). All vectors and matrices in the protocol are over $\mathbb{F}$.

Typically, $w_G = 8$, $\mathbb{F} = GF(2^8)$, and records are an integer number of bytes, so that s is a multiple of 8, and $m \cdot w_G = s$ exactly.

Protocol: To query the server for record i_0, a client creates the elementary vector $\mathbf{e}_{i_0}$ with a 1 in the i_0^{th} place, and 0 everywhere else. She then creates ℓ Shamir secret shares $\mathbf{v}_1, \ldots, \mathbf{v}_\ell$ for $\mathbf{e}_{i_0}$ in the field $\mathbb{F}$.

Each server is then sent one of these shares. The communication cost from the client to each server is then $n \cdot w_G$ bits.

The server simply multiplies their query vector $\mathbf{v_j}$ by the database D to get a response vector $\mathbf{r_j}$, and sends it back to the client. This makes the communication cost from each server to the client $m w_G = s$ bits.

In this protocol, we assume that some number of servers $k \leq \ell$ respond to the query. Even if $k \neq \ell$, meaning that not all servers responded, the client may still be able to recover the database record. This is because the use of Shamir secret sharing in the query makes the server responses Shamir secret shares for the database record D_{i_0}. This implies that the client only needs $k > t$ of the responses (where $t < \ell$) to successfully recover the record.

Similarly, we also do not need to assume that all of the servers are behaving correctly. The client can treat the responses as Reed-Solomon error correction codewords and use a Reed-Solomon decoding algorithm to recover the database record D_{i_0}. As shown by Devet et al. [12], the client can decode the database record in polynomial time as long as the number of Byzantine servers v is bounded by $v < k - t - 1$. They also show that this bound is the optimal bound on the number of tolerable Byzantine servers.

The Shamir secret shares are generated from a degree-t polynomial where $t < k$. By the properties of Shamir secret sharing, any coalition of at most t servers will not gain any information about the secret $\mathbf{e}_{i_0}$. However, if at least $t + 1$ of the servers collude, they will be able to discover $\mathbf{e}_{i_0}$; that is, the query is information-theoretically private assuming that at most t servers are allowed to collude. We note that there is a trade off between the level of robustness and the privacy level—the client can chose a value of t to provide the wanted privacy up to and including $t = \ell - 1$ (all but one of the servers colluding), but then there is no robustness.

For more details on this protocol, see the extended version of this paper [11, Appendix B].

Advantages and Disadvantages: As discussed above, the main advantage of the G07 protocol over other protocols is that is it robust and can handle missing and/or incorrect server responses. This allows us to combat some stronger adversarial servers that maliciously alter their responses in an attempt to block the client from recovering the database record. We note that the AG07 single-server CPIR scheme has no robustness since there is only one server and missing or incorrect responses from that server can not be overcome.

The G07 protocol has low communication cost and computation time. It is also very simple to implement on the server side. A series of works since 2011 have shown that Goldberg's protocol is faster than the trivial protocol [23] and have added improvements to the performance by using distribution of computation [10] and advanced error-correction algorithms [12].

This protocol sacrifices some level of privacy to gain robustness. Because of this we need to assume that there is no collusion between some number of servers. In some settings, it is unclear how this requirement can be enforced or detected. This uncertainty may make this protocol less desirable than others with different privacy guarantees.

Adaptation for Hybrid Security: When he introduced his IT-PIR scheme in 2007 [16], Goldberg proposed an extension to create a scheme whose privacy relied on a hybrid of information-theoretic and computational primitives. This extended scheme provides information-theoretic protection of the query as long as no more than t servers collude, but retains computational protection when any number of the servers collude.

This is accomplished by encrypting the query with an additive homomorphic cryptosystem—G07 used the Pailler cryptosystem. The client will encrypt the query before it is sent to the servers. When the servers receive the query, they multiply it by the database, but use the homomorphic property. In the case of the Pailler cryptosystem, the server would use multiplication in the place of addition and exponentiation in the place of scalar multiplication. The response that the client receives is decrypted before the regular G07 decoding operations are performed.

Though this hybrid scheme relies on two assumptions for privacy (the information-theoretic assumption that no more than t servers collude and the assumption that adversaries do not have the computational resources to break the additive homomorphic cryptosystem used), as long as one of them holds, the protocol still guarantees perfect privacy of the query.

This added protection comes at an extreme cost, however: the hybrid version of G07 is *3–4 orders of magnitude slower* [16] than the pure information-theoretic version. In the next section, we will introduce a new approach to hybrid PIR that combines the benefits of CPIR and IT-PIR without the overhead of previous proposals.

4   Hybrid PIR

In this work, we propose a hybrid protocol that combines a multiple-server IT-PIR protocol with a single-server CPIR protocol. Our goal is to incorporate the positive aspects of each protocol into our hybrid protocol, while mitigating the negative aspects of each. In particular, we want to join the low communication and computation cost of multiple-server IT-PIR schemes with the recursion of single-server CPIR schemes to improve the communication cost of PIR queries relative to both classes of protocols.

Our scheme will use a recursive depth of d as in the AG07 CPIR scheme. However, the first layer of recursion will be performed using the chosen multiple-server IT-PIR protocol. On each server, the remainder of the recursive steps will be done on the result of each previous step using the chosen recursive single-server CPIR scheme.

4.1   Notation

Our hybrid protocol will use the notation outlined in Sections 1.2, 2.1, and 3.1 as well as:

- Ψ is the multiple-server IT-PIR protocol being used.
- Φ is the single-server recursive CPIR protocol being used.

- γ_u is the number of virtual records that the database is split into for the uth step of recursion of the hybrid scheme. It is required that $n \leq \prod_{u=1}^{d} \gamma_u$.

- δ_u is the number of actual records in each virtual record at the uth step of recursion of the hybrid scheme. If the database does not evenly split, dummy records are appended to the end of the database to make each virtual record the same size.

- π_u is the index of the virtual record that the client's desired actual record i_0 is in at the uth step of recursion.

We outline how to optimally choose the values for γ_u and δ_u in Section 5.1.

4.2 Protocol

Our protocol is generalized to use the implementer's choice of inner protocols. We use Ψ to denote the multiple-server IT-PIR inner protocol and use Φ to denote the single-server recursive CPIR inner protocol. We use this notation because our protocol is very well suited for a modular implementation. That is, an implementation of this scheme could easily swap inner protocols for other suitable protocols.

Algorithm 4.1 outlines how to generate a query for this protocol. To query the database servers, the client must determine the index π_u of the virtual record that her desired record i_0 is contained in, at each step u of the recursion. She then creates a multiple-server IT-PIR Ψ-query for index π_1 and sends each server its part of the query. Then for each remaining recursive step $u \in \{2, \ldots, d\}$, she creates single-server CPIR Φ-queries for index π_u and sends this same query to each of the servers.

Algorithm 4.2 outlines the server-side computations for this protocol. In each recursive step u, the server splits the database into γ_u virtual records, each containing δ_u actual records. For the first step, the server uses the IT-PIR Ψ server computation algorithm. For the remainder of the steps, the server uses the CPIR Φ server computation algorithm. The result of the last recursive step is sent back to the client.

We note that we can somewhat improve the performance of this scheme by starting the server-side computations for each recursive step before reading the queries for subsequent recursive steps, thus overlapping computation and communication.

When the client receives the servers' responses, she applies the corresponding decoding algorithms using the information stored during query generation in reverse order.

Algorithm 4.1. Hybrid Query Generation

Input: Desired record index: i_0

1. For each recursive step $u \in \{1, \ldots, d\}$ find the index of the virtual record π_u that record i_0 belongs to.
2. Generate a multiple-server Ψ-query Q_1 for index π_1 and send each server its part of the query.
3. **for** $u = 2 \rightarrow d$ **do**
4.   Generate a single-server Φ-query Q_u for index π_u and send each server a copy of the query.

Algorithm 4.2. Hybrid Server Computation

Input: Query from client: $Q_1, \ldots, Q_d$

1. Split the database D into $D^{(1)}$, a virtual database of γ_1 consecutive virtual records, each containing δ_1 actual records.
2. Apply the Ψ-query Q_1 to database $D^{(1)}$ using the Ψ server computation algorithm. The result is R_1 which will be used as the database for the next recursive step.
3. **for** $u = 2 \to d$ **do**
4.   Split the result R_{u-1} into $D^{(u)}$, a virtual database of γ_u consecutive virtual records, each containing the encoding of δ_u actual records
5.   Apply the Φ-query Q_u to database $D^{(u)}$ using the Φ server computation algorithm to get result R_u.
6. Send the final result R_d to the client.

Algorithm 4.3. Hybrid Response Decoding

Input: Responses from the servers: $X_1^{(d)}, \ldots, X_k^{(d)}$

1. **for** $u = d \to 2$ **do**
2.   **for** $j = 1 \to k$ **do**
3.   Decode $X_j^{(u)}$ from server j using the Φ single-server decoding algorithm to get result $X_j^{(u-1)}$.
4. Decode $X_1^{(1)}, \ldots, X_k^{(1)}$ simultaneously using the Ψ multiple-server decoding algorithm to recover the database record D_{i_0}.

That is, she first uses the information from query Q_d to decode the received responses. Treating the results of that decoding as virtual responses themselves, she uses information from Q_{d-1} to decode those, and so on until she uses information from Q_1 to decode the final step. This yields the desired record. The procedure for decoding server responses for this protocol is outlined in Algorithm 4.3. We note that for all but the last step of decoding, the result from each server must be decoded separately using the single-server decoding algorithm for protocol Φ. In the last step of decoding, all server results are decoded simultaneously using the multiple-server decoding algorithm for protocol Ψ.

5   Analytical Evaluation

This evaluation of the hybrid scheme uses the G07 IT-PIR scheme for Ψ and the AG07 CPIR scheme for Φ.

5.1   Communication

The communication cost of the response from the server to the client is simply

$$C_{down} = 6^{d-1}s.$$

If we combine the communication costs for the queries at each recursive step, we get the following total cost for the query (in bits) from the client to each server:

$$C_{up} = \gamma_1 w_G + \sum_{u=2}^{d} \left(6N^2 w_{AG} \cdot \gamma_u\right).$$

To optimize C_{up}, we first find the optimal choices for the γ_u values for any given d.

After the first recursive step the result will encode $\delta_1 = \lceil \frac{n}{\gamma_1} \rceil$ records. We can optimize the CPIR query sizes by splitting the database at each remaining step into $\gamma_u = {}^{(d-1)}\!\sqrt{\delta_1}$ virtual records. The cost becomes:

$$C_{up} = \gamma_1 w_G + \sum_{u=2}^{d} \left(6N^2 w_{AG} \cdot \left(\frac{n}{\gamma_1}\right)^{\frac{1}{d-1}}\right).$$
$$= \gamma_1 w_G + (d-1) \cdot 6N^2 w_{AG} \cdot \left(\frac{n}{\gamma_1}\right)^{\frac{1}{d-1}}$$

We then find the value of γ_1 that minimizes C_{up} to be:

$$\gamma_1 = \left(\frac{6N^2 w_{AG}}{w_G} {}^{(d-1)}\!\sqrt{n}\right)^{\frac{d-1}{d}}.$$

Therefore, at recursive step u, we split the database as follows:

$$\gamma_u = \begin{cases} \left(\frac{6N^2 w_{AG}}{w_G} {}^{(d-1)}\!\sqrt{n}\right)^{\frac{d-1}{d}} & : u = 1 \\ \left(\frac{n}{\gamma_1}\right)^{\frac{1}{d-1}} & : 2 \le u \le d \end{cases}$$

$$\delta_u = \left(\frac{n}{\gamma_1}\right)^{\frac{d-u}{d-1}}$$

With these values, our query communication cost simplifies to:

$$C_{up} = d \left(6N^2 w_{AG}\right)^{\frac{d-1}{d}} \sqrt[d]{w_G} \sqrt[d]{n}.$$

We observe that both the query and response cost functions (C_{up} and C_{down}) are concave up in d. Therefore, the combined communication cost can be minimized for some depth d. Since d is an integer, we evaluate the cost functions at each d starting at 1 and incrementing until we find a value for d such that the cost at d is less than the cost at $d+1$. This value of d is our optimal depth.

Note that the combined cost function should ideally, if such information is available, take the bandwidths of both directions of our connection into account and that the different directions may have different bandwidths. This is accomplished with a simple linear weighting, such as $4C_{down} + C_{up}$ if the downstream bandwidth is 4 times that of the upstream.

Table 1 shows a comparison of the communication cost for each of the protocols in this paper.

Table 1. A comparison of the communication costs (in bits) for the PIR protocols discussed in this paper

Protocol	Query Cost	Response Cost
AG07 [2]	$\left(6N^2 w_{AG}\right) n$	$6s$
Recursive AG07 [2]	$d\left(6N^2 w_{AG}\right)\sqrt[d]{n}$	$6^d s$
G07 [16]	$\ell w_G n$	ℓs
Our hybrid (with AG07 and G07)	$\ell d\left(6N^2 w_{AG}\right)^{\frac{d-1}{d}}\sqrt[d]{w_G}\sqrt[d]{n}$	$\ell 6^{d-1} s$

If we use our hybrid protocol with a depth of $d = 1$, then we are simply using the G07 protocol (with no CPIR component) and so will clearly have the same amount of communication as the G07 protocol. Since we choose the value of d that minimizes the communication cost for our hybrid protocol, we only use $d > 1$ if doing so results in a lower communication cost. Hence when we use a depth of $d > 1$, we will have a lower communication cost than the G07 scheme. Therefore, our hybrid scheme will not have a higher communication cost than G07 for any depth. For typical values of the parameters, we find that for 1 KB records, we will select $d > 1$ (and so strictly outperform G07) whenever $n > 160,000$. For 10 KB records, we see an improvement for $n > 240,000$.

Comparing the formulas in Table 1, we see that the upstream cost of our hybrid protocol is no worse than that of Recursive AG07 when $\ell^d \leq \frac{6N^2 w_{AG}}{w_G}$ (= 37500 for the recommended parameters), and similarly for the downstream cost when $\ell \leq 6$. For many reasonable PIR setups, these inequalities are easily satisfied. Even if they are not, however, the computational savings of our scheme over Recursive AG07 (see below) more than makes up for the difference. A slight complication in the analysis arises in cases in which the optimal recursive depth d differs between the Recursive AG07 scheme and our hybrid scheme; however, we will see in Section 6 that our scheme nonetheless outperforms the Recursive AG07 scheme.

5.2   Computation

Unlike our analysis of communication, we do not have simple expressions for our computation costs. In this section we reason about the computational cost of our protocol compared to others; in Section 6.2, below, we directly measure the computation costs of our scheme using empirical experimentation. The key observation, however, is that the slower CPIR protocol is being performed over a *much smaller database* than the original. The protocol effectively consists of IT-PIR over the whole database of n records, followed by recursive CPIR over a sub-database of δ_1 records.

Query Encoding: AG07 is expensive when generating the query because it involves matrix multiplications. However, G07 is relatively cheap because it is essentially just generating random values and evaluating polynomials. We expect the hybrid scheme will be better than AG07 for this step because it replaces one iteration with the cheap

G07 scheme encoding. Our hybrid scheme may also be faster in this stage than G07 because of the addition of recursion. As when recursion is added to the AG07 protocol, we change the request from one large (size n) query into d much smaller (size a constant multiple of $\sqrt[d]{n}$) queries.

Server Computation: The AG07 scheme is also expensive compared to the G07 scheme for server-side computation. This is because AG07 uses matrix-by-matrix multiplication for the bulk of its work, whereas G07 uses vector-by-matrix multiplication. Our hybrid scheme will use the relatively cheap server computation of G07 for the first iteration where the database is its full size. The subsequent iterations will use a much smaller subset of the database, so using AG07's server computation will not add much additional expense.

Response Decoding: The last recursive step of decoding for our hybrid scheme will take the same amount of computation as the G07 scheme. Since we have $d - 1$ steps of AG07 decoding as well, our hybrid protocol will not outperform G07 in the decoding step. Our hybrid protocol will also need to do any AG07 decoding once for every server at every recursive step. However, the response being decoded at each recursive step is smaller than that of the recursive AG07 protocol by a factor of 6 in our hybrid scheme. Therefore, when $d > 1$, the decoding for our hybrid protocol will be comparable to that of recursive AG07.

If there are a significant number of Byzantine servers—those who attempt to maliciously alter the result of the query—then the decoding time will be increased for the G07 iteration of our hybrid scheme, though this increase will not be very significant compared to the server computation of the G07 scheme [12].

5.3 Privacy

The AG07 scheme keeps the client's query private as long as the servers are computationally bounded and as long as the Hidden Lattice Problem and the Differential Hidden Lattice Problem are indeed hard to solve. Our hybrid scheme relies on these assumptions for perfect privacy.

The G07 scheme keeps the query private as long as no more than t servers are colluding to find the contents of the query. Our hybrid scheme also relies on this non-collusion assumption for perfect privacy.

One advantage of our hybrid scheme is that if the privacy assumptions for one of the inner protocols is broken, then the query will still be partially private as long as we use depth $d > 1$. For example, if the G07 non-collusion assumption is broken, then the colluding servers will be able to find out a subset of the database that the desired record is in, but they will not find out which record in that subset is the wanted one as long as the AG07 assumptions still hold. We similarly have partial privacy if the AG07 computational assumptions are broken and the G07 non-collusion assumptions still hold.

This "defence in depth" is a benefit because it may dull some of the fears about using a scheme that a user thinks does not adequately enough guarantee privacy. For example, if someone does not feel that the non-collusion assumption is adequate enough for the G07 scheme, they may be more comfortable using this hybrid scheme because they know that even in the event that too many servers collude, they will still maintain some privacy.

Unlike the hybrid protection extension to G07 (Section 3.1), our protocol does not provide perfect privacy if one of the two privacy assumptions fails. The advantages of using our protocol over hybrid G07 are a significant reduction in computation time and, as will be illustrated in Section 6.1, improved communication cost.

5.4 Robustness

As stated previously, the G07 scheme has the ability to correct for servers not responding or responding incorrectly. The single-server AG07 scheme, however, does not have any robustness.

In 2012, Devet et al. [12] observed that the G07 protocol can be slightly modified to be able to withstand up to $v < k - t - 1$ misbehaving servers, with no extra computation or communication cost over the original protocol, in a typical setting where clients aim to fetch multiple records from the database. (The original G07 bound [16] is $v < k - \sqrt{kt}$ when only one record is retrieved.)

An advantage of using G07 in our hybrid protocol is that our hybrid protocol retains exactly the same robustness properties as that scheme: any misbehaviour will be detected at the Ψ IT-PIR multiple-server decoding step.

6   Implementation and Empirical Evaluation

We have implemented these protocols as an extension to the Percy++ [15] library, an implementation of Goldberg's scheme from Section 3.1. We incorporated both the AG07 CPIR scheme and our hybrid scheme. Our implementation will be available in the next release of Percy++.

The implementation of our hybrid PIR system combines the implementations of the two inner protocols (G07 and AG07), using them as black boxes. Given all of the other parameters, our implementation will find the optimal depth (d) and the best way to split the database for the first (IT-PIR) iteration of the scheme (γ_1) to minimize the communication cost.

All of our multi-server queries were run on $\ell = 4$ servers and we used $t = 1$ for the G07 privacy parameter. For our client machine, we used a 2.4 GHz Intel Xeon 8870, and each server machine was a 2.0 GHz Intel Xeon E5-2650. All computations reported here were done in a single thread, so that the reported times reflect total CPU time. However, all of the computations are almost completely parallelizable [10], and using multiple cores would greatly reduce end-to-end latency, though not total CPU time.

6.1   Communication

The plots in Figure 1 illustrate the amount of communication needed for our hybrid scheme and the schemes of which it is comprised. We see that our hybrid protocol uses less communication than that of AG07, and no more than that of G07, verifying the analysis in Section 5.1, above.

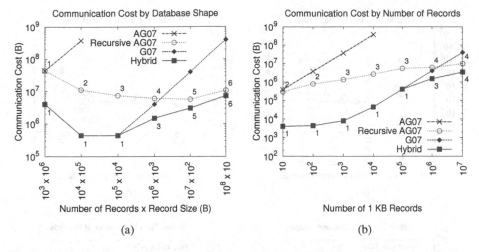

Fig. 1. Comparison of communication used by each scheme. Plot (a) shows the communication used for queries on a 1 GB database for different database shapes. In plot (b), the record size is fixed at 1 KB and we see the communication for different numbers of records. Non-recursive AG07 imposes a limit of approximately 10,000 records so we do not have data points for larger numbers of records. Error bars are present for all data points, but may be too small to see. The datapoint labels for the Hybrid and Recursive AG07 schemes indicate the recursive depth used.

6.2 Computation

Figure 2 illustrates computation time involved in all three of the computational parts of a PIR system.

Query Encoding: Our experimental results show us that the encoding time is very much related to the size of a PIR request. This is evidenced by how similar Figure 2b is to Figure 1b (the communication associated with the same tests). The query encoding time for G07 is linear in the number of records. On the other hand, the query encoding time for the AG07 scheme is dominated by the dth root of the number of records. Because of this, for larger numbers of records, the hybrid protocol encodes queries faster than G07.

Server Computation: As expected, Figures 2c and 2d show that the server computation time of our hybrid PIR system is very comparable to that of the G07 protocol. The figures also show that our hybrid system performs its server computation approximately 2 orders of magnitude faster than Recursive AG07. As noted above, this time is also highly parallelizable; the times reported in the figure use only a single thread, and so represent total CPU time.

Response Decoding: Figures 2e and 2f show us that when we have a depth of at least 2 for the hybrid PIR system (i.e. we have at least one iteration of AG07) , the

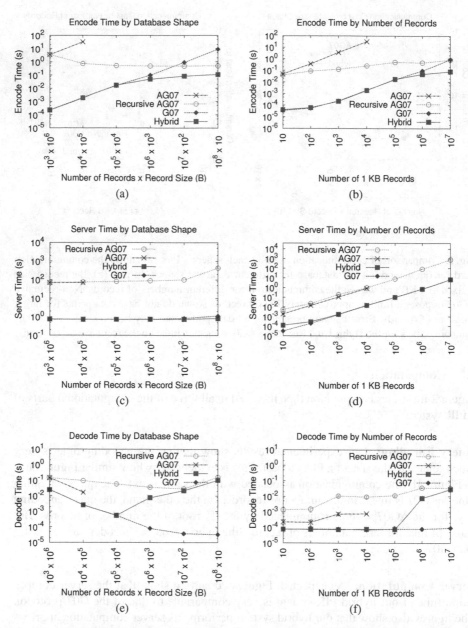

Fig. 2. Comparison of the time used by the schemes at each computation step. Plots (a,c,e) show the computation time for queries on a 1 GB database for different database shapes. In plots (b,d,f), the record size is fixed at 1 KB and we see the computation time for different numbers of records. Non-recursive AG07 imposes a limit of approximately 10,000 records so we do not have data points for larger numbers of records. Error bars are present for all data points, but may be too small to see.

decoding time approaches that of recursive AG07. This is because, unlike the server computation where the cheap G07 computation is being done on the first iteration when the database is large, the cheap G07 decoding is happening on the last iteration, when the response has been reduced in size by $d - 1$ iterations of AG07 decoding. For this reason, the decoding step of our hybrid PIR system is comparable to that of recursive AG07 and not the quicker G07. Even so, we note that the time of the decoding step is quite insignificant compared to the server computation step of a query.

6.3 Total Query Time

In Figure 3 we plot the total time for a query on our hybrid PIR system as well as its component protocols. We show the total time for three different connection speeds between the client and server(s). Figures 3a and 3b use a connection with 9 Mbps download and 2 Mbps upload. This connection was used by Olumofin and Goldberg [23] to represent a home user's connection in 2010. Using the same source [24], we represent a home user in 2014 in Canada or the U.S. with 20 Mbps download and 5 Mbps upload in Figures 3c and 3d. Figures 3e and 3f model a connection over 100 Mbps Ethernet.

Our results show us that the total query time needed for our hybrid PIR system is similar or better than that of G07. We also see that the total query time of recursive AG07 is approximately 2 orders of magnitude larger than that of our system.

These plots also illustrate that our hybrid PIR system does not use much communication time. This is because the total query time of the hybrid system does not improve much when the network capacity is increased. Contrast this with G07 when there are a large number of records—in this case we see a significant improvement in total query time as the network capacity increases.

7   Future Work

Parallel Server Computation. We note that the bulk of the computation is on the server side of the protocol. Devet [10] describes experiments showing that the G07 protocol is almost completely parallelizable: using m threads or worker processes will improve the computation latency of G07 by a factor of m. We believe similar results are attainable for our hybrid system and as future work we intend to implement distributed server computation for this scheme.

AG07 using GPUs. Aguilar Melchor et al. [1] demostrate how the AG07 scheme can be made much faster by implementing the server-side computations on GPUs instead of CPUs. Our implementation does not include this feature, but we plan on implementing it in the future and investigating how much this will speed up our hybrid protocol.

Security of AG07. AG07's privacy guarantees rely on the hardness of the Hidden Lattice Problem and the Differential Hidden Lattice Problem, as specified by Aguilar Melchor and Gaborit [2]. According to Aguilar Melchor et al. [1] and Olumofin et al. [23] the security of this scheme is not well understood. Future work could involve investigating the security of the scheme and either developing a security proof or altering the scheme to make it provably secure.

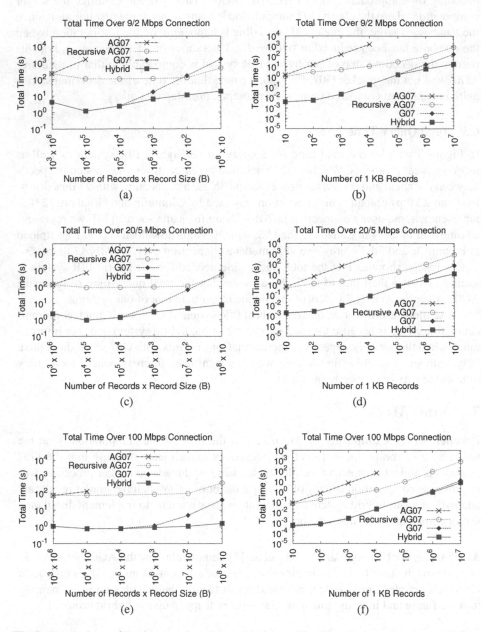

Fig. 3. Comparison of total query time for each scheme. Plots (a,c,e) show the time used for queries on a 1 GB database for different database shapes. In plots (b,d,f), the record size is fixed at 1 KB and we see the time for different numbers of records. Non-recursive AG07 imposes a limit of approximately 10,000 records so we do not have data points for larger numbers of records. Error bars are present for all data points, but may be too small to see. Connections specified as A/B Mbps indicate A Mbps download bandwidth and B Mbps upload bandwidth.

8   Conclusion

We introduce a hybrid Private Information Retrieval protocol that combines the low communication and computation costs of multiple-server IT-PIR protocols with the ability of single-server CPIR protocols to do recursion. We show that our protocol inherits several positive aspects of both types of protocols and mitigates the negative aspects. In particular, our protocol maintains partial privacy of client query information if the assumptions made by one of the inner protocols is broken.

We have implemented our protocol as part of the open-source Percy++ library for PIR, and using this implementation, demonstrated that our protocol performs as well or better than PIR schemes by Aguilar Melchor and Gaborit and by Goldberg. Our hybrid scheme is particularly effective when the number of records in a database is large relative to the size of each record—a situation that arises naturally in a number of network scenarios, including TLS certificate checking, private LDAP lookups, sensor networks, and more.

Acknowledgements. We thank Ryan Henry for the idea that inspired us to explore this new type of Hybrid PIR. We gratefully acknowledge NSERC and ORF for funding this research. This work benefited from the use of the CrySP RIPPLE Facility at the University of Waterloo.

References

1. Aguilar Melchor, C., Crespin, B., Gaborit, P., Jolivet, V., Rousseau, P.: High-Speed Private Information Retrieval Computation on GPU. In: SECURWARE, pp. 263–272. IEEE (2008)
2. Aguilar-Melchor, C., Gaborit, P.: A Lattice-Based Computationally-Efficient Private Information Retrieval Protocol. In: WEWORC 2007 (July 2007)
3. Asonov, D.: Private Information Retrieval: An overview and current trends. In: ECDPvA Workshop (2001)
4. Beimel, A., Ishai, Y., Malkin, T.: Reducing the Servers' Computation in Private Information Retrieval: PIR with Preprocessing. J. Cryptology 17(2), 125–151 (2004)
5. Chaum, D., Carback, R., Clark, J., Essex, A., Popoveniuc, S., Rivest, R.L., Ryan, P.Y.A., Shen, E., Sherman, A.T., Vora, P.L.: Scantegrity II: End-to-end verifiability by voters of optical scan elections through confirmation codes. IEEE Transactions on Information Forensics and Security 4(4), 611–627 (2009)
6. Chor, B., Goldreich, O., Kushilevitz, E., Sudan, M.: Private Information Retrieval. In: 36th Annual IEEE Symposium on Foundations of Computer Science (FOCS 1995), pp. 41–50 (October 1995)
7. Chor, B., Gilboa, N., Naor, M.: Private Information Retrieval by Keywords. Technical Report TR CS0917, Department of Computer Science, Technion, Israel (1997)
8. Chor, B., Kushilevitz, E., Goldreich, O., Sudan, M.: Private Information Retrieval. J. ACM 45, 965–981 (1998)
9. Danezis, G., Dingledine, R., Mathewson, N.: Mixminion: Design of a Type III Anonymous Remailer Protocol. In: IEEE Symposium on Security and Privacy, pp. 2–15. IEEE Computer Society (2003)
10. Devet, C.: Evaluating Private Information Retrieval on the Cloud. Technical Report 2013-05, CACR (2013), http://cacr.uwaterloo.ca/techreports/2013/cacr2013-05.pdf

11. Devet, C., Goldberg, I.: The Best of Both Worlds: Combining Information-Theoretic and Computational PIR for Communication Efficiency. Technical Report 2014-07, CACR, http://cacr.uwaterloo.ca/techreports/2014/cacr2014-07.pdf
12. Devet, C., Goldberg, I., Heninger, N.: Optimally Robust Private Information Retrieval. In: 21st USENIX Security Symposium (2012)
13. Dingledine, R., Mathewson, N., Syverson, P.: Tor: The Second-Generation Onion Router. In: 13th USENIX Security Symposium (2004)
14. Gertner, Y., Goldwasser, S., Malkin, T.: A Random Server Model for Private Information Retrieval or How to Achieve Information Theoretic PIR Avoiding Database Replication. In: Rolim, J.D.P., Serna, M., Luby, M. (eds.) RANDOM 1998. LNCS, vol. 1518, pp. 200–217. Springer, Heidelberg (1998)
15. Goldberg, I.: Percy++ project on SourceForge, http://percy.sourceforge.net (accessed February 2014)
16. Goldberg, I.: Improving the Robustness of Private Information Retrieval. In: 2007 IEEE Symposium on Security and Privacy, pp. 131–148 (2007)
17. Henry, R., Olumofin, F.G., Goldberg, I.: Practical PIR for Electronic Commerce. In: ACM Conference on Computer and Communications Security, pp. 677–690 (2011)
18. Kikuchi, H.: Private Revocation Test using Oblivious Membership Evaluation Protocol. In: 3rd Annual PKI R&D Workshop (2004)
19. Kushilevitz, E., Ostrovsky, R.: Replication Is Not Needed: Single Database, Computationally-Private Information Retrieval. In: FOCS, pp. 364–373 (1997)
20. Laurie, B., Langley, A., Kasper, E.: Certificate Transparency. RFC 6962 (June 2013)
21. Mittal, P., Olumofin, F., Troncoso, C., Borisov, N., Goldberg, I.: PIR-Tor: Scalable Anonymous Communication Using Private Information Retrieval. In: 20th USENIX Security Symposium, pp. 475–490 (2011)
22. Olumofin, F., Goldberg, I.: Privacy-Preserving Queries over Relational Databases. In: Atallah, M.J., Hopper, N.J. (eds.) PETS 2010. LNCS, vol. 6205, pp. 75–92. Springer, Heidelberg (2010)
23. Olumofin, F., Goldberg, I.: Revisiting the Computational Practicality of Private Information Retrieval. In: Danezis, G. (ed.) FC 2011. LNCS, vol. 7035, pp. 158–172. Springer, Heidelberg (2012)
24. Ookla: Net Metrics for Canada and the United States, http://www.netindex.com (accessed February 2014)
25. Ryan, P.Y.A., Schneider, S.A.: Prêt à Voter with Re-encryption Mixes. In: Gollmann, D., Meier, J., Sabelfeld, A. (eds.) ESORICS 2006. LNCS, vol. 4189, pp. 313–326. Springer, Heidelberg (2006)
26. Santesson, S., Myers, M., Ankney, R., Malpani, A., Galperin, S., Adams, C.: X.509 Internet Public Key Infrastructure Online Certificate Status Protocol - OCSP. RFC 6960 (June 2013)
27. Sassaman, L., Cohen, B.: The Pynchon Gate: A Secure Method of Pseudonymous Mail Retrieval. In: Proceedings of the Workshop on Privacy in the Electronic Society (WPES 2005), pp. 1–9 (2005)
28. Sermersheim, J.: Lightweight Directory Access Protocol (LDAP): The Protocol. RFC 4511 (June 2006)
29. Shamir, A.: How to share a secret. Commun. ACM 22, 612–613 (1979)
30. Sion, R., Carbunar, B.: On the Computational Practicality of Private Information Retrieval. In: Proceedings of the Network and Distributed Systems Security Symposium (2007)
31. Xively: Public Cloud for the Internet of Things, http://www.xively.com (accessed February 2014)

Social Status and the Demand for Security and Privacy

Jens Grossklags[1] and Nigel J. Barradale[2]

[1] College of Information Sciences and Technology,
The Pennsylvania State University, USA
[2] Department of Finance,
Copenhagen Business School, Denmark

Abstract. High-status decision makers are often in a position to make choices with security and privacy relevance not only for themselves but also for groups, or even society at-large. For example, decisions about security technology investments, anti-terrorism activities, and domestic security, broadly shape the balance between security and privacy. However, it is unclear to what extent the mass of individuals share the same concerns as high-status individuals. In particular, it is unexplored in the academic literature whether an individual's status position shapes one's security and privacy concerns.

The method of investigation used is experimental, with 146 subjects interacting in high- or low-status assignments and the subsequent change in the demand for security and privacy being related to status assignment with a significant t-statistic up to 2.9, depending on the specification. We find that a high-status assignment significantly increases security concerns. This effect is observable for two predefined sub-dimensions of security (i.e., personal and societal concerns) as well as for the composite measure. We find only weak support for an increase in the demand for privacy with a low-status manipulation.

We complement these results with a second experiment on individuals' time preferences with 120 participants. We show that the high-status manipulation is correlated with increased patience, i.e., those individuals exhibit more robust long-term appreciation of decisions. Given that many security and privacy decisions have long-term implications and delayed consequences, our results suggest that high-status decision makers are less likely to procrastinate on important security investments, and are more likely to account for future risks appropriately. The opposite applies to privacy and low-status roles.

Keywords: Privacy, Security, Social status, Time Preferences, Experiment, Laboratory.

1 Introduction and Research Objectives

With the heightened impact of a broad range of cybercriminal activites and the threat from diffuse terrorist groups, countermeasures and policy activities

E. De Cristofaro and S.J. Murdoch (Eds.): PETS 2014, LNCS 8555, pp. 83–101, 2014.

that influence the balance between privacy and security have become central societal issues. Many commentators have argued that there is an inherent trade-off related to these two concepts. The common adage is that better security always necessitates concessions on the side of privacy [45].

This belief has been challenged by several security and privacy researchers and advocates. Further, computer scientists have worked on key technologies to gather security-relevant information without unduly impacting individuals' privacy, e.g., in the context of video surveillance [40]. Progress has also been made to disambiguate important overgeneralizations about the privacy-security trade-off. For example, Solove provided a succinct discussion of the nothing-to-hide argument [43].

In contrast, our knowledge about the behavioral trade-off, or to put it differently, the joint demand for security and privacy, remains lackluster. Most studies focus on either security or privacy, but rarely on both variables at the same time. For example, starting with Westin's surveys, countless studies have reported a typically moderate to high average concern for privacy in the subject population (see, for example, [32]). Similarly, the perceived threat of terrorism and cyber-crime is reflected by a heightened overall concern for security (e.g., [15,55]). From an economic perspective, some studies document the existence of a positive (but usually small) willingness-to-pay for additional privacy or information security measures [22,39,48].

Even less is known about factors that moderate the trade-off between security and privacy, and that might be able to explain the apparent heterogeneity of individuals' preferences and behaviors. Our research targets this problem area. In particular, we argue that the relative social status of an individual is an important factor influencing concerns for security and privacy.

Social status may be broadly defined as power and influence hierarchy of the members of a society with accompanying dominance and submissive behaviors [6,7]. Social status is thus a relative, rather than absolute, measure. Social status may include measures of socioeconomic status such as occupation, education, income and wealth. Further, intelligence, age and ethnicity may function as status cues that lead to power and influence within groups [50].

Our method of investigation is experimental with subjects being assigned a role with high or low status, respectively. This allows us to demonstrate causation (instead of merely statistical correlation) from a low/high-status assignment to a shift in the variables under observation. In this paper, we present results from two experiments.

First, we study the impact of the social status manipulation on the demand for security and privacy. We subdivide security concerns into societal and personal dimensions [8].

Second, we report results from a parallel investigation into individuals' time preferences. Specifically, we measure the level of patience, which is the willingness to delay pleasure for an ultimately greater benefit.

Lower socioeconomic status is correlated with less patience (or more impatience), whether it is measured using education, income, or even age [37].

Similarly, many field behaviors that are more prevalent in low-status groups are associated with a high level of impatience, including lack of exercise, smoking and body mass index [10], substance abuse [31,38], and delinquency in juveniles [53]. This literature demonstrates the importance of impatience in shaping unhealthy behaviors, with individuals from lower status groups more frequently procrastinating on important investments into their future wealth or health, or seeking immediate gratification when patience would be to their benefit. However, the existing literature is merely correlational with regards to status and does not demonstrate causation from status to impatience.

Together, the two experiments contribute to a better understanding of how subjects from different social status categories perceive threats to their privacy and security, and whether they are likely able to act upon their preferences in an effective manner.

First, privacy and security decisions by high-status individuals can be aligned or misaligned with the interests of low-status individuals. Our work suggests that social status differences contribute to a misalignment of these interests. Second, effective privacy and security decision-making usually involves the economic evaluation of positive or negative consequences over time [2,3]. For example, revealing data on a social networking site may have short-term benefits, but may also increase the individual's vulnerability to cybercrime (e.g., social phishing [28]) or mass surveillance. However, such negative events typically happen at an unspecified later date. Decision-makers need to be able to account for such scenarios to be able to make privacy and security decisions that limit their exposure to negative events in the future. However, a higher degree of impatience (as evidenced with low-status individuals) would hinder the correct evaluation of such scenarios [18].

The remainder of the paper is structured as follows. We discuss related work in Section 2. In Section 3, we discuss the experimental setup in detail. In Section 4, we present the results of the experiments. Finally, we engage in a discussion of the results and present concluding remarks in Sections 5 and 6, respectively. The Appendix includes the key elements of the experimental instructions and survey measures.

2   Background

Going back to Westin's seminal work [51], the study of individuals' valuation of privacy has been identified as a complex issue and continues to present researchers with theoretical challenges and contradictory empirical revelations (see, for example, Solove [44] and Spiekermann et al. [46]). A number of review articles have summarized findings about the various factors that influence individuals' perceptions, preferences and behaviors regarding privacy (see, for example, Brandimarte and Acquisti [9] and Hui and Png [27]).

Capturing this complexity (and lessons learned) in an adequate decision-making model may appear as an insurmountable task. However, Acquisti and Grossklags provided a high level classification of important factors [3]. First, individuals are hampered in their decision-making due to information boundaries in the marketplace (such as asymmetric or incomplete information). Second, individuals suffer from their bounded rationality and have to avail themselves of learned or innate heuristics to respond in complex privacy scenarios (such as, for example, by applying *rational ignorance* about too complex matters). Third, certain psychological biases lead to systematic deviations of expected behaviors (e.g., time-inconsistent discounting).

Responding to the third factor, work by Acquisti and colleagues has shown that privacy preferences are malleable, i.e., preferences can be *easily* changed or influenced (see, for example, the previously cited review article [9]). Our work is related to these findings, however, we argue that privacy and security preferences are dependent on the relative social status of an individual within a target population.

Given our careful reading of the related work, our approach is novel from at least three perspectives. First, by utilizing a test-manipulation-retest methodology we can demonstrate causality with respect to privacy and security preferences as a result of the manipulation of social status in the subject population. We are not aware of many studies in the privacy and security fields that apply this methodology (see [4] for an example in the security education context). Second, as described in the introduction, the relative social status of an individual may depend on many important factors such as wealth, professional achievement, and education/skills. It is, therefore, a central aspect of our society that has not, yet, found adequate consideration in the privacy/security literature. Third, we conduct an experiment measuring privacy and security preferences at the same time; a timely topic given the recent revelations about mass surveillance that demand a sophisticated response from decision-makers in business and policy, and the general population.

3   Experimental Setup

In the following, we present the essential building blocks of the two experiments (see Figure 1).

3.1   Overview

Similar to clinical trials for new drugs and experiments in psychology and biology, we conduct measurements (in the form of a survey) of variables of interest before and after a manipulation. This test-manipulation-retest methodology has been applied less often in social science and economic research. The main benefit is that it allows us to clearly address questions of causation between important behavioral measures.

In the first experiment, we measured subjects' privacy and security concerns. The key survey instrument in the second experiment is addressing individuals' time preferences, i.e., how patient are individuals when they are presented with delayed payments. We varied the questions between the test and retest phase to

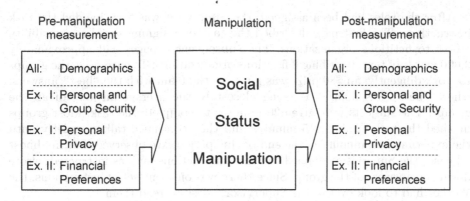

Fig. 1. Overview of Experiments

avoid individuals anchoring on specific responses (i.e., to avoid a carryover effect from the first survey stage to the second survey stage).[1]

3.2 Social Status Manipulation

The status manipulation utilized is similar to others in the literature (see, for example, [5,23,42,54]), with two subjects working together on a shared task. One subject is assigned to a high-status role (i.e., the Supervisor) and the other subject to a low-status role (i.e., the Worker).

For the manipulation, subjects were seated in same-sex pairs.[2] After completing the initial questionnaire, the experimenter approached each pair and offered the subject seated closest to the aisle a choice between two pieces of paper. The subject could not see the contents of the paper until after he or she had selected it. The other piece of paper was then given to the second person in the pair. The two pieces of paper described the roles of Supervisor and Worker that the subjects would take in a 2-person work group. These role instructions are included in the Appendix. In brief, the Supervisor was responsible for writing down the group's answers to the task, and the Worker was responsible for advising and helping the Supervisor. To eliminate bias due to the top or bottom piece of paper being chosen more frequently, the order of the two pieces of paper was alternated; if the Supervisor description was on top for one pair, then the Worker description would be on top for the next pair. The verbal instructions given to the subjects were minimal. Subjects were paid the same amount.

---

[1] Common across both experiments, we also included demographic variables and measures of affect (emotion). The latter we do not discuss in detail in this paper.

[2] This requirement was introduced to eliminate a potential confound related to the interaction of participants with different genders. For example, previous experimental research has provided evidence for performance differences in competitive environments when individuals were part of either same-sex and mixed-sex groups [19].

After the roles had been assigned, the Supervisor was then handed the task instructions. The first page described the task of assigning social responsibility scores to fictitious organizations. The subsequent 5 pages had approximately 2,000 words of text describing 8 fictitious organizations. To encourage the groups to work diligently, an $80 prize was given to the team with the "best" answers, where "best" was defined as being closest to the average answers of all the groups. The subjects were given 20 minutes to complete the task. Most groups finished the task in about 15 minutes and then continued talking quietly until the experimenter announced the end of this period. We observed that in almost all cases the Supervisor retained the task instructions and, as instructed, wrote down the answers of the group. Since there was only one set of instructions, the Worker had to look over to the Supervisor's desk to read them.

The experimental setup was designed to isolate the status interaction as the manipulated factor. Hence the two subjects were treated equally, apart from the instructions, and the assignment of roles was transparently random. There was no attempt to devalue either subject or to suggest the Supervisor in any way deserved the role by being "better" than the Worker. Since social status was manipulated, we refer to the Supervisors as the High-Status Group and the Workers as the Low-Status Group.

3.3   Measures for Security and Privacy Experiment

We measured security concern for two different dimensions. First, we considered how participants evaluated security risks from a societal perspective. Specifically, we asked "how concerned are you about the following internet security issues as they may affect society in general?" The sub-questions targeted issues such as terrorism, domestic wiretapping, online crime, child pornography. Second, we asked a number of questions to address individuals' personal sense of security. We asked "how concerned are you about the following internet security issues as they may affect you personally?" The sub-questions addressed security issues related to the usage of the Internet and personal computers such as viruses, spyware, and online banking. The personal security questions were modeled after surveys conducted, for example, by the National Cyber Security Alliance (e.g., [35]), and inspired by academic research on, e.g., phishing [14], and spyware [20].

The question about privacy was focused on potential concerns about information revelation by the subjects themselves. We asked "how comfortable [you] would be providing [a certain] type of information to Web sites." The information categories included the subject's full name, social security number, political orientation etc. This measure of privacy concern was first introduced by Ackermann et al. [1] and reutilized, for example, by Acquisti and Grossklags [3] and Spiekermann et al. [46].

All sub-questions were presented to the participants with a 9-point scale to accurately state the level of their concerns (examples are given in the Appendix). We then averaged the data for each category of questions to derive three quasi-continuous (9-point) rating scales (i.e., Likert-type scales) for social security concerns, personal security concerns, and privacy concerns, respectively. The summary statistics are provided in Table 1. As previously stated, to reduce anchoring and potential carryover effects, we asked different sub-questions before and after the experimental manipulation.

3.4 Measures for Discounting Experiment

The financial questions are broadly modeled after those of Thaler [47], with the subjects being told they had received a hypothetical prize from their bank with a fixed delay. The subjects were then asked for the amount of money they would need to receive now to make them indifferent compared to receiving the larger amount with a fixed delay. The subjects were asked for their indifference point over amounts that varied widely in magnitude (from tens of dollars to thousands of dollars) and for fixed delays of 1 week, 2 months, and 2 years. To reduce anchoring, slightly different payment amounts were presented after, compared to before, the experimental manipulation.

These financial questions are matching tasks, as defined by Frederick et al. [17]. The subjects were required to state the amount of money that would make them indifferent to the proposed payout. We selected this in preference to a choice task, where subjects make a choice between two alternatives. Choice tasks generate a coarse filtration of preferences unless many questions are asked, and since the experimental manipulation was expected to have only a moderate effect on preferences, it was considered important to have tightly defined financial preferences. Choice tasks allow real, versus hypothetical, decisions to be made, usually with one of the choices having some probability of actually being paid. But the large magnitude of some payment amounts would make such real payments impractical. Other researchers find little difference between the real and hypothetical answers, e.g., [29,30,34], obviating the need for real rewards. Choice tasks can also be easier to understand than matching tasks and, indeed, several subjects reported difficulty understanding the financial questions. This was perhaps the main disadvantage of using a matching task.

The financial questions allowed us to estimate discount factors for each subject for the three time periods (1 week, 2 months, and 2 years) for the questions asked before and after the experimental manipulation. For each future payment amount, we took the subject's immediate value and then divided by the future amount to calculate a discount factor for that payment. For example, the subjects were asked how much they would need to receive now to make them indifferent to receiving $80 in 2 months. If the subject stated they would need to receive $60 now, then their discount factor for that payment would be 0.75 ($60/$80). The discount factors for each time period were then averaged for each subject, as presented in Table 3.

3.5 Apparatus and Subject Payments

The questionnaires were conducted on computers using z-Tree [16]. The experimental manipulation was a group interaction with instructions given on paper. The complete experimental sessions lasted just under an hour and the subjects were paid $15 for their participation (plus a potential bonus payment as discussed above; the bonus payment was divided equally between the Supervisor and Worker).

Our research protocol and apparatus has been reviewed and approved by an Institutional Review Board for experiments with human subjects.

4   Data and Results

4.1   Subject Recruiting and Demographics

A total of 266 undergraduate students from the University of California at Berkeley participated in the experiments which were held at the Experimental Social Science Laboratory (Xlab). The experiments were advertised to a pool of students who previously indicated their interest to participate in economic studies.

Table 1. Summary statistics for the demand for security and privacy

	Security	Personal	Societal	Privacy
No. Obs.	146	146	146	146
Mean	6.482	6.988	5.976	5.331
StDev	1.491	1.638	1.778	1.486
Skew	-0.626	-1.040	-0.398	-0.044
Kurtosis	0.315	0.932	-0.178	0.016

For the security and privacy experiment, we successfully invited 146 individuals. We did not exclude any subjects from the analysis. Of the 146 participants, 96 (64.4%) were female. On average, participants had already gained over two years of college experience which is roughly equivalent to the level of junior students in the United States undergraduate system.

For the discounting experiment, we recruited 120 subjects. The 9 subjects who answered zero to any of the financial questions were excluded from the analysis because placing a zero value on future cash flows indicates that they may not have fully understood the questions. This left 111 subjects whose responses we analyze. Of the 111 participants, 64 (57.7%) were female. Similar to the group of participants in the security/privacy experiment, participants had (on average) already gained over two years of college experience equivalent to the level of junior students.

4.2   Results for the Security and Privacy Experiment

The summary statistics for the security and privacy experiment are reported in Table 1. For these static measurements, security concerns trump privacy concerns by about one point on the 9-point rating scale, and personal security concerns are somewhat larger than societal security concerns. On average, individuals are more than "somewhat concerned" about security, and less than "somewhat comfortable" to share personal information online which (i.e., these levels constitute the middle points of the given rating scales; see selected questions and scales in the Appendix).

Table 2. Impact of experimental manipulation on the demand for security and privacy

Change in Dependent Variables:	Security	Personal	Societal	Privacy
Supervisor	0.425	0.335	0.514	0.061
Worker	0.068	-0.006	0.143	0.248
Difference	0.356	0.341	0.371	-0.187
Robust Standard Error	0.124	0.152	0.177	0.158
(t-statistic)	2.876	2.244	2.095	-1.189
p-value	0.005**	0.026*	0.038*	0.237

To test the impact of the experimental manipulation, we conducted an ordinary least-squares (OLS) regression with Huber-White (robust) standard errors [25,52]. Regressions with robust standard errors are a standard approach in economics and finance to account for data with some imperfections and minor concerns about failure to meet assumptions about normality, heteroscedasticity, or some observations that exhibit large residuals, leverage or influence [11].

The experimental manipulation leads to a relative increase of security concerns for the high-status assignment (see Table 2). This effect is statistically significant for the two components of security concern as well as the composite measure. In contrast, privacy concerns are relatively higher for subjects in the low-status condition, but this effect is not statistically significant.

4.3   Results for the Discounting Experiment

Table 3 captures the discount factors observed for the 111 experimental subjects that supplied us with valid data. As expected, participants' indifference point for equating an amount now in comparison with a delayed fixed payment is decreasing with an increase in advertised delay. That is, individuals' indifference point for receiving an amount now instead of a dollar after one week is about 82 cents. Whereas a payment delay of two years pushes the indifference point down to about 62 cents. Put differently, individuals are satisfied with lower monetary amounts now when facing longer delays. This effect is rational since a longer delay prevents individuals from accomplishing alternative objectives (such as purchasing goods or investing the money) for a longer period of time.

However, individuals behave less rationally concerning the magnitude of their discounting choices. Equating 82 cents now with a one dollar payment after one week resembles an extraordinarily large discount rate. The same applies to the other two time intervals.

Taken together, participants consistently adapt their valuation when shifting between different delay options, however any delay at all is treated very harshly.

Table 3. Summary statistics for discounting behavior

	1 Week	2 Months	2 Years	Average
No. Obs.	111	111	111	111
Mean	0.821	0.785	0.624	0.744
StDev	0.235	0.218	0.250	0.203
Skew	-1.591	-1.307	-0.492	-0.875
Kurtosis	1.824	1.117	-0.575	0.014

In general, this will lead subjects to seek rewards that are available now, and delay investments that yield benefits in the future. Similar findings have been reported in a survey study by Acquisti and Grossklags [3].

Our analysis regarding the impact of the experimental manipulation follows the same approach as outlined in Section 4.2. When evaluating the impact of the experimental manipulation, we observe that the different status assignments lead to relative changes in the discounting behavior. The high-status Supervisors experience an increase in the value of the delayed payments with, for example, the value of $1.00 in 1 week increasing by $0.010. Conversely, the low status Workers experience a decrease in the value of the delayed payments with, for example, the value of $1.00 in 1 week decreasing by $0.049. The difference between the preference changes of the Supervisors and Workers is $0.059 for the 1 week period and $0.056 for the 2 month period; both are statistically significant. Furthermore, the average difference across the 3 time periods is $0.051, which is statistically significant at the 1% level. Hence this experiment demonstrates that a low, rather than high, status level leads to a relatively greater focus on immediate rewards.

Table 4 also enables us to estimate the impact of the social status manipulation on an impulsiveness metric that is defined as one minus the 1-week discount factor. The average initial metric is 0.179 (1.00 − 0.821). Following the status manipulation, the high status group's impulsiveness falls to 0.169 (0.179−0.010) while the low status group's impulsiveness increases to 0.228. The level of impulsiveness is 35 percent (i.e., 0.228/0.169 − 1.00) higher for the low-status role compared to the high-status role as a result of the status manipulation.

Table 4. Impact of experimental manipulation on discounting factor

Change in Dependent Variables	1 Week	2 Months	2 Years	Average
Supervisor	0.010	0.026	0.020	0.018
Worker	-0.049	-0.030	-0.018	-0.032
Difference	0.059	0.056	0.037	0.051
Robust Standard Error	0.025	0.024	0.027	0.019
(t-statistic)	2.317	2.309	1.395	2.632
p-value	0.021*	0.021*	0.163	0.008**

5   Discussion

Our results are derived from an experimental laboratory study. We designed a controlled environment to carefully isolate and manipulate an important factor, and created experimental manipulations to demonstrate causation as a result of these manipulations. Experimental economics studies that intersect with the field of computer science have become more popular in recent years, and our work contributes to this literature [21].

Our experiment is run in the tradition of experimental economics [41]. According to the standard in this research field, the experiment has taken place in a laboratory which exclusively runs experiments without deception, and we did not utilize any such techniques [36].

With our experiment, we did not aim for an experimental environment that closely mimics a realistic privacy and security decision-making situation. Our research question is novel in the literature, and we attempted to create a relatively abstract experimental setup that will be the basis for follow-up studies which can be conducted outside the laboratory, or with a more complex decision-making environment in the laboratory. For example, as a next step, a status manipulation within the framework of a valuation of private information study would be suitable [22].

Our experimental subjects were drawn from a standard student pool for experiments. While the degree of their privacy and security concerns may not have been fully representative of the wider population (e.g., students may be more computer literate), it is reasonable to assume that their preferences changed in response to the same stimuli that other types of subjects would react to [24]. Hence, our manipulation has relevance for the wider policy discussion. Nevertheless, a useful validation step would be to conduct the experiment with different subject populations; maybe even drawn from societies that differ from the Western cultures [24].

Exploring our research question in a more complex laboratory environment or outside the laboratory may give us insights about the relative importance of the observed factors in relation to other real-world factors. However, the lack of control and the need to consider multiple decision-making factors makes these approaches a less suitable first research step. Research exists to guide researchers into the direction of incrementally increasing the realism of studies inside and outside the laboratory [33].

Returning to our experimental findings, we provide robust evidence for the assertion that high-status decision-makers are likely to express higher concerns for security issues than low-status individuals. This applies to personal and societal concerns. Questions about personal concerns included whether participants were concerned about using an internet café with unencrypted data transfer, or about a virus deleting data from their hard disk. Questions about societal matters included whether individuals were concerned about governments snooping on their citizens, or whether they were concerned about terrorists using the Internet for attacks. Questions about personal concerns were aimed at affecting the individual more directly, whereas the questions about societal concerns addressed issues of broader concerns.

As with most experimental results, the findings may appear easy to rationalize in hindsight and, indeed, they are consistent with observations about the real world [49]. After all, individuals of high social status (which also include those with high socioeconomic status) may feel, for example, that they have more to protect (e.g., according to absolute measures of net wealth, but also other measures of social status). In contrast, one could argue that low-status individuals may feel more concerned about any loss due to security incidents. By providing actual data, our experimental finding is, therefore, from a psychological perspective surprising and provides insights into the reasoning of individuals from different social status categories.

We also find initial evidence for a second observation, i.e., that low-status assignments trigger a relatively higher demand for privacy. This observation is, however, not statistically significant (presumably for lack of power) and requires follow-up research. Assuming that this evidence would be validated in future research, it can be partly explained with individuals' desire to shield themselves from scrutiny if they perceive themselves as deviating from a more desirable state [26]. Participants with a low-status assignment may have found themselves at a disadvantage relative to their partners and this effect then triggered an increased demand for privacy.

We also noted that effective privacy and security decision-making usually involves the economic evaluation of decisions that may cause positive or negative consequences over long periods of time [2,3]. For example, investing into additional security measures now, may deter an attack or may defend an individual against an intrusion attempt at a much later time. From previous research, we know that individuals suffer from a desire for immediate gratification and exhibit often signs of procrastination. Our results from the experiment on time preferences shed light at the question whether individuals from different social status categories share the same magnitude of impatience in their decision-making. We find that low-status individuals are significantly more impatient, and we measure the strength of this effect on tasks that involve monetary comparisons.

Combining the findings from the two experiments, we conclude that high-status individuals are less prone to procrastinate on important security investments (or also privacy-enhancing activities) that address their personal and societal concerns. In contrast, low-status individuals are more likely failing to take appropriate actions that reflect their increased concerns for privacy due to their heightened tendency for procrastination. These findings have direct implications for the utilization of security and privacy-enhancing technologies. For example, while individuals may be capable to state their specific concerns about security and privacy, the likelihood to act to protect themselves may differ based on the level of impatience. This is a further factor that contributes to the explanation of the gap between privacy preferences and privacy behaviors exhibited in previous experimental research [46].

Security and privacy decisions taken by individuals will affect others through externalities. For example, individuals on social networking sites may (through their actions) reveal private information about their peers to undesirable third-parties. Similarly, individuals who suffer from security breaches may have their resources being abused for spam or may contribute to the weakening of the defenses of an organization.

In addition, individuals may act as decision-makers for groups or even larger populations, and may exercise power and influence over these groups. Typically, such positions are associated with a higher relative social status. Our findings may also apply to these scenarios. That is, high-status individuals may focus on their own heightened concerns for security; and may not appropriately consider the increased privacy-concerns of low-status individuals. It is, therefore, conceivable that the privacy and security interests of different social status categories are misaligned. Another finding is that high-status decision-makers will also be more patient in their actions, and less prone to procrastinate on decisions. Depending on what privacy and security measures are considered this could be a benefit or a disadvantage from the perspective of low-status individuals.

In practice, (self-)regulatory efforts in the domains of privacy and security are subject to many factors of influence. Our findings are one contributory factor for decision-making in the public domain, but need to be considered in light of the increasing complexity of privacy and security policy [13].

6 Conclusions

By introducing social status as a mediating factor in a test-manipulation-retest study format we were able to demonstrate causality between high/low-status assignments and their relative impact on the demand for security and privacy, and timing preferences.

Our results complement the sparse empirical literature on the privacy/security trade-off (e.g., [39]) and shift the focus away from mere descriptive work on privacy and security concerns towards studies that increase our understanding of the impact of several important mediating variables.

Our research is timely given the heated debate about the appropriate balance between the enactment of (secret) security measures and the protection of privacy and civil liberties. In particular, the report and recommendations of the Presidents Review Group on Intelligence and Communications Technologies clearly highlight the various battlegrounds related to the unprecedented use of mass surveillance technologies [12].

High-status individuals are typically in the position to make decisions for many others who may have other personal preferences. Our findings highlight one contributory factor of why high-status decision-makers may favor security measures at the expense of civil liberties and privacy.

Acknowledgments. We want to thank the anonymous reviewers, Kelly Caine, Alice Marwick, Salil Vadhan, Jonathan Berk, Ulrike Malmendier, and Christine Parlour for their detailed comments on our research project and/or this paper. Our research benefited from the feedback received during a presentation at the Fourth Annual Privacy Law Scholars Conference, and seminars given at

École Polytechnique Fédérale de Lausanne, Harvard University, Université Paris-Sud, Copenhagen Business School, Stockholm School of Economics, University of Melbourne, George Washington University, and the University of California at Berkeley. The experiments were conducted at and partially supported by the Experimental Social Science Laboratory at the University of California at Berkeley.

References

1. Ackerman, M., Cranor, L., Reagle, J.: Privacy in e-commerce: Examining user scenarios and privacy preferences. In: Proceedings of the ACM Conference on Electronic Commerce (EC 1999), pp. 1–8 (1999)
2. Acquisti, A., Grossklags, J.: Privacy attitudes and privacy behavior: Losses, gains, and hyperbolic discounting. In: Camp, J., Lewis, S. (eds.) The Economics of Information Security, pp. 165–178. Kluwer Academic Publishers (2004)
3. Acquisti, A., Grossklags, J.: Privacy and rationality in individual decision making. IEEE Security & Privacy 3(1), 26–33 (2005)
4. Anandpara, V., Dingman, A., Jakobsson, M., Liu, D., Roinestad, H.: Phishing IQ tests measure fear, not ability. In: Dietrich, S., Dhamija, R. (eds.) FC 2007 and USEC 2007. LNCS, vol. 4886, pp. 362–366. Springer, Heidelberg (2007)
5. Anderson, C., Berdahl, J.: The experience of power: Examining the effects of power on approach and inhibition tendencies. Journal of Personality and Social Psychology 83, 1362–1377 (2002)
6. Barradale, N.: Social incentives and human evolution, Available at SSRN, Paper No. 1520206 (2009)
7. Barradale, N.: Essays in Social Status and Finance. PhD thesis, University of California, Berkeley (2010)
8. Bilgin, P.: Individual and societal dimensions of security. International Studies Review 5(2), 203–222 (2003)
9. Brandimarte, L., Acquisti, A.: The economics of privacy. In: Peitz, M., Waldvogel, J. (eds.) The Oxford Handbook of the Digital Economy, pp. 547–571. Oxford University Press (2012)
10. Chabris, C., Laibson, D., Morris, C., Schuldt, J., Taubinsky, D.: Individual laboratory-measured discount rates predict field behavior. Journal of Risk and Uncertainty 37, 237–269 (2008)
11. Chen, X., Ender, P., Mitchell, M., Wells, C.: Regression with Stata. Stata Web Books (2003),
http://www.ats.ucla.edu/stat/stata/webbooks/reg/default.htm
12. Clarke, R., Morell, M., Stone, G., Sunstein, C., Swire, P.: Liberty and security in a changing world: Report and recommendations of The Presidents Review Group on Intelligence and Communications Technologies (December 2013)
13. Davies, S.: When privacy reform gets as dirty as environmental reform, we're all in trouble. The Privacy Surgeon (June 2013), Blog article available at http://www.privacysurgeon.org/
14. Dhamija, R., Tygar, J., Hearst, M.: Why phishing works. In: Proceedings of the SIGCHI Conference on Human Factors in Computing Systems (CHI 2006), pp. 581–590 (2006)
15. Drakos, K., Müller, C.: Terrorism risk concern in Europe. Economics Letters 112(2), 195–197 (2011)

16. Fischbacher, U.: z-tree: Zurich toolbox for ready-made economic experiments. Experimental Economics 10(2), 171–178 (2007)
17. Frederick, S., Loewenstein, G., O'Donoghue, T.: Time discounting and time preference: A critical review. Journal of Economic Literature 40, 351–401 (2002)
18. Ghafurian, M., Reitter, D.: Impatience, risk propensity and rationality in timing games. In: Proceedings of the 36th Annual Conference of the Cognitive Science Society, CogSci (2014)
19. Gneezy, U., Niederle, M., Rustichini, A.: Performance in competitive environments: Gender differences. Quarterly Journal of Economics 118(3), 1049–1074 (2003)
20. Good, N., Dhamija, R., Grossklags, J., Aronovitz, S., Thaw, D., Mulligan, D., Konstan, J.: Stopping spyware at the gate: A user study of privacy, notice and spyware. In: Proceedings of the Symposium On Usable Privacy and Security (SOUPS 2005), pp. 43–52 (2005)
21. Grossklags, J.: Experimental economics and experimental computer science: A survey. In: Proceedings of the Workshop on Experimental Computer Science (ExpCS 2007) (2007)
22. Grossklags, J., Acquisti, A.: When 25 cents is too much: An experiment on willingness-to-sell and willingness-to-protect personal information. In: Proceedings of the Sixth Workshop on Economics of Information Security (WEIS 2007) (2007)
23. Hall, J., Carter, J., Horgan, T.: Status roles and recall of nonverbal cues. Journal of Nonverbal Behavior 25, 79–100 (2001)
24. Henrich, J., Heine, S., Norenzayan, A.: The weirdest people in the world? Behavioral and Brain Sciences 33(2-3), 61–83 (2010)
25. Huber, P.: The behavior of maximum likelihood estimates under nonstandard conditions. In: Proceedings of the Fifth Berkeley Symposium on Mathematical Statistics and Probability, pp. 221–233 (1967)
26. Huberman, B., Adar, E., Fine, L.: Valuating privacy. IEEE Security & Privacy 3(5), 22–25 (2005)
27. Hui, K., Png, I.: Economics of privacy. In: Hendershott, T. (ed.) Handbook of Information Systems and Economics, pp. 471–497. Elsevier (2006)
28. Jagatic, T., Johnson, N., Jakobsson, M., Menczer, F.: Social phishing. Communications of the ACM 50(10), 94–100 (2007)
29. Johnson, M., Bickel, W.: Within-subject comparison of real and hypothetical money rewards in delay discounting. Journal of the Experimental Analysis of Behavior 77, 129–146 (2002)
30. Kachelmeier, S., Shehata, M.: Examining risk preferences under high monetary incentives: Experimental evidence from the People's Republic of China. American Economic Review 82, 1120–1141 (1992)
31. Kirby, K., Petry, N., Bickel, W.: Heroin addicts have higher discount rates for delayed rewards than non-drug-using controls. Journal of Experimental Psychology 128, 78–87 (1999)
32. Kumaraguru, P., Cranor, L.: Privacy indexes: A survey of Westin's studies, Available as ISRI Technical Report CMU-ISRI-05-138 (2005)
33. Levitt, S., List, J.: What do laboratory experiments measuring social preferences reveal about the real world? The Journal of Economic Perspectives 21(2), 153–174 (2007)
34. Madden, G., Raiff, B., Lagorio, C., Begotka, A., Mueller, A., Hehli, D., Wegener, A.: Delay discounting of potentially real and hypothetical rewards: II. Between- and within-subject comparisons. Experimental and Clinical Psychopharmacology 12, 251–261 (2004)

35. NCSA/Norton (National Cyber Security Alliance and Norton by Symantec). 2010 NCSA/Norton by Symantec Online Safety Study (2010), http://www.staysafeonline.org/

36. Ortmann, A., Hertwig, R.: The costs of deception: Evidence from psychology. Experimental Economics 5(2), 111–131 (2002)

37. Reimers, S., Maylor, E., Stewart, N., Chater, N.: Associations between a one-shot delay discounting measure and age, income, education and real-world impulsive behavior. Personality and Individual Differences 47(8), 973–978 (2009)

38. Reynolds, B.: A review of delay-discounting research with humans: Relations to drug use and gambling. Behavioural Pharmacology 17, 651–667 (2006)

39. Robinson, N., Potoglou, D., Kim, C., Burge, P., Warnes, R.: Security, at what cost? Quantifying people's trade-offs across liberty, privacy and security (2010)

40. Schiff, J., Meingast, M., Mulligan, D., Sastry, S., Goldberg, K.: Respectful cameras: Detecting visual markers in real-time to address privacy concerns. In: Senior, A. (ed.) Protecting Privacy in Video Surveillance, pp. 65–89. Springer (2009)

41. Smith, V.: Economics in the laboratory. Journal of Economic Perspectives 8(1), 154–158 (1994)

42. Snodgrass, S.: Further effects of role versus gender on interpersonal sensitivity. Journal of Personality and Social Psychology 62, 154–158 (1992)

43. Solove, D.: "I've got nothing to hide" and other misunderstandings of privacy. San Diego Law Review 44, 745–772 (2007)

44. Solove, D.: Understanding Privacy. Harvard University Press, Cambridge (2008)

45. Solove, D.: Nothing to Hide: The False Tradeoff between Privacy and Security. Yale University Press, New Haven (2011)

46. Spiekermann, S., Grossklags, J., Berendt, B.: E-privacy in 2nd generation e-commerce: Privacy preferences versus actual behavior. In: Proceedings of the ACM Conference on Electronic Commerce (EC 2001), pp. 38–47 (2001)

47. Thaler, R.: Some empirical evidence on dynamic inconsistency. San Diego Law Review 8, 201–207 (1981)

48. Tsai, J., Egelman, S., Cranor, L., Acquisti, A.: The effect of online privacy information on purchasing behavior: An experimental study. Information Systems Research 22(2), 254–268 (2011)

49. Watts, D.: Everything is obvious: How common sense fails us. Crown Business, New York (2012)

50. Webster, M.: Working on status puzzles. In: Thye, S., Skvoretz, J. (eds.) Advances in Group Processes, pp. 173–215. Elsevier Ltd. (2003)

51. Westin, A.: Privacy and freedom. Atheneum, New York (1970)

52. White, H.: A heteroskedasticity-consistent covariance matrix estimator and a direct test for heteroskedasticity. Econometrica 48(4), 817–838 (1980)

53. White, J., Moffitt, T., Caspi, A., Bartusch, D., Needles, D., Stouthamer-Loeber, M.: Measuring impulsivity and examining its relationship to delinquency. Journal of Abnormal Psychology 103, 192–205 (1994)

54. Wojciszke, B., Struzynska-Kujalowicz, A.: Power influences self-esteem. Social Cognition 25, 472–494 (2007)

55. Youn, S., Lee, M.: The determinants of online security concerns and their influence on e-transactions. International Journal of Internet Marketing and Advertising 5(3), 194–222 (2009)

A   Appendix: Experimental Materials

A.1   Instructions for Worker

CONGRATULATIONS! You have been assigned to the role of WORKER in your group. You are expected to help the other group member, the SUPERVISOR, in a decision-making task. The task involves making a series of decisions concerning the social responsibility of organizations. While all decisions are the responsibility of the SUPERVISOR, you should have an important contribution by giving the SUPERVISOR a second opinion and generally acting in a supporting role.

The pay for each group member has been set at $15 for the experiment. In addition, your group may receive a performance bonus of $80, to be split equally. When you are finished reading these instructions, please turn the sheet over and display it prominently at your workspace so the experimenter can see your role. Then read the instructions for the social responsibility task. The SUPERVISOR will write down the answers to the questions on that task.

(On reverse, in large font:) WORKER

A.2   Instructions for Supervisor

CONGRATULATIONS! You have been assigned to the role of SUPERVISOR in your group. You are responsible for the performance of your group in a decision-making task. The task involves making a series of decisions concerning the social responsibility of organizations. The other group member, the WORKER, is expected to help you and provide a second opinion, but all decisions are your responsibility.

The pay for each group member has been set at $15 for the experiment. In addition, your group may receive a performance bonus of $80, to be split equally. When you are finished reading these instructions, please turn the sheet over and display it prominently at your workspace so the experimenter can see your role. Then read the instructions for the social responsibility task. As the SUPERVISOR, you will write down the answers to the questions on that task.

(On reverse, in large font:) SUPERVISOR

A.3   Task Instructions

Organizations vary in their level of social responsibility. They go to different lengths to protect the interests of local communities, the environment, their employees, their suppliers and customers, and the disadvantaged members of society. Ratings of social responsibility can be based either on objective criteria or on the public's perception of the organization. Surveys are one method of eliciting the public's perception of social responsibility, and those surveys may be completed in a group setting.

Your task is to rate organizations on their social responsibility. You will be given descriptions of fictitious organizations that you will rate on a scale of 1-9, where 9 denotes an organization that is extremely socially responsible. As a reward for performance, the group that has the best answers will be given a bonus payment of $80. The "best answers" are defined as those closest to the average of all the groups completing the exercise. Hence, one strategy is to rate each organization based on your expectation of the average response for all the groups.

Please discuss the answers quietly in your group. No communication with other groups is allowed. To prevent cheating, each group has a different set of questions, with organizations shown in a different order and assigned different letters. Write your rating for each organization immediately below the description of the organization.

You will have approximately 2 minutes to rate each organization. The experimenter will let you know when there are 5 minutes and 1 minute remaining on the task. At the completion of the task, you must stop writing and hand back the questions and answers.

A.4   Discounting Experiment Question

You have won a NOW-or-LATER Prize in a lottery organized by your bank. The bank will either pay you a smaller amount NOW or a larger amount LATER (assume there is no risk of the payment not happening).

Consider the following LATER amounts and dates. For each, you must decide on the NOW amount that would make you indifferent between receiving the NOW amount and the LATER amount.

(If the NOW amount is too high, you would rather receive that. If it is too low, you would rather receive the LATER amount. You will be indifferent somewhere between the two.)

(Note there is no "correct" answer - the question is merely asking about your preference.)

- $4,400 in 2 months vs. $ Now:
- $2,500 in 2 years vs. $ Now:
- $1,900 in 1 week vs. $ Now:
- $240 in 1 week vs. $ Now:
- $300 in 2 years vs. $ Now:
- $27 in 1 week vs. $ Now:
- $48 in 2 years vs. $ Now:
- $80 in 2 months vs. $ Now:
- $730 in 2 months vs. $ Now:

A.5   Questions for Security and Privacy Experiment

How concerned are you about the following internet security issues as they may affect society in general? (1 = Not concerned at all; 5 = somewhat concerned; 9 = Very concerned)

- The use of the internet by race-hate groups to spread propaganda
- Oppressive governments using the internet to snoop on their populations
- Social networking sites being used by pedophiles to contact children
- The limited resources of law enforcement agencies to deter online crime
- Online users bullying and intimidating one another
- Profits from internet activities funding organized crime groups
- The vulnerability of the national internet infrastructure to attack by hostile governments and terrorists
- The use of the internet by terrorist groups to organize attacks

How concerned are you about the following internet security issues as they may affect you personally? (1 = Not concerned at all; 5 = somewhat concerned; 9 = Very concerned)

- People using the internet to withdraw money from your bank account
- Using internet cafes with unencrypted data transfer
- Employers searching for information about you online
- Your ISP selling your data
- Spyware becoming installed on your computer
- Your computer being taken over as part of a botnet
- A virus deleting data from your hard disk

When visiting Web sites that collect information, many people find there is some information that they generally feel comfortable providing, some information they feel comfortable providing only under certain conditions, and some information that they never or rarely feel comfortable providing. For each of the types of information in the left most column, please indicate how comfortable you would be providing that type of information to Web sites. (1 = Very comfortable; 5 = Somewhat comfortable; 9 = Not comfortable at all)

- Full name
- Home address
- Your weight
- Outside work and study interests
- Social network user name/address
- Social security number
- Political orientation
- Driving record
- High school grades

C3P: Context-Aware
Crowdsourced Cloud Privacy

Hamza Harkous, Rameez Rahman, and Karl Aberer

École Polytechnique Fédérale de Lausanne (EPFL), Switzerland
{hamza.harkous,karl.aberer}@epfl.ch, rrameez@gmail.com

Abstract. Due to the abundance of attractive services available on the cloud, people are placing an increasing amount of their data online on different cloud platforms. However, given the recent large-scale attacks on users data, privacy has become an important issue. Ordinary users cannot be expected to manually specify which of their data is sensitive, or to take appropriate measures to protect such data. Furthermore, usually most people are not aware of the privacy risk that different shared data items can pose. In this paper, we present a novel conceptual framework in which privacy risk is automatically calculated using the sharing context of data items. To overcome ignorance of privacy risk on the part of most users, we use a crowdsourcing based approach. We use *Item Response Theory* (IRT) on top of this crowdsourced data to determine the sensitivity of items and diverse attitudes of users towards privacy. First, we determine the feasibility of IRT for the cloud scenario by asking workers feedback on *Amazon mTurk* on various sharing scenarios. We obtain a good fit of the responses with the theory, and thus show that IRT, a well-known psychometric model for educational purposes, can be applied to the cloud scenario. Then, we present a lightweight mechanism such that users can crowdsource their sharing contexts with the server and determine the risk of sharing particular data item(s) privately. Finally, we use the Enron dataset to simulate our conceptual framework and also provide experimental results using synthetic data. We show that our scheme converges quickly and provides accurate privacy risk scores under varying conditions.

1 Introduction

1.1 Motivation and Challenges

Cloud computing platforms have become a ubiquitous presence in our digital lives. Given the pervasiveness of useful cloud services such as storage, online document editing, media streaming, etc., data which would normally be on the user's local machine, now invariably lies in the cloud. Recent large scale leakage of data [1] has raised serious concerns about users privacy. Prior to designing privacy mechanisms, it is important to identify the challenges of privacy provision in the cloud, which can inform potential solutions. In particular, we notice three major stumbling blocks towards privacy provision in the cloud:

E. De Cristofaro and S.J. Murdoch (Eds.): PETS 2014, LNCS 8555, pp. 102–122, 2014.

a) **Privacy vs Services Dilemma:** To tackle privacy concerns, some cloud computing companies provide the users with the option of client-side encryption to protect the data before it leaves the users' device, thus preventing any other entity from data decryption, including the cloud provider itself. However, while this approach eliminates most of the data privacy concerns, its main disadvantage is that the user cannot readily utilize existing cloud services. For some services, attempts exist at designing alternatives that operate over encrypted data, benefiting from the recent breakthroughs in homomorphic encryption [2]. In addition to resulting in services orders of magnitude less efficient than their counterparts, homomorphic encryption is provably not sufficient for constructing several essential services involving multiple users [3]. Furthermore, resorting to homomorphic encryption as the ultimate solution requires rewriting most of the cloud applications' code to operate over the encrypted data. New versions of existing LaTeXcompilers, photo filters, music recommenders, etc., based on homomorphic encryption, will need to be programmed with the goal of keeping all data private, which is evidently non-realistic.

b) **Difficulty of manually assessing data privacy levels:** Users cannot be expected to individually assess the sensitivity level for each item before they share it as that can require a lot of investment in terms of time and effort, coupled with technical expertise. A recent survey [4] has shown that, in one out of four organizations, the management has little or no understanding of what constitutes sensitive data. Evidently, this fraction is expected to be significantly higher for individual users.

c) **General lack of awareness about privacy:** This includes limited notions about privacy being restricted to hiding 'sensitive' content, such as personal identification numbers, credit card details etc. Often, the metadata associated with the data item, the location and device from which the item is shared, the entity with whom the data is shared, etc., can be as important as the content of the data itself.

In our solution for privacy provision in the cloud, we seek to overcome these above hurdles.

1.2   Approach and Contributions

How do we address the 'stumbling blocks' that we identified in Section 1.1? First, we show how we can use a centralized solution to facilitate crowdsourcing for privacy *without requiring revelation of users preferences*. We argue that to achieve this, cryptographic methods are infeasible, and we present a novel design that allows users to reveal their preferences to the central server privately. We show how an existing psychologically grounded method for analyzing users preferences and data properties, can be rigorously used to analyze this crowdsourced information. Users can then reap the benefits of this crowdsourced information as the server analyzes it to provide them with sensitivity indicators when they share new data.

By crowdsourcing the solution, users are no longer isolated individuals who lack privacy awareness. They can now be guided by the *Wisdom of the Crowd.*

Also, they do not have to exert manual effort to find the sensitivity associated with each item they share, as the server can guide them automatically. Furthermore, they need not worry about getting stuck with 'bad' crowdsourced information, i.e., about majority of users being as clueless about privacy as them. This is because the psychometric method we use for analyzing this information, Item Response Theory, ensures that computed parameters of data items do not only apply to a specific sample of people. The solution would ensure, for example, that sharing compromising photos of oneself with the public is deemed risky even when majority of the people in the system are doing so. Only a few conservative users in the system are enough to keep the system risk-averse. Finally, we validate our design with both simulation and empirical data, thus showing the feasibility of our solution.

Specifically, we make the following main contributions in this paper:

- We propose a privacy framework, which is specific to the cloud scenario and incorporates the nuances of data sharing within cloud, such as the *Privacy vs Services Dilemma* and *Lack of Privacy Awareness and Effort* on part of most users.
- We create a realistic vocabulary for a personal cloud, and use it to create 'Human Intelligence Tasks' on the *Amazon Mechanical Turk*. We measure people's responses, in terms of their privacy attitudes, against the *Item Response Theory* (IRT) and find a good fit. We thereby demonstrate that Item Response Theory, a well-used psychometric model for diverse purposes, can be applied fruitfully in the cloud scenario.
- Our solution depends on crowdsourcing the contexts and policies associated with shared items. The sensitivity associated with different items is determined by grouping together same (or similar) contexts and analyzing different policies set by people with different privacy attitudes. However, we also have to ensure the privacy of this aggregated context information. Towards that aim, we provide a lightweight mechanism based on *K-Anonymity* [5] for privately calculating similarity between items in a centralized way, without depending on infeasible cryptographic methods.
- We perform a set of experiments using synthetic data, with various graphs for user activities, item distribution, and types of users (honest vs. malicious).
- Finally, we use the *Enron* email dataset for evaluating our framework. This dataset gives us a good model of users sharing activities and the diversity of data items (and their contexts). Under both datasets, we show that our scheme bootstraps quickly and provides accurate privacy scores in varying conditions.

2   System Model

2.1   Interacting Entities

We consider a system involving interactions between two types of entities: *end-users* and *cloud service providers (CSPs)*. The end-user can play one of two roles: *data sharer* or *data observer* while the cloud provider can only be a data observer. A data sharer is an end-user who shares *data items* she possesses. A data observer is any entity that is given access to observe the shared items by the data sharer.

We assume that the user sends her data to a single CSP, called the *intermediary* that acts as the repository for this user's data. The user can select to give other CSPs access to her data through that CSP (e.g. when the latter has an API that the other CSPs can use). The interaction between these two types of entities is in the form of data sharing operations. Each such operation is initiated by an end-user s_0 who shares a data item d (e.g. document, picture, etc.) with a CSP or another user s_1. Additionally, the data sharer intends from the sharing operation to obtain a certain service of interest from the CSP, such as music streaming, document viewing, file syncing, etc. The network is dynamic, in the sense that these entities can enter and leave the network, and the user items can be shared over time, not necessarily concurrently.

2.2 Threat Model

We assume that the user is interested in hiding her sensitive data from the CSPs. Existing privacy threat models consider an adversary who attempts at discovering quantifiable sensitive information, such as location, browsing history, credit card information, etc. In our model, we do not set an a priori definition of sensitive information due to the heterogeneity of the shared data items we consider. Instead, we develop a protocol that quantifies the sensitivity of a certain sharing operation (determined by its context), based on the privacy policies that people use. Furthermore, we assume that the CSP is *honest but curious*, in the sense it follows the protocol, but it can arbitrarily analyze the protocol transcript offline to infer extra information.

2.3 Our Conceptual Framework

We now discuss the key concepts and components that underlie our conceptual framework for privacy provision in the cloud.

Context Vocabulary. In Section 3, we use the notion of *Context vocabulary* to define the contexts of items shared in a given domain. A context accounts for the content features of the items, the metadata associated with it, and the environment of the sharing operation (e.g. data observers, device used, etc.).

Sharing Policy. People can share different data items with different policies, where a policy is in the range $[0, 1]$ and 0 signifies full transparency while 1 signifies full obscurity. We discuss this in more detail in Section 3.2.

Crowd-Sourcing. In our framework, after each sharing operation, the context of the item and the policy applied are eventually aggregated at the cloud via a privacy preserving mechanism. This aggregation is required so that the *Lack of Privacy Awareness* may be overcome, and individual decisions could be guided by the *Wisdom of the Crowd*.

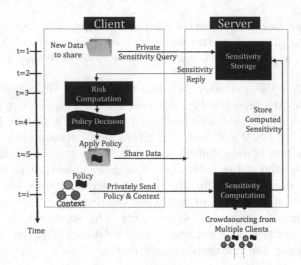

Fig. 1. Sequence diagram of the system

Risk Evaluation. Based on the processing and analysis of the crowdsourced information, the system can guide others about the privacy risk that is posed by sharing different items in different contexts. Towards that aim, we use *Item Response Theory* (IRT) which is a well-known psychometric function that has been widely used in psychology, education, public health, and computer adaptive testing.

Policy Recommendation. The final component in our framework is a suite of risk mitigation applications. By this, we mean system recommended policies that can guide the general user in minimizing risk while still availing services. In this work, we do not focus on Policy Recommendation and leave it for future work.

In Figure 1, we show a sequence diagram summarizing the steps taken in one run of the system. The client contacts the server with a private query about the sensitivity of the current context (t=1), in a way that the server remains oblivious about the actual context. Upon receiving the response with the sensitivity (t=2), the client locally computes the privacy risk of sharing the data (t=3) and decides on the relevant privacy policy (t=4). Next, the client sends the data at t=5. At a later round (t=i), the client sends the context along with the used policy after it makes sure that the server cannot associate the context with the actual sharing operation. The server determines the similarity of this item with other items that users have crowdsourced to it. Using psychometric functions, the server computes the sensitivity associated with the item being shared, which is used to respond to future sensitivity queries.

3   Context Vocabulary and Sharing Policies

We begin by describing the fundamental building blocks of our framework, which refer to the context in which an item is shared and the policy with which the item is shared.

Fig. 2. An example vocabulary for data sharing in the personal cloud

3.1   Context Vocabulary

We introduce the technical notion of 'Context', which includes the metadata associated with a particular data item, user supplied information about the data item (such as tags), and the environment features in which the data is being shared (such as the device information or the relationship with the observer). Furthermore, 'Context' also includes information extracted through content analysis of the data item, such as topic modeling statistics in case of a text document and face recognition in the case of images.

For an illustration of 'Context', consider a case where Bob shares a *word document* about *financial risk* authored by *sharer* (i.e. Bob himself) on Bob's *laptop* and shared with a *colleague*. The words in italics capture the context of the data item. For a specific domain, 'Context Vocabulary' is the set of all fields that can be used to represent any shared item in that domain. Put another way, the context vocabulary is the vocabulary that can be used to represent all possible contexts in a given domain. We give an example of such a vocabulary in Figure 2.

The general template for a context of an item would be a tuple of the general form $(field1=value1,\ field2=value2,\dots)$, containing f fields. Thus, the context of the data item in the above example would be $(data\_type=word\ document,\ topic=financial\ risk,\ device=laptop,\ author=sender,\ observer=colleague)$.

It should be noted that there are usually two kinds of fields associated with a data item. The first are those which are by default associated with the data item, e.g., *data type*, and other metadata information, e.g., *author*, which are available (or can be extracted by anyone) if the data item is shared completely transparently as in plaintext. We term these *explicit* fields. The second are defined by the sharer while sharing the data item, e.g., *observer*, *topic*, *device*, or other tags that might be associated with the data item. We term these *implicit* fields.

We note here that it is not necessary (or even usual) for all data items to have all context fields available. An item's context is defined by whatever fields are available. For example if we have a *pdf* file which does not have its *author* present, then obviously the file's context would not include the author. Put another way, the value of the author field would be considered empty.

3.2 Sharing Policies

When a user decides to share a data item, it does so with a policy. This policy ranges from 0 to 1, where 0 signifies full transparency while 1 signifies full obscurity. For example, if the user decides to encrypt a file, then this would be symbolized by a policy value of 1. On the other hand, sharing an unencrypted file while hiding some meta-data fields (such as e.g., author, modified_by etc) would result in a policy value between 0 and 1.

4 Crowd-Sourcing and Risk Evaluation

As shown in Figure 1, a client can privately query the server about the sensitivity of a specific sharing operation and get a response based on that. In this section, we describe these parts of our framework in more detail. Informally speaking, the privacy guarantee that we achieve throughout is that, at any time, the server has multiple contexts that can be associated with each sharing operation. Accordingly, the context of each operation is never deterministically disclosed to the server.

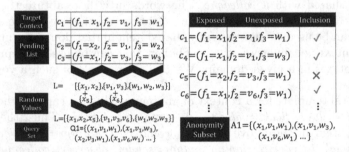

Fig. 3. *QuerySet* formation and anonymity subset definition

4.1 Privacy Aware Querying

Directly sending the context to the server allows it to associate the sharing operation with that context, which we aim to avoid. Instead, we describe a scheme, where the client queries the server about multiple dummy contexts, in a way that hides the actually requested one.

***QuerySet* Formation.** We denote by *targetContext* the context for which the client is querying. This context is sent as part of a *QuerySet*, containing other contexts, which we term as *homonyms*. As shown in Figure 3, suppose that the *targetContext* is $c_1 : (f_1 = x_1, f_2 = v_1, f_3 = w_1)$. The client forms a list of alternative values for each field, e.g. $L = [\{x_1, x_2, x_5\}, \{v_1, v_3, v_6\}, \{w_1, w_2, w_3\}]$ so that, in total, each field has k possible values. Then the homonyms are formed by producing the cartesian product of all the sets in L. This results in contexts having different combinations of field values.

The choice of the alternative values is not totally at random. In order to allow *targetContexts* to appear faster in multiple *QuerySets*, thus approaching the privacy condition formalized in this section, the client keeps a *Pending List (PL)*, containing previously queried *targetContexts*. It selects at random a fraction of $t \times k$ values[1] from *PL* when available and fills the rest of the values from the domain of each field.

The client sends this *QuerySet* to the server. The server, on receiving a *Query-Set*, responds with a subset of all those contexts for which it knows the sensitivity[2]. If the sensitivity of the *targetContext* is also returned by the server, the client decides to apply a policy on the data item based on this; otherwise the client can choose to do the same uninformed. In both cases, the actual data item is sent afterwards to the server. Once the server receives the actual data item, it can easily infer the *exposed* part of the *targetContext*. This part includes those *explicit* fields as defined in Section 3.1, which the client did not choose to hide. It is evident to notice that, by the construction of the *QuerySet*, the server is not able to deterministically infer any field of the *unexposed* part of the context (containing all *implicit* fields and those *explicit* fields which have been hidden by the client). In particular, the server has k possible values for each such field. Moreover, assuming there are u fields in the unexposed part, we will have k^u contexts that match the exposed part of the *targetContext*. We call this set of contexts the *Anonymity Subset (A_i)* of the *targetContext* c_i, and we illustrate its contents with an example in Figure 3. With respect to the server, one of the elements of this subset is the *targetContext*, but no element can be ruled out without further information.

We now add the following definition:

Definition 1. *We say that a context c can be **validly associated** with the sharing operation of item d_i if c has appeared in A_i and if the server cannot assert with certainty that c exclusively belongs to one or more anonymity subsets other than A_i.*

Hence, at this stage, we have the following guarantee:

Guarantee 1. At the querying phase, the server receives k^u contexts that can be validly associated with the current sharing operation.

Crowdsourcing. Up till now, we have shown how the client privately queries the server about the sensitivity. In order to compute this sensitivity, the server relies on crowdsourcing, through *privately* collecting *targetContexts* along with the corresponding policies (together called the *Crowdsourcing Information (CI)*) from different clients. We alternatively say that a context c is *crowdsourced* when $CI(c)$ is sent to the server. The client should not send dummy information as in the querying phase in order to not affect the accuracy of the sensitivity computation. Thus, we now present the scheme in which client sends the CI in

---

[1] k is a constant ($0 < k < 1$) (we take $t = 2/3$ in our experiments).
[2] We shall discuss how the server calculates this sensitivity in Section 4.2.

a way that continues to maintain Guarantee 1 for all the sharing operations. As a result, the server will be able to know, for example, that a client *Bob* shared a *financial document* with a *colleague* in an *plaintext form*, but it will not be able to link the document topic or his relationship with the observer to a specific sharing operation.

One way this guarantee might be weakened is if the client sends the *CI* in a way that allows the server to discover the anonymity subset in which the context was the *targetContext*. For example, sending $CI(c)$ after c has appeared in a single anonymity subset A_1 will reveal to the server that c corresponds to data d_1. Hence, the first intuitive measure for preventing this association is to wait until a context appears in multiple anonymity subsets before sending the *CI*.

However, this measure is not sufficient. Consider the case of two contexts c_x and c_y, both only appearing in anonymity subsets A_4 and A_6. Suppose that we require that a context appears in at least two anonymity subsets before it is sent. Then, both $CI(c_x)$ and $CI(c_y)$ will be sent directly after item d_6 (with anonymity subset A_6) is sent. At this point, the server is sure that one of c_x and c_y is the *targetContext* for A_4 and the other for A_6. All of the other $k^u - 2$ contexts that have appeared in A_4 and A_6 are no more possible candidates for being the actual *targetContext* from the viewpoint of the server. Hence, Guarantee 1 for these two sharing operations is weakened as the $k^u - 2$ contexts are now deterministically associated with other anonymity subsets. The guarantee will be weakened further if there was a third item d_8 that has been subsequently sent, with its context c_8 appearing in A_4 and A_8. From the server's viewpoint, A_4 is no more a valid possibility for c_8 due to the mapping deduced when c_x and c_y were sent. Therefore, the server can deterministically associate A_8 to c_8, and the whole context for d_8 is revealed. The main weakness in this naive method is that it does not account for the fact the server can link multiple sending instances and reduce the possibility of mapping to a single case. Our strategy to counteract that and keep Guarantee 1 is to verify that crowdsourcing the next context preserves the property that each sent context item is still validly associated with all the anonymity subsets it has appeared in.

At this point we add another definition:

Definition 2. *We say that there is a **valid mapping** from a list of contexts to a list of anonymity subsets if each context in the former can be validly associated with a distinct anonymity subset from the latter.*

Suppose the client has just completed the sharing operation i, and is attempting to crowdsource the contexts that have not been sent yet, which are kept in its *Pending List (PL$_i$)*. We also denote by SL_i the *Sent List*, containing all contexts that have been crowdsourced previously, and by G_i the group of all client's anonymity subsets up to (and including) A_i. Towards achieving Guarantee 1, a context $c \in PL_i$ can be crowdsourced only when the following two conditions are true:

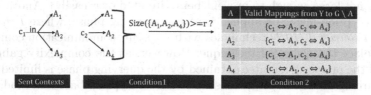

Fig. 4. Checking privacy conditions before crowdsourcing context c_2

1. c appears in at least r anonymity subsets
2. For each $A \in G_i$, there exists a valid mapping from the list $SL'_i = SL \bigcup \{c\}$ of contexts to the list $G_i \setminus A$ of anonymity subsets.

Going back to the previous example, after each of c_x and c_y has appeared in two anonymity subsets, condition 1 is satisfied. However, condition 2 is not satisfied since excluding A_4 will lead to $G \setminus A4 = \{A6\}$, and then we cannot map each context to a distinct anonymity set.

Figure 4 illustrates with another example how the two conditions can be verified. For each *targetContext*, the client maintains a list of the anonymity subsets it has appeared in. In addition, it maintains two lists: $U1$, containing the *targetContexts* that have not satisfied the first condition yet[3], and $S1U2$, containing the list of items that have satisfied the first condition but not the second. The figure shows a valid mapping that exists for each anonymity subset in G when c_2 is considered for crowdsourcing. It is worth noting that $PL = U1 \bigcup S1U2$. Also, as discussed in Section 4.1, when the contexts of PL appear in more anonymity subsets, the above privacy conditions will be satisfied faster; hence, they were used in the construction of the *QuerySet*.

Lemma 1. *Checking conditions 1 and 2 allows to preserve Guarantee 1.*

Proof. Consider any context that is about to be crowdsourced. Condition 2 implies that for each $A \in G$, there is a possibility that the *targetContext* of A has not been sent yet. Hence, each context in $c \in SL'$, can still be *validly associated* with all the r subsets it appeared in. Let Z_i be the list of all contexts that appeared in the elements of G_i. It is evident that there is no new information being sent about the contexts in $Z \setminus SL'$. Therefore, all the contexts in Z_i can still be validly associated with the anonymity subsets they appeared in. Accordingly, Guarantee 1 is preserved.   □

Discussion: We note that an alternative scheme for crowdsourcing that includes encrypting the context before sharing it would not work. In our framework, the server is required to use a similarity function to match the context with other ones sent by people in order to compute the context sensitivity. Even if we encrypt the context before we send it, the server will be able to know it by computing its similarity with all the possible contexts in the vocabulary (as the

---

[3] Regardless of whether the second condition is satisfied.

latter are not large enough to prevent being iterated over easily). Another place where encryption might be applied is at the querying phase, where *Private Information Retrieval (PIR)* techniques with constant communication complexity might replace the *QuerySet* technique. However, as the complexity gain is absent, and the privacy guarantee obtained by the querying phase is limited by the crowdsourcing phase, we do not resort to the encryption-based method, which is more complex to implement.

4.2   Sensitivity and Risk Evaluation

When the server receives the crowdsourcing information, it seeks to determine the sensitivity associated with this item based on same or similar items shared with different policies in the past by different users. The client, upon receiving this sensitivity, locally computes the privacy risk of sharing. In this paper, for computing the sensitivity, we use *Item Response Theory* (IRT), a well-known psychometric function, which we describe next.

Sensitivity Computation by the Server. Item Response Theory (IRT) is a modern test theory typically used for analyzing questionnaires to relate the examinees' probability of answering a question correctly (or in general a correct response probability P_{ij}) to two elements: (1) the difficulty of the question (or in general a latent threshold parameter β_i of item i) and (2) the examinees' abilities to answer questions (or in general a latent parameter θ_j for each person j). In contrast to *Classical Test Theory (CTT)*, which measures a person's ability based on averages and summations over the items, IRT has two distinguishing features: (1) the group invariance of calculated item parameters (i.e. a single item's parameters do not only apply to the current user sample, assuming the social norms won't vary significantly) and (2) the item invariance of a person's latent trait (i.e. the trait is invariant with respect to the items used to determine it) [6].

In this work, we apply IRT by mapping the item's difficulty to the sensitivity, the user's trait to the privacy attitude (or willingness to expose the items), and the response probability to the policy level of the item (similar to previous works [7,8]).

We focus on the unidimensional IRT models, which make three main assumptions about the data: (1) unidimensionality (i.e. there is a single underlying trait θ that determines the person's response), (2) local independence (i.e. for each underlying trait θ, there is no association between responses to different items), and (3) model fit (i.e. the estimated item and person parameters can be used to reproduce the observed responses) [9]. An IRT model is termed as *dichotomous* if the responses to the questions are binary ones (correct/incorrect) and *polytomous* if there are multiple levels of the response (e.g. a five-level Likert scale with responses: strongly disagree/disagree/neutral/agree/strongly agree).

The Rasch model, one of the most common IRT models, assumes that the probability of correct response is a function of θ and β only and that the items are equally discriminative for testing the underlying trait. It is particularly advantageous with smaller sample sizes, due to its simplicity and few parameters, and, as we show in Section 5.1, it also fits well in the scenario of cloud data sharing. The parameters of the dichotomous Rasch model for an item i and a person with parameter θ are related by the following function, called the *Item Response Function (IRF)*:

$$P_i = \frac{1}{1 + e^{-(\theta - \beta_i)}} \tag{1}$$

With polytomous models, we will make the assumption that the policies chosen by the users are on the same scale for all the items. It is similar to the case of Likert scale, where the same set of categories are applied for each item in the test. Accordingly, the most suitable model for us, and whose fit to the cloud scenario will be demonstrated in Section 5.1, is the Rasch Rating Scale Model. For estimating the parameters of the different models, we used *Marginal Maximum Likelihood estimation*, which is an expectation-maximization algorithm. The estimation technique relies on having enough responses for multiple items by different people. For more details about item response theory models, the reader is referred to the following works [6,9,10].

Risk Computation by the Client. The sensitivity is an indication of the magnitude of privacy loss incurred when data is lost. The client can combine this measure with another measure of the *likelihood* that this event happens, using information that is kept locally, such as the level of *trust* for the current observer, the level of *protection* (i.e. the policy), etc. The privacy risk is then a combination of the sensitivity and the likelihood.

5   Evaluation and Experiments

5.1   Experiments for Validating IRT

Since we shall be using Item Response Theory (IRT) to calculate the sensitivity of shared items, the first question that needs to be answered is this: *Can IRT be meaningfully applied in the cloud scenario in which people share data items in a variety of contexts?* In order to investigate this and to empirically ground our design and subsequent experiments, we validated IRT for the cloud scenario using real people's feedback on Amazon Mechanical Turk. Next, we explain our methodology for this validation.

Methodology. We created a realistic vocabulary for the personal cloud, and, based on it, we developed a list of questions that we submitted as *Human Intelligence Tasks* (HITS) on Amazon mTurk[4]. We created two separate HITs for the dichotomous and polytomous cases of IRT. For the dichotomous case, we asked 96 questions to which we received answers from 81 people. For the polytomous

---

[4] The vocabulary and the survey are available online: http://goo.gl/xjuvvj

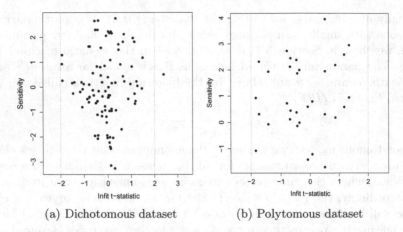

(a) Dichotomous dataset   (b) Polytomous dataset

Fig. 5. Bond-and-Fox Pathway Map on the mTurk data (a dot represents a context item)

case (with 3 categories), we asked 16 questions to which we received answers from 50 people[5]. Here each question represents a *context item* while the users responses represent their *policies* for sharing in the given context.

We analyzed the results using the eRm Package in R [12]. For testing the model fit, we used the standardized (STD) and the mean square (MSQ) infit statistics. An infit statistic is a weighted fit statistic derived from the squared standardized residual between the observed data and the one predicted by the model [13]. The STD infit indicates whether the data fits the model *perfectly* and is also an approximate t-statistic. In Figure 5, we show the STD infit statistic in the two cases of dichotomous and polytomous items, along with the sensitivity value of items (threshold values in the polytomous case) in each graph, also called the *Bond-and-Fox Pathway Map*. We notice that all the values in the polytomous case and all but one in the dichotomous case lie between -2 and 2, which are the typically acceptable bounds [13]. We also derived the MSQ infit which serves as an indication of whether the data fits the model *usefully*, i.e. if it is productive for measurement. We found that the MSQ infit was in the range [0.7, 1.312] for dichotomous items and [0.683,1.287] for polytomous items, which are both within the typically accepted [0.5, 1.5] range [13].

Having shown the applicability of IRT to the cloud sharing scenario, we proceed to the evaluation of our framework.

5.2   Synthetic Datasets

In this section we detail our methodology for evaluating our framework with synthetic data, followed by the experimental results and discussion.

Methodology. The context items in this dataset were generated by selecting a generic vocabulary with 5 fields per context. Each field of a context had 5

---

[5] The numbers of respondents is generally considered a good number for testing IRT[11].

possible values for a total of 3125 possible contexts. From these contexts, we selected 200 ones at random. There are 500 sharers (or people) who share these items. In total, for each experiment we allocated 30000 sharing instances, each of which represents a data item (corresponding to the context item) shared by a certain person with another person at a specific time. The item to share at each instance is drawn according to a predetermined item distribution (zipf with exponent 2, or uniform, depending on the experiment). In our implementation, the distance (and hence similarity) between each pair of contexts is based on considering the hamming distance over their fields[6]. The people connections for sending data were modeled using two types of graphs: (i) small world (using the Watts-Strogatz model with a base degree of 2 and $\beta = 0.5$) and (ii) random (with average degree of 4). Our simulation is a discrete event based simulation, punctuated by sharing events. The person who instantiates a sharing event is selected randomly from the graph, weighted by her degree, so that people who have more neighbors share more items than those with less. The data receiver is selected randomly from the list of neighbors of the sender. Each person sends data at a time rate modeled by a Poisson process so that the time between her two sharing instances is exponentially distributed with an average of 3,6, or 12 hours, depending on the experiment.

At each sharing instance, the context item's *QuerySet* is sent according to our scheme. The server maintains clusters of contexts it receives, grouped according to a *similarity parameter* (whose value of 1 implies that each cluster's contexts differ by one field from their cluster center, etc.). When the server receives a new context, it either maps it to an existing cluster or assigns it as the center of a new one. All the contexts of a certain cluster are assumed to have the same sensitivity. The server replies with all the sensitivities it knows for the clusters to which the contexts in the *QuerySet* were mapped. If the reply contains the requested item, this is considered as a *Hit*.

In the crowdsourcing phase, upon receiving new *Crowdsourcing Information (CI)* from a client, the server matches it to a cluster S and tries to compute the sensitivity for S if it is not yet computed. To achieve an acceptable sample for IRT, we require that (1) S has a minimum of 15 contexts with their policies, (2) that there are 4 other clusters satisfying requirement 1, and (3) that each of these 4 clusters has at least 8 *CIs* by people who have also sent *CIs* appearing in S. The sensitivities are computed using the *marginal maximum likelihood estimation* technique. In all the experiments, unless otherwise stated, the default setting is a small world social network with zipf item distribution, six hours average sharing interval, and a similarity parameter of 1. In addition, the value for parameter r is equal to k, which is 3 by default. Hence, k is the anonymity parameter we use henceforth.

---

[6] System designers can use any similarity measure best suited for their needs, e.g., those dealing specifically with semantic similarity. However, that is beyond the scope of this work.

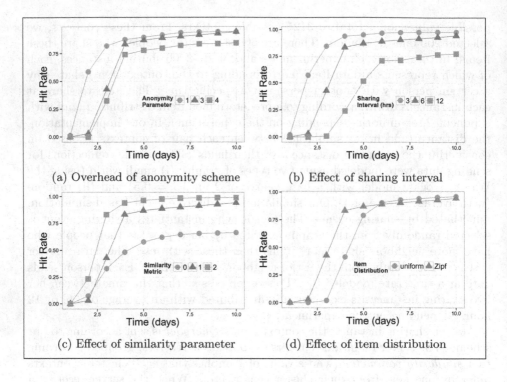

(a) Overhead of anonymity scheme   (b) Effect of sharing interval

(c) Effect of similarity parameter   (d) Effect of item distribution

Fig. 6. Synthetic dataset graphs

Results and Discussion. Figure 6a shows the Hit Rate of users queries over time, where Hit Rate is defined as:

$$HitRate = \frac{\# \ of \ queried \ items \ with \ available \ sensitivity}{total \ \# \ of \ queried \ items} \tag{2}$$

The Hit Rate is calculated per day unless otherwise specified. In Figure 6a we can see that the Hit Rate for anonymity parameter 3 is better than the Hit Rate for 4. As discussed earlier, anonymity parameter k implies that a *targetContext* for sensitivity must have appeared in k different anonymity subsets and that k different values for each field in the *targetContext* must be present in the *QuerySet*. The above conditions suggest that lower the anonymity parameter value, more *targetContexts* would be sent to the server for crowdsourcing, and thus more quickly would IRT be able to respond with sensitivity values.

The anonymity parameter 1 implies no anonymity at all. We plot this curve to see the 'overhead' of our K-anonymity scheme on top of the time required by IRT. Simply put, the curve for the anonymity parameter 1 represents the time it takes IRT to provide Hit Rates when there is no anonymity scheme in place. Thus the difference between the curves for anonymity parameters 1 and 3 represents the overhead of our anonymity scheme in terms of reduced Hit Rate. However, we see that the curve for 3 converges to the same Hit Rate as 1 in ten days time. This suggests that our anonymity scheme bootstraps quickly and does not pose significant overhead[7]

Figure 6b shows the Hit Rate with different sharing intervals in hours. An interval of 3 means that all users query for the sensitivity of an item every 3 hours on average. It can be seen from the Figure that initially, longer the interval, the slower the increase in the Hit Rate. This is most noticeable around the 5th day, when the Hit Rate with an interval 12 is still around 0.5 and lags significantly behind. Eventually, as the server collects more and more items, the Hit Rates of all sharing intervals converge to similar values.

Figure 6c shows the Hit Rate with different similarity parameters. Similarity parameter has been defined in Section 5.2 A similarity parameter of 0 signifies that there is no (zero) difference between two context items while calculating sensitivity[8]. Precisely, what this means is that to calculate the sensitivity of an item, IRT would require other items, which are exactly the same as this item, to have been shared with different policies. A similarity parameter 1 implies that two items that differ by a distance of 1 would be considered the same while 2 implies that items differ by a distance of 2 would be considered the same. This in turn implies that IRT would be able to more quickly calculate the sensitivity of an item (as opposed to case 0) since there would be more items which are considered the same. Thus we can see in Figure 6c that Hit Rate with similarity parameter 0 is the worst since IRT does not have enough items for calculation.

In Figure 6d, we investigate the effects of the 'item distribution' on the Hit Rate. By 'item distribution' we mean the distribution of the context items, i.e., the different contexts in which users share data. This is an important feature because different organizations and different systems would naturally have different item distribution. For our experiments, we use two different item distributions. One is the *zipf* distribution, which has been shown to be most common in social networks [14]. The other is the *random* distribution in which all context items are randomly distributed. A look at the Figure 6d reveals that a *zipf* distribution 'bootstraps' faster than a random distribution. The Hit Rate with random distribution lags behind zipf by a day, i.e., it reaches the same Hit Rate a day later, till the fifth day. We argue this is because, given a *zipf* distribution, users share more similar items, and thus the crowdsourcing is more effective, and IRT is able to calculate the sensitivity of items quickly. Given a random distribution, it takes more time for IRT to accumulate enough similar items for the calculation of sensitivity. However, as the times goes by and more items are accumulated, both random and zipf converge to around the same values.

In Figure 7a we observe the effect of changing the underlying social network. We use two graphs for the social network structure: small world and random. These affect the sharing patterns of the users. We see that the effect of the underlying graphs on the Hit Rate is not significant and both lead to similar values, with the small world doing slightly better than the random network.

---

[7] This overhead can be further reduced through bootstrapping the system with initial data collected from surveys, thus increasing the Hit Rate at the beginning.

[8] This was the case for example in the experiments for validating IRT in Section 5.1.

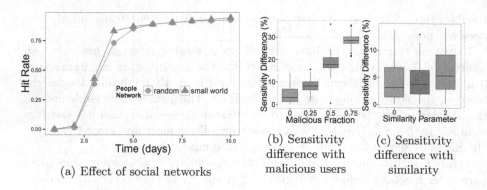

(a) Effect of social networks

(b) Sensitivity difference with malicious users

(c) Sensitivity difference with similarity

Fig. 7. Hit rate and sensitivity difference under various conditions

Finally, Figures 7b and 7c show the effect of malicious users and changing similarity parameters on the sensitivity values. For this particular set of experiments, we begin by assigning different sensitivity values to the items and also different attitudes to the users. As the experiment runs, the policy of the users on sharing the items is dictated by their attitude and the item sensitivity given at the beginning. The sensitivity of the items is then calculated by our scheme. We then measure the absolute difference between the actual sensitivity of the items and the calculated sensitivity. Ideally, there should be no significant difference between the actual sensitivity and the calculated sensitivity. However, differences could arise under certain conditions. The first condition is the presence of *malicious users*. A malicious user sends random policies for items, i.e., she does not have a fixed attitude but rather a random and unpredictable one.

Figure 7b shows the effect of such malicious users on our scheme. The figure shows the box plots for each item's normalized sensitivity difference in terms of percentage. We observe that when there are no malicious users, the difference is pretty low (in the range [2%, 6%]), with most items calculated sensitivity very near the actual sensitivity (the individual dots represent the outliers). This keeps getting progressively worse as the proportion of malicious users increases. Finally, with a fraction of 0.75 malicious users, most of the items' calculated sensitivity differs by as much as 30% from the actual sensitivity.

In Figure 7c, we see that the effect of different similarity parameters on the calculated sensitivity. We can see that, with similarity parameters 0 and 1, the difference between actual and calculated sensitivity is very low. The reader will recall that similarity parameter 0 means that two items would only be grouped together if they are identical. Therefore, when IRT calculates sensitivity value of an item, it does so on the basis of other identical items for which it has received policies from different users. Thus the calculated sensitivity value would be in high agreement with actual sensitivity. With increasing similarity parameter values, the system would group together items which are not identical, therefore sacrificing accuracy in sensitivity calculation. We observe that the difference of actual and calculated sensitivity with similarity parameter 2 is greater than 0 and 1. However, as we discussed while explaining the results of Figure 6c, a

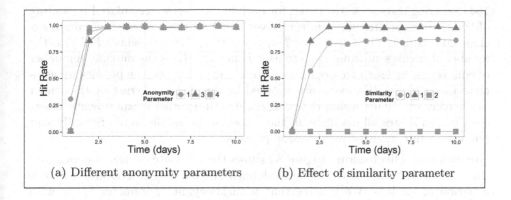

(a) Different anonymity parameters   (b) Effect of similarity parameter

Fig. 8. Enron dataset graphs

higher value for the similarity parameter signifies a better Hit Ratio. Therefore, we discover that there is a *tradeoff* between accuracy of calculated sensitivity and Hit Rate, as far as similarity parameter is concerned.

5.3 Enron Experiments

We want to evaluate our scheme in a realistic setting. However, as there is no dataset of users sharing activities in the cloud that is publicly available, we use the Enron email dataset. Sharing data of various types with certain entities in the cloud is analogous to sharing attachments via emails. Specifically, what we get from this dataset, is a variety of items (hence variety of contexts in which real people share these items with others) and also the level of trust that they have in each other. We explain these points as well as our data extraction and analysis methodology below.

Methodology. The dataset was obtained from (http://info.nuix.com/ Enron.html) in the form of 130 personal storage folders (pst). It was processed using the PST File Format SDK[9] and the MIME++ toolkit[10]. We only considered emails with attachments, whose metadata was extracted using the GNU Libextractor library[11]. Precisely, the main metadata we extracted from files is: (revision history, last saved by, resource type, file type, author name, and creator). We then collected all the email addresses mentioned in the dataset and grouped the ones corresponding to the same person, based on the patterns of occurrence of email aliases. Next, the emails of each person were used to obtain the list of companies she is affiliated with according to the email domain, filtering out public email services (e.g. AOL, Yahoo). We matched all the processed metadata with a specific vocabulary we created for the Enron Dataset. In total the obtained dataset contained 2510 people sharing 184 distinct contexts over

---

[9] http://pstsdk.codeplex.com/
[10] http://www.hunnysoft.com/mimepp/
[11] http://www.gnu.org/software/libextractor/

19415 sharing instances. Moreover, for each file sender, we calculated a measure of the trust associated with each receiver based on the frequency of emails exchanged with her. The trust value $T(i,j) = F(i,j)/Max(i)$, where $F(i,j)$ is the number of emails sent from user i to user j, and $Max(i)$ is the maximum number of emails sent by user i to any receiver. In our experiments, the policies we associate with each sending event are dictated by this degree of trust by the sender in the receiver. We use a similar timing scale as the synthetic experiments, where each person shares all his items in the sequence the emails were originally sent but with a rate modeled as a Poisson process.

Results and Discussion. Figure 8a shows the Hit Rate of users queries over time, where Hit Rate is the same as defined in Equation 2. The graph is over a period of 10 days. We can see that with anonymity parameter 1, i.e. with no anonymity scheme in place, the Hit Rate jumps very quickly. However, anonymity parameter 3 and 4 eventually catch up and all the curves show a Hit Rate of 1 by the third day. We argue that this improvement in Hit Rate over the case of synthetic experiments (see Figure 6a) is because the sharing contexts in the Enron dataset are not diverse and more similar items are collected faster, thus leading to an increase in the Hit Rate.

In Figure 8b we can see that with the similarity parameter equal to 2, the Hit Rate remains at 0 consistently. Our investigation into this reveals to us the reason behind this strange result. We discover that the context items shared in the Enron dataset are not very diverse. Hence, having a similarity value of 2 means that most items are clustered together since most items in the Enron dataset differ from each other by at most 2 fields. As most items are clustered in very few clusters, this means that IRT is not able to work since it does not find enough different items to sensitivity calculation. The number of different items that IRT requires for working differs on the implementation being used. Our implementation requires that there must be at least 5 different items for IRT to work. In case of similarity 2, these clusters are not available.

However, with similarity 1, enough clusters are found and this in turn implies that IRT would be able to more quickly calculate the sensitivity of an item (as opposed to case 0) since there would be more items which are considered the same. Therefore, similarity 1 shows better Hit Rate than similarity 0.

These results suggest that using IRT in a scenario where most people share similar items, the similarity parameter should be low. However, we note that the Enron dataset, being an email dataset, does not have the same diversity as would be available in a cloud setting. Thus, we have shown the feasibility of our scheme using synthetic and empirical data.

6   Related Work

One of the relevant attempts at privacy risk estimation was in the field of social networks. Liu and Terzi [7] used IRT in quantifying the privacy risk of exposing user profile items on Facebook (e.g. birthday, political affiliation, etc.). Kosinki et al. [8] also modeled the process of information disclosure in Facebook using

IRT and found correlations between disclosure scores and personality traits. Our work is distinct from these in that IRT is shown to apply in the case of privacy aware sharing in the cloud and in that it utilizes context extraction to work with any data file, without being limited to a predefined set of profile items.

The concerns about the privacy of user data in the cloud were confirmed by Ion et al. [15] through surveys highlighting the users' beliefs about the intrinsic insecurity of the cloud. A client-centric system was also developed by Ion et al. [16], enabling users to share text and image files on web-based platforms while keeping the data encrypted and hiding the fact that confidential data has been exchanged from a casual observer. From one angle, our work is complementary to theirs as we design the framework to help users decide on what data to keep confidential. From another perspective, our work is distinct as we allow multiple levels of privacy policies that can be controlled by the user.

The work by Garg et al. [17] highlights the *peer produced privacy* paradigm, which treats privacy as a community good and considers individuals who share the risk of information sharing. The authors argue that such an approach can result in more socially optimal privacy decisions. Our work shares similar motivations, among which are the suboptimal privacy decisions taken by average users and the inability of users to keep track of the changing contextual factors affecting privacy. We envision that extensions of our work can exploit this paradigm for producing socially optimal privacy policy recommendations.

The concept of contextual privacy has also received significant attention recently. Nissenbaum's work (e.g. [18]) was one of the notable contributions that called for articulating context-based rules and expectations and to embed some of them in law. Several works have developed context-aware systems for privacy preservation in scenarios like sensor data sharing [19] and mobile social networks [20].

7 Future Work

In this paper, we have provided a novel framework for preserving the privacy of data shared to the cloud. One of the future directions we are planning to investigate is further improving the privacy guarantee of our scheme to resist probabilistic attacks by a server trying to link a context with a sharing operation. Moreover, we are currently investigating alternative techniques to IRT, such as *Bayesian Networks*, that can also serve to model people's privacy aware sharing. Also, developing techniques for recommending privacy policies to users is one of the main pillars of the final system. As of writing, we are working on developing the first prototype for our system, which will be released in the near future.

Acknowledgment. The research leading to these results has received funding from the EU in the context of the project *CloudSpaces*: Open Service Platform for the Next Generation of Personal clouds (FP7-317555).

References

1. Greenwald, G., MacAskill, E.: NSA Prism program taps in to user data of Apple, Google and others. The Guardian 7(6), 1–43 (2013)
2. Gentry, C.: A fully homomorphic encryption scheme. PhD thesis, Stanford University (2009)
3. Van Dijk, M., Juels, A.: On the impossibility of cryptography alone for privacy-preserving cloud computing. In: Proceedings of the 5th USENIX Conference on Hot Topics in Security, pp. 1–8 (2010)
4. Protiviti: Knowing how – and where – your confidential data is classified and managed. Technical report, Protiviti Inc. (2013)
5. Sweeney, L.: k-anonymity: A model for protecting privacy. International Journal of Uncertainty, Fuzziness and Knowledge-Based Systems 10(05), 557–570 (2002)
6. Baker, F.B.: The basics of item response theory. ERIC (2001)
7. Liu, K., Terzi, E.: A framework for computing the privacy scores of users in online social networks. ACM Transactions on Knowledge Discovery from Data 5(1), 6 (2010)
8. Quercia, D., Casas, D.L., Pesce, J.P., Stillwell, D., Kosinski, M., Almeida, V., Crowcroft, J.: Facebook and privacy: The balancing act of personality, gender, and relationship currency. In: International AAAI Conference on Weblogs and Social Media (2012)
9. Reeve, B.B., Fayers, P.: Applying item response theory modeling for evaluating questionnaire item and scale properties. Assessing Quality of Life in Clinical Trials: Methods of Practice 2, 55–73 (2005)
10. Nering, M.L., Ostini, R.: Handbook of polytomous item response theory models. Taylor & Francis (2011)
11. Linacre, J.M.: Sample size and item calibration stability. Rasch Measurement Transactions 7(4), 328 (1994)
12. Mair, P., Hatzinger, R.: Extended rasch modeling: The erm package for the application of irt models in r. Journal of Statistical Software 20(9), 1–20 (2007)
13. De Ayala, R.J.: Theory and practice of item response theory. Guilford Publications (2009)
14. Lewis, K., Kaufman, J., Gonzalez, M., Wimmer, A., Christakis, N.: Tastes, ties, and time: A new social network dataset using facebook.com. Social Networks 30(4), 330–342 (2008)
15. Ion, I., Sachdeva, N., Kumaraguru, P., Čapkun, S.: Home is safer than the cloud!: Privacy concerns for consumer cloud storage. In: Proceedings of the Seventh Symposium on Usable Privacy and Security, pp. 13:1–13:20 (2011)
16. Ion, I., Beato, F., Čapkun, S., Preneel, B., Langheinrich, M.: For some eyes only: Protecting online information sharing. In: Proceedings of the Third ACM Conference on Data and Application Security and Privacy, pp. 1–12 (2013)
17. Garg, V., Patil, S., Kapadia, A., Camp, L.J.: Peer-produced privacy protection. In: IEEE International Symposium on Technology and Society, pp. 147–154 (2013)
18. Nissenbaum, H.: A contextual approach to privacy online. Daedalus 140(4), 32–48 (2011)
19. Pallapa, G., Di Francesco, M., Das, S.K.: Adaptive and context-aware privacy preservation schemes exploiting user interactions in pervasive environments. In: IEEE International Symposium on a World of Wireless, Mobile and Multimedia Networks, pp. 1–6 (2012)
20. Bilogrevic, I., Huguenin, K., Agir, B., Jadliwala, M., Hubaux, J.P.: Adaptive information-sharing for privacy-aware mobile social networks. In: Proceedings of the 2013 ACM International Joint Conference on Pervasive and Ubiquitous Computing, pp. 657–666 (2013)

Forward-Secure Distributed Encryption*

Wouter Lueks[1], Jaap-Henk Hoepman[1], and Klaus Kursawe[2]

[1] Radboud University Nijmegen, Nijmegen, The Netherlands
{lueks,jhh}@cs.ru.nl
[2] The European Network for Cyber Security, The Hague, The Netherlands
klaus.kursawe@ecns.eu

Abstract. Distributed encryption is a cryptographic primitive that implements revocable privacy. The primitive allows a recipient of a message to decrypt it only if enough senders encrypted that same message. We present a new distributed encryption scheme that is simpler than the previous solution by Hoepman and Galindo—in particular it does not rely on pairings—and that satisfies stronger security requirements. Moreover, we show how to achieve key evolution, which is necessary to ensure scalability in many practical applications, and prove that the resulting scheme is forward secure. Finally, we present a provably secure batched distributed encryption scheme that is much more efficient for small plaintext domains, but that requires more storage.

1 Introduction

Revocable privacy [6,14] has been proposed as a means for balancing security and privacy. A system implements revocable privacy if "the architecture of the system guarantees that personal data is revealed only if a predefined rule has been violated" [6]. For an in-depth discussion of the complex interactions between security and privacy, and the value of revocable privacy therein we refer to [6].

The distributed encryption scheme proposed by Hoepman and Galindo [7] is a primitive that can be used to implement revocable privacy. In particular it can be used to implement the rule "if a person or an object generates more than k events, its identity should be revealed." To do so, senders in the distributed encryption scheme encrypt the corresponding identity for every event that occurs. The scheme guarantees that the recipient of these ciphertexts can recover the identity only if it can combine k ciphertext shares, i.e., encryptions, of the same message created by different senders. We refer to [9] for other applications, but for the purpose of this paper we will examine the following two in more detail:

1. Consider the notarized sale of valuable objects like houses. Objects that change hands frequently may indicate fraud or money laundering and may therefore be

---

* This research is supported by the research program Sentinels as project 'Revocable Privacy' (10532). Sentinels is being financed by Technology Foundation STW, the Netherlands Organization for Scientific Research (NWO), and the Dutch Ministry of Economic Affairs. This research is conducted within the Privacy and Identity Lab (PI.lab) and funded by SIDN.nl (http://www.sidn.nl).

E. De Cristofaro and S.J. Murdoch (Eds.): PETS 2014, LNCS 8555, pp. 123–142, 2014.

suspicious. A distributed encryption scheme can be used to identify the suspicious sales, while learning nothing about the others. To do so, every notary encrypts a record of every transaction under the distributed encryption scheme and submits the ciphertext share to a central authority. The authority can then recover only the details of the suspicious objects.

2. A distributed encryption scheme can enforce speed limits in a privacy-friendly manner as follows. Place automatic number plate recognition (ANPR) systems at the start and end of a stretch of highway, like in the SPECS system [13]. Suppose that a car is speeding if it takes at most t seconds to traverse this stretch. The ANPR systems generate ciphertext shares for every passing car. The system restarts after time t, so speeding cars generate two shares instead of one. They can be detected with a distributed encryption scheme with two senders and threshold one. To reliably detect speeding cars, the detection system needs to run multiple, staggered instances of the distributed encryption scheme. The higher the number of parallel instances, the better the accuracy. See Sect. 7 for the details.

The second application is especially challenging: the time frames are short and the number of observations is high. In this paper we propose two new schemes that can deal with these situations much more efficiently than the distributed encryption scheme by Hoepman and Galindo [7].

In the speed-limiting application, two-way interaction between the cars and ANPR systems is infeasible: adding communication facilities to cars would be costly. Therefore, distributed encryption schemes should be non-interactive to offer privacy in these situations. Techniques based on k-times anonymous credentials [2] and threshold encryption schemes—see [7] for a detailed discussion—are thus not appropriate. Also, when using a distributed encryption scheme the senders can immediately encrypt their observations. Storing a plaintext copy, as would be needed for a secure multi-party computation between the senders, is therefore not necessary. We see this as an advantage. The non-interactivity does imply, however, that the senders have to be trusted, and that framing is possible otherwise.

Our first contribution is a simpler distributed encryption scheme that does not use pairings, and satisfies stronger security requirements than the original scheme by Hoepman and Galindo [7]. We present this scheme in Sect. 4. We extend it with a non-trivial key-evolution method [5] to forward-securely [8] generate as many keys as necessary while keeping the key-size constant, see Sect. 5. The ability to restart the system with fresh keys is important in almost all applications, including the speed-limiting example, because it ensures that only shares generated within the same time frame can be combined. Hoepman and Galindo's original solution requires that the keys for every time frame are generated in advance, and therefore scales less well.

Our second contribution is a batched distributed encryption scheme. It addresses the issue of inefficiency in traditional distributed encryption schemes in practice. In the speed-limiting use case, for example, the cost to recover all encrypted plaintexts from a set of ciphertexts shares is exponential: the only option is to try all possible combinations of shares. Our batched solution, which we present in Sect. 6, is much more efficient, at the cost of increased storage requirements. The amount of storage is linear in the number of plaintexts. Hence this solution is feasible only if the domain is small, as is the case for license plates. Nevertheless, we believe this to be a worthwhile trade-off.

Finally, in Sect. 7 we analyze the performance of our schemes, suggest additions to our scheme that may be useful in practice and present conclusions.

2   The Idea

The idea of our new distributed encryption scheme is that a ciphertext share can be generated by first encoding the plaintext, and then transforming the ciphertext into a ciphertext share. If enough of these ciphertext shares are collected, the combiner can recover the plaintext.

Let G be a cyclic group of prime order q, such that DDH is hard in G. The protocol uses an injection $\chi : \{0,1\}^{\ell_p} \to G$ to encode plaintexts elements into group elements. The function χ^{-1} is the inverse of χ, i.e., $\chi^{-1}(\chi(p)) = p$. This mapping is redundant, i.e., with high probability a random group element $g \in G$ has no inverse under χ^{-1}. We construct this map in the next section.

Every sender i is given a secret share $s_i \in Z_q$, corresponding to a k-out-of-n Shamir secret sharing of a *publicly known* value, 1. Let f be the corresponding degree $k-1$ secret-sharing polynomial, i.e., $f(0) = 1$ and $s_i = f(i)$. Sender i produces a ciphertext share for plaintext p as follows. First, it encodes the plaintext into a generator $\chi(p) \in G$. Then, it uses its secret share to produce the ciphertext share $\alpha_i = \chi(p)^{s_i}$. Given enough of these shares for the same plaintext, the exponents can be removed, and the original ciphertext can be recovered. More precisely, consider a set $\{\alpha_{i_1}, \ldots, \alpha_{i_k}\}$ of shares with $I = \{i_1, \ldots, i_k\}$ the set of indices, then there exist Lagrange coefficients $\lambda_{i_1}^I, \ldots, \lambda_{i_k}^I$ such that $\sum_{i \in I} \lambda_i^I s_i = f(0) = 1$. So, we can calculate

$$\alpha = \prod_{i \in I} \alpha_i^{\lambda_i^I} = \chi(p)^{\sum_{i \in I} s_i \lambda_i^I} = \chi(p)^{f(0)} = \chi(p).$$

Then, $p = \chi^{-1}(\alpha)$. If the shares do not belong to the same plaintext the resulting encoding will, with high probability not be an encoding of a plaintext element, and therefore fail to decode using χ^{-1}.

If χ is not redundant, the scheme is insecure. Let $p = \chi^{-1}(g)$ and $p' = \chi^{-1}(g^2)$. Then given a share $\alpha_i = \chi(p)^{s_i} = g^{s_i}$ it is trivial to make a share $\alpha_i' = \chi(p')^{s_i} = g^{2s_i} = (g^{s_i})^2$ for p' without help of the sender. As will become clear later, this breaks the scheme.

3   Preliminaries

We first recall some definitions. The security of our new distributed encryption schemes requires the following problem to be hard.

Definition 1 (Decisional Diffie-Hellman problem). *The Decisional Diffie-Hellman problem (DDH) in a group G of order q takes as input a tuple $(g, A = g^a, B = g^b, C = g^c) \in G^4$ and outputs 'yes' if $c = ab \pmod q$, and else 'no.'*

We define Lagrange coefficients as used in Shamir's secret sharing scheme [12].

Definition 2 (Lagrange coefficients). *For a set $I \subseteq \{1,\ldots,n\}$ and field $\mathbf{Z}_q$ with $q > n$, we define the Lagrange polynomials $\lambda_i^I(x)$ as $\lambda_i^I(x) = \prod_{t \in I \setminus \{i\}} \frac{x-t}{i-t} \in \mathbf{Z}_q^*[x]$, and the Lagrange coefficients as $\lambda_i^I = \lambda_i^I(0)$. Then, for any polynomial $P \in \mathbf{Z}_q[x]$ of degree at most $|I| - 1$, $P(x) = \sum_{i \in I} P(i) \lambda_i^I(x)$ and $P(0) = \sum_{i \in I} P(i) \lambda_i^I$.*

Notation. We write $|A|$ to denote the cardinality of the set A, $[n]$ to denote the set $\{1,\ldots,n\}$ and $x \parallel y$ to denote the concatenation of the strings x and y. Finally, $x \in_R A$ denotes that x is drawn uniformly at random from the set A.

Redundant Injective Map. We now describe how to construct the map χ described in the previous section. The first step is a redundant injective map.

Definition 3. *We call a map $\psi : A \to B$, with inverse $\psi^{-1} : B \to A \cup \{\bot\}$ a redundant injective map with security parameter ℓ_H if it satisfies the following properties:*

Computable *The functions ψ and ψ^{-1} are efficiently computable.*
Reversible *For all $a \in A$ we have $\psi^{-1}(\psi(a)) = a$.*
Redundant *For any $b \in_R B$ we have $\psi^{-1}(b) = \bot$ with probability $1 - 2^{-\ell_H}$.*

The redundancy prevents the attack described at the end of Sect. 2, but requires $|B|$ to be at least $2^{\ell_H} |A|$. In our scheme, B must be a group. We therefore use the following group encoding that maps strings to group elements.

Definition 4. *A group encoding $(\phi, \phi^{-1}, \{0,1\}^\ell, \mathbf{G}, E)$ consists of a bijective function $\phi : \{0,1\}^\ell \to E \subset \mathbf{G}$ and its inverse ϕ^{-1}. The functions ϕ and ϕ^{-1}, and membership tests in E run in polynomial time, and $|\mathbf{G}| / |E|$ is polynomial in ℓ.*

The Elligator map [1] is one such encoding, where $|\mathbf{G}| / |E| \approx 2$, and the group is an elliptic curve.

Definition 5. *Our Redundant Injective Map consists of the three algorithms* RIM.GEN, RIM.MAP *and* RIM.UNMAP—*the latter two correspond to χ and χ^{-1}.*

RIM.GEN$(1^{\ell_p}, 1^{\ell_H}, (\phi, \phi^{-1}, \{0,1\}^{\ell_p + \ell_H}, \mathbf{G}, E))$ *Given a plaintext size ℓ_p, a security parameter ℓ_H, and a group encoding $(\phi, \phi^{-1}, \{0,1\}^{\ell_p + \ell_H}, \mathbf{G}, E)$, it outputs two cryptographic hash functions $H_1 : \{0,1\}^{\ell_p} \to \{0,1\}^{\ell_H}$ and $H_2 : \{0,1\}^{\ell_H} \to \{0,1\}^{\ell_p}$.*
RIM.MAP(p) *This function takes as input a plaintext $p \in \{0,1\}^{\ell_p}$ and returns the group element $\phi(p \oplus H_2(r) \parallel r) \in E \subset \mathbf{G}$ where $r = H_1(p)$.*
RIM.UNMAP(c) *Given a group element $c \in \mathbf{G}$ this function returns $\bot$ if $c \notin E$. Else, it sets $b_1 \parallel b_2 = \phi^{-1}(c)$ and $p = b_1 \oplus H_2(b_2)$. If $H_1(p) = b_2$ it returns p, else it returns $\bot$.*

Computability and reversibility are clearly satisfied. For any $c \in_R E$ the inverse $b_1 \parallel b_2 = \phi^{-1}(c)$ is uniformly distributed over $\{0,1\}^{\ell_p + \ell_H}$. Therefore, since H_1 is a hash-function, $H_1(b_1 \oplus H_2(b_2)) = b_2$ with probability $2^{-\ell_H}$, so the map is redundant.

We need the following lemma in our security proof.

Lemma 1. *Our Redundant Injective Map from Definition 5 is programmable in the random oracle model for H_1 and H_2. This means that we can adaptively ensure that* RIM.MAP$(p) = g$ *for any* $p \in \{0,1\}^{\ell_p}$ *and* $g \in_R E$ *with overwhelming probability, provided that H_1 was not queried with p.*

Proof. Suppose we wish to set RIM.MAP$(p) = b_1 \| b_2 = \phi^{-1}(g)$. We set $H_1(p) = b_2$. Then, since b_2 is random, with overwhelming probability it was not queried before and we can set $H_2(b_2) = p \oplus b_1$. Since b_1 and b_2 are random, so is $p \oplus b_1$, therefore, the outputs are set to random values as required.   □

4 A New DE Scheme

Our new DE scheme, which we sketched in Sect. 2, directly creates shares of the plaintext instead of shares of an identity-based decryption key that decrypts the plaintext, as in Hoepman and Galindo's scheme [7]. The resulting scheme is simpler and no longer requires pairings. Furthermore, the new structure allows us to define a non-trivial key-evolution method, which seems impossible for the original scheme without compromising forward security. We formally introduce this scheme now.

4.1 Syntax

First, we recall the syntax of a key-evolving distributed encryption scheme from [7]. Note that we have made the safety requirement explicit.

Definition 6 (Key-evolving Distributed Encryption). *A k-out-of-n key-evolving distributed encryption scheme with lifetime divided into s stages, or (k,n,s)-KDE scheme, consists of the following four algorithms.*

KDE.GEN$(1^\ell, k, n, s, \ell_p)$ *This key generation algorithm takes as input a security parameter 1^ℓ, a threshold k, the number of senders n, the number of stages s and a plaintext size ℓ_p.[1] For each sender it generates initial encryption keys $S_{1,1}, \ldots, S_{1,n}$ and returns these, the system parameters, and the plaintext space $\mathscr{P}$.*

KDE.UPDKEY$(S_{\sigma,i})$ *The key update function KDE.UPDKEY takes as input $S_{\sigma,i}$ and outputs the key $S_{\sigma+1,i}$ for the next stage. This function aborts if $\sigma + 1 > s$.*

KDE.ENC$(S_{\sigma,i}, p)$ *Given an encryption key $S_{\sigma,i}$ and a plaintext p, this function returns a ciphertext share c.*

KDE.COMB(C) *Given a set $C = \{c_1, \ldots, c_k\}$ consisting of k ciphertext shares, the function KDE.COMB(C) either returns a plaintext p or ERROR.*

Every key-evolving distributed encryption scheme must satisfy the following correctness and safety requirements.

CORRECTNESS *Create the encryption keys $S_{\sigma,1}, \ldots, S_{\sigma,n}$ by running the algorithm KDE.GEN and then repeatedly updating them using KDE.UPDKEY to reach the required stage σ. For all plaintexts p and pairwise disjoint senders i_j we have KDE.COMB$(C) = p$ if $C = \{\text{KDE.ENC}(S_{\sigma,i_1}, p), \ldots, \text{KDE.ENC}(S_{\sigma,i_k}, p)\}$.*

---

[1] In the original description the plaintext size was implicit.

SAFETY   *Generate $S_{\sigma,1}, \ldots, S_{\sigma,n}$ as for correctness. If $C = \{KDE.ENC(S_{\sigma,i_1}, p_{i_1}), \ldots,$*
    KDE.ENC$(S_{\sigma,i_k}, p_{i_k})\}$ with not all p_i equal, then with overwhelming probability
    KDE.COMB$(C) = $ ERROR.

To make the system secure in practice, senders need to get their keys in a secure manner, and, to ensure forward security, senders have to destroy the old key after updating it.

A distributed encryption scheme is a special case of a key-evolving distributed encryption scheme.

Definition 7 (Distributed Encryption). *A k-out-of-n distributed encryption scheme, or (k, n)-DE scheme, is a $(k, n, 1)$-KDE scheme were the functions are called DE.GEN, DE.ENC and DE.COMB instead.*

4.2   Security Definition

We define the forward security of a key-evolving distributed encryption scheme by recalling its security game. We present the security game by Hoepman and Galindo [7] in a slightly more general setting: plaintexts that have been queried before may be used in the challenge phase, provided this does not lead to a trivial win for the adversary.

Definition 8 (KDE forward-security game). *Consider a (k, n, s)-KDE key-evolving distributed encryption scheme with security parameter 1^ℓ given by the four algorithms KDE.GEN, KDE.UPDKEY, KDE.ENC and KDE.COMB. Define the following game between a challenger and an adversary $\mathscr{A}$.*

Setup   *The challenger runs KDE.GEN$(1^\ell, k, n, s)$ to obtain $(S_{1,1}, \ldots, S_{1,n})$ and sends a description of the plaintext space $\mathscr{P}$ and system parameters to the adversary.*

Find   *The challenger initializes the current stage σ to 1, and the set of corrupted senders $I_{1,c}$ to the empty set. The adversary can issue the following three types of queries:*

  – *A corrupt(i) query is only allowed before any encryption query enc(i, p) has been made for the current stage. If the query is allowed, the challenger sends $S_{\sigma,i}$ to the adversary and it adds i to $I_{\sigma,c}$.*
  – *On encryption queries enc(i, p), where $i \in [n]$, $i \notin I_{\sigma,c}$ and $p \in \mathscr{P}$, the adversary receives the ciphertext KDE.ENC$(S_{\sigma,i}, p)$.*
  – *On next-stage queries next$()$, the challenger updates the encryption keys of senders $i \in \{1, \ldots, n\} \setminus I_{\sigma,c}$ by setting $S_{\sigma+1,i} \leftarrow$ KDE.UPDKEY$(S_{\sigma,i})$. The adversary is responsible for updating the keys of the other senders $i \in I_{\sigma,c}$. Finally, the challenger sets $I_{\sigma+1,c} \leftarrow I_{\sigma,c}$ and $\sigma \leftarrow \sigma + 1$.*

Challenge   *The adversary $\mathscr{A}$ outputs a challenge stage number $\sigma^\star < s$, indices $I_{nc} = \{i_1, \ldots, i_t\}$ corresponding to senders from which it wants to receive challenge ciphertexts and two equal length plaintexts $p_0, p_1 \in \mathscr{P}$. Let r denote the cardinality of $I_{\sigma^\star,c}$ and C_0 and C_1 denote the senders at which plaintexts p_0 and p_1 were queried respectively in stage $\sigma^\star$. The challenger aborts if the challenge is not valid, i.e., if one of the following conditions holds*

  – *p_0 or p_1 was queried at a challenge sender, i.e., if $(C_0 \cup C_1) \cap I_{nc} \neq \emptyset$;*
  – *a challenge sender was already corrupted, i.e., if $I_{nc} \cap I_{\sigma^\star,c} \neq \emptyset$; or*
  – *too many shares are known to the adversary for either p_0 or p_1. This is the case if $\max(|C_0 \cup I_{\sigma^\star,c}|, |C_1 \cup I_{\sigma^\star,c}|) + |I_{nc}| \geq k$.*

Finally, the challenger chooses $\beta \in_R \{0,1\}$ *and returns a challenge ciphertext share*
$c_{\sigma*,i} = \text{DE.ENC}(E_{\sigma*,i}, p_\beta)$ *for each* $i \in I_{nc}$.
Guess *The adversary* $\mathscr{A}$ *outputs a guess* $\beta' \in \{0,1\}$. *The adversary wins if* $\beta = \beta'$.
The advantage of adversary $\mathscr{A}$ *is given by* $\mathbf{Adv}_{\mathscr{A}}^{\text{KDE}}(1^\ell) = 2 |\Pr[\beta' = \beta] - 1/2|$. *An KDE*
scheme is called forward secure *if* $\mathbf{Adv}_{\mathscr{A}}^{\text{KDE}}(1^\ell)$ *is negligible for every PPT adversary*
$\mathscr{A}$.

The solution by Hoepman and Galindo is only secure in a more restricted attacker
model (which they call the static adversary model), where the attacker announces up
front which senders it will corrupt in what stage, what the challenge stage σ^* is, and
which senders it will query in this challenge phase. Our scheme does not need these
restrictions.

4.3 A New Distributed Encryption Scheme

In Sect. 2 we gave a sketch of our new distributed encryption scheme. Here we fill out
the details. Correctness and safety follow from the earlier discussion.

Definition 9 (DE scheme). *The new distributed encryption (DE) scheme is given by the*
following algorithms, where RIM.GEN, RIM.MAP *and* RIM.UNMAP *are as in Def. 5.*
DE.GEN$(1^\ell, k, n, \ell_p)$ *Create a group* $\mathbf{G}$ *of prime order* q, *where* $q \approx 2^\ell$, *such that*
   DDH is hard in $\mathbf{G}$, *and create a group encoding* $\delta = (\phi, \phi^{-1}, \{0,1\}^{\ell_p+\ell}, \mathbf{G}, E)$.
   Call RIM.GEN$(1^{\ell_p}, 1^\ell, \delta)$ *to setup the redundant injective map. Let* $\mathscr{P} = \{0,1\}^{\ell_p}$
   be the plaintext space. Share the public value 1 *using Shamir's k-out-of-n secret*
   sharing as follows. Choose $\varepsilon_1, \ldots, \varepsilon_{k-1} \in_R \mathbf{Z}_q$ *and define the* $k-1$ *degree polyno-*
   mial $f(x) = 1 + \sum_{i=1}^{k-1} \varepsilon_i x^i$, *then* $f(0) = 1$. *Every sender* i *is given a share* $S_i = (i, s_i)$
   where $s_i = f(i)$. *Output* S_i *for each sender, and publish* $(\mathbf{G}, q, E, \phi, \phi^{-1}, \mathscr{P})$.
DE.ENC(S_i, p) *Given an encryption key* $S_i = (i, s_i)$ *let* $\alpha_i = \text{RIM.MAP}(p)^{s_i}$. *Return*
   $c_i = (i, \alpha_i)$.
DE.COMB(C) *Let* $C = \{c_{i_1}, \ldots, c_{i_k}\}$. *Each share* c_{i_j} *is parsed as* (i_j, α_{i_j}). *Construct*[2]
   $I = \{i_1, \ldots, i_k\}$, *let* $c = \prod_{i \in I} (\alpha_i)^{\lambda_i^I}$ *and return* RIM.UNMAP(c).

In Sect. 7.1 we sketch how to handle arbitrary-length plaintexts.

4.4 Security of the DE Scheme

In this section we sketch the proof of the following theorem.

Theorem 1. *In the random oracle model for* H_1 *and* H_2 *the new distributed encryption*
scheme from Def. 9 is secure assuming the DDH assumption holds in the group $\mathbf{G}$.

We first give an ideal model for this scheme, and show that in this model the DE scheme
is secure. We then prove that the ideal model and the actual scheme are indistinguishable, hence proving the security of the actual scheme as well.

---

[2] The index i_j is part of c_j to be able to explicitly reconstruct I and thus compute $\lambda_{i_j}^I$ given a set
   C.

The Ideal Scheme. In the ideal scheme the secret sharing is made specific to the plaintext. So, sender i uses a plaintext-specific secret share $s_i^{(p)}$ to construct a ciphertext share $\alpha_i = \text{RIM.MAP}(p)^{s_i^{(p)}}$ for plaintext p. For each p, the secret shares $s_1^{(p)}, \ldots, s_n^{(p)}$ form a random k-out-of-n sharing of the secret 1.

The reader may wonder at this point, if it still suffices to use a degree $k-1$ polynomial. Traditional uses of a secret sharing scheme suggest that the degree should be k instead, since one secret share is already known. This is not the case, for the following two reasons. First, knowing the secret itself does not help in the recovery as the generator, i.e., the encryption of the plaintext, is actually unknown. Second, while it is possible to guess the generator, thus giving k shares in total, an extra share is needed to verify that guess.

Lemma 2. *The ideal DE scheme is secure.*

Proof. By construction of the secret shares we only need to consider the shares for the challenge plaintexts p_0 and p_1; all others are completely independent. After the challenge the attacker knows at most $k-1$ ciphertext shares. Hence, no information is leaked as with only $k-1$ shares, both sets of shares are equally likely to combine to $\text{RIM.MAP}(p_0)$ as they are to $\text{RIM.MAP}(p_1)$. In fact, for each set of shares there exists a kth share that reconstructs the desired value. □

Indistinguishability of Ideal and Real Scheme. Suppose an attacker can break DDH, i.e., given $(g, A = g^a, B = g^b, C = g^c)$ it can decide whether $c = ab$. Then it can break our scheme as follows. It picks three different plaintexts p, p_0, p_1, and calculates $g = \text{RIM.MAP}(p)$ and $A = \text{RIM.MAP}(p)^{s_i}$, for the latter it uses one query. Then it sets $B = \text{RIM.MAP}(p_0)$ and obtains $C = \text{RIM.MAP}(p_d)^{s_i}$ as a response to its challenge query on p_0 and p_1. Now, $d = 0$ if and only if $c = ab$ in the DDH problem, thus breaking the DE security as well.

The indistinguishability proof that we present here shows that any attacker has to solve a DDH problem. The proof is in the hybrid model, see Fig. 1. Queries for the first $\kappa - 1$ plaintexts will be answered using ideal shares, then the κth plaintext will get either ideal or real shares depending on whether $c = ab$ in the DDH instance, and the remaining plaintext will have real shares. We use Lem. 1 to ensure that the correct generators are used for those plaintexts. Induction on κ shows that any distinguisher between ideal and real shares thus solves the DDH instance.

To construct the shares corresponding to the different senders while still ensuring proper secret-sharing we duplicate the DDH instance, combine it with the corrupted shares, and derive the remaining shares based on the underlying secret sharing scheme.

Lemma 3. *In the random oracle model for H_1 and H_2 (as used by the redundant injective mapping), the ideal and the real DE schemes are indistinguishable provided the DDH assumption holds in $\mathbf{G}$.*

Proof. For this proof we use a hybrid scheme that is parametrized by κ. Let $(g, A = g^a, B = g^b, C = g^c)$ be a DDH instance for $\mathbf{G}$, our task is to decide whether $c = ab$.

senders   senders

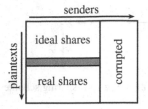   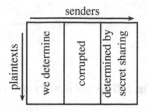

Fig. 1. The table on the left shows which type of secret shares are used to answer the queries for the plaintexts while the table on the right shows how these answers are constructed

This proof is in the random oracle model for H_1 and H_2, so the adversary has oracle access to each of them. Let $\mathscr{P}_Q = (p_1, \ldots, p_{q_E})$ be the plaintexts queries made by the adversary to the H_1 oracle.

In the hybrid scheme, the ciphertext shares corresponding to plaintexts in the set $\mathscr{P}_I = \{p_1, \ldots, p_{\kappa-1}\}$ will be created using ideal shares, whereas the ciphertext shares for plaintexts in $\mathscr{P}_R = \{p_{\kappa+1}, \ldots, p_{q_E}\}$ will be created using the real shares, see Fig. 1. If $c = ab$ (of the DDH instance) then the hybrid scheme uses real shares for p_κ and ideal shares otherwise. Any distinguisher for the two variants will thus solve the DDH instance. Induction over κ completes the proof.

We now show how to play the security game. Initially we generate $\gamma_p \in_R \mathbf{Z}_q$ for all $p \in \mathscr{P}_R$ such that $g^{\gamma_p} \in E$ and we generate $\gamma_{p_\kappa} \in_R \mathbf{Z}_q$ such that $A^{\gamma_{p_\kappa}} \in E$. This is possible since $|\mathbf{G}| / |E|$ is polynomial and can be done without knowing the queries in advance. As queries for p's come in to the H_1 oracle, use Lemma 1 to set $\mathrm{RIM.MAP}(p) = g^{\gamma_p}$ for $p \in \mathscr{P}_R$ and to set $\mathrm{RIM.MAP}(p_\kappa) = A^{\gamma_{p_\kappa}}$. All other queries are answered normally.

Then we play the game as follows. The attacker only makes corruption queries at the start of the game. For every corrupt(i) query, add i to I_c and generate an arbitrary secret-share $s_i \in_R \mathbf{Z}_q$ and send $S_i = (i, s_i)$ to the challenger.

We now consider three cases of enc(i, p) queries. The first, where $p \in \mathscr{P}_I$, for which the answers will be using ideal shares, the second when $p = p_\kappa$ and the third when $p \in \mathscr{P}_R$, for which the answers will be using real shares.

Without loss of generality, we assume that the r corrupted senders are numbered $k - r, \ldots, k - 1$, see Fig. 1. As we cannot play with the corrupted senders, the corresponding shares are always given by enc(i, p) = $\mathrm{RIM.MAP}(p)^{s_i}$ for $i > n - r$ and all plaintexts $p \in \mathscr{P}$.[3] This determines r shares. Furthermore, $\mathrm{RIM.MAP}(p)^1$ is also a valid share, giving $r + 1$ determined shares. In the following we show how to answer the enc(i, p) queries with $1 \le i \le k - (r + 1)$ for all three cases.

For plaintexts $p \in \mathscr{P}_I$ generate ideal secret shares $s_i^{(p)}$ for senders $1 \le i \le k - (r + 1)$. The ciphertext shares are given by enc(i, p) = $\mathrm{RIM.MAP}(p)^{s_i^{(p)}}$.

For the remaining plaintexts we use the DDH instance $(g, A = g^a, B = g^b, C = g^c)$ to compute the answers to the enc(i, p) queries. First, create an extension as follows. Generate $d_i, e_i \in_R \mathbf{Z}_q$ for $1 \le i \le k - (r + 1)$ and set $B_i = B^{d_i} g^{e_i}$ and $C_i = C^{d_i} A^{e_i}$. It can be shown that $(g, A, B_i = g^{b_i}, C_i = g^{c_i})$ are DDH tuples such that $c_i = ab_i$ when

---

[3] In this proof we omit the sender's index and just write enc(i, p) = $\mathrm{RIM.MAP}(p)^{s_i}$.

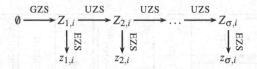

Fig. 2. Graphical representation of an evolving zero-sharing scheme

$c = ab$ in the original problem, and $c_i \in_R \mathbf{Z}_q$ otherwise [10]. We then act as if $s_i = b_i$ for $1 \leq i \leq k - (r+1)$.

For p_κ the ciphertext shares for $1 \leq i \leq k - (r+1)$ are given by $\text{enc}(i, p_\kappa) = C_i^{\gamma_{p_\kappa}}$. If $c_i = ab_i$ then we have $\text{enc}(i, p_\kappa) = (g^{a\gamma_{p_\kappa}})^{b_i} = \text{RIM.MAP}(p_\kappa)^{s_i}$, making the shares real. Otherwise, the c_i's are random, thus the shares are ideal.

For all other plaintexts $p \in \mathscr{P}_R$ the ciphertexts for $1 \leq i \leq k - (r+1)$ are given by $c_{pi} = B_i^{\gamma_p} = (g^{\gamma_p})^{b_i} = \text{RIM.MAP}(p)^{s_i}$, as desired.

We now determined k shares for every plaintext p, the responses for senders $k, \dots, n$, see Fig. 1, are calculated from these by interpolating the exponents

$$\text{enc}(i, p) = \text{RIM.MAP}(p)^{1\lambda_0^I(i)} \text{enc}(1, p)^{\lambda_1^I(i)} \cdots \text{enc}(k-1, p)^{\lambda_{k-1}^I(i)}$$

We have now described how to answer the queries.

Since DDH is hard, two subsequent hybrid schemes are indistinguishable. Thus, the ideal scheme and the real scheme are indistinguishable as well. $\qquad \square$

5   Forward-Secure DE Scheme

The keys of our DE scheme consist of Shamir secret shares, to create a forward secure scheme we need to forward-securely evolve these shares. In this section we show how to do this. When we combine this technique with our new distributed encryption schemes the result is forward secure. In this section we prove this for the scheme in Sect. 4. In the next section we prove this for the batched scheme.

5.1   A Key-evolution Scheme

The scheme we present in this section forward securely generates sharings of the value 0. It combines ideas from Cramer *et al.* [4] and Ohkubo *et al.* [11]. We take the following approach, see also Fig. 2. Time is split into stages. Every sender i has an internal state $Z_{\sigma,i}$ for the current stage σ. The states of all senders combined implicitly define a zero-sharing polynomial z_σ. The states are constructed in such a way that every sender can, without interacting with other senders, derive its zero-share $z_{\sigma,i} = z_\sigma(i)$ for that stage. To move to the next stage, every party can individually update the internal state. After destroying the previous internal state it is not possible to retrieve any information on it from the current internal state.

Syntax. The informal description of the scheme captured in the previous section can be formalized as follows.

internal	$Z_{\sigma,1} \cdots Z_{\sigma,r}$	$Z_{\sigma,r+1} \cdots Z_{\sigma,n}$
external	$\overline{z_{\sigma,1}} \cdots \overline{z_{\sigma,r}}$	$\overline{z_{\sigma,r+1}} \cdots \overline{z_{\sigma,n}}$

Fig. 3. The highlighted section illustrate the adversary's view for a set of corrupted senders $I_c = \{1, \ldots, r\}$. In the next stage, $\sigma + 1$, the adversary gets the complete internal state.

Definition 10 (Evolving zero-sharing). *The next three algorithms describe an evolving zero-sharing scheme. See also Fig. 2.*
 - GZS$(k, n, s, \mathcal{K})$ *takes as input the threshold k, the number of senders n, the number of stages s, and secret sharing field $\mathcal{K}$. It outputs initial states $Z_{1,1}, \ldots, Z_{1,n}$.*
 - UZS$(Z_{\sigma,i})$ *is a non-interactive protocol that takes as input the current state $Z_{\sigma,i}$ and outputs a new state $Z_{\sigma+1,i}$ or aborts.*
 - EZS$(Z_{\sigma,i})$ *takes as input the current state $Z_{\sigma,i}$ and outputs a zero share $z_{\sigma,i}$.*

This definition describes a non-interactive scheme because our use cases require this. Interactive schemes are easier to build, but are not considered in this paper.

Intuitively, forward security requires that no matter what an adversary learns in later stages, it cannot use this knowledge to obtain additional information on the current stage. We formalize this notion for evolving zero-sharing schemes, which we call transparency, as we need it to prove forward-security of our key-evolving distributed encryption scheme.

Consider a stage σ. Clearly, an adversary has the biggest advantage in learning more about stage σ, if it gets the complete state of the system in stage $\sigma + 1$. The following definition formalizes the notion that every zero-sharing polynomial in stage σ is equally likely, as long as it matches the view the adversary already had obtained through corruptions—note this fixes the polynomial if the adversary has corrupted $k - 1$ senders. The adversary gets access to the full zero-sharing polynomial in stage σ. We note that this is very liberal, as in the actual combination with the DE schemes the zero-shares will be kept secret.

Definition 11 (Transparency). *Let k be the threshold, n the total number of senders, q the group order and s the maximum number of stages. Let an evolving zero-sharing given by the algorithms GZS, UZS and EZS be defined for these parameters. Let $Z_{\sigma,1}, \ldots, Z_{\sigma,n}$ be the result of calling GZS and then running UZS $\sigma - 1$ times for each sender. Furthermore, let $z_{\sigma,i} = $ EZS$(Z_{\sigma,i})$ and $Z_{\sigma+1,i} = $ UZS$(Z_{\sigma,i})$. Let $\mathscr{A}$ be an adversary. It outputs a set $I_c \subset [n]$ of senders corrupted in stage σ and receives*
 - *the internal state $Z_{\sigma,i}$, for all senders $i \in I_c$,*
 - *the external state $\overline{z_{\sigma,i}}$ for all senders, and*
 - *the internal state $Z_{\sigma+1,i}$ for all senders,*
see also Fig. 3. We say the evolving zero sharing scheme is transparent *if adversary $\mathscr{A}$ cannot distinguish the following two situations:*
 1. *the normal situation with $\overline{z_{\sigma,i}} = z_{\sigma,i}$ and*
 2. *a situation in which the secret changes, i.e. $\overline{z_{\sigma,i}} = z_{\sigma,i} + z(i)$ where z is a degree $k - 1$ zero-sharing polynomial, such that $z(i) = 0$ for all $i \in I_c$.*

Key-evolution Scheme. We follow Cramer *et al.* [4] in constructing a zero-sharing polynomial in such a way that sender i can only evaluate the polynomial at the point i. For every set $A \subset [n]$ of cardinality $n - (k - 2)$ we define the $k - 1$ degree polynomial $g_A(x) = x \prod_{i \in [n] \setminus A}(x - i)$. Our zero-sharing polynomial is then given by

$$z_\sigma(x) = \sum_{\substack{A \subset [n] \\ |A| = n - (k-2)}} r_{\sigma,A} \cdot g_A(x),$$

where a factor $r_{\sigma,A}$ is known only to the senders $i \in A$. Note that by construction, z is of degree $k - 1$ and $z_\sigma(0)$ is indeed 0. It can be shown that $k - 2$ colluding parties cannot recover $z_\sigma(x)$. Furthermore, for every zero-sharing polynomial z of degree $k - 1$, there exist values for the $r_{\sigma,A}$s such that $z_\sigma(x) = z(x)$. This gives the following scheme.

Definition 12 (Evolving zero-sharing scheme). *Let ℓ_h be a security parameter and let $h_1 : \{0,1\}^{\ell_h} \to \{0,1\}^{\ell_h}$ and $h_2 : \{0,1\}^{\ell_h} \to \mathbf{Z}_q$ be hash functions. The evolving zero-sharing scheme is implemented as follows.*
- GZS$(k, n, s, \mathbf{Z}_q)$ *For each $A \subset [n]$ of cardinality $n - (k - 2)$ generate a random share $\bar{r}_{1,A} \in_R \{0,1\}^{\ell_h}$ and for each sender i set $Z_{1,i} = (\bar{r}_{1,A})_{A \ni i}$.*
- UZS$(Z_{\sigma,i})$ *This algorithm is non-interactive. First, parse $Z_{\sigma,i}$ as $(\bar{r}_{\sigma,A})_{A \ni i}$, and set $\bar{r}_{\sigma+1,A} = h_1(\bar{r}_{\sigma,A})$ for A such that $i \in A$. Then return $Z_{\sigma+1,i} = (\bar{r}_{\sigma+1,A})_{A \ni i}$.*
- EZS$(Z_{\sigma,i})$ *To derive the zero-share parse $Z_{\sigma,i}$ as $(\bar{r}_{\sigma,A})_{A \ni i}$. Then, set $r_{\sigma,A} = h_2(\bar{r}_{\sigma,A})$ for A such that $i \in A$ and determine*

$$z_{\sigma,i} = z_\sigma(i) = \sum_{\substack{A \subset [n] \\ |A| = n - (k-2)}} r_{\sigma,A} \cdot g_A(i).$$

Finally, return $z_{\sigma,i}$.

The construction and the proof of the following lemma are inspired by the Ohkubo *et al.* scheme [11]. See the appendix for the proof.

Lemma 4. *The evolving zero-sharing scheme from Def. 12 is transparent in the random oracle model for h_2.*[4]

5.2   A Key-Evolving DE Scheme

In this section we build a key-evolving DE scheme using the evolving zero-sharing scheme of the previous section. The latter scheme generates as many distributed zero-sharing polynomials as we want. By adding the constant polynomial $g(x) = 1$ to this polynomial we obtain the key-sharing polynomial in our DE scheme.

Definition 13 (KDE scheme). *The key-evolving distributed encryption (KDE) scheme is constructed from the new distributed encryption scheme given by the algorithms* DE.GEN, DE.ENC *and* DE.COMB, *and the evolving zero-sharing scheme from Definition 12 given by the algorithms* GZS, UZS *and* EZS. *It is defined by the following four algorithms.*

---

[4] Actually, it is not really necessary to use a random oracle for this part of the proof. In fact, one can use k-wise independent functions, see for example Canetti *et al.* [3], and thus prove this lemma in the standard model.

- KDE.GEN$(1^\ell, k, n, s, \ell_p)$ *The* KDE.GEN *algorithm first runs* DE.GEN$(1^\ell, k, n, \ell_p)$
  to obtain $(\mathbf{G}, q, E, \phi, \phi^{-1}, \mathscr{P})$, *which it outputs as well. Here group* $\mathbf{G}$ *is of order*
  q. *It then calls* GZS$(k, n, s, \mathbf{Z}_q)$ *to obtain* $Z_{1,1}, \ldots, Z_{1,n}$, *sets* $s_{1,i} = 1 + $ EZS$(Z_{1,i})$ *and*
  outputs $S_{1,i} = (i, s_{1,i}, Z_{1,i})$ *for each sender.*
- KDE.UPDKEY$(S_{\sigma,i})$ *Let* $S_{\sigma,i} = (i, s_{\sigma,i}, Z_{\sigma,i})$. *It then sets* $Z_{\sigma+1,i} = $ UZS$(Z_{\sigma,i})$ *and*
  $s_{\sigma+1,i} = 1 + $ EZS$(Z_{\sigma+1,i})$ *and returns* $S_{\sigma+1,i} = (i, s_{\sigma+1,i}, Z_{\sigma+1,i})$ *or aborts if* UZS
  aborts.
- KDE.ENC$(S_{\sigma,i}, p)$. *Let* $S_{\sigma,i} = (i, s_{\sigma,i}, Z_{\sigma,i})$. *To encrypt a plaintext* p *algorithm*
  KDE.ENC *returns the result of* DE.ENC$((i, s_{\sigma,i}), p)$.
- KDE.COMB(C) *To combine ciphertexts* KDE.COMB *runs* DE.COMB(C).

Efficiency. The evolving zero-sharing scheme has complexity $\binom{n}{k-2}$ in both space and time to store and evaluate the zero-shares. While this number is exponential, it is almost always much smaller than the cost of combining in a real scenario (see Table 1 on page 139). In particular, it is comparable to recovering a single plaintext in the batched scheme which we will present in the next section. Furthermore, its space complexity is independent of the number of stages, which is a big gain with respect to the original scheme [7] where the space complexity is linear in the number of stages. In many practical applications this number will be a lot bigger than $\binom{n}{k-2}$.

Security. The security of the KDE scheme can easily be reduced to that of the DE scheme by using the properties of the evolving zero-sharing scheme. We give a sketch of the proof; we refer to App. B for the full proof.

Theorem 2. *The new KDE scheme is* (k, n, s)-*KDE secure provided that the DE is* $(k, n, 1)$-*KDE secure and the evolving zero-sharing scheme is transparent. The proof is in the random oracle model for* h_2[5].

Proof (Sketch). We reduce the security of the KDE scheme to that of the DE scheme. To setup the system we generate random $\bar{r}_{1,A}$s. We guess the challenge phase $\sigma^\star$ and simulate all stages except $\sigma^\star$, where we use our DE oracle. To ensure that this is not detected we must ensure that corrupted hosts have the correct secret shares. We do this by modifying $h_2(\bar{r}_{\sigma^\star,A})$ in the random oracle model on $\bar{r}_{\sigma^\star,A}$ that were not yet known to the adversary. Then queries in stage $\sigma^\star$ can be answered by our DE oracle. The distribution of the secret shares does not correspond to the initial $\bar{r}_{1,A}$s, however, the transparency of the evolving zero-sharing scheme ensures this cannot be detected. □

This proof easily translates to other evolving zero-sharing schemes where the challenge phase can be incorporated.

6   Efficient Solutions for Small Domains

As was already analyzed by Hoepman and Galindo [7], any distributed encryption solution will be rather inefficient. The main culprit is the combination phase. We do not

---

[5] Again, it is not really necessary to use a random oracle for this proof either. However, the security of the DE scheme uses non-standard assumptions anyway.

add indicators, like the hash of a plaintext, to the ciphertexts as they allow an attacker to trivially test if they belong to given plaintext. Therefore, it is not clear which shares might belong to the same plaintext. The only solution is to try all combinations of k shares, from different senders, of the received shares. Depending on the situation this can become prohibitive. We now propose a variant of our new scheme that is much more efficient for small plaintext domains.

The crucial difference is that we will now operate in a batched setting. At the end of a stage the sender generates a share for *every* plaintext. It generates a proper share for every plaintext it needs to send, as before, and a random value for all other plaintexts. Now we know directly which shares belong to a given plaintext. This reduces the exponential term in the combing phase considerably. Also, since the plaintext is known a priori, the only remaining task of the combiner is to determine whether this plaintext was encrypted by a sufficient number of senders. In particular we can replace the integrity preserving encryption scheme with a hash function.

6.1 Syntax

For small plaintext spaces, the following definition of a *batched key-evolving distributed encryption* scheme makes sense.

Definition 14 (Batched KDE). *A k-out-of-n batched key-evolving distributed encryption scheme with lifetime divided into s stages, or (k,n,s)-BKDE scheme, consists of the following four algorithms.*

BKDE.GEN$(1^\ell, k, n, s, \mathscr{P})$ *Given the security parameter 1^ℓ, the threshold k, the number of senders n, the number of stages s and a plaintext space $\mathscr{P}$ it generates initial encryption keys $S_{1,1}, \ldots, S_{1,n}$ for each sender $i \in [n]$. It returns these encryption keys as well as the system parameters.*

BKDE.ENC$(S_{\sigma,i}, P)$ *Given an encryption key $S_{\sigma,i}$ corresponding to sender i at stage σ and a set of plaintexts $P \subset \mathscr{P}$, this function returns a vector C_i of ciphertext shares of length $|\mathscr{P}|$.*

BKDE.UPDKEY$(S_{\sigma,i})$ *The key update function takes as input $S_{\sigma,i}$ and outputs the key $S_{\sigma+1,i}$ for the next stage. This function aborts if $\sigma + 1 > s$.*

BKDE.COMB$(C_1, \ldots, C_n, s)$ *Given the ciphertext share vectors $C_1, \ldots, C_n$ produced by the senders, the function BKDE.COMB returns a set of plaintexts P.*

A key-evolving batched distributed encryption scheme must satisfy the following combined correctness and safety requirement.

CORRECTNESS & SAFETY *Let the encryption keys $S_{\sigma,i}$ be generated as described above. Let $C_i = \text{BKDE.ENC}(S_{\sigma,i}, P_i)$ for each sender i and for all $P_i \subset \mathscr{P}$. Then the result P of $\text{BKDE.COMB}(C_1, \ldots, C_n)$ is such that $p \in P$ if $p \in P_i$ for at least k different P_i.*

6.2 Security Definition

The following game captures the security properties of our protocol.

Definition 15 (Batched KDE forward-security game). *Consider a (k,n,s)-BKDE batched key-evolving distributed encryption scheme. The batched KDE forward-security* *game is very similar to the KDE forward-security game for a (k,n,s)-KDE scheme. We only note the changes. The algorithms* BKDE.GEN *and* BKDE.UPDKEY *replace the algorithms* KDE.GEN *and* KDE.UPDKEY.

Setup *First, the adversary outputs a plaintext space $\mathcal{P}$ it wants to attack, then the setup phase runs as before.*

Find *In the find phase the adversary is allowed to make* bcorrupt(i), bnext$()$ *and* benc(i,P) *queries. The first two are implemented using* corrupt(i) *and* next$()$ *respectively. On input of a query* benc(i,P_i), *where $i \in [n]$, $i \notin I_{\sigma,c}$ and $P \subset \mathcal{P}$, the challenger sends the vector* BKDE.ENC$(S_{\sigma,i},P_i)$ *to the adversary.*

Challenge *If the challenge on p_0 and p_1 at hosts I_{nc} is valid (see Definition 8) the challenger chooses $\beta \in_R \{0,1\}$, sets $C = $ BKDE.ENC$(S_{\sigma^*,j}, \{p_\beta\})$, and returns the ciphertext share C_{p_β} to the challenger for each $j \in I_{nc}$.*

Guess *The guess phase is unchanged.*

The adversary $\mathcal{A}$'s advantage is defined as $\mathbf{Adv}_{\mathcal{A}}^{\mathrm{BKDE}}(1^\ell) = |\Pr[\beta' = \beta] - 1/2|$. An BKDE scheme is called forward secure *if $\mathbf{Adv}_{\mathcal{A}}^{\mathrm{BKDE}}(1^\ell)$ is negligible for every PPT adversary $\mathcal{A}$.*

6.3   The Scheme

In the batched scheme a sender will output a complete vector of ciphertext shares $(c_{pi})_{p\in\mathcal{P}}$ at the end of a stage. Let $H : \{0,1\}^* \to \mathbf{G}$ be a cryptographic hash function. An element c_{pi} equals $H(p)^{s_i}$ when sender i been asked to encrypt p, and $c_{pi} \in_R \mathbf{G}$ otherwise. Intuitively, when the secret shares are unknown, these two are indistinguishable. The full scheme is given by the following definition. Note the similarities with our new KDE scheme.

Definition 16 (Batched KDE scheme). *Let* (GZS, UZS, EZS) *be an evolving zero-sharing scheme. The following algorithms define a batched key-evolving distributed encryption (BKDE) scheme.*

BKDE.GEN$(1^\ell, k, n, s, \mathcal{P})$ *Generate a cyclic group $\mathbf{G}$ such that its order q is of size ℓ bits. Then construct a hash function $H : \{0,1\}^* \to \mathbf{G}$. Create the secret sharing of zero by calling* GZS$(k,n,s,\mathbf{Z}_q)$ *to obtain $Z_{1,1}, \ldots, Z_{1,n}$. Let $s_{1,i} = 1 + $ EZS$(Z_{1,i})$. Output $S_{1,i} = (s_{1,i}, Z_{1,i})$ for each sender, together with a description of $\mathbf{G}$ and the hash function H.*

BKDE.ENC$(S_{\sigma,i}, P)$ *Let $S_{\sigma,i} = (s_{\sigma,i}, Z_{\sigma,i})$, and let $C_i = (c_{pi})_{p\in\mathcal{P}}$ be the resulting ciphertext share vector such that for all $p \in \mathcal{P}$*

$$c_{pi} = \begin{cases} H(p)^{s_{\sigma,i}} & \text{if } p \in P \\ h \in_R \mathbf{G} & \text{otherwise.} \end{cases}$$

BKDE.UPDKEY$(S_{\sigma,i})$ *Let $S_{\sigma,i} = (s_{\sigma,i}, Z_{\sigma,i})$. Set $Z_{\sigma+1,i} = $ UZS$(Z_{\sigma,i})$ and $s_{\sigma+1,i} = 1 + $ EZS$(Z_{\sigma+1,i})$. Return $S_{\sigma+1,i} = (s_{\sigma+1,i}, Z_{\sigma+1,i})$ or abort if UZS does.*

BKDE.COMB$(C_1, \ldots, C_n)$ *For each $p \in \mathcal{P}$, do the following. Consider all shares $(c_{p1}, \ldots, c_{pn})$ corresponding to plaintext p from senders 1 trough n. For all possible combinations of index sets $I \subseteq \{1, \ldots, n\}$ of size k verify whether*

$$\prod_{i \in I} (c_{pi})^{\lambda_i^I} = H(p)^1 = H(p).$$

If so, add p to the set of plaintexts to return.

The structure of this scheme is similar to that of our new DE and KDE schemes. Correctness and safety are easy to check. The security proofs of the DE and KDE schemes can readily be adapted to this setting directly by replacing the redundant injective map by one hash function in the random oracle model. We will not do this here. Instead we prove that the security of the BKDE scheme can be reduced to that of the KDE scheme. This theorem is slightly weaker as it requires us to also model H_1 and H_2 in the random oracle model. However, it nicely illustrates how the schemes relate.

Theorem 3. *The batched key-evolving distributed encryption scheme is (k,n,s)-BKDE secure, provided that the KDE scheme is (k,n,s)-KDE secure. The proof is in the random oracle model for H, H_1 and H_2.*

Proof. Suppose we have an adversary $\mathcal{A}$ against the batched scheme, then we build an adversary $\mathcal{B}$ against the KDE scheme. First, $\mathcal{A}$ requests a plaintext space $\mathcal{P}$ for the batched scheme. Then, $\mathcal{B}$ gets a description of the group and the plaintext space $\mathcal{P}'$ from its challenger. It forwards the group description to $\mathcal{A}$. Furthermore, it chooses a hash function $H' : \mathcal{P} \to \mathcal{P}'$ onto the plain text space required by the KDE scheme. Then we answer its queries as follows.

Adversary $\mathcal{B}$ answers a bcorrupt(i) query from $\mathcal{A}$ with the result of a corrupt(i) query to its oracle. On input of a bnext(i) query $\mathcal{B}$ makes a next$()$ query to its oracle. Adversary $\mathcal{B}$ answers a hash query $H(x)$ with $H(x) = \mathrm{RIM.MAP}(H'(x))$.

The answer C_i to a batched encryption query benc(i, P_i) is constructed as follows:

$$c_{pi} = \begin{cases} \mathrm{enc}(i, H'(p)) & \text{if } p \in P_i \\ h \in_R \mathbf{G} & \text{otherwise} \end{cases}$$

By choice of $H(x)$ this is indeed correct, as

$$\mathrm{enc}(i, H'(p)) = \mathrm{RIM.MAP}(H'(p))^{s_{\sigma,i}} = H(p)^{s_{\sigma,i}},$$

as desired. The challenge made by $\mathcal{A}$ is forwarded to $\mathcal{B}$'s challenge oracle, and the results relayed back. The advantage of $\mathcal{A}$ against the BKDE scheme is the same as $\mathcal{B}$'s advantage against the KDE scheme.   □

7   Analysis and Conclusions

7.1   Practical Considerations

We propose two small extensions that can improve the scheme in practice. Our scheme works only with fixed-length plaintexts. It is, however, possible to handle longer plaintexts as well. First, append a hash of the message to authenticate the message as a whole. Then, split the message into appropriately sized chunks and run the DE scheme for each

Table 1. Performance comparison between the KDE scheme and the batched KDE (BKDE) scheme. The time complexity gives the approximate number of combine actions needed. The space complexity gives the number of ciphertext shares stored. Here m is the average number of plaintexts encrypted by each sender.

		KDE		BKDE	
	Parameters	Time	Space	Time	Space
Formula		$\binom{n}{k}m^k$	nm	$\binom{n}{k}|\mathscr{P}|$	$n|\mathscr{P}|$
Speed limiting	$n = 2, |\mathscr{P}| = 10^7$ $k = 2, m = 600$	$1 \times 360 \cdot 10^3$	$2,250$	$1 \times 10 \cdot 10^6$	$50 \cdot 10^6$
Canvas cutters	$n = 8, |\mathscr{P}| = 10^7$ $k = 4, m = 400$	$70 \times 26 \cdot 10^9$	$3,200$	$70 \times 10 \cdot 10^6$	$80 \cdot 10^6$

of them. After recovering the multiple blocks, combine them and check the hash before outputting the plaintext. This procedural extension allows encrypting arbitrary length plaintexts.

The second improvement deterministically encrypts the message with the public key of the combiner before running the DE scheme itself. This ensures that only the combiner—which is still assumed to be honest—can successfully recover the encrypted plaintexts even if ciphertexts leak.

7.2 Performance

Tab. 1 shows the two methods' time complexity, in terms of combine operations, and the space complexity, in terms of stored ciphertext shares. It also gives numbers for two specific use cases. In both, we assume the total number of vehicles is 10 million, like in the Netherlands. For the first, a speed-monitoring example, we choose the parameters to monitor a 20 kilometer stretch of highway—for simplicity, we assume there are no exits—with one ANPR system placed at the beginning, and one at the end. We set the epoch length to 10 minutes. Every minute, we start a parallel instance of the system. This setting guarantees that every car going at least $120/(9/60) \approx 133$ km/h will generate two shares in the same epoch, and is thus always caught, while cars going between 120 km/h and 133 km/h may be caught. Using 20 parallel instances, instead of 10, will lower this bound to 126 km/h.

Suppose that 600 cars pass the ANPR systems during an epoch. The regular KDE scheme is more efficient in this setting due to the relatively low number of shares. In fact, it can be optimized significantly, because the first station needs to create a share for only the newest epoch, instead of all parallel ones. This modification reduces the combining cost by another factor of 10. In this setting, our key-evolution schemes ensure that the senders do not need to store $60 \cdot 24$ keys for every day the system is operational, instead they store only two.

The second use case comes from Hoepman and Galindo [7]. They describe a scenario where criminals, so-called canvas-cutters, frequently visit rest stops along a highway, cut open the canvas on lorries, and rob them. The criminals can typically be recognized by looking for cars that visit rest stops rather frequently. Suppose we monitor 8 rest stops, and consider a car suspicious if it visits at least 4 within a 4 hour period. Suppose 400 (different) cars visit each rest stop per period. Here, the BKDE scheme is clearly better. The exponential factor in the regular scheme quickly drives up the number of combines needed. In fact, this would be exacerbated if traffic increases. Nevertheless, these cases also illustrate that if storage is an issue, or fewer shares are expected, then it is better to use the non-batched scheme.

7.3 Conclusion

In this paper, we presented a new distributed encryption scheme that is simpler than previous solutions, and uses weaker assumptions. Furthermore, we described a key-evolving variant that offers proper key evolution and is therefore forward secure. Additionally, we demonstrated a batched variant of our new distributed encryption scheme that is much more efficient for small plaintext domains.

None of the known distributed encryption schemes offer semantic security; senders always produce the same ciphertext for a given plaintext. It would be very interesting to see solutions that use randomization to avoid this problem.

References

1. Bernstein, D.J., Hamburg, M., Krasnova, A., Lange, T.: Elligator: elliptic-curve points indistinguishable from uniform random strings. In: Sadeghi, A.R., Gligor, V.D., Yung, M. (eds.) ACM Conference on Computer and Communications Security, pp. 967–980. ACM (2013)
2. Camenisch, J., Hohenberger, S., Kohlweiss, M., Lysyanskaya, A., Meyerovich, M.: How to win the clonewars: efficient periodic n-times anonymous authentication. In: Juels, A., Wright, R.N., De Capitani di Vimercati, S. (eds.) ACM Conference on Computer and Communications Security, pp. 201–210. ACM (2006)
3. Canetti, R., Halevi, S., Katz, J.: A forward-secure public-key encryption scheme. J. Cryptology 20(3), 265–294 (2007)
4. Cramer, R., Damgård, I., Ishai, Y.: Share conversion, pseudorandom secret-sharing and applications to secure computation. In: Kilian, J. (ed.) TCC 2005. LNCS, vol. 3378, pp. 342–362. Springer, Heidelberg (2005)
5. Franklin, M.K.: A survey of key evolving cryptosystems. International Journal of Security and Networks 1(1/2), 46–53 (2006)
6. Hoepman, J.H.: Revocable privacy. ENISA Quarterly Review 5(2) (June 2009)
7. Hoepman, J.H., Galindo, D.: Non-interactive distributed encryption: a new primitive for revocable privacy. In: Chen, Y., Vaidya, J. (eds.) Proceedings of the 10th Annual ACM Workshop on Privacy in the Electronic Society, WPES 2011, Chicago, IL, USA, October 17, pp. 81–92. ACM (2011)
8. Itkis, G.: Forward security – adaptive cryptography: Time evolution. In: Bidgoli, H. (ed.) Handbook of Information Security, pp. 927–944. John Wiley and Sons (2006)
9. Lueks, W., Everts, M.H., Hoepman, J.H.: Revocable privacy 2012 – use cases. Tech. Rep. 35627, TNO (2012)
10. Naor, M., Reingold, O.: Number-theoretic constructions of efficient pseudo-random functions. J. ACM 51(2), 231–262 (2004)

11. Ohkubo, M., Suzuki, K., Kinoshita, S.: Efficient Hash-Chain Based RFID Privacy Protection Scheme. In: International Conference on Ubiquitous Computing – Ubicomp, Workshop Privacy: Current Status and Future Directions, Nottingham, England (September 2004)
12. Shamir, A.: How to share a secret. Commun. ACM 22(11), 612–613 (1979)
13. Speed Check Services: SPECS3 network average speed check solutions, http://www.speedcheck.co.uk/images/SCS_SPECS3_Brochure.pdf (accessed: January 27, 2013)
14. Stadler, M.: Cryptographic Protocols for Revocable Privacy. Ph.D. thesis, Swiss Federal Institute of Technology, Zürich (1996)

A   Proof of Lemma 4

Proof. Let $Z_{\sigma,i} = (\bar{r}_{\sigma,A})_{A \ni i}$ and let $z_\sigma(x)$ be the zero-sharing polynomial in stage σ, corresponding to situation one. Now, we show how to change this to $z_\sigma(x) + z(x)$ by modifying the random oracle for h_2. Let $r = |I_c|$, and w.l.o.g. assume that $I_c = \{n - r + 1, \ldots, n\}$. Since $z(i)$ is zero for all $i \in I_c$ the polynomial is fully determined by $c = k - 1 - r$ extra values. We need to ensure that

$$z_{\sigma,i} + z(i) = \sum_{\substack{A \subset [n] \\ |A| = n - (k-2)}} r_{\sigma,A} g_A(i) = \underbrace{\sum_{A \cap I_c \neq \emptyset} r_{\sigma,A} g_A(i)}_{\text{fixed}} + \underbrace{\sum_{A \cap I_c = \emptyset} r_{\sigma,A} g_A(i)}_{\text{not fixed}}.$$

The fixed part contains values that are known to the adversary, and hence cannot be changed. The not-fixed part can, however, be changed. Consider the sets:

$$A_i = [n] \setminus (\{1, \ldots, i-1, i+1, \ldots c\} \cup I_c)$$

for $i \in [c]$. These sets are such that only set A_i influences the value for sender i, i.e.

$$z_{\sigma,i} + z(i) = \left[\sum_{\substack{A \subset [n] \\ |A| = n - (k-2), \forall j: A \neq A_j}} r_{\sigma,A} g_A(i) \right] + r_{\sigma,A_i} g_{A_i}(i), \tag{1}$$

for $i \in [c]$. Let $r_{\sigma,A} = h_2(\bar{r}_{\sigma,A})$ for all $A \neq A_i$ as always. Then choose the r_{σ,A_i}s such that equation (1) holds for $i \in [c]$. Finally, set $h_2(\bar{r}_{\sigma,A_i})$ to the new value r_{σ,A_i}. This cannot be detected by the adversary due to the one-wayness of h_1, so the situations are indistinguishable. □

B   Full Proof of Theorem 2

Proof. Suppose we have an adversary $\mathscr{A}$ against the KDE scheme. We then build an adversary $\mathscr{B}$ against the underlying DE scheme. Adversary $\mathscr{B}$ receives the system parameters from the challenger and forwards them to $\mathscr{A}$. Next, adversary $\mathscr{B}$ makes a guess σ^* for the challenge stage and initializes the set of corrupted senders I_c to $\emptyset$.

Adversary $\mathscr{B}$ will fully simulate all stages, except stage σ^*, where it will use its oracle to answer the queries. For all $A \subset [n]$, such that $|A| = n - (k-2)$ generate $\bar{r}_{1,A} \in_R \{0,1\}^{\ell_h}$.

We now look into the details of the evolving zero-sharing scheme. By generating $\bar{r}_{1,A}$'s we have completely fixed the system, but we still need to ensure that epoch $\sigma^\star$ can be answered using our oracles. To this end we will change the value of the hash function $h_2(\bar{r}_{\sigma^\star,A_i})$ for specific sets A_i belonging to corrupted parties i. These sets A_i will be chosen in such a way, that $\bar{r}_{\sigma^\star,A_i}$ is not known to any previously corrupted party.

We handle corrupt(i) queries in or before stage $\sigma^\star$ as follows. Let I_c be the set of senders that were corrupted earlier and $f_{\sigma^\star}$ the secret-sharing polynomial induced by the values $\bar{r}_{\sigma^\star,A}$. First, we corrupt sender i using our oracle to obtain its internal state $(i, s_{\sigma^\star,i}) = $ corrupt(i). We need to ensure that $f_{\sigma^\star}(i) = s_{\sigma^\star,i}$. Pick a set A_i of cardinality $n - (k-2)$ such that $I_c \cap A_i = \emptyset$ and $i \in A_i$. This is possible, since the constraints in the challenge phase require $|I_c \cup \{i\}| < k$, therefore, $|I_c|$ will be at most $k-2$. For all other sets $A \ni i$ obtain $r_{\sigma^\star,A} = h_2(\bar{r}_{\sigma^\star,A})$ as usual. Then choose $r_{\sigma^\star,A_i}$ such that:

$$s_{\sigma^\star,i} = f_{\sigma^\star}(i) = 1 + \sum_{\substack{A \subset [n] \\ |A| = n-k+1}} r_{\sigma^\star,A} \cdot g_A(i).$$

By the choice of the set A_i the coefficient $\bar{r}_{\sigma^\star,A_i}$ is not known to any corrupted host, hence we can use the random oracle model to ensure that $h_2(\bar{r}_{\sigma^\star,A_i}) = r_{\sigma^\star,A_i}$. With very high probability this will not be detected by the adversary as the $\bar{r}_{\sigma^\star,A_i}$s are random. Finally, we return $(i, (\bar{r}_{\sigma^\star,A})_{A \ni i})$ to the adversary.

Now $\mathscr{B}$ proceeds as follows. For all stages except $\sigma^\star$ it knows the complete state of the system, and can thus answer all $\mathscr{A}$'s queries. For epoch $\sigma^\star$, all corrupted hosts will, by construction of the hash-function, have the correct secret shares for this epoch. All other queries can be answered by the oracle.

The transparency of the evolving zero-sharing scheme ensures that it is not possible for the adversary to detect that we do something different in stage $\sigma^{\star 6}$.

In the challenge phase $\mathscr{A}$ will announce its challenge phase σ'. If $\sigma' \neq \sigma^\star$ then $\mathscr{B}$ aborts. Otherwise, $\mathscr{B}$ will pass the challenge from $\mathscr{A}$ on to its own oracle. Finally, $\mathscr{B}$ outputs whatever $\mathscr{A}$ outputs. Adversary $\mathscr{B}$ has the same advantage as $\mathscr{A}$ up to a factor $1/s$ for guessing the stage. This proves the result. $\square$

---

[6] This proof only changes h_2 for corrupted hosts, whereas the proof of Lemma 4 (see Appendix A) changes h_2 for non-corrupted hosts, so they can indeed be combined.

I Know Why You Went to the Clinic: Risks and Realization of HTTPS Traffic Analysis

Brad Miller[1], Ling Huang[2], A.D. Joseph[1], and J.D. Tygar[1]

[1] UC Berkeley, USA
[2] Intel Labs, USA

Abstract. Revelations of large scale electronic surveillance and data mining by governments and corporations have fueled increased adoption of HTTPS. We present a traffic analysis attack against over 6000 webpages spanning the HTTPS deployments of 10 widely used, industry-leading websites in areas such as healthcare, finance, legal services and streaming video. Our attack identifies individual pages in the same website with 90% accuracy, exposing personal details including medical conditions, financial and legal affairs and sexual orientation. We examine evaluation methodology and reveal accuracy variations as large as 17% caused by assumptions affecting caching and cookies. We present a novel defense reducing attack accuracy to 25% with a 9% traffic increase, and demonstrate significantly increased effectiveness of prior defenses in our evaluation context, inclusive of enabled caching, user-specific cookies and pages within the same website.

1   Introduction

HTTPS is far more vulnerable to traffic analysis than has been previously discussed by researchers. In a series of important papers, a variety of researchers have shown a number of traffic analysis attacks on SSL proxies [1,2], SSH tunnels [3,4,5,6,7], Tor [3,4,8,9], and in unpublished work, HTTPS [10,11]. Together, these results suggest that HTTPS may be vulnerable to traffic analysis. This paper confirms the vulnerability of HTTPS, but more importantly, gives new and much sharper attacks on HTTPS, presenting algorithms that decrease errors 3.9x from the best previous techniques. We show the following novel results:

- Novel attack technique capable of achieving 90% accuracy over 500 pages hosted at the same website, as compared to 60% with previous techniques
- Impact of caching and cookies on traffic characteristics and attack performance, affecting accuracy as much as 17%
- Novel defense reducing accuracy to 25% with 9% traffic increase; significantly increased effectiveness of packet level defenses in the HTTPS context

We evaluate attack, defense and measurement techniques on websites for healthcare (Mayo Clinic, Planned Parenthood, Kaiser Permanente), finance (Wells Fargo, Bank of America, Vanguard), legal services (ACLU, Legal Zoom) and streaming video (Netflix, YouTube).

E. De Cristofaro and S.J. Murdoch (Eds.): PETS 2014, LNCS 8555, pp. 143–163, 2014.

We design our attack to distinguish minor variations in HTTPS traffic from significant variations which indicate distinct webpages. Minor traffic variations may be caused by caching, dynamically generated content, or user-specific content including cookies. To distinguish minor variations, our attack employs clustering and Gaussian similarity techniques to transform variable length traffic into a fixed width representation. Due to similarity with the Bag-of-Words approach to text analysis, we refer to our technique as Bag-of-Gaussians (BoG). We augment our technique with a hidden Markov model (HMM) leveraging the link structure of the website and further increasing accuracy. Our approach achieves substantially greater accuracy than attacks developed by Panchenko *et al.* (Pan) [8], Liberatore and Levine (LL) [6], and Wang *et al.* [9].[1]

We also present a novel defense technique and evaluate several previously proposed defenses. In the interest of deployability, all defenses we evaluate have been selected or designed to require minimal state. Our evaluation demonstrates that some techniques which are ineffective in other traffic analysis contexts have significantly increased impact in the HTTPS context. For example, although Dyer *et al.* report exponential padding as decreasing accuracy of the Panchenko classifier from 97.2% to 96.6% on SSH tunnels with website homepages [5], we observe a decrease from 60% to 22% in the HTTPS context. Our novel defense reduces the accuracy of the BoG attack from 90% to 25% while generating only 9% traffic overhead.

We conduct our evaluations using a dataset of 463,125 page loads collected from 10 websites during December 2013 and January 2014. Our collection infrastructure includes virtual machines (VMs) which operate in four separate collection modes, varying properties such as caching and cookie retention across the collection modes. By training a model using data from a specific collection mode and evaluating the model using a different collection mode, we are able to isolate the impact of factors such as caching and user-specific cookies on analysis results. We present these results along with insights into the fundamental properties of the traffic itself.

Our evaluation spans four website categories where the specific pages accessed by a user reveal private information. The increased importance of contents over existence of communication is present in traditional privacy concepts such as patient confidentiality or attorney-client privilege. We examine three websites related to healthcare, since the page views of these websites have the potential to reveal whether a pending procedure is an appendectomy or an abortion, or whether a chronic medication is for diabetes or HIV/AIDS. We also examine legal websites, offering services spanning divorce, bankruptcy and wills and legal information regarding LGBT rights, human reproduction and immigration. As documented by Chen *et al.*, specific pages accessed within financial websites may reveal income levels, investment and family details; hence we examine three financial websites [12]. Lastly, we examine two streaming video sites, as the Netflix privacy breach demonstrates the importance of streaming video privacy.

---

[1] To facilitate further research, code and data from this work are available for download at http://secml.cs.berkeley.edu/pets2014.

Table 1. Prior works have focused almost exclusively on website homepages accessed via proxy. Cheng and Danezis work is preliminary and unpublished. Note that "?" indicates the author did not specify the property.

Author	Privacy Technology	Page Set Scope	Page Set Size	Accuracy (%)	Cache	Cookies	Traffic Composition	Analysis Primitive	Active Content
Miller	HTTPS	Closed	6388	90	On	Individual	Single Site	Packet	On
Hintz [1]	SSL proxy	Closed	5	100	?	Individual	Homepages	Request	?
Sun [2]	SSL proxy	Open	2,000 100,000	75 (TP) 1.5 (FP)	Off	Universal	Single Site	Request	Off
Cheng [10]	HTTPS	Closed	489	96	Off	Individual	Single Site	Request	Off
Danezis [11]	HTTPS	Closed	?	89	n/a	n/a	Single Site	Request	n/a
Herrmann [3]	SSH tunnel	Closed	775	97	Off	Universal	Homepages	Packet	?
Cai [4]	SSH tunnel	Closed	100	92	Off	Universal	Homepages	Packet	Scripts
Dyer [5]	SSH tunnel	Closed	775	91	Off	Universal	Homepages	Packet	?
Liberatore [6]	SSH tunnel	Closed	1000	75	Off	Universal	Homepages	Packet	Flash
Bissias [7]	SSH tunnel	Closed	100	23	?	Universal	Homepages	Packet	?
Wang [9]	Tor	Open	100 1000	95 (TP) .06 (FP)	Off	Universal	Homepages	Packet	Off
Wang [9]	Tor	Closed	100	91	Off	Universal	Homepages	Packet	Off
Cai [4]	Tor	Closed	100	78	On	Universal	Homepages	Packet	Scripts
Cai [4]	Tor	Closed	800	70	Off	Universal	Homepages	Packet	Scripts
Panchenko [8]	Tor	Closed	775	55	Off	Universal	Homepages	Packet	Off
Panchenko [8]	Tor	Open	5 1,000	56-73 (TP) .05-.89 (FP)	Off	Universal	Homepages	Packet	Off
Herrmann [3]	Tor	Closed	775	3	Off	Universal	Homepages	Packet	?
Coull [13]	Anonymous Trace	Open	50 100	49 .18	On	Universal	Homepages	NetFlow	Flash & Scripts

2 Prior Work

In this section we review attacks and defenses proposed in prior work, as well as the contexts in which work is evaluated. Comparisons with prior work are limited since much work has targeted specialized technologies such as Tor.

Table 1 presents an overview of prior attacks. The columns are as follows:

Privacy Technology The protection mechanism analyzed for traffic analysis vulnerability. Note that some authors considered multiple mechanisms.

Page Set Scope *Closed* indicates the evaluation used a fixed set of pages known to the attacker in advance. *Open* indicates the evaluation used traffic from pages both of interest and unknown to the attacker. Whereas open conditions are appropriate for Tor, closed conditions are appropriate for HTTPS.

Page Set Size For closed scope, the number of pages used in the evaluation. For open scope, the number of pages of interest to the attacker and the number of background traffic pages, respectively.

Accuracy For closed scope, the percent of pages correctly identified. For open scope, the true positive (TP) rate of correctly identifying a page as being within the censored set and false positive (FP) rate of identifying an uncensored page as censored.

Cache *Off* indicates caching disabled. *On* indicates default caching behavior.

Cookies *Universal* indicates that training and evaluation data were collected on the same machine or machines, and consequently with the same cookie values. *Individual* indicates training and evaluation data were collected on separate machines with distinct cookie values.

Traffic Composition *Single Site* indicates the work identified pages within a website or websites. *Homepages* indicates all pages used in the evaluation were the homepages of different websites.

Analysis Primitive The basic unit on which traffic analysis was conducted. *Request* indicates the analysis operated on the size of each object (e.g. image, style sheet, etc.). *Packet* indicates meta-data observed from TCP packets. *NetFlow* indicates network traces anonymized using NetFlow.

Active Content Indicates whether Flash, JavaScript, Java or any other plugins were enabled in the browser.

Several works require discussion in addition to Table 1. Chen *et al.* study side-channel leaks caused by AJAX in web applications. As Chen focuses on traffic generated after a page loads, we view the work as both complimentary and orthogonal [12]. Danezis focused on the HTTPS context, but evaluated his technique using HTTP server logs at request granularity, removing any effects of fragmentation, concurrent connections or pipelined requests [11]. Cheng *et al.* also focused on HTTPS and conducted an evaluation which parsed request sizes from unencrypted HTTP traffic at a website intentionally selected for its static content [10]. Like Cheng and Danezis, Sun *et al.* and Hintz *et al.* assume the ability to parse entire object sizes from traffic [1,2]. For these reasons, we compare our work to Liberatore and Levine, Panchenko *et al.* and Wang *et al.* as these are more advanced and recently proposed techniques.

Herrmann [3] and Cai [4] both conduct small scale preliminary evaluations which involve enabling the browser cache. These evaluations only consider website homepages and all pages are loaded in a fixed, round-robin order. Herrmann additionally increases the cache size from the default to 2GB. We evaluate the impact of caching on pages within the same website, where caching will have a greater effect due to increased page similarity, and load pages in a randomized order for greater cache state variation.

Separate from attacks, we also review prior work relating to traffic analysis defense. Dyer *et al.* conduct a review of low level defenses operating on individual packets [5]. Dyer evaluates defenses using data released by Liberatore and Levine and Herrmann *et al.* which collect traffic from website homepages on a single machine with caching disabled. In this context, Dyer finds that low level defenses are ineffective against attacks which examine features aggregated over multiple packets. Our evaluation finds that low level defenses are considerably more effective in the HTTPS context.

In addition to the packet level defenses evaluated by Dyer, many defenses have been proposed which operate at higher levels with additional cost and implementation requirements. These include HTTPOS [14], traffic morphing [15] and BuFLO [4,5]. HTTPOS manipulates features of TCP and HTTP to affect packet size, object size, pipelining behavior, packet timing and other properties. BuFLO sends a constant stream of traffic at a fixed packet size for a pre-set minimum amount of time. Given the effectiveness and advantages of packet level level defenses in our evaluation context, we do not further explore these higher level approaches in our work.

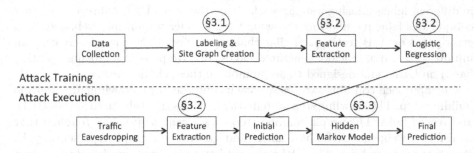

Fig. 1. The dashed line separates training workflow from attack workflow. Bubbles indicate the section in which the system component is discussed. Note that the attacker may conduct training in response to a victim visiting a website, recording victim traffic and inferring contents after browsing has occurred.

3   Attack Presentation

Figure 1 presents the workflow of the attacker as well as the subsections in which we discuss his efforts. In section 3.1, we present a formalism for labeling webpages and generating a link graph relating labeled webpages. Section 3.2 presents the core of our classification approach: Gaussian clustering techniques that capture significant variations in traffic and allow logistic regression to robustly identify objects that reliably differentiate pages. Having generated isolated predictions, we then leverage the site graph and sequential nature of the data in section 3.3 with a hidden Markov model (HMM) to further improve accuracy.

Throughout this section we depend on several terms defined as follows:

Webpage A set of resources loaded by a browser in response to a user clicking a link or entering a URL into the browser address bar. Webpages representing distinct resources are considered *the same* if a user would likely view their contents as substantially similar, regardless of the specific URLs fetched while loading the webpages or dynamic content such as advertising.

Sample A traffic instance generated when a browser displays a webpage.

Label A unique identifier assigned to sets of webpages which are the same. For example, webpages differing only in advertising receive the same label. Samples are labeled according to the webpage in the sample's traffic.

Website A set of webpages such that the URLs which cause each webpage to load in the browser are hosted at the same domain.

Site Graph A graph representing the link structure of a website. Nodes correspond to labels assigned to webpages within the website. Edges correspond to links, represented as the set of labels reachable from a given label.

3.1   Label and Site Graph Generation

Although initially appealing, URLs are poorly suited to labeling webpages within a website. URLs may contain arguments which do not impact content and result in different labels aliasing webpages which are the same. URL redirection further complicates labeling, allowing the same URL to refer to multiple webpages (e.g. error pages or A/B testing). Similar challenges affect web crawlers, creating an infinite web of dynamically generated pages [16]. We present a labeling solution based on URLs and designed to accommodate these challenges.

Our approach contains two phases, each composed of a crawling and a graph building step. The crawling step systematically visits the website to gather URLs and record links. The graph building step uses a *canonicalization function* that transforms webpage URLs into labels and generates a graph representing the structure of the website. The URLs observed and site graph produced in the first phase guide the second, larger crawl which is necessary to observe the breadth of non-deterministic URL redirections. We present our approach below.[2]

Execute Initial Crawl. The crawl can be implemented as either a depth- or breadth-first search, beginning at the homepage and exploring every link on a page up to a fixed maximum depth. We perform a breadth first search to depth 5. This crawl will produce a graph $G = (U, E)$, where U represents the set of URLs seen as links during the crawl, and $E = \{(u, u') \in U \times U \mid u \text{ links to } u'\}$ represents links between URLs in U.

Canonicalize Initial Graph. First, we construct a canonicalization function of the form $C : U \to L$, where C denotes the canonicalization function, U denotes the initial set of URLs, and L denotes the set of labels. We then use our canonicalization function to produce an initial site graph $G' = (L, E')$ where L represents the set of labels on the website and E' represents links. We construct E' as follows:

$$E' = \{(C(u), C(u')) \mid (u, u') \in E\} \tag{1}$$

We define a reverse canonicalization function $R : L \to \mathcal{P}(U)$ such that

$$R(l) = \{u \in U \mid C(u) = l\} \tag{2}$$

Note that $\mathcal{P}(X)$ denotes the *power set* of X, which is the set of all subsets of X.

Execute Primary Crawl. The primary crawl allows the attacker to more fully observe the URL redirection behavior of the website. The attacker conducts the primary crawl in a series of browsing sessions; we fixed the length of each session to 75 labels. The attacker builds browsing sessions using a random walk through G', prioritizing labels not yet visited. The attacker then executes each browsing session by visiting a URL u for each label l such that $u \in R(l)$. The attacker records the value of document.location once u and all associated resources are done loading to identify any URL redirections. U' denotes the set of final URLs which are observed in document.location. We define a new function $T : U \to \mathcal{P}(U')$ such that $T(u) = \{u' \in U' \mid u \text{ resolved at least once to } u'\}$. We use this to define a new translation $T' : L \to \mathcal{P}(U')$ such that

---

[2] A more detailed description of the crawling infrastructure, canonicalization process and graph generation is available on arXiv [17].

Table 2. "Selected Subset" denotes the subset of the initial site graph randomly selected for inclusion in our evaluation, "Avg. Links" denotes the average number of links per label, and "URLs" indicates the number of URLs seen as links in the preliminary site graph corresponding to an included label.

Website	Initial Site Graph G'			Selected Subset			Final Site Graph G'''	
	URLs	Labels	Avg. Links	URLs	Labels	Avg. Links	Labels	Avg. Links
ACLU	54398	28383	130.5	1061	500	41.7	506	44.7
Bank of America	1561	613	30.2	1105	500	30.3	472	43.2
Kaiser Permanente	1756	780	29.7	1030	500	22.6	1037	141.1
Legal Zoom	5248	3973	26.8	602	500	11.8	485	12.2
Mayo Clinic	33664	33094	38.1	531	500	12.5	990	31.0
Netflix	8190	5059	13.8	2938	500	6.2	926	9.0
Planned Parenthood	6336	5520	29.9	662	500	24.8	476	24.4
Vanguard	1261	557	28.4	1054	500	26.7	512	30.8
Wells Fargo	4652	3677	31.2	864	500	17.9	495	19.5
YouTube	64348	34985	7.9	953	500	4.3	497	4.24

$$T'(l) = \bigcup_{u \in R(l)} T(u) \tag{3}$$

Refine Initial Graph To produce the final site graph, we construct a new canonicalization function $C' : U' \to L'$, where U' denotes the final set of URLs and L' denotes a new set of labels. The final graph G''' must maintain the property that for any browsing path in the initial graph G' and any URL redirections in T', after canonicalization with C' the path must also be valid in the final graph. Therefore, the attacker defines an intermediary graph $G'' = (U', E'')$ such that E'' is defined as

$$E'' = \{(u, u') \mid u \in T'(l) \wedge u' \in T'(l') \, \forall \, (l, l') \in E'\} \tag{4}$$

We apply our canonicalization function C' to produce a final graph $G''' = (L', E''')$ where

$$E''' = \{(C'(u), C'(u')) \, \forall \, (u, u') \in E''\} \tag{5}$$

guaranteeing that we have strictly increased the connectivity of the site graph.

In the interest of balancing, given available resources, the amount of collection modes, samples of each label, websites surveyed, and pages included from each website, we selected a 500 page subset of each initial site graph. Consequently, we were able to complete data collection in about four weeks during December 2013 and January 2014 using four virtual hosts. We initialize the selected subset to include the label corresponding to the homepage, and iteratively expand the subset by adding a randomly selected label reachable from the selected subset via the link structure of the initial site graph until 500 labels are selected. The set of links for the graph subset is defined as any links occurring between the 500 selected labels. Table 2 presents properties of the initial site graph G', selected subset, and the final site graph G''' for each of the 10 websites we survey.

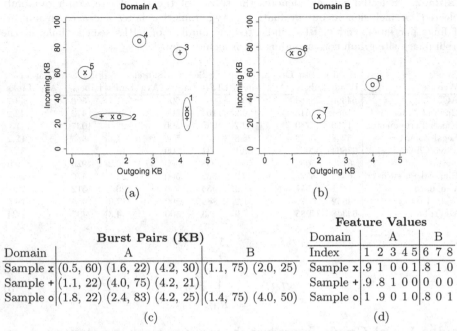

Fig. 2. Table 2c displays the burst pairs extracted from three hypothetical samples. Figures 2a and 2b show the burst pair clusters. Figure 2d depicts the Bag-of-Gaussians features for each sample. Our Gaussian similarity metric enables our attack to distinguish minor traffic variations from significant differences.

Note that the second crawl also serves as the data collection process; samples are labeled as $C'(u') \in L'$ where u' denotes the value of `document.location` when the sample finished loading. Each model uses only redirections observed in training data when generating the site graph used by the HMM for that model.

3.2   Feature Extraction and Machine Learning

This section presents our individual sample classification technique. First, we describe the information which we extract from a sample, then we describe processing to produce features for machine learning, and finally describe the application of the learning technique itself.

We initially extract traffic burst pairs from each sample. Burst pairs are defined as the collective size of a contiguous outgoing packet sequence followed by the collective size of a contiguous incoming packet sequence. Intuitively, contiguous outgoing sequences correspond to requests, and contiguous incoming sequences correspond to responses. All packets must occur on the same TCP connection to minimize the effects of interleaving traffic. For example, denoting outgoing packets as positive and incoming packets as negative, the sequence

[+1420, +310, -1420, -810, +530, -1080] would result in the burst pairs [1730, 2230] and [530, 1080]. Analyzing traffic bursts removes any fragmentation effects. Additionally, treating bursts as pairs allows the data to contain minimal ordering information and go beyond techniques which focus purely on packet size distributions.

Once burst pairs are extracted from each TCP connection, the pairs are grouped using the second level domain of the host associated with the destination IP of the connection. All IPs for which the reverse DNS lookup fails are treated as a single "unknown" domain. Pairs from all samples from each domain undergo k-means clustering to identify commonly occurring and closely related tuples. We fit a Gaussian distribution to each cluster using a maximum likelihood estimates of the mean and covariance.[3] We then treat each cluster as a feature dimension, producing our fixed width feature vector. Features are extracted from samples by computing the extent to which each Gaussian is represented in the sample.

Figure 2 depicts the feature extraction process using a fabricated example involving three samples and two domains. Clustering results in five clusters for Domain A and three clusters for Domain B, ultimately producing an eight-dimensional feature vector. Sample x has traffic tuples in clusters 1, 2, 5, 6 and 7, but no traffic tuples in clusters 3, 4, 8, so its feature vector has non-zero values in dimensions 1, 2, 5, 6, 7, and zero values in dimensions 3, 4, 8. We create feature vectors for samples + and o in a similar fashion.

Analogously to the Bag-of-Words document processing technique, our approach projects a variable length vector of tuples into a finite dimensional space where each dimension "occurs" to some extent in the original sample. Whereas occurrence is determined by word count in Bag-of-Words, occurrence in our method is determined by Gaussian likelihood. For this reason, we refer to our approach as Bag-of-Gaussians (BoG).

We specify our approach formally as follows:

- Let X denote the entire set of tuples from a sample, with $X^d \subseteq X$ denoting the set all tuples observed at domain d.
- Let Σ_i^d, μ_i^d denote the covariance and mean of Gaussian i at domain d.
- Let F denote all features, with F_i^d denoting feature i from domain d.

$$F_i^d = \sum_{x \in X^d} \mathcal{N}(x | \Sigma_i^d, \mu_i^d) \tag{6}$$

To determine the best number of Gaussian features for each domain, we divide the training data into two parts to train and evaluate models using K values of 4000, 1000 and 500. We then retrain using all training data and the best performing K values for each domain.

Once Gaussian features have been extracted from each sample the feature set is augmented to include counts of packet sizes observed over the entire trace. For

---

[3] For clusters where all samples occur at the same point, we set the covariance matrix to a scalar matrix with $\lambda = N^{-1}$, where N denotes the size of the cluster.

example, if the lengths of all outgoing and incoming packets are between 1 and 1500 bytes, we add 3000 additional features where each feature corresponds to the total number of packets sent in a specific direction with a specific size. We linearly normalize all features to be in the range $[0, 1]$ and train a model using L2 regularized multi-class logistic regression with the `liblinear` package [18]. We use $C = 128$ for all sites as we observed varying C did not improve accuracy enough for any site to justify the additional computational cost.

3.3   Hidden Markov Model

The basic attack presented in section 3.2 classifies each sample independently. In practice, samples in a browsing session are not independent since the link structure of the website guides the browsing sequence. We leverage this ordering information, contained in the site graph produced in section 3.1, to improve results using a hidden Markov model (HMM). Recall that a HMM for a sequence of length N is defined by a set of latent (unknown) variables $Z = \{z_n \mid 1 \leq n \leq N\}$, a set of observed variables $X = \{x_n \mid 1 \leq n \leq N\}$, transition matrix A such that $A_{i,j} = P(z_{n+1} = j | z_n = i)$, an initial distribution π such that $\pi_j = P(z_1 = j)$ and an emission function $E(x_n, z_n) = P(x_n | z_n)$.

To apply the HMM, we treat sample labels as latent variables and the traffic contained in the samples as observed variables. We then use the Viterbi algorithm to find the most likely sequence of labels Z visited by a user given the observed traffic X produced by the user. Given a traffic sample, the logistic regression model specifies the likelihood of each label and acts as the emission function E required by the Viterbi algorithm. We assume in the initial distribution π that the user is equally likely to begin browsing with any label in the website, and construct the transition matrix A such that if the site graph contains a link from label i to label j, then $A_{i,j} = N_i^{-1}$, where N_i denotes the number of links leading from label i. If there is no link leading from label i to label j, then $A_{i,j} = 0$.

4   Impact of Evaluation Conditions

In this section we demonstrate the impact of evaluation conditions on accuracy results and traffic characteristics. First, we present the scope, motivation and experimental methodology of our investigation. Then, we present the results of our experiments on four attack implementations, with the most affected attack decreasing accuracy from 68% to 51%. We discuss attack accuracy only insofar as is necessary to understand the impact of evaluation conditions; we defer a full attack evaluation to section 5.

Cache Configuration. The browser cache improves page loading speed by storing previously loaded web resources; this poses two challenges to traffic analysis. Providing content locally decreases the total amount of traffic, reducing the information available for use in an attack. Additionally, differences in browsing history cause differences in cache contents and further vary network traffic. Since privacy tools such as Tor frequently disable caching, many prior evaluations have disabled caching as well [19]. General HTTPS users are unlikely to modify cache settings, so we evaluate the impact of enabling caching to default settings.

User-Specific Cookies. If an evaluation collects all data with either the same browser instance or repeatedly uses a fresh browser image, there are respective assumptions that the attacker and victim will either share the same cookies or use none at all. While a traffic analysis attacker will not have access to victim cookies, privacy technologies which begin all browsing sessions from a clean browsing image effectively share the *null cookie*. We compare the performance of evaluations which use the same (non-null) cookie value in all data, different (non-null) cookie values in training and evaluation, a null cookie in all data, and evaluations which mix null and non-null cookies.

Pageview Diversity. Many evaluations collect data by repeatedly visiting a fixed set of URLs from a single machine and dividing the collected data for training and evaluation. This approach introduces an unrealistic assumption that an attacker will be able to collect separate training data for each victim, visiting the exact same set of webpages as the victim. We examine the impact of allowing the victim to intersperse browsing of multiple websites, including websites outside our attacker's monitoring focus.[4]

Webpage Similarity. Since HTTPS usually allows an eavesdropper to learn the domain a user is visiting, our evaluation focuses on differentiating individual webpages within a website protected by HTTPS. Differentiating webpages within the same website may pose a greater challenge than differentiating website homepages. Webpages within the same website share many resources, increasing caching and decreasing data available for analysis. We examine the relative traffic volumes of browsing both website homepages and webpages within a website.

To quantify the impact of evaluation conditions on accuracy results, we design four modes for data collection designed to isolate specific effects. Our approach assumes that data will be gathered in a series of browsing sessions, each consisting of a fixed number of samples. The four modes are as follows:

1. Cache disabled, new virtual machine (VM) for each browsing session
2. Cache enabled, new VM for each browsing session
3. Cache enabled, persistent VM for all browsing sessions, single site per VM
4. Cache enabled, persistent VM for all browsing sessions, all sites on same VM

We fixed the session length to 75 samples and collected at least 16 samples of each label under each collection mode. The first two modes differ only with respect to cache configuration and begin each browsing session with a fresh VM image to eliminate any cookie persistence in browser or machine state. In effect the second, third and fourth modes each represent a distinct cookie value, with the second mode representing a null cookie and the third and fourth modes

---

[4] This is different from the open-world vs. closed-world distinction in section 2, as we assume that the attacker will train a model for each website in its entirety and identify the correct model based on traffic destination. Here, we are concerned with effects on browser cache or personalized content which may impact traffic analysis.

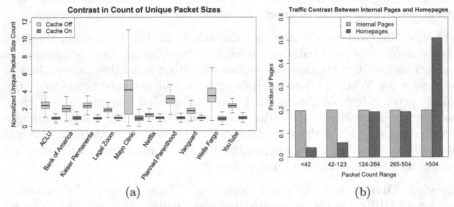

(a)   (b)

Fig. 3. Impact of evaluation conditions on traffic characteristics. Figure 3a presents the increase in number of unique packet sizes per sample of a given label caused by disabling the cache. For each label l we determine the mean number l_m of unique packet sizes for samples of l with caching enabled, and normalize the unique packet size counts of all samples of label l using l_m. We present the normalized values for all labels separated by cache configuration. Figure 3b presents the decrease in traffic volume caused by browsing webpages internal to a website as compared to website homepages. Similar to the effect of caching, the decreased traffic volume is likely to increase classification errors.

having actual, distinct, cookie values set by the site. The third and fourth modes differ in pageview diversity. In the context of HTTPS evaluations, the fourth mode most closely reflects the behavior of actual users and hence serves as evaluation data, while the second and third modes generate training data.

Our analysis reveals that caching significantly decreases the number of unique packet sizes observed for samples of a given label. We focus on the number of unique packet sizes since packet size counts are a commonly used feature in traffic analysis attacks. Figure 3a contrasts samples from the first and second collection modes, presenting the effect of caching on the number of unique packet sizes observed per label for each of the 10 websites we evaluate. Note that the figure only reflects TCP data packets. We use a normalization process to present average impact of caching on a *per-label basis* across an *entire website*, allowing us to depict for each website the expected change in number of unique packet sizes for any given label as a result of disabling the cache.

Since prior works have focused largely on website homepages, we present data demonstrating a decrease in traffic when browsing webpages within a website. Figure 3b presents the results of browsing through the Alexa top 1,000 websites, loading the homepage of each site, and then loading nine additional links on the site at random with caching enabled. By partitioning the total count of data packets transferred in the loading of webpages internal to a website into five equal size buckets we see that there is a clear skew towards homepages generating more traffic. Similar to the traffic increase from disabled caching, the increased traffic of website homepages is likely to increase accuracy.

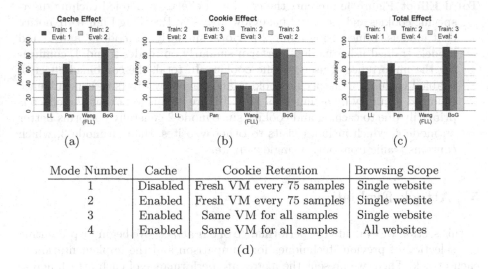

Fig. 4. "Train: X, Eval: Y" indicates training data from mode X and evaluation data from mode Y as shown in Table 4d. For evaluations which use a privacy tool such as the Tor browser bundle and assume a closed world, training and evaluating using mode 1 is most realistic. However, in the HTTPS context training using mode 2 or 3 and evaluating using mode 4 is most realistic. Figure 4c presents differences as large as 17% between these conditions, demonstrating the importance of evaluation conditions when measuring attack accuracy.

Beyond examining traffic characteristics, our analysis shows that factors such as caching, user-specific cookies and pageview diversity impact attack accuracy measurements. We examine each of these factors by training a model using data from a specific collection mode, and comparing model accuracy when evaluated on a range of collection modes. Since some models must be trained and evaluated using the same collection mode we must select a portion of the data from each mode for training and leave the remainder for evaluation. We perform a three-fold evaluation for each attack, varying the evaluation data used for each fold. Figure 4 presents the results of our analysis:

Cache Effect Figure 4a compares the performance of models trained and evaluated using mode 1 to models trained and evaluated using mode 2. As these modes differ only by enabled caching, we see that caching has moderate impact and can influence reported accuracy by as much as 10%.

Cookie Effect Figure 4b measures the impact of user-specific cookies by comparing the performance of models trained and evaluated using browsing modes 2 and 3. We observe that both the null cookie in mode 2 and the user-specific cookie in mode 3 generally perform 5-10 percentage points better when the evaluation data is drawn from the same mode as the training data. This suggests that any difference in cookies between training and evaluation conditions will impact accuracy results.

Total Effect Figure 4c presents the combined effects of enabled caching, user-specific cookies and increased pageview diversity. Recalling Figure 4b, notice that models trained using mode 2 perform similarly on modes 3 and 4, and models trained using mode 3 perform similarly on modes 2 and 4, confirming the importance of user-specific cookies. In total, the combined effect of enabled caching, user-specific cookies and pageview diversity can influence reported accuracy by as much as 17%. Figure 4b suggests that the effect is primarily due to caching and cookies since mode 2 generally performs better on mode 4, which includes visits to other websites, than on mode 3, which contains traffic from only a single website.

5   Attack Evaluation

In this section we evaluate the performance of our attack. We begin by presenting the selection of previous techniques for comparison and the implementation of each attack. Then, we present the aggregate performance of each attack across all 10 websites we consider, the impact of training data on attack accuracy, and the performance each attack at each individual website.

We select the Liberatore and Levine (LL), Panchenko *et al.* (Pan), and Wang *et al.* attacks for evaluation in addition to the BoG attack. The LL attack offers a view of baseline performance achievable from low level packet inspection, applying naive Bayes to a feature set consisting of packet size counts [6]. We implemented the LL attack using the naive Bayes implementation in `scikit-learn` [20]. The Pan attack extends size count features to include additional features related to burst length as measured in both packets and bytes as well as total traffic volume [8]. For features aggregated over multiple packets, the Pan attack rounds feature values to predetermined intervals. We implement the Pan attack using the `libsvm` [21] implementation of the RBF kernel support vector machine with the C and γ parameters specified by Panchenko. We select the Pan attack for comparison to demonstrate the significant benefit of Gaussian similarity rather than predetermined rounding thresholds. The BoG attack functions as described in section 3. We implement the BoG attack using the k-means package from `sofia-ml` [22] and logistic regression with class probability output from `liblinear` [18], with `Numpy` [23] performing intermediate computation.

The Wang attack assumes a fundamentally different approach from LL, Pan and BoG based on string edit distance [9]. There are several variants of the Wang attack which trade computational cost for accuracy by varying the string edit distance function. Wang reports that the best distance function for raw packet traces is the Optimal String Alignment Distance (OSAD) originally proposed by Cai *et al.* [4]. Unfortunately, the edit distance must be computed for each pair of samples, and OSAD is extremely expensive. Therefore, we implement the Fast Levenshtein-Like (FLL) distance,[5] an alternate edit distance function proposed

---

[5] Note that the original attack rounded packet sizes to multiples of 600; we operate on raw packet sizes as we found this improves attack accuracy in our evaluation.

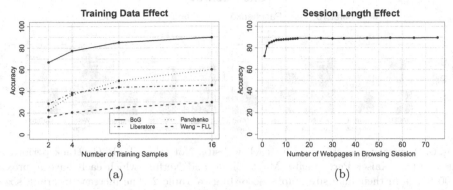

Fig. 5. Performance of BoG attack and prior techniques. Figure 5a presents the performance of all four attacks as a function of training data. Figure 5b presents the accuracy of the BoG attack trained with 16 samples as a function of browsing session length. At one sample, the HMM has no effect and reveals the effectiveness of the BoG attack without the HMM. Note that the BoG attack achieves 90% accuracy as compared to 60% accuracy with the best prior work.

by Wang which runs approximately 3000x faster.[6] Since Wang demonstrates that FLL achieves 46% accuracy operating on raw packet traces, as compared to 74% accuracy with OSAD, we view FLL as a rough indicator of the potential of the OSAD attack. We implement the Wang - FLL attack using `scikit-learn` [20].

We now examine the performance of each attack implementation. We evaluate attacks using data collected in mode 4 since this mode is most similar to the behavior of actual users. We consider both modes 2 and 3 for training data to avoid any bias introduced by using the same cookies as seen in evaluation data or browsing the exact same websites. As shown in Figure 4, mode 2 performs slightly better so we train all models using data from mode 2.

Consistent with prior work, our evaluation finds that accuracy of each attack improves with increased training data, as indicated by Figure 5a. Note that since we only collect 16 samples of each label in each collection mode, we are unable to conduct a multi-fold evaluation since all data is required for a single 16 training sample model. Notice that the Pan attack is most sensitive to variations in the amount of training data, and the BoG attack continues to perform well even at low levels of training data. In some cases an attacker may have ample opportunity to collect training data, although in other cases the victim website may attempt to actively resist traffic analysis attacks by detecting crawling behavior and engaging in cloaking, rate limiting or other forms of blocking.

---

[6] OSAD has $O(mn)$ runtime where m and n represent the length of the strings, whereas FLL runs in $O(m + n)$. Wang et al. report completing an evaluation with 40 samples of 100 labels each in approximately 7 days of CPU time. Since our evaluation involves 10 websites with approx. 500 distinct labels each and 16 samples of each label for training and evaluation, we would require approximately 19 months of CPU time (excluding any computation for sections 4 or 6).

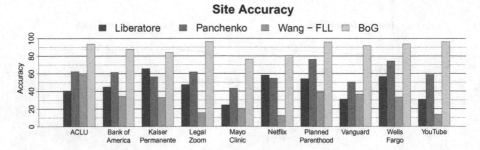

Fig. 6. Accuracy of each attack for each website. Note that the BoG attack performs the worst at Kaiser Permanente, Mayo Clinic and Netflix, which each have approx. 1000 labels in their final site graphs according to Table 2. The increase in graph size during finalization suggests potential for improved performance through better canonicalization to eliminate labels aliasing the same webpages.

The BoG attack derives significant performance gains from the application of the HMM. Figure 5b presents the BoG attack accuracy as a function of the browsing session length. Although we collect browsing sessions which each contain 75 samples, we simulate shorter browsing sessions by applying the HMM to randomly selected subsets of browsing sessions and observing impact on accuracy. At session length 1 the HMM has no effect and the BoG attack achieves 71% accuracy, representing the improvement over the Pan attack resulting from the Gaussian feature extraction. The HMM accounts for the remaining performance improvement from 71% accuracy to 90% accuracy. We achieve most of the benefit of the HMM after observing two samples in succession, and the full benefit after observing approximately 15 samples. Although any technique which assigns a likelihood to each label for each sample could be extended with a HMM, applying a HMM requires solving the labeling and site graph challenges which we present novel solutions for in section 3.

Although the BoG attack averages 90% accuracy overall, only 4 of the 10 websites included in evaluation have accuracy below 91%. Figure 6 presents the accuracy of each attack at each website. The BoG attack performs the worst at Mayo Clinic, Netflix and Kaiser Permanente. Notably, the number of labels in the site graphs corresponding to each of these websites approximately doubles during the finalization process summarized in Table 2 of section 3. URL redirection causes the increase in labels, as new URLs appear whose corresponding labels were not included in the preliminary site graph. Some new URLs may have been poorly handled by the canonicalization function, resulting in labels which alias the same content. Although we collected supplemental data to gather sufficient training samples for each label, the increase in number of labels and label aliasing behavior degrade measured accuracy for all attacks.

Despite the success of string edit distance based attacks against Tor, the Wang - FLL attack struggles in the HTTPS setting. Wang's evaluation is confined to Tor, which pads all packets into fixed size cells, and does not effectively explore edit distance approaches applied to unpadded traffic. Consistent with

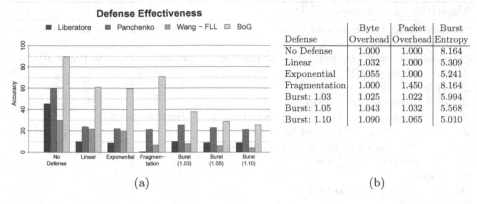

Fig. 7. Figure 7a presents the impact of defenses on attack accuracy. Figure 7b presents defense costs and entropy of burst sizes. The Burst defense is a novel proposal, substantially decreasing accuracy at a cost comparable to a low level defense. Entropy provides useful but limited insight into defense effectiveness, as rare values minimally impact entropy but may uniquely identify content.

the unpadded nature of HTTPS, we observe that Wang's attack performs best on unpadded traffic in the HTTPS setting. Despite this improvement, the Wang - FLL technique may struggle because edit distance treats all unique packet sizes as equally dissimilar; for example, 310 byte packets are equally similar to 320 byte packets and 970 byte packets. Additionally, the application of edit distance at the packet level causes large objects sent in multiple packets to have proportionally large impact on edit distance. This bias may be more apparent in the HTTPS context than with website homepages since webpages within the same website are more similar than homepages of different websites. Replacing the FLL distance metric with OSAD or Damerau-Levenshtein would improve attack accuracy, although the poor performance of FLL suggests the improvement would not justify the cost given the alternative techniques available.

6 Defense

This section presents and evaluates several defense techniques, including our novel Burst defense which operates between the application and TCP layers to obscure high level features of traffic while minimizing overhead. Figure 7 presents the impacts and costs of the defenses we consider. We find that evaluation context significantly impacts defense performance, as we observe increased effectiveness of low level defenses in our evaluation as compared to prior work [5]. Additionally, we find that the Burst defense offers significant performance improvements while maintaining many advantages of low level defense techniques.

We select defenses for evaluation on the combined basis of cost, deployability and effectiveness. We select the linear and exponential padding defenses from Dyer *et al.* as they are reasonably effective, have the lowest overhead, and are

---

Algorithm 1. Threshold Calculation

Precondition: *bursts* is a set containing the length of each burst in a given direction in defense training traffic
Precondition: *threshold* specifies the maximum allowable cost of the Burst defense
 1: *thresholds* ← *set*()
 2: *bucket* ← *set*()
 3: **for** *b* **in** sorted(*bursts*) **do**
 4:     *inflation* ← len(*bucket* + *b*) ∗ max(*bucket* + *b*)/sum(*bucket* + *b*)
 5:     **if** *inflation* ≥ *threshold* **then**
 6:         *thresholds* ← *thresholds* + max(*bucket*)
 7:         *bucket* ← *set*() + *b*
 8:     **else**
 9:         *bucket* ← *bucket* + *b*
10:     **end if**
11: **end for**
12: **return** *thresholds* + max(*bucket*)

Algorithm 2. Burst Padding

Precondition: *burst* specifies the size of a directed traffic burst
Precondition: *thresholds* specifies the thresholds obtained in Algorithm 1
 1: **for** *t* **in** sorted(*thresholds*) **do**
 2:     **if** *t* ≥ *burst* **then**
 3:         **return** *t*
 4:     **end if**
 5: **end for**
 6: **return** *burst*

---

implemented statelessly below the TCP layer. The linear defense pads all packet sizes up to multiples of 128, and the exponential defense pads all packet sizes up to powers of 2. Stateless implementation at the IP layer allows for easy adoption across a wide range of client and server software stacks. Additionally, network overhead is limited to minor increases in packet size with no new packets generated, keeping costs low in the network and on end hosts. We also introduce the fragmentation defense which randomly splits any packet which is smaller than the MTU, similar to portions of the strategy adopted by HTTPOS [14]. Fragmentation offers the deployment advantages of not introducing any additional data overhead, as well as being entirely supported by current network protocols and hardware. We do not consider defenses such as BuFLO or HTTPOS given their complexity, cost and the effectiveness of the alternatives we do consider [5,14].

The exponential defense slightly outperforms the linear defense, decreasing the accuracy of the Pan attack from 60% to 22% and the BoG attack from 90% to 60%. Notice that the exponential defense is much more effective in our evaluation context than Dyer's context, which focuses on comparing website homepages loaded over an SSH tunnel with caching disabled and evaluation traffic collected on the same machine as training traffic. The fragmentation defense is extremely effective against the LL and Wang - FLL attacks, reducing accuracy to below 1% and 7% for each respective attack, but less effective against the Pan and BoG attacks as these attacks perform TCP stream reassembly. Since TCP stream reassembly is expensive and requires complete access to traffic, the fragmentation defense may be a superior choice against many adversaries in practice.

Although the fragmentation, linear and exponential defenses offer the deployment advantages of functioning statelessly below the TCP layer, their effectiveness is limited. The Burst defense offers greater protection, operating between the TCP layer and application layer to pad contiguous bursts of traffic up to predefined thresholds uniquely determined for each website. Reducing the number of thresholds allows the Burst defense to achieve greater privacy at the expense of increased padding.

Algorithms 1 and 2 present the training and application of the Burst defense respectively. Unlike the BoG attack which considers bursts as a tuple, for the purposes of the Burst defense (and Figure 7b) we define a burst as a contiguous sequence of packets in the same direction on the same TCP connection. Hence, we apply Algorithm 1 in each direction. We evaluate the Burst defense for *threshold* values 1.03, 1.05 and 1.10, with the resulting cost and performance shown in Figure 7. The Burst defense outperforms defenses which operate solely at the packet level by obscuring features aggregated over entire TCP streams. Simultaneously, the Burst defense offers deployability advantages over techniques such as HTTPOS since the Burst defense is implemented between the TCP and application layers. The cost of the Burst defense compares favorably to defenses such as HTTPOS, BuFLO and traffic morphing, reported to cost at least 37%, 94% and 50% respectively [4,15].

7 Discussion and Conclusion

This work examines the vulnerability of HTTPS to traffic analysis attacks, focusing on evaluation methodology, attack and defense. Although we present novel contributions in each of these areas, many open problems remain.

Our examination of evaluation methodology focuses on caching and user-specific cookies, but does not explore factors such as browser differences, operating system differences, mobile/tablet devices or network location. Each of these factors may contribute to traffic diversity in practice, likely degrading attack accuracy. Additional future work remains in the area of attack development. To date, all approaches have assumed that the victim browses the web in a single tab and that successive page loads can be easily delineated. Future work should investigate actual user practice in these areas and impact on analysis results. For example, while many users have multiple tabs open at the same time, it is unclear how much traffic a tab generates once a page is done loading. Additionally, we do not know how easily traffic from separate page loadings may be delineated given a contiguous stream of user traffic.

Defense development and evaluation also require further exploration. Attack evaluation conditions and defense development are somewhat related since conditions which favor attack performance will simultaneously decrease defense effectiveness. Defense evaluation under conditions which favor attack creates the appearance that defenses must be complex and expensive, effectively discouraging defense deployment. To increase likelihood of deployment, future work must investigate necessary defense measures under increasingly realistic conditions since realistic conditions may substantially contribute to effective defense.

References

1. Hintz, A.: Fingerprinting Websites Using Traffic Analysis. In: Dingledine, R., Syverson, P.F. (eds.) PET 2002. LNCS, vol. 2482, pp. 171–178. Springer, Heidelberg (2003)
2. Sun, Q., Simon, D.R., Wang, Y.-M., Russell, W., Padmanabhan, V.N., Qiu, L.: Statistical Identification of Encrypted Web Browsing Traffic. In: Proc. IEEE S&P (2002)
3. Herrmann, D., Wendolsky, R., Federrath, H.: Website Fingerprinting: Attacking Popular Privacy Enhancing Technologies with the Multinomial Naive-Bayes Classifier. In: Proc. of ACM CCSW (2009)
4. Cai, X., Zhang, X.C., Joshi, B., Johnson, R.: Touching From a Distance: Website Fingerprinting Attacks and Defenses. In: Proc. of ACM CCS (2012)
5. Dyer, K.P., Coull, S.E., Ristenpart, T., Shrimpton, T.: Peek-a-Boo, I Still See You: Why Efficient Traffic Analysis Countermeasures Fail. In: IEEE S&P (2012)
6. Liberatore, M., Levine, B.N.: Inferring the Source of Encrypted HTTP Connections. In: Proc. ACM CCS (2006)
7. Bissias, G.D., Liberatore, M., Jensen, D., Levine, B.N.: Privacy Vulnerabilities in Encrypted HTTP Streams. In: Danezis, G., Martin, D. (eds.) PET 2005. LNCS, vol. 3856, pp. 1–11. Springer, Heidelberg (2006)
8. Panchenko, A., Niessen, L., Zinnen, A., Engel, T.: Website Fingerprinting in Onion Routing Based Anonymization Networks. In: Proc. ACM WPES (2011)
9. Wang, T., Goldberg, I.: Improved Website Fingerprinting on Tor. In: Proc. of ACM WPES 2013 (2013)
10. Cheng, H., Avnur, R.: Traffic Analysis of SSL Encrypted Web Browsing (1998), http://www.cs.berkeley.edu/~daw/teaching/cs261-f98/projects/final-reports/ronathan-heyning.ps
11. Danezis, G.: Traffic Analysis of the HTTP Protocol over TLS, http://research.microsoft.com/en-us/um/people/gdane/papers/TLSanon.pdf
12. Chen, S., Wang, R., Wang, X., Zhang, K.: Side-Channel Leaks in Web Applications: A Reality Today, a Challenge Tomorrow. In: Proc. IEEE S&P (2010)
13. Coull, S.E., Collins, M.P., Wright, C.V., Monrose, F., Reiter, M.K.: On Web Browsing Privacy in Anonymized NetFlows. In: Proc. USENIX Security (2007)
14. Luo, X., Zhou, P., Chan, E.W.W., Lee, W., Chang, R.K.C., Perdisci, R.: HTTPOS: Sealing Information Leaks with Browser-side Obfuscation of Encrypted Flows. In: Proc. of NDSS (2011)
15. Wright, C.V., Coull, S.E., Monrose, F.: Traffic Morphing: An Efficient Defense Against Statistical Traffic Analysis. In: NDSS (2009)
16. To infinity and beyond? No! http://googlewebmastercentral.blogspot.com/2008/08/to-infinity-and-beyond-no.html
17. Miller, B., Huang, L., Joseph, A.D., Tygar, J.D.: I Know Why You Went to the Clinic: Risks and Realization of HTTPS Traffic Analysis (2014), http://arxiv.org/abs/1403.0297

18. Fan, R.-E., Chang, K.-W., Hsieh, C.-J., Wang, X.-R., Lin, C.-J.: LIBLINEAR: A Library for Large Linear Classification. JMLR (9), 1871–1874 (2008)
19. Torbutton FAQ, https://www.torproject.org/torbutton/torbutton-options.html.en (accessed May 2012)
20. Scikit-learn, http://scikit-learn.org/stable/
21. Chang, C.-C., Lin, C.-J.: LIBSVM: A Library for Support Vector Machines. ACM Transactions on TIST 2(3) (2011)
22. Sofia-ml, http://code.google.com/p/sofia-ml/
23. Numpy, http://www.numpy.org/

I Know What You're Buying:
Privacy Breaches on eBay

Tehila Minkus[1] and Keith W. Ross[1,2]

[1] Dept. of Computer Science and Engineering, NYU, USA
[2] NYU Shanghai, China
{tehila,keithwross}@nyu.edu

Abstract. eBay is an online marketplace which allows people to easily engage in commerce with one another. Since the market's online nature precludes many physical cues of trust, eBay has instituted a reputation system through which users accumulate ratings based on their transactions. However, the eBay Feedback System as currently implemented has serious privacy flaws. When sellers leave feedback, buyers' purchase histories are exposed through no action of their own. In this paper, we describe and execute a series of attacks, leveraging the feedback system to reveal users' potentially sensitive purchases. As a demonstration, we collect and identify users who have bought gun-related items and sensitive medical tests. We contrast this information leakage with eBay users' privacy expectations as measured by an online survey. Finally, we make recommendations towards better privacy in the eBay feedback system.

1   Introduction

Online commerce has introduced new risks and rewards for consumers. It offers ease and convenience, allowing for in-depth comparison shopping from the comfort of one's home computer or mobile device. However, the impersonal and intangible nature of online transactions gives rise to trust-based issues as well: how can users know that they will actually receive the goods they bought? Will the goods arrive intact and in a timely fashion? In response to these issues, online marketplaces have instituted reputation systems, where parties to the market are rated based on their behavior in transactions.

eBay is somewhat unique among online marketplaces in that its reputation system is symmetric: not only can buyers rate sellers, sellers can also provide feedback on the users who have bought their wares. At first, this seems like a helpful mechanism; users receive recognition for prompt payment, and a sense of reciprocity may motivate them to contribute feedback to their seller in return. This makes the reputation system robust and popular. However, as we will show in this paper, the current implementation has some serious privacy implications.

In this research, we explore the privacy issues that are byproducts of the symmetric and public nature of the eBay feedback system. We first describe the *purchase history attack*: given a user's eBay username, we show how to discover his purchases by correlating his feedback page with the feedback pages of the

E. De Cristofaro and S.J. Murdoch (Eds.): PETS 2014, LNCS 8555, pp. 164–183, 2014.

sellers with whom he has interacted. If the attacker knows the real identity of the username in question, this is potentially a serious privacy breach. If he does not know the identity, we show that the attacker may still be able to link the username to an online social network and identify the buyer.

We also show how a large set of eBay buyer usernames can be indirectly obtained from eBay. Given such a large set, an attacker can execute the *broad profiling attack*, namely, determine the purchase history for each of the users in the large set. The attacker can then perform the *category attack*, namely, determine a subset of users who have purchased items in a specific sensitive category, such as gun equipment or medical tests. If the attacker makes the data from the broad profiling attack publicly available, then a third-party can also use side information to de-anonymize a specific target user, giving rise to the *side-information attack*.

In particular, we make the following contributions:

- Show how it is possible to recover a user's purchase history given his eBay username, despite the privacy measures included in the system.
- Describe several attacks compromising the privacy of eBay users. We discuss three variations: the *broad profiling attack*, the *category attack*, and the *side-information attack*.
- Provide a landscape of user beliefs and expectations regarding eBay privacy, based on a survey of nearly 1,000 subjects.
- Recommend several modifications to the feedback system to allow for better privacy on eBay.

This paper is organized as follows: in Section 2, we introduce the eBay feedback system and some preliminaries. In Section 3, we explain how an attacker can discover the purchase history of a target. In Section 4, we present the broad profiling attack. In Section 5, we describe the category attack, using purchases of gun-related items and medical tests as illustrations. We also briefly discuss the side information attack. Section 6 examines eBay users' privacy expectations via a survey. In Section 7, we make recommendations to mitigate the risk of privacy attacks. Section 8 summarizes related work. Finally, in Section 9, we conclude.

2   Preliminaries

In this paper, we examine the privacy leaks inherent in eBay's feedback system. This section describes the eBay feedback system. We also discuss the ethical considerations involved in this research.

2.1   Description of the eBay Feedback System

Feedback Interface. The eBay feedback page for a given user is accessible at http://feedback.ebay.com/ws/eBayISAPI.dll? ViewFeedback2&userid= <username>, where <username> is replaced with the username in question.

A viewer need not sign in to access a specific user's feedback page; it is entirely public. As shown in Figure 1, there are several tabs allowing one to filter the feedback shown. One may view all feedback, feedback left on purchases, feedback left on sales, or feedback left for others by the user.

Of particular interest to our work is the tab entitled "Feedback as a Buyer". This tab displays the feedback left by all sellers from whom the user has made a purchase. Each entry includes the feedback rating (uniformly positive, due to the policies detailed above), the specific feedback message, the seller's username, and the date and time when the feedback was left. In order to protect the user's privacy, *no item description or link to the item page is included on the buyer's feedback page*.

Another tab, entitled "Feedback Left for Others" displays the feedback that the user has left for others. When the user in question is a seller, this primarily contains the feedback he or she has left for customers. Each record includes the item description, a link to the item page, the feedback left, and a pseudonym for the user. *The user's actual username is not included.*

It is especially important to note that the item's link can posted even when the buyer does not leave any feedback for the transaction. If the seller leaves feedback (which is estimated to happen in 60-78% of transactions, see Section 8), then the purchase effectively becomes public through no action of the buyer, as we will show.

Public Feedback as a Default. As just described, an eBay user's feedback profile contains a list of the feedback he has given and received. Generally, the comments are public. However, if a user chooses to have a private profile, only his aggregate feedback score is visible; no individual feedback records are shown. eBay states the following regarding feedback profiles[1]:

> Feedback Profiles are public by default. Members have the option of making their Feedback Profiles private. However, it's important to remember that keeping your profile public builds trust by letting potential trading partners see what others have said about you.
>
> When you choose the "private" setting for your Feedback Profile:
> – You can't sell items on eBay.
> – Only the Feedback comments are hidden from other members. Your Feedback Score - the number of positive, neutral, and negative Feedback ratings you've received - is still public.

Private Listings.   Though sellers cannot hide their own feedback history, they can provide additional privacy to buyers by creating a listing with private feedback. Feedback on such a listing will be visible on the seller's and buyer's feedback page, but no description or link will be attached to the feedback. Additionally, the bidding history for a private auction is hidden. In all other ways, such as product search and sale procedure, the listing follows standard procedure.

---

[1] http://pages.ebay.com/help/feedback/profile-public-private.html

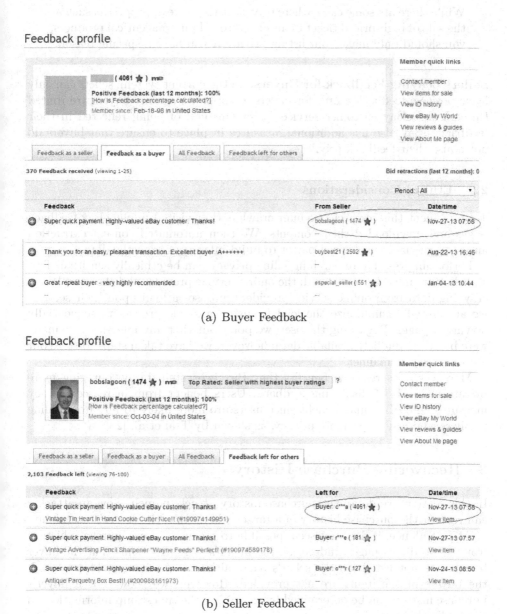

(a) Buyer Feedback

(b) Seller Feedback

Fig. 1. Condensed versions of the buyer and seller feedback pages. We have removed the buyer's username and profile picture from the buyer's profile.

Interestingly, eBay advocates limited use of this feature[2]:

> While there are some cases where private listings are appropriate, such as the sale of high-priced ticket items or approved pharmaceutical products, you should only make your listing private if you have a specific reason.

Sellers Leaving Feedback for Buyers. In the current system, sellers can only leave positive feedback scores for buyers; complaints against buyers are routed through the eBay customer service system instead of being reflected in their feedback. eBay also has additional measures in place to ensure that buyers do not abuse their feedback privileges.[3]

2.2   Ethical Considerations

To implement this research, we built crawlers that visited public eBay feedback pages and downloaded their contents. We then automated content extraction and storage via a customized parser to build inferences from the data.

Performing real-life research in online privacy can be ethically sensitive. Two stakeholders must be considered: the online service provider and the user. While crawling data from online service providers imposes a load upon their servers, we attempted to minimize the load by using a single process to sequentially download pages. Regarding the user, we point out that any inferences we made were based on publicly available data; however, we have taken steps to store our data in a secure manner.

Moreover, this research benefits the eBay ecosystem by encouraging more private methods of displaying feedback. Users benefit from increased privacy measures, and eBay may benefit since users are more likely to buy from online retailers who visibly promote privacy, as shown by Tsai et al. [28].

3   Recovering Purchase History

In this section, we detail the purchase history attack, namely, how an attacker can recover the purchase history of a target when given the target's username.

At first glance, it does not seem possible to recover a user's purchase history from the feedback pages. Indeed, on the buyer's page, the items that the buyer bought are not listed; on the seller's page, although the items sold are listed, the buyers of the items are not provided. However, we show that a buyer's purchase history can be determined by exploiting the timestamp information on the feedback pages.

Each feedback record is displayed with a timestamp, both on the seller's page and the buyer's page. This allows for linking of feedback records from a seller's account to a buyer's account through the following process:

---

[2] http://pages.ebay.com/help/sell/private.html
[3] http://pages.ebay.com/services/forum/sellerprotection.html

1. Retrieve the user's feedback page.
2. Extract the seller's name and the timestamp for each feedback entry.
3. For each feedback entry, visit the seller's page. Then search among the feedback listings for feedback with an identical timestamp. Retrieve the item link and description.
4. Output the list of the user's sale records.

However, in some cases a seller may have left feedback for more than one purchase simultaneously (perhaps through an automated system). Thus, relying solely on the timestamp may introduce false records into the target's purchase history. To study this issue, we examined 5,580 randomly chosen purchases. We found that 49% of the timestamps on buyers' pages matched with only one distinct listing from the seller's feedback page. On average, each buyer feedback record matched the timestamps of 6.5 records from the seller's feedback; the median was 2 matches. In one specific case, the timestamp on one buyer's corresponded to as many as 279 feedback records from the seller in question. (The buyer in this case had made several purchases from a seller who used an automated system to post large batches of feedback.) To resolve this ambiguity that occurs in approximately half of the transactions, we extend the above attack by leveraging the pseudonyms included in the seller's feedback page.

While the seller's feedback page uses only a pseudonym to identify the buyers, each user's pseudonym remains consistent across the site. eBay assigns pseudonyms according to a specific algorithm: randomly select two character's from the user's real username and insert three asterisks in between them to form the pseudonym[4]. This allows an attacker to definitively rule out any pseudonyms that could not be generated by a specific username. For example, if the targeted user goes by the user ID "catlady24", then the pseudonym "u***v" cannot correspond to that user.

The number of possible pseudonyms per username is bounded by $n(n-1)$, where n is the length of the username. As such, the pseudonym is not random, but is rather chosen from a relatively small space of potential pseudonyms.

Based on this additional data, we modify the above process for purchase recovery for a given user to reduce false associations:

1. Retrieve the user's feedback page.
2. Extract the seller's name and the timestamp for each feedback entry.
3. For each feedback entry, visit the seller's page. Then search among the feedback listings for feedback with an identical timestamp. Retrieve the item link and description.
4. When all the purchases are retrieved, remove all feedback entries which have pseudonyms that could not be generated by the username.

By utilizing the pseudonym as a heuristic to rule out listings with invalid pseudonyms, we were able to reduce the number of potential matches in our

---

[4] http://community.ebay.com/t5/Bidding/Bid-History-Changes-including-a-b-userIDs/m-p/2443087#M26865

sample database by roughly 70%. However, after filtering by timestamp and invalid pseudonyms, there were still false matches remaining in the database, with an average of 1.9 potential matches for each listing in a buyer's feedback. To reduce the number of false matches, we leverage the fact that a user's pseudonym is consistent across the feedback system. Since each user has only one actual pseudonym in the system, we attempt to find this pseudonym and thus eliminate any potential matches using other pseudonyms. In our sample database, 73% of users had more than one potential pseudonym remaining at this point in the process. We aim to resolve this ambiguity with the following steps:

5. If more than one pseudonym remains among the buyer's matched records:
   (a) Conduct a vote where each seller nominates the pseudonym that dominates its corresponding records for the user.
   (b) Select as the correct pseudonym the one which has the most votes.
   (c) Eliminate all records which use a different pseudonym
6. Output the list of the user's sale records.

Through the steps above, it is possible to recover both a user's purchase history and their pseudonym, given their real username. Not only does this allow one to see the user's past purchase behavior, it makes it easier to monitor future behavior since the attacker has learned the user's persistent pseudonym.

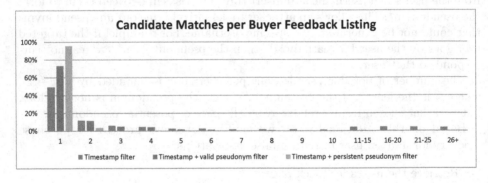

Fig. 2. The distribution of matches found per buyer feedback listing when using the different filtering methods. The precision of the matches increases considerably with the more advanced filtering methods.

When testing the database of 5,580 feedback records, extending the technique with pseudonym information enabled us to match 96% of buyers' feedback records to a single seller feedback record complete with purchase details. Likewise, we were able to learn a single persistent pseudonym for 96% of the sampled users. Figure 2 shows the how the modifications to the filtering method reduce the number of matches found per purchase.

4 Broad Purchase Profiling

To further illustrate the privacy leakage potential of the eBay feedback system, we introduce a broad purchase profiling attack where we find users on eBay and associate their purchase history with a real name drawn from Facebook.

4.1 Motivation

The ability to collect widespread eBay purchase data and associate it to real people is of use to several actors. Advertisers and content publishers would like to collect user purchasing behavior in order to present targeted ads, and marketers would like to analyze which purchases are bought together in order to aim their products at specific segments. Additionally, companies providing background checks for employers or insurance companies may want to include purchasing behavior in their classification methods. Finally, malicious parties may want to build detailed dossiers on eBay users in order to enable sophisticated spear phishing attempts.

In each of these cases, eBay feedback information can be utilized to engineer a privacy breach by inferring potentially sensitive facts about users which were not previously known. The association of these records to real people constitutes a privacy liability.

4.2 Execution

Given a list of eBay user IDs, we detail how to infer the name and purchase history of each user. Here, we make the assumption that the attacker has access to a substantial amount of computing and bandwidth resources. Also, when crawling eBay, we assume the attacker is clever enough to introduce sufficient delays between queries so that eBay does not block his requests; to expedite the attack, he may also use multiple IP addresses.

The first step of the attack involves identification of users' real names. To accomplish this, we leveraged the Facebook Graph API[5], a tool for building applications integrated with the Facebook social graph. (Using the Graph API via a browser does not require a developer account; however, integrating it into an automated crawler program requires developer and app tokens, which can be accessed for free after a short sign-up procedure requiring only a Facebook account.)

To test each eBay username for a match, we sent an HTTP request to `http://graph.facebook.com/<username>`, where `<username>` was replaced with the eBay username in question. If a match was found, then a response (pictured in Figure 3) was received, detailing the matched account's name, gender, locale, a unique numerical Facebook ID, and (in most cases) a link to their profile.

---

[5] `http://developers.facebook.com/docs/reference/api/`

This produced a list of eBay user IDs and corresponding potential real names. To recover the users' feedback history, we followed the process in Section 3, but with a slight modification to reduce the network and processing overhead. Instead of individually retrieving the sellers on a buyer-by-buyer basis, and thus perhaps retrieving duplicate pages, each buyer page was parsed to compile a comprehensive list of all sellers who had engaged with our list of buyers. We then downloaded each seller's page once and proceeded with the above methods of matching purchase histories to users.

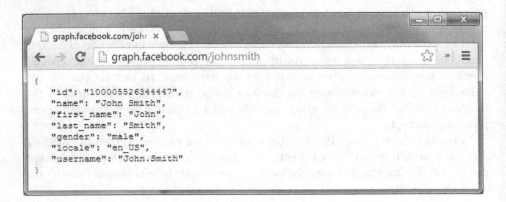

Fig. 3. A sample response from the Facebook Graph tool. Note that the tool performs some simple string-matching to match the term "johnsmith" with the account "John.Smith".

4.3   Results

We began with a list of 130,991 usernames. In order to limit the extent of our crawling, we first attempted to match the usernames to Facebook accounts and names before proceeding with purchase profiling. 22,478 matches were found, for a match rate of 17.2% (see Table 1). It is important to note that this method does not conclusively match accounts. For example, the accounts using a common name such as "bob123" on Facebook and eBay may very well belong to two different people [22]. As such, the match rate of 17.2% should be considered an upper bound which includes some false positives.

The 22,478 usernames were then used to recover their recent purchase history. In total, this produced a list of 414,483 purchases, for an average of approximately 18 purchases per customer. Matching the information from user feedback with seller feedback provided item descriptions and links, based on the timestamp and pseudonym information.

In summary, we were able to match 17% of 130,991 users with a potential real name on Facebook. For the matched users, we discovered on average 18 purchases per person, complete with purchase description.

Table 1. The number of user IDs, Facebook names matched, and the match rate for each experiment

Case Study	List of User IDs	Names Found	Match Rate
Broad user profiling	130,991	22,478	17.2%
Gun accessories	228,332	35,262	15.4%
Pregnancy tests	27,261	4,694	17.2%
H.I.V. tests	221	37	16.7%

4.4 Collecting Usernames

The above method assumes that the attacker has access to a large set of eBay usernames. An attacker can obtain a list of eBay usernames through several avenues:

- **eBay social features:** eBay provides a feature where buyers can follow sellers. Each seller's list of followers is publicly accessible at `http://www.ebay.com/usr/<sellername>/followers`, where `<sellername>` is replaced with the seller's user ID. The buyer IDs are provided in cleartext. This enables an attacker to crawl buyers' user IDs by iteratively visiting a seller page to collect followers and then collecting more sellers from each of the follower's feedback pages.
- **Seller's names:** eBay users can both buy and sell; many eBay users engage in both activities. It is possible to discover eBay sellers via the search interface. By searching for many items, one can thus compile an extensive list of eBay sellers and then determine their purchase histories. As we show via a survey in Section 6, 60% of eBay users have sold at least one item; therefore, this approach can expose many usernames.
- **Username reuse:** the attacker can use a list of usernames that are publicly available on some other service (such as Twitter or Facebook[6]). By using the feedback interface as an oracle, the attacker can determine if the usernames are in use at eBay as well.
- **Social engineering:** the attacker can sell popular items on eBay to collect eBay usernames (since sellers can view the usernames of users who purchased from them).
- **Brute force:** the attacker can generate potential usernames and use the feedback interface as an oracle to determine if the usernames are in use.

5 Category and Side Information Attack

Beyond exposing the feedback history of many users, the feedback history can also be exploited to generate a list of users who have engaged in specific, potentially sensitive categories of transactions. In this section, we elaborate an attack

---

[6] `http://www.facebook.com/directory/`

to reveal users who have bought specific items from eBay. This more vividly demonstrates the privacy risks embodied in the eBay feedback system.

This method can be accomplished using the basic techniques laid out in Section 4. Here, we introduce some modifications to streamline the attack further. Using the eBay search interface, it is possible to perform keyword search for completed sales of a specific item. This provides a list of sellers who sell the merchandise in question. This list allows the attacker to reduce the network overhead of his attack; instead of attempting to discover the purchase history of all the user IDs in his database, he can restrict his search to the users who have interacted with the sellers who sell this item. The process would be as follows:

1. Using eBay's keyword search, curate a list of sellers who have sold the item in question.
2. For each buyer in the database, download their feedback page.
3. For each buyer's feedback, discard any feedback not related to a seller on the list.
4. For the remaining records, recover the purchase history as detailed in Section 3.

We now introduce a few case studies that are enabled by this approach.

5.1   eBay Gun Registry

Gun control and ownership in the United States is a highly charged topic, as illustrated by the public uproar in December 2012 when a newspaper in Westchester County, NY published a list of local gunowners and their addresses [30]. Readers and residents considered this to be a massive privacy breach and the paper later removed the list [11].

Crawling eBay to find gun owners could be of interest to several parties. Firstly, law enforcement or private investigators may want to search for unregistered gun owners. Secondly, background check providers or data aggregators may want to include gun ownership in their records. In certain municipalities, a list of registered gun owners in a county can be accessed by filing a Freedom of Information request; however, the approach described here has several advantages. Firstly, it leaves no legal trail, a fact which may be appealing to actors (both criminal and innocent) operating outside of the legal framework. Secondly, it can help to uncover unregistered gun owners who have purchased gun supplies or accessories online. Thirdly, since guns are generally registered at the local level, compiling an extensive list would require many FOIA requests to different authorities; this approach is not subject to such limitations.

We began our data collection of eBay users by searching eBay for purveyors of gun accessories. (Actual firearms are not sold on eBay, so we use purchase of firearm accessories, such as holsters, as a proxy for gun ownership.) A search of "gun holster" on eBay's web site enabled us to curate a list of 11 sellers who sell firearm accessories at high volume.

Using a second external list of usernames, we narrowed down the users to those who had interacted with the identified gun-accessory sellers. For each matched purchase, a simple text-based classifier was applied to ascertain that the purchase was gun-related. Afterwards, we used Facebook's Graph tool to find potential names for each buyer.

Based on a list of 11 firearms-accessory sellers, we found records of 292,827 gun accessory purchases, made by 228,332 unique buyers. After matching for names on Facebook, we had names and sale records for 35,262 suspected gun owners.

5.2   Medical Test Purchases

In this second case study, we present an attack against users who have purchased sensitive medical tests, namely pregnancy or fertility tests and H.I.V. tests.

As a health-related issue, pregnancy is a private concern for many people. Pregnant women may wish to keep their reproductive status secret for a variety of reasons: they may be concerned about the pregnancy's medical viability, afraid of job discrimination or social stigma, or desirous of quietly ending the pregnancy without censure. In nearly all cases, expectant parents prefer to have control over who gains access to their news. This issue was highlighted when the retail giant Target began to track buyers' purchases in order to predict pregnancy among buyers (and subsequently advertise to them); buyers were unsettled by the fact that a retail store had estimated their due date even before they had told their parents [8]. Pregnancy is clearly private information, and people who are pregnant or trying to conceive deserve privacy for related purchases.

Even more private is H.I.V.-positive status. People with H.I.V. may find themselves subject to discrimination in a number of ways due to social stigma related both to the disease itself and its associated risk factors. As such, it is of prime importance that purchases related to H.I.V. testing remain hidden from the public eye.

These attacks were executed in the same manner as the gun registry attack. Specifically, we collected a list of eBay accounts that sell tests for these medical conditions and then matched them against a list of users' feedback pages to find users who had bought these items. Having found eBay usernames, we then fed these identifiers to the Graph API to find matching Facebook accounts and real names.

After building a list of pregnancy test sellers, comparing with a list of usernames and feedback, and filtering out non-fertility-related purchases, we had collected a list of 27,261 unique eBay users that purchased fertility-related tests. (We use this term to include ovulation tests, pregnancy tests, and gender-prediction tests.) Of these users, we found 4,694 matching Facebook accounts for a matching rate of 17.2%. This supplied us with a list of nearly 5,000 real names for potentially pregnant people.

The number of users returned for the targeted pregnancy test crawl was much smaller than the number returned for the gun crawl. This can be explained by the observation that, as of the the time of writing, there are more than 15 as many listings on eBay for the search "gun holster" than for the search term "pregnancy test." This indicates a a greater market for gun accessories than for medical tests on eBay, enabling a larger-scale crawl for gun-related purchases.

The crawl for buyers of H.I.V. test yielded much more meager results, for a number of reasons. Firstly, H.I.V. is a much rarer condition than pregnancy, and therefore is not as commonly tested. Secondly, H.I.V. tests are significantly more expensive than pregnancy tests and therefore less likely to be bought often. Thirdly, H.I.V. tests are commonly administered in a medical setting, not at home (unlike pregnancy tests). Fourthly, many sellers of H.I.V. tests had taken precautions to keep the listings private.

Nonetheless, an extensive crawl did discover 221 unique users who had purchased H.I.V. tests online. 37 of these users were matched to accounts and names on Facebook. Of the matched users with a specified gender, 28% were female and 72% were male; this correlates roughly with the general rates of H.I.V. infection in the USA [4].

5.3   Side Information Attack

We now briefly describe another possible attack, utilizing side information. For concreteness, we state this problem in terms of employer who is suspicious of his employee with regard to health, interests, or other sensitive information that could be revealed in eBay purchase data. The employer knows that his employee uses eBay, but he does not know his employee's eBay user name. Finally, suppose he has some side information; namely, that his employee made a specific purchase on a specific day.

Now assume that an attacker has carried out the broad profiling attack on a set of users containing the employee and makes the corresponding database publicly available on a website.

For each piece of side-channel purchase data that the boss knows about his employee, he can narrow down the set of prospective matches. Intuitively, the more side information he has, the smaller the set of candidate matches will become. Once he has a small enough set of candidate matches, he can then attempt to pinpoint a specific username as corresponding to his target. This enables him to learn the entire purchase history of his target, and it also makes it easy for him to continue monitoring any future eBay purchases made by the employee.

6   User Expectations for Privacy on eBay

Are users aware of the eBay feedback policies, and how accessible do they expect their purchase data to be? We conducted a survey of eBay users on Amazon Mechanical Turk[7], a crowdsourcing microtask market, to answer these questions. To maintain a uniform high quality of responses, we followed the guidelines established by Kelley and Patrick [14] while designing our survey to make sure that users stayed engaged, attentive, and honest.

---

[7] http://www.mturk.com

6.1 Survey Design

Our questions were designed to answer a few specific questions about eBay users' expectation and behavior.

– Are usernames considered private information by users?
– Is eBay a place where people purchase sensitive items?
– Whom do users expect to be able to see their purchase history?

We limited participation in our study to US-based Mechanical Turk workers. We screened subjects to make sure they were actually users of eBay. We also incorporated demographic questions. Each worker was paid $0.25 for a multiple-choice survey that took 3 or 4 minutes to complete.

6.2 Survey Results

We gathered 1114 responses from Mechanical Turk. After removing "click spam" as detected by attention-measuring questions, we had 913 responses. To assess the representative qualities of our sample, we compared the reported demographics to those measured by the Google AdWords Display Planner Tool[8]. The gender proportions of our sample exactly matched the eBay users measured by AdWords, and the sample also followed the general age trends reported by AdWords, albeit with less precision. Some variance may be due to the generally younger population of Mechanical Turk workers, as measured by Ross [24]. Overall, the sample proved to be highly representative of the general eBay population.

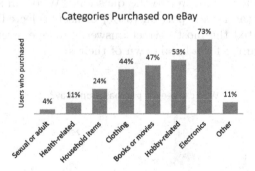

Fig. 4. The percentage of users who have bought items from specific categories on eBay

Purchase Behavior on eBay. Do users buy sensitive items on eBay? We asked our subjects if they had purchased items from several categories, listed in Figure 4. Notably, 10.7% of users answered that they had bought health-related items on eBay, and 4.3% of users had bought sexual/adult items on eBay.

---

[8] https://adwords.google.com/da/DisplayPlanner/Home

While we consider health- and adult-related purchases to be uniformly private information, there may also be sensitive purchases made in other categories. In order to gain a broader view of how users view eBay, we asked them to answer the following question: "If I need to buy something sensitive or embarrassing, I would probably buy it from..." The available answers were "a physical store," "eBay," and "other (please specify)." eBay edged out physical stores as the most likely place to buy sensitive items. 38.6% of users chose eBay, 35.6% of users chose a physical store, and 25.8% chose other. From these numbers, it is clear to see that users see eBay as a leading way to easily and anonymously conduct transactions that may be embarrassing or sensitive.

Users and Feedback. Do eBay users leave feedback? Do they understand the way it works? Our survey included a series of questions about usage and perception of the feedback system. 50.7% of the respondents reported that they leave feedback all the time, with only 10.7% answering that they never leave feedback. The remaining respondents have left feedback somewhat often (17.4%) or a few times (21.1%). Despite their extensive use of the feedback system, users did not seem to understand the complexities of the system. Only 18% of users correctly agreed with the statement that "sellers cannot leave negative feedback for buyers on eBay". 66.4% disagreed with the statement, and 15.7% were not sure. This is despite the fact that 63.3% of the users reported that they had sold at least one item on eBay.

Privacy Expectations. Users understood that feedback was public: 76.6% of users agreed with the statement that "anyone can see the feedback that sellers leave on my account." However, it was unclear to many users just how this related to their purchase privacy. In answer to the question, "Who can see the purchases I make on eBay?" the largest portion (38%) of users selected "just me." Only 8.7% of users selected the most correct answer, "anyone, even if they are not signed in." See Figure 5 for a breakdown of their answers.

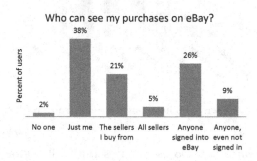

Fig. 5. Users selected one answer that they believed to best include who could view their purchases on eBay. The correct answer is highlighted.

7   Recommendations

In many ways, eBay's system for buyer reputation seems to be an artifact of an older era. Since 2008, the feedback system on eBay allows sellers to leave only positive feedback for buyers. As such, a buyer's feedback score reflects merely the quantity, not the quality, of his transactions.

Additionally, buyers' reputations matter less to the success of the eBay marketplace than those of sellers. In contrast to sellers, who can easily defraud consumers by failing to ship or shipping incorrect items, buyers have a much more limited scope of possible fraud. While a buyer might fail to pay, eBay policy advises sellers not to ship their wares until buyers have paid. Additionally, there are internal methods by which sellers can report fraudulent buyers.

Allowing sellers to leave feedback about buyers may benefit the eBay marketplace by encouraging buyers to then reciprocate with feedback about the buyers. Moreover, since feedback from purchases counts towards the user's general feedback score, it may give experienced eBay shoppers an advantage when they first begin to sell goods on eBay. However, it is unclear why feedback left by sellers for buyers should be made public. Since the feedback is uniformly positive, it does not offer helpful guidance for future transactions. Considering the privacy leakage which public buyer reputations enable, we make the following recommendations:

- **Recommendations to eBay:** We recommend that the Private Listing option should become the default listing method. This removes any visible link between the buyers and sellers. Alternatively, we propose that eBay use a non-persistent pseudonym for buyers on the sellers' feedback pages; this would make it harder to link feedback. Additionally, the timestamp of the feedback left could be generalized (for example, by displaying only the date) in order to make linkage attacks more difficult.
- **Recommendations to buyers:**
  Buyers on eBay can make their feedback profile private by changing a setting in their Feedback Forums page[9]. However, accounts with private feedback profiles cannot be used for selling. We therefore recommend that eBay users maintain two separate accounts, a private profile for buying and a public account for selling. (However, this does not obviate the need for an eBay policy change, since it prevents a user's selling account from reaping the benefits of the positive feedback he has earned as a buyer on eBay.)
  We also recommend that users avoid reusing usernames across different websites in order to retain stronger pseudonymity.
- **Recommendations to sellers:** eBay offers a selling option called a Private Listing[10] which operates exactly like a regular listing while keeping all buyer information anonymous. This is a way for sellers to offer their buyers all buying benefits while retaining privacy. Other users cannot see the list of bids on the item, and all feedback on the item is anonymous for feedback

---

[9] http://pages.ebay.com/help/feedback/profile-public-private.html
[10] http://pages.ebay.com/help/sell/private.html

profile views. The listing is included in searches as usual, and it has no extra fees associated with it.

8   Related Work

Feedback and Reputational Systems. The eBay reputation system has been studied in depth by the economics and management science communities to assess the impact of ratings on sale statistics. Lucking-Reiley et al. [17] found that increases in negative ratings were associated with significantly lower selling prices. While Resnick et al. [23] found that the impact of reputation was inconsistent across areas, Houser et al. [12] found that better seller reputations tended to raise prices in auctions.

How widely is the eBay feedback system used? Do buyers and sellers take the time to submit ratings and comments? Based on a 1999 dataset of more than 30,000 postcard sales, Resnick et al. [23] found that 52.1% of buyers and 60.8% of sellers left feedback on transactions. In 2008, Dellarocas and Wood [7] found in a study of over 50,000 rare coins that 78% of sellers and 68% of buyers left feedback on a purchase. 20% of the auctions in their dataset had feedback from sellers only, with no feedback from buyers (as opposed to feedback from both, neither, or only the buyer).

Klein [15] found that buyers' fear of retaliatory feedback from sellers led them to leave feedback at the last available moment, and may have even suppressed feedback rates due to fear of retaliation. Chwelos and Dehar [5] found that the two-way nature of the system, where sellers and buyers rate one another, has a dual effect: it encourages buyers to leave more feedback, but it also inflates positive feedback. Klein et al. [16] suggest that removing the ratings of buyers would create a less sugar-coated feedback system while introducing little risk, since there is little need for the seller to trust buyers in any case.

Deanonymization. Robust data anonymization has been a high-profile problem since 2006, when a woman was identified based on her "de-identified" queries in the publicly released AOL search logs [3]. External data sources were also used by Narayanan and Shmatikov [19] to reidentify the anonymous NetFlix dataset with matching members on IMDB, using only the sparse vector of movies watched and reviewed. Approaches for deanonymization of social networks are presented by Backstrom et al. [2], Narayanan and Shmatikov [20], and Wondracek et al. [29]. Goga et al. [10] correlate user accounts from Twitter, Flickr, and Yelp by using only temporal, geographic, and language features.

These attacks have given rise to several frameworks with the aim of providing a more disciplined and guarantee-based approach to data anonymization. These approaches add anonymity at the expense of specificity; namely, they generalize the dataset until there are fewer distinctive records. The first of these approaches, by Sweeney, was k-anonymity [27], which iteratively generalizes information until there are at least k records present in the dataset that match any specific tuple. More recently, Machanavajjhala et al. [18] proposed l-diversity, which

extends k-anonymity to disallow uniform generalizations about specific populations. Finally, differential privacy, by Dwork [9], advocates systematically adding
Laplacian noise to query answers in order to provide numeric privacy guarantees
that can quantify the risk of a privacy breach.

Username Reuse. While users are warned about the dangers of password reuse
across online accounts (see for example Ives et al. [13]), there is little work
discussing the phenomenon of username reuse. Perito et al. [22] research the
entropy of usernames, finding that certain usernames are more unique (and thus
more traceable) than others. Using measures such as Levenshtein Distance and
TF/IDF, they were able to achieve a recall of 71% in matching related usernames.

Privacy-Preserving Reputation Systems. For the most part, reputation systems
have focused on accountability rather than privacy. However, there are cases
where reviewers may wish to hide their identity, both from other users and
from a centralized authority. This has led to the research topic of decentralized
reputation systems [26]. Schemes have been implemented to retain properties
such as security against forged reviews and persistent reputations in the face of
multiple pseudonyms to allow for anonymity [1].

   Notably, Pavlov et al. [21] propose a decentralized system allowing for privacy
on the reviewer's part as well as easy additive aggregation of users' reputations
from across the decentralized system. This deals with the problem of privacy
from the reviewer's perspective; however, it does not focus on privacy breaches
from the viewpoint of the party receiving feedback.

   Schiffner et al. [25] point out theoretical limits on the utility of any fully private
reputational system. Consequently, in [6], Clauß et al. construct a reputation
system that conforms to the more relaxed privacy definition of k-anonymity.

Our Contributions Existing research has explored the utility of reputation systems; however, there has not been any in-depth investigation into the privacy
implications of the eBay feedback system. What risks are inherent in its setup,
and how can they be exploited? How does this comply with user expectations
of privacy? In this work, we explore these questions and offer recommendations
based on our findings.

9   Conclusion

This research brings to light several important issues. Firstly, we show how an
attacker can determine a target's purchases if he knows the target's eBay username. Though the feedback interface does not explicitly link buyers to purchases,
we leverage feedback timestamps and pseudonym information to infer a list of
purchases made by a user. We present several classes of attacks complete with
case studies to show how serious the breach is. In the feedback history attack, we
show how to recover one user's history. In the broad profiling attack, we modify the technique to recover purchase histories of many users. In the category

attack, we show how to collect a list of users who have bought specific items. We demonstrate this attack by uncovering buyers of gun accessories, pregnancy tests, and H.I.V. tests. Subsequently, we examine user expectations of privacy on eBay and find a serious clash with reality; eBay is much less private than users believe. Finally, we recommend several techniques to mitigate the privacy risks of the system.

Acknowledgements. This work was supported in part by the NSF under grants CNS-1318659 and 0966187. The views and conclusions contained in this document are those of the authors and should not be interpreted as necessarily representing the official policies, either expressed or implied, of any of the sponsors.

References

1. Androulaki, E., Choi, S.G., Bellovin, S.M., Malkin, T.: Reputation systems for anonymous networks. In: Borisov, N., Goldberg, I. (eds.) PETS 2008. LNCS, vol. 5134, pp. 202–218. Springer, Heidelberg (2008)
2. Backstrom, L., Dwork, C., Kleinberg, J.: Wherefore art thou r3579x?: anonymized social networks, hidden patterns, and structural steganography. In: Proceedings of the 16th International Conference on World Wide Web, pp. 181–190. ACM (2007)
3. Barbaro, M., Zeller, T., Hansell, S.: A face is exposed for aol searcher no. 4417749. New York Times (August 9, 2006)
4. CDC. H.i.v. incidence (May 22, 2013)
5. Chwelos, P., Dhar, T.: Caveat emptor: Differences in online reputation mechanisms. Technical report, Working Paper, Sauder School of Business, University of British Columbia (2006)
6. Clauß, S., Schiffner, S., Kerschbaum, F.: k-anonymous reputation. In: Proceedings of the 8th ACM SIGSAC Symposium on Information, Computer and Communications Security, pp. 359–368. ACM (2013)
7. Dellarocas, C., Wood, C.A.: The sound of silence in online feedback: Estimating trading risks in the presence of reporting bias. Management Science 54(3), 460–476 (2008)
8. Duhigg, C.: How companies learn your secrets. New York Times (February 16, 2012)
9. Dwork, C.: Differential privacy. In: Bugliesi, M., Preneel, B., Sassone, V., Wegener, I. (eds.) ICALP 2006. LNCS, vol. 4052, pp. 1–12. Springer, Heidelberg (2006)
10. Goga, O., Lei, H., Parthasarathi, S.H.K., Friedland, G., Sommer, R., Teixeira, R.: Exploiting innocuous activity for correlating users across sites. In: Proceedings of the 22nd International Conference on World Wide Web, pp. 447–458. International World Wide Web Conferences Steering Committee (2013)
11. Goodman, J.D.: Newspaper takes down map of gun permit holders. The New York Times (January 18, 2013)
12. Houser, D., Wooders, J.: Reputation in auctions: Theory, and evidence from ebay. Journal of Economics & Management Strategy 15(2), 353–369 (2006)
13. Ives, B., Walsh, K.R., Schneider, H.: The domino effect of password reuse. Communications of the ACM 47(4), 75–78 (2004)

14. Kelley, P.G.: Conducting usable privacy & security studies with amazon's mechanical turk. In: Symposium on Usable Privacy and Security, SOUPS (2010)
15. Klein, T., Lambertz, C., Spagnolo, G., Stahl, K.O.: Last minute feedback. Centre for Economic Policy Research (2006)
16. Klein, T.J., Lambertz, C., Spagnolo, G., Stahl, K.O.: The actual structure of ebay's feedback mechanism and early evidence on the effects of recent changes. International Journal of Electronic Business 7(3), 301–320 (2009)
17. Lucking-Reiley, D., Bryan, D., Prasad, N., Reeves, D.: Pennies from ebay: The determinants of price in online auctions. The Journal of Industrial Economics 55(2), 223–233 (2007)
18. Machanavajjhala, A., Kifer, D., Gehrke, J., Venkitasubramaniam, M.: l-diversity: Privacy beyond k-anonymity. ACM Transactions on Knowledge Discovery from Data (TKDD) 1(1), 3 (2007)
19. Narayanan, A., Shmatikov, V.: Robust de-anonymization of large sparse datasets. In: IEEE Symposium on Security and Privacy, pp. 111–125. IEEE (2008)
20. Narayanan, A., Shmatikov, V.: De-anonymizing social networks. In: IEEE Symposium on Security and Privacy, pp. 173–187. IEEE (2009)
21. Pavlov, E., Rosenschein, J.S., Topol, Z.: Supporting privacy in decentralized additive reputation systems. In: Jensen, C., Poslad, S., Dimitrakos, T. (eds.) iTrust 2004. LNCS, vol. 2995, pp. 108–119. Springer, Heidelberg (2004)
22. Perito, D., Castelluccia, C., Kaafar, M.A., Manils, P.: How unique and traceable are usernames? In: Fischer-Hübner, S., Hopper, N. (eds.) PETS 2011. LNCS, vol. 6794, pp. 1–17. Springer, Heidelberg (2011)
23. Resnick, P., Zeckhauser, R.: Trust among strangers in internet transactions: Empirical analysis of ebay's reputation system. Advances in Applied Microeconomics 11, 127–157 (2002)
24. Ross, J., Irani, L., Silberman, M., Zaldivar, A., Tomlinson, B.: Who are the crowdworkers?: shifting demographics in mechanical turk. In: CHI 2010 Extended Abstracts on Human Factors in Computing Systems, pp. 2863–2872. ACM (2010)
25. Schiffner, S., Pashalidis, A., Tischhauser, E.: On the limits of privacy in reputation systems. In: Proceedings of the 10th Annual ACM Workshop on Privacy in the Electronic Society, pp. 33–42. ACM (2011)
26. Srivatsa, M., Xiong, L., Liu, L.: Trustguard: countering vulnerabilities in reputation management for decentralized overlay networks. In: Proceedings of the 14th International Conference on World Wide Web, pp. 422–431. ACM (2005)
27. Sweeney, L.: k-anonymity: A model for protecting privacy. International Journal of Uncertainty, Fuzziness and Knowledge-Based Systems 10(05), 557–570 (2002)
28. Tsai, J.Y., Egelman, S., Cranor, L., Acquisti, A.: The effect of online privacy information on purchasing behavior: An experimental study. Information Systems Research 22(2), 254–268 (2011)
29. Wondracek, G., Holz, T., Kirda, E., Kruegel, C.: A practical attack to de-anonymize social network users. In: IEEE Symposium on Security and Privacy, pp. 223–238. IEEE (2010)
30. Worley, D.R.: The gun owner next door: What you don't know about the weapons in your neighborhood. The Journal News (December 24, 2012)

Quantifying the Effect of Co-location Information on Location Privacy

Alexandra-Mihaela Olteanu[1], Kévin Huguenin[1], Reza Shokri[2],
and Jean-Pierre Hubaux[1]

[1] School of Computer and Communication Sciences, EPFL, Switzerland
{alexandramihaela.olteanu,kevin.huguenin,jean-pierre.hubaux}@epfl.ch
[2] Department of Computer Science, ETH Zurich, Switzerland
reza.shokri@inf.ethz.ch

Abstract. Mobile users increasingly report their *co-locations* with other users, in addition to revealing their locations to online services. For instance, they tag the names of the friends they are with, in the messages and in the pictures they post on social networking websites. Combined with (possibly obfuscated) location information, such co-locations can be used to improve the inference of the users' locations, thus further threatening their location privacy: as co-location information is taken into account, not only a user's reported locations and mobility patterns can be used to localize her, but also those of her friends (and the friends of their friends and so on). In this paper, we study this problem by quantifying the effect of co-location information on location privacy, with respect to an adversary such as a social network operator that has access to such information. We formalize the problem and derive an optimal inference algorithm that incorporates such co-location information, yet at the cost of high complexity. We propose two polynomial-time approximate inference algorithms and we extensively evaluate their performance on a real dataset. Our experimental results show that, even in the case where the adversary considers co-locations with only a single friend of the targeted user, the location privacy of the user is decreased by up to 75% in a typical setting. Even in the case where a user does not disclose any location information, her privacy can decrease by up to 16% due to the information reported by other users.

Keywords: Location privacy, co-location, statistical inference, social networks.

1 Introduction

Increasingly popular GPS-equipped mobile devices with Internet connectivity allow users to enjoy a wide range of online location-based services while on the go. For instance, mobile users can search for nearby points of interest and get directions, possibly in real time, to their destinations. Location-based services raise serious privacy concerns as a large amount of personal information can be inferred from a user's whereabouts. The research community has extensively

E. De Cristofaro and S.J. Murdoch (Eds.): PETS 2014, LNCS 8555, pp. 184–203, 2014.

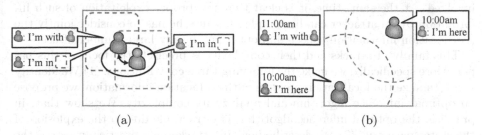

Fig. 1. Examples showing how co-location information can be detrimental to privacy. (a) A user reports being in a given area, and a second user reports being in another (overlapping) area and that she is co-located with the first user. By combining these pieces of information, an adversary can deduce that both users are located in the intersection of the two areas, thus narrowing down the set of possible locations for both of them. (b) Two users (initially apart from each other, at 10am) declare their exact individual location. Later (at 11am), they meet and report their co-location without mentioning where they are. By combining these pieces of information, the adversary can infer that they are at a place that is reachable from both of the initially reported locations in the amount of time elapsed between the two reports.

studied the problem of location privacy; more specifically, location-privacy protection mechanisms (so-called LPPMs), that can anonymize and obfuscate the users' locations before sending them to online location-based services, have been proposed [16]. In addition, formal frameworks to quantify location privacy in the case where users disclose their (possibly obfuscated) locations have been proposed [19,20]. In such frameworks, the mobility profiles of the users play an important role in the inference of the users' locations, namely in a localization attack.

In parallel, social networks have become immensely popular. Every day, millions of users post information, including their locations, about themselves, but also about their friends. An emerging trend, which is the focus of this paper, is to report co-locations with other users on social networks, e.g., by tagging friends on pictures they upload or in the messages they post. Our preliminary survey involving 132 Foursquare users, recruited through Amazon Mechanical Turk, reveals that 55.3% of the participants do report co-locations in their check-ins and that for the users who do so, on average, 2.84%±0.06 of their check-ins do contain co-location information. In fact, co-location information can be obtained in many different ways, such as automatic face recognition on pictures (which can contain the time and location at which the picture was taken in their EXIF data), Bluetooth-enabled device sniffing and reporting neighboring devices. Similarly, users who connect from the same IP address are likely to be attached to the same Internet access point, thus providing evidence of their co-location.

Attacks exploiting both location and co-location information (as mentioned in [22]) can be quite powerful, as we show in this paper. Figure 1 depicts and describes two example situations in which co-location can improve the performance of a localization attack, thus degrading the location-privacy of the users involved. At the same time, it is clear that the proper exploitation of such information by an attacker can be complex because he has to consider jointly the (co-)location information collected about a potentially large number of users.

This family of attacks and their complexity is precisely the focus of this paper. More specifically, we make the following three contributions. (1) We identify and formalize the localization problem with co-location information, we propose an optimal inference algorithm and analyze its complexity. We show that, in practice, the optimal inference algorithm is intractable due to the explosion of the state space size. (2) We describe how an attacker can drastically reduce the computational complexity of the attack by means of well-chosen approximations. We present two polynomial-time heuristics, the first being based on a limited set of considered users and the second relying on an independence approximation. (3) We extensively evaluate and compare the performance of these two heuristics in different scenarios, with different settings, based on a mobility dataset. Our experimental results show that, even in the case where the adversary considers co-locations with only a single friend of the targeted user, the median location privacy of the user is decreased by up to 75% in a typical setting. Even in the case where a user does not disclose any location information, her privacy can decrease by up to 16% due to the information reported by other users. A paramount finding of our work is that users partially lose control over their location privacy as co-locations and individual location information disclosed by other users substantially affect their own location privacy. To the best of our knowledge, this is the first work to quantify the effects of co-location information, that stems from social relationships, on location privacy; thus making a connection between privacy implications of social networks and location privacy.

The remainder of the paper is organized as follows. In Section 2, we define and formalize the system model. In Section 3, we present the optimal localization attack for N users and assess its complexity. In Section 4, we show how this complexity can be reduced by means of approximations. In Section 5, we report on the experimental evaluation of the localization attack with co-locations. In Section 6, we survey the related work. In Section 7, we conclude the paper and suggest directions for the future work.

2   System Model and Formalization

We consider a set of mobile users who move in a given geographical area. While on the go, users make use of some online services to which they communicate potentially obfuscated location (*i.e.,* where they are) and accurate co-location information (*i.e.,* who they are with). We consider that a curious service provider (referred to as the adversary) wants to infer the location of the users from this information, hence tracking them over time. In order to carry out the inference attack, based on which the location privacy of the users is evaluated, the adversary would model the users as described below. Our model is built upon [20] and uses similar notations. Figure 2 gives an overview of the considered scenario.

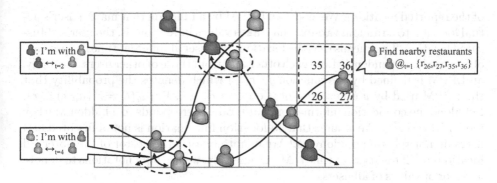

Fig. 2. Scenario of (co-)location exposure. Three users move in a given geographical area. They communicate their potentially obfuscated locations and accurate co-location information to a service provider (*i.e.*, the adversary) who wants to infer their locations.

2.1 Users

We consider a set $\mathcal{U} = \{u_1, \ldots, u_N\}$ of N mobile users who move within a given geographical area that is partitioned into M regions (locations) $\mathcal{R} = \{R_1, \ldots, R_M\}$. Time is discrete and we consider the state of the system (including the locations of the users) at the successive time instants $\{1, \ldots, T\}$. The region in which a user $u \in \mathcal{U}$ is at time instant $t \in \{1, \ldots, T\}$ is called the *actual location* of the user and is denoted by $a_u(t)$. The mobility of the users is modeled by a first order time-homogeneous Markov chain. We denote by $p_u(\rho, r)$ the probability that user u moves from region ρ to region r during one time instant, and by $\pi_u(r)$ the probability that user u is in region r at time t (*i.e.*, the stationary distribution of p_u). We call a co-location the fact that two users are at the same location at some point in time. The fact that users u and v are co-located at time t means that $a_u(t) = a_v(t)$; we denote by $u \leftrightarrow_t v$ the fact that a co-location between users u and v at time t is reported, and we denote by $c_u(t)$ the set of all reported co-locations that involve user u at time t. We define $C_t = \bigcup_{u \in \mathcal{U}} c_u(t)$ and $C = \bigcup_{t=1..T} C_t$.

2.2 Location-Privacy Protection Mechanisms

In order to protect their privacy, users rely on location-privacy protection mechanisms (LPPM) for obfuscating their individual location information before they communicate it to an online service provider. We denote by $u @_t r'$ the fact that user u reports being at location r' at time t to the online service. The online service observes only the obfuscated location of the users, which we denote by $o_u(t)$ for a user u at time t. We denote by $\mathcal{R}'$ the set of obfuscated locations; typically $\mathcal{R}'$ is the power set of $\mathcal{R}$, as LPPMs can return a set of locations instead of a single one. Typical LPPMs replace the actual location of a user with another location (*i.e.*, adding noise to the actual location) or merge several regions (*i.e.*, reducing the granularity of the reported location). We model an LPPM by a function that maps a user's actual location to a random variable that takes values in $\mathcal{R}'$, that is, the user's obfuscated location. This means that the locations of a user at different time instants are obfuscated independently from each other and from those of other users. Formally, an LPPM is defined by the function $f_u(r, r')$ which denotes the probability that the LPPM used by u obfuscates location r to r', i.e., $\Pr\left(o_u(t) = r' \mid a_u(t) = r\right)$. Let alone the co-location information, our model corresponds to a hidden Markov model (HMM) [1]. We assume that co-location information is not obfuscated and users do not rely on pseudonyms.[1] We denote by $\mathbf{o}(t)$ the vector of the observed locations of all the users at time t. More generally, we use bold notations to denote a vector of values of all users.

2.3   Adversary

The adversary, typically an online service provider (or an external observer who has access to this information, *e.g.*, another user of the social network), has access to the observed locations and co-locations of one or several users and seeks to locate users, at a given time instant, namely carry out a *localization attack*. Because the locations of the users are not independent, given the co-location information, when attacking the location of a given user, the adversary takes into account information potentially about all the users. The attack is performed *a posteriori*, meaning that the adversary has access to the observed traces over the complete period, namely $\{\mathbf{o}(t)\}_{t=1..T}$ and C, at the time of the attack. In addition to the observations during the time period of interest (*i.e.*, $\{1, \ldots, T\}$), the adversary has access to some of the users' past location traces, from which he builds individual mobility profiles for these users, under the form of transition probabilities $\{p_u\}_{u \in \mathcal{U}}$. See [20] for more details about the knowledge construction, in particular on how the mobility profiles can be built from obfuscated traces with missing locations. The mobility profiles constitute, together with the knowledge of the LPPMs used by the users (including their parameters), the adversary's *background knowledge* $\mathcal{K} = \{p_u, f_u\}_{u \in \mathcal{U}}$.

The output of a localization attack that targets a user u at a time instant t, is a *posterior probability distribution* over the set $\mathcal{R}$ of locations.

$$h_t^u(r) \triangleq \Pr\left(a_u(t) = r \mid \{\mathbf{o}(t)\}_{t=1..T}, C, \mathcal{K}\right) . \tag{1}$$

2.4   Location Privacy Metric

The location privacy $\mathrm{LP}_u(t)$ of a user u at time t, with respect to a given adversary, is captured by the expected error of the adversary when performing a localization attack [20]. Given the output $h_t^u(\cdot)$ of the localization attack, the location privacy writes:

$$\mathrm{LP}_u(t) \triangleq \sum_{r \in \mathcal{R}} h_t^u(r) \cdot d(r, a_u(t)) , \tag{2}$$

---

[1] Note that even if pseudonyms are used, the identity of the users can be inferred by using their social network [18] or their locations [20].

where $d(\cdot, \cdot)$ denotes a distance function on the set $\mathcal{R}$ of regions, typically the Haversine distance between the centers of the two regions.

3   Optimal Localization Attack

Without co-location information (as in [20]) and under the assumptions described in the previous section, the localization problem translates to solving a HMM inference problem, for which the *forward-backward* algorithm is a known solution. Essentially, the forward-backward algorithm defines forward and backward variables that take into account the observations before and after time t, respectively. The forward variable is the joint probability of location of user at time t and all the observations up to, and including, time t. The backward variable is the conditional probability of all observations after time t, given the actual location of user at that time instant. Then, the posterior probability distribution of the possible locations for the targeted user is obtained by combining (*i.e.*, multiplying and normalizing) the forward and backward variables. With co-location information, the locations of the users are not mutually independent: as soon as two users are co-located at some point in time t, their locations, before and after time t, become dependent. Actually, the fact that two users meet a same third user (even if they meet her at different time instants) suffices to create some dependencies between their locations; this means that, to perform the localization attack on a user, the adversary must take into account the locations (*i.e.*, the obfuscated location information and the co-location information) of all the users who are connected to u by a *chain* of co-location (*i.e.*, the connected component of u in the co-location graph). Formally speaking, it means that the adversary cannot rely only on the *marginal* distributions of the users' location; instead he must consider the *joint* distributions. In other words, co-locations turn N disjoint inference problems (*i.e.*, HMM problems solved by the forward-backward algorithm) into a joint inference problem.

To solve the localization problem, we consider the users jointly; we show that it translates to an HMM problem that we solve using a forward-backward algorithm. For a set $\mathcal{U}$ of users and a time t, we define the following forward and backward variables:

$$\alpha_t^{\mathcal{U}}(\mathbf{r}) \triangleq \Pr\left(\mathbf{o}(1)\ldots,\mathbf{o}(t), C_1,\ldots, C_t, \mathbf{a}(t) = \mathbf{r} \,|\, \mathcal{K}\right) \tag{3}$$

$$\beta_t^{\mathcal{U}}(\mathbf{r}) \triangleq \Pr\left(\mathbf{o}(t+1)\ldots,\mathbf{o}(T), C_{t+1},\ldots, C_T \,|\, \mathbf{a}(t) = \mathbf{r}, \mathcal{K}\right) , \tag{4}$$

where $\mathbf{r}$ denotes a vector of size N, *i.e.*, $\mathbf{r} \in \mathcal{R}^N$, and represents the actual locations of all users at a single time instant. These variables can be defined recursively (over t) and, unlike in the case where no co-location observations are available, their expressions involve the co-location information. More specifically, it can be proved that for all $\mathbf{r} \in \mathcal{R}^N$, we have[2]

---

[2] For the sake of simplicity and clarity, we define the variables at $t = 0$ even though no observations are made at this time instant.

$$\alpha_t^{\mathcal{U}}(\mathbf{r}) = \begin{cases} \pi_{\mathcal{U}}(\mathbf{r}) & \text{if } t = 0 \\ \dfrac{\mathbf{1}_t(\mathbf{r}, C)}{\sum_{C'} \mathbf{1}_t(\mathbf{r}, C')} \cdot f_{\mathcal{U}}(\mathbf{r}, \mathbf{o}(t)) \sum_{\rho \in \mathcal{R}^N} \alpha_{t-1}^{\mathcal{U}}(\rho) \cdot p_{\mathcal{U}}(\rho, \mathbf{r}) & \text{if } t > 0 \end{cases} \quad (5)$$

and

$$\beta_t^{\mathcal{U}}(\mathbf{r}) = \begin{cases} \displaystyle\sum_{\rho \in \mathcal{R}^N} \dfrac{\mathbf{1}_t(\rho, C)}{\sum_{C'} \mathbf{1}_t(\rho, C')} \cdot \beta_{t+1}^{\mathcal{U}}(\rho) \cdot p_{\mathcal{U}}(\mathbf{r}, \rho) \cdot f_{\mathcal{U}}(\rho, \mathbf{o}(t+1)) & \text{if } t < T \\ 1 & \text{if } t = T \end{cases}$$

$$(6)$$

where for $\mathbf{r} = (r_1, \dots, r_N) \in \mathcal{R}^N$, $\rho = (\rho_1, \dots, \rho_N) \in \mathcal{R}^N$, $\mathbf{r}' = (r_1', \dots, r_N') \in \mathcal{R}'^N$, $\pi_{\mathcal{U}}(\mathbf{r}) = \prod_{i=1}^N \pi_{u_i}(r_i)$, $f_{\mathcal{U}}(\mathbf{r}, \mathbf{r}') = \prod_{i=1}^N f_{u_i}(r_i, r_i')$, $p_{\mathcal{U}}(\rho, \mathbf{r}) = \prod_{i=1}^N p_{u_i}(\rho_i, r_i)$, and $\mathbf{1}(\cdot, \cdot)$ is the indicator function that returns 1 if the locations of the users are *consistent* with the co-location information reported at time t, and 0 otherwise. That is, formally,

$$\mathbf{1}_t(\mathbf{r}, C) = \begin{cases} 1 & \text{if } \forall (u_i \leftrightarrow_t u_j) \in C_t, \ r_i = r_j \\ 0 & \text{otherwise} \end{cases}. \quad (7)$$

In other words, the indicator function captures whether the users for which a co-location was reported are indeed at the same locations in $\mathbf{r}$. As the adversary has no knowledge about the way co-locations are reported, the distribution of the sets of reported co-locations, given the actual locations of the users, is modeled with a uniform distribution.

The intuition behind Equation (5) is that the forward variable at time t can be expressed recursively, with respect to time, by combining, for all possible locations of the users at time $t - 1$: (1) the joint probability that the users were at location ρ at time $t - 1$ and reported the obfuscated locations observed by the adversary up to time $t - 1$ (this is captured by $\alpha_{t-1}^{\mathcal{U}}$), (2) the joint probability that the users move from the locations ρ to the locations $\mathbf{r}$ (this is captured by $p_{\mathcal{U}}$), (3) the joint probability that the users obfuscate their locations $\mathbf{r}$ to that observed by the adversary $\mathbf{o}(t)$ (this is captured by $f_{\mathcal{U}}$) and that the locations $\mathbf{r}$ of the users are consistent with the co-locations reported at time t. Because users obfuscate their locations independently from each other, the joint obfuscation probability is the product of the individual obfuscation probabilities (hence the expression of $f_{\mathcal{U}}$). The same applies to $p_{\mathcal{U}}$. The same intuition lies behind Equation (6).

The indicator function $\mathbf{1}_t(\cdot, \cdot)$ accounts for the co-location information in the localization attack by ruling out the *impossible* (*i.e.*, inconsistent with the reported co-locations) user locations, hence further narrowing down the set of possible locations for the users involved in a co-location. Schematically speaking (with a deterministic vision, for the sake of clarity), the set of possible locations for a user u_i (at time t), co-located with a user u_j, consists of the locations that can be obfuscated into the location reported by u_i at time t and that can be reached (according to u_i's mobility profile) from a possible location of u_i at time

$t - 1$ **and** that can be obfuscated into the location reported by u_j at time t **and** that can be reached (according to u_j's mobility profile) from a possible location of u_j at time $t - 1$.

Finally, the posterior probability distribution of the users' locations can be computed based on the forward and backward variables, by using the following formula, for $u_i \in \mathcal{U}$ and at time t:

$$
h_t^{u_i}(r) = \Pr\left(a_{u_i}(t) = r \mid \{o(t)\}_{t=1..T}, C, \mathcal{K}\right) = \frac{\displaystyle\sum_{\mathbf{r} \in \mathcal{R}^N \mid r_i = r} \alpha_t^{\mathcal{U}}(\mathbf{r}) \cdot \beta_t^{\mathcal{U}}(\mathbf{r})}{\displaystyle\sum_{\mathbf{r} \in \mathcal{R}^N} \alpha_t^{\mathcal{U}}(\mathbf{r}) \cdot \beta_t^{\mathcal{U}}(\mathbf{r})} . \tag{8}
$$

We now evaluate the complexity of the joint localization attack. The first observation is that the size of the state space (*i.e.*, the locations of all users) is M^N. To attack a user at time t, the adversary needs to compute the values of α *up to* time t and the values of beta *down to* time t.[3] At each time instant, the adversary needs to compute the values of these two variables for all possible values of their inputs $\mathbf{r} \in \mathcal{R}^N$ (there are M^N possible values for $\mathbf{r}$). The computation of each of these values requires summing over the M^N possible locations ρ at time $t - 1$; for each of the possible locations, the computation of one element of the sum takes $\Theta(N)$ operations. Therefore, the computation of the forward and backward variables, at all time instants, for all possible values of the localizations is $\Theta(NTM^{2N})$ operations. Note that the complexity is the same whether the adversary attacks one or all the users at one or all time instants. In fact, the adversary can pre-compute the h_t^u for all u and all t with a complexity that is dominated by that of the computations of the forward and backward variables. In summary, the complexity of the localization attack on one or all of the users in $\mathcal{U}$ is

$$
c_{\mathrm{opt}}(N, T, M) = \Theta(NTM^{2N}) . \tag{9}
$$

The complexity of the optimal localization attack is prohibitively high and prevents its use for the entire set of users of a mobile social network; the optimal localization attack is tractable only for small values of N, *i.e.*, 2 and 3. In the next section, we propose heuristics for performing low-complexity approximate localization attacks.

4   Approximate Localization Attack

We propose two low-complexity heuristics for performing approximate localization attacks. Essentially, the first selects a small set of users to consider when

---

[3] The best way to do this is to use dynamic programming, *i.e.*, compute the α_t (and storing its values) iteratively for increasing t and compute the β_t (and store the values) iteratively for decreasing t.

attacking a target user and performs an optimal joint localization attack on this small set of users (*i.e.*, considering only the co-locations between these users). The intuition behind this heuristic is that the locations of a user are significantly correlated with those of only a limited number of users (*e.g.*, a few co-workers during work hours, and her family and close friends the rest of the time). The second makes use of individual forward-backward variables (one for each user of the entire set of users) and computes their values at each time instant, based on the considered user's individual variable at time $t - 1$ and the reported locations of the users co-located with her at time t, hence disregarding the dependencies stemming from past co-locations. The intuition behind this heuristic is that the dependency between two users' locations fades relatively quickly over time after they meet.

4.1   Heuristic 1: Limited User Set Approximation

As discussed in Section 3, the optimal localization attack can be efficiently performed only on small sets of users. This is because location of a target user u depends on locations of *all* other users that are connected to u in the co-location graph (where there is an edge between two users u and v if $u \leftrightarrow_t v$ for some time t). The rationale of our first approximation is to limit the number of users, on which the target user's location depends, and to consider only those that have high location correlation with u. Concretely, we choose the user(s) that have the largest number of reported co-locations with the targeted user and we perform an optimal localization attack on the resulting set of users. We call these users the *co-targets* of the targeted user. Depending on his computational power, the adversary can choose one or two such users (*i.e.*, $N = 2$ or $N = 3$) to attack the target with. The co-targets of a user u are chosen as follows:

$$\text{co-target}_1(u) \triangleq \underset{v \in \mathcal{U} \setminus \{u\}}{\text{argmax}} |\{t \in \{1, \ldots, T\} \mid u \leftrightarrow_t v\}| \tag{10}$$

$$\text{co-target}_2(u) \triangleq \underset{v \in \mathcal{U} \setminus \{u,u'\}}{\text{argmax}} |\{t \in \{1, \ldots, T\} \mid u \leftrightarrow_t v\}| + |\{t \in \{1, \ldots, T\} \mid u' \leftrightarrow_t v\}|$$

$$\tag{11}$$

where $u' = \text{co-target}_1(u)$ and $|\cdot|$ denotes the cardinality of the set. More specifically, the first co-target of a user u is the user with whom u has the more reported co-locations during the time interval considered for the localization attack. The second co-target of u is chosen so as to maximize the number of co-locations with u **plus** the number of co-locations with u's first co-target. Note that the set of considered users can be different for every targeted user; in particular $v = \text{co-target}_1(u) \not\Rightarrow u = \text{co-target}_1(v)$. The complexity of this heuristic is $\Theta(TM^4)$ for $N = 2$ and $\Theta(TM^6)$ for $N = 3$ (obtained by replacing N by its value in the generic expression (9) of the complexity of the optimal attack).

4.2   Heuristic 2: Independence Approximation

As discussed in Section 3, the need to jointly consider the locations of all the users, which cause the explosion of the state space size and thus the high complexity of the attack, stems from the fact that their locations are not independent as soon as co-locations are reported. The rationale behind our second heuristic is to ignore the mobility profiles of the co-located users, hence alleviating the need to take into account their past locations, which causes the state space explosion) and to consider only their reported co-locations to improve the inference of the target user's location at the considered time instant. This comes down to considering the locations reported by the users co-located with u, as if u had reported these obfuscated locations herself (as depicted in Figure 1a). We define individual forward and backward variables for each user and we couple them upon co-locations, as follows:

$$\hat{\alpha}_t^u(r) \triangleq \begin{cases} \pi_u(r) & \text{if } t = 0 \\ \displaystyle\prod_{u'|u \leftrightarrow_t u'} f_{u'}\left(r, o_{u'}(t)\right) \cdot f_u\left(r, o_u(t)\right) \cdot \sum_{\rho \in \mathcal{R}} \hat{\alpha}_{t-1}^u(\rho)\, p_u(\rho, r) & \text{otherwise} \end{cases} \quad (12)$$

and

$$\hat{\beta}_t^u(r) \triangleq \begin{cases} 1 & \text{if } t = T \\ \displaystyle\sum_{\rho \in \mathcal{R}} \hat{\beta}_{t+1}^u(\rho)\, p_u(r, \rho)\, f_u(\rho, o_u(t+1)) \prod_{u'|u \leftrightarrow_{t+1} u'} f_{u'}(\rho, o_{u'}(t+1)) & \text{otherwise} \end{cases}$$
$$(13)$$

Finally, when performing a localization attack on user u, the posterior distributions of the locations of the users co-located with u at time t are taken into account. More specifically, we estimate the probability distribution of user u's location at time t by

$$\hat{h}_t^u(r) \triangleq \frac{\hat{\alpha}_t^u(r) \cdot \hat{\beta}_t^u(r) \cdot \displaystyle\prod_{u'|u \leftrightarrow_t u'} \hat{\alpha}_t^{u'}(r)\, \hat{\beta}_t^{u'}(r)}{\displaystyle\sum_{r' \in \mathcal{R}} \left(\hat{\alpha}_t^u(r')\, \hat{\beta}_t^u(r') \prod_{u'|u \leftrightarrow_t u'} \hat{\alpha}_t^{u'}(r')\, \hat{\beta}_t^{u'}(r') \right)} . \quad (14)$$

We now compute the complexity of this heuristic. To perform a localization attack on a user, the adversary needs to compute the individual variables of all the users that are connected to the target by a chain of co-location, that is N users at most. The computation of a value $\hat{\alpha}$ and $\hat{\beta}$ (for a given t and a given r), in the worst case (*i.e.*, when all the users are co-located), takes $\Theta(NM)$ operations; and TM such values need be computed for each user. Therefore, the complexity of this heuristic is $\Theta(N^2TM^2)$.

5   Experimental Evaluation

We evaluate the effect of co-locations on users' location privacy, with respect to the various localization attacks presented in the previous sections, by using a dataset of real mobility traces.

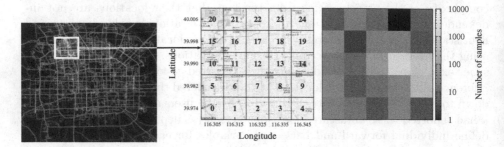

Fig. 3. Illustration of the dataset used in the evaluation. Most traces are located in the region of Beijing (left); we focus on a small active area that corresponds to the campus of the Tsinghua University and we partition it by using a 5 × 5 square grid (middle). The heat-map (right) shows the number of samples in each region (logscale).

5.1   Dataset, Methodology and Experimental Setup

The dataset was collected by Microsoft Research Asia, in the framework of the GeoLife project [24]. It comprises the GPS traces (*i.e.,* sequences of time-stamped latitude-longitude couples, sampled at a rate of one point every 1-5 seconds) of 182 users, collected over a period of over three years. The GPS traces are scattered all over the world; but most of them are located in the region of Beijing, China. We processed the data as follows, in order to fit in our formalism.

Space Discretization. We select the area of ∼4.4 km × 4.4 km, within Beijing, that contains the largest number of GPS samples, and we filter out GPS samples that are outside of this area. This geographic area corresponds to the campus of the Tsinghua University (longitude ranging from 116.3 to 116.35 and latitude ranging from 39.97 to 40.01, see Figure 3). We partition the selected area into 25 regions by using a 5×5 square grid. The GPS coordinates of each sample are translated into the region (*i.e.,* the grid cell) they fall into.

Time Discretization. We split the continuous time interval into one-hour time sub-intervals, which correspond to time instants in our formalism. For each time sub-interval t and for each user u, we set the user's actual location in that time interval (*i.e.,* $a_u(t)$) to the region corresponding to the sample that is the closest to the midpoint of the considered time sub-interval. If a user's trace does not contain any sample in a given time sub-interval, the user's actual location is set to a dummy region $r_\perp$, leaving us with partial user traces.

Co-location Generation. As the dataset does not contain explicit co-location information reported by the users, we use synthetic co-locations that we generate as follows: At each time instant, we generate a co-location between two users if their discretized actual locations are the same (and different from $r_\perp$). Because in real-life not all such situations correspond to actual co-location and because even actual co-locations are not necessarily reported, in our evaluation we take into account only a proportion ω (ranging from 0% to 100%) of the synthetic co-locations.

For each user, we compute the number of co-locations she has with every other user in the dataset, across the full user traces. We keep only the users for which there exists another user with whom they have at least 200 co-locations. For these users, we consider their *common* time interval (*i.e.*, the longest time interval during which all these users have at least one sample); we obtained an interval of $\sim$6000 hours. Within the common interval, we sample 10 short traces of 300 continuous hours such that (1) all users have at least 10% of valid samples (*i.e.*, , different from $r_{\perp}$) and (2) all users have at least 20 co-locations with their co-target$_1$ (as defined in Equation (11)). This leaves us with a total of 5 users.

User Mobility Profiles Construction.   We build the mobility profiles $\{p_u\}_{u \in \mathcal{U}}$ of the users based on their entire discretized traces by counting the transitions from any region to any region (in $\mathcal{R}$) in one time instant.

Obfuscation.   We consider that users report a single (or none), potentially obfuscated, location at each time instant.[4] This means that the set $\mathcal{R}'$ in which the obfuscated location $o_u(\cdot)$ takes values is $\mathcal{R} \cup \{r_{\perp}\}$. We consider, for each user u, that two location-privacy protection mechanisms are used together: First, the location is hidden (*i.e.*, obfuscated to $r_{\perp}$) with a probability λ_u and then, if the location has not been hidden, it is replaced by a region (chosen uniformly at random) at a distance of at most d_u from the user's actual discretized location (*i.e.*, a region). If the actual location of a user is not known (*i.e.*, set to $r_{\perp}$), the LPPM returns $r_{\perp}$ with probability 1. In our evaluation, we vary λ_u from 0 to 1 and we set d_u to the size of one grid cell; this means that, if it is not hidden, a user's location is obfuscated either to its actual value (with probability 0.2) or to one of the four adjacent regions (*e.g.*, 2, 6, 8 and 12 for region 7 in Figure 3), each with probability 0.2.

Privacy Evaluation.   We evaluate the location privacy of the users, and the effect of co-locations on it, based on the metric defined in (2). For each user and for each short trace, we generate 20 random obfuscated traces (remember that obfuscation is a random process) and we perform a localization attack on each of them. We compute the average location privacy of each user across the different obfuscated traces and across the different time instants. Time instants for which the location of a user is not known (*i.e.*, set to $r_{\perp}$) are not taken into account in the computation of their average over time.

Limitations.   Due to the synthetic nature of the reported location and co-location information in our data source, our experimental setup does not per-fectly reflect on a real usage case. Therefore, the results presented in this section cannot directly be interpreted as the magnitude of the threat in real-life. Yet, we believe that it suffices to get insight into the effect of co-locations on location

---

[4] We make this assumption because of the limited size of the considered grid and we leave the case where LPPMs output a *set* of locations to future work.

privacy, the sources of privacy loss, and the relative performance of the proposed heuristics. Also, the number of users considered in our evaluation (*i.e.*, 5) is relatively small. Hence, the results may not be representative of the entire population. In order to overcome the aforementioned shortcomings, we intend to collect a large-scale dataset from an existing social network. We also intend to run experiments on large grids (*i.e.*, larger than the 5×5 grid used in the evaluation).

5.2   Experimental Results

We now experimentally evaluate the algorithms, presented in Section 4, in different scenarios, with different settings. The goal of our evaluation is to assess the raw performance of our heuristics, but also to compare them. In addition, we analyze the effect of the different parameters of the model (including the individual LPPM settings of the users and the *differences* between the individual LPPM settings of the users) and of the set of co-locations considered in the localization attack.

Effects of Co-locations and LPPM Settings. We begin our evaluation by analyzing the effect of (1) the proportion ω of reported co-location and (2) the LPPM settings (*i.e.*, w/ or w/o obfuscation and the location hiding probability λ, assumed to be the same across users) in the case of two users, *i.e.*, the target user and her first co-target are considered jointly in an optimal localization attack, namely the limited user set approximation with $N = 2$. The results are depicted in Figure 4. The left sub-figure shows the case where no obfuscation is used (*i.e.*, the users disclose their *actual* locations with probability $1-\lambda$ and hide them completely otherwise), whereas the right sub-figure shows the case where obfuscation is used (*i.e.*, the users disclose their *obfuscated* locations, specifically a region chosen uniformly at random among the actual location and the four immediate neighboring regions, with probability $1 - \lambda$ and hide them otherwise). The top graphs show a box-plot representation (*i.e.*, first quartile, median, third quartile and outliers) of the users' location privacy expressed in terms of the expected error of the adversary, in kilometers (left axis) and in proportion of the size of the considered geographic area (right axis). For each couple of values (λ, ω), we draw one box-plot to aggregate the data-points obtained for all users and for all the 20 randomly generated obfuscated versions of each of the considered actual trace. Note that without obfuscation, the case $\lambda = 0$ leads to zero privacy as users *always* disclose their *actual* locations. It can be observed that the proportion of reported co-locations consistently decreases the location privacy of the users. To quantify this decrease, we plot (middle and bottom graphs) the privacy loss caused by the use of co-location information, with respect to the case where co-locations are ignored (or not available), *i.e.*, $\omega = 0\%$. We show both the median absolute privacy loss (in kilometers, middle graph) and the median relative privacy loss (in percentage of the privacy in the case $\omega = 0\%$, bottom graph). Note that the median privacy loss is **not** equal to the difference of the median privacy. Consider for example, the case $\lambda = 0.4$ and $\omega = 50\%$:

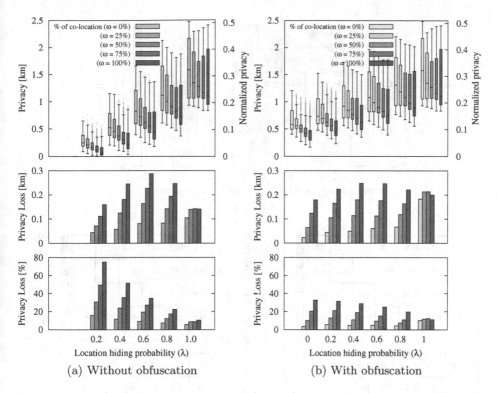

Fig. 4. Privacy (top), absolute privacy loss (middle) and relative privacy loss (bottom) for the limited user set attack with $N = 2$ users. The privacy *loss* is expressed wrt the case where no co-locations are reported ($\omega = 0\%$); the histograms show median values. Co-location information decreases privacy. The relative privacy loss is higher for small values of the hiding probability and without obfuscation.

in the case without obfuscation the median privacy loss is approximately 125m, which corresponds to a decrease of 25%. The median absolute privacy loss can go up to 290m ($\lambda = 0.6$, $\omega = 100\%$) and the median relative privacy loss up to 75% ($\lambda = 0.2$ and $\omega = 100\%$). We observe the same trend, with a more modest loss, in the case where obfuscation is used. For the rest of the evaluation, we focus on the case where users do obfuscate their locations and report $\omega = 50\%$ of the co-locations.

Effects of the differences of Individual LPPM Settings. Here, we analyze the effect of the differences, in the users' LPPM settings, on the location privacy (loss) due to co-locations. To do so, we focus on the case of two users, a target and her co-target, both who obfuscate their location but with different hiding probabilities λ_{target} and $\lambda_{\text{co-target}}$. We perform a joint optimal localization attack. The results are depicted in Figure 5 under the form of heat-maps that represent the target user's location privacy (a) as well as her absolute (b) and relative (c)

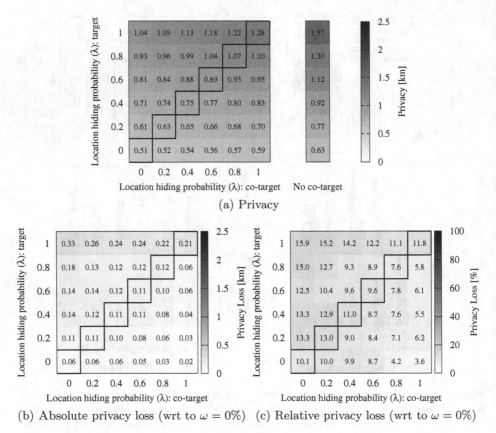

(a) Privacy

(b) Absolute privacy loss (wrt to $\omega = 0\%$)   (c) Relative privacy loss (wrt to $\omega = 0\%$)

Fig. 5. Median values of the target's location privacy (loss), for the limited user set attack with $N = 2$ users, when the target and her co-target have different values of λ (with obfuscation and $\omega = 50\%$). The diagonals correspond to the values of Figure 4b.

privacy loss (wrt the case $\omega = 0\%$) as functions of the respective LPPM settings $\lambda_{\text{co-target}}$ (x-axis) and λ_{target} (y-axis).

A first observation is that co-locations always decrease the privacy of the target (*i.e.*, all values in Figure 5b are positive) and that the more information the co-target discloses, the worse the privacy of the target is (*i.e.*, the cells of the heat-map depicted in Figure 5a become lighter, when going from right to left on a given row).

The diagonals of the heat-maps correspond to the case $\lambda_{\text{co-target}} = \lambda_{\text{target}}$, which is depicted in more details in Figure 4. The region of the heat-map above the diagonal corresponds to the case where the target is more *conservative*, in terms of her privacy attitude, than her co-target (*i.e.*, $\lambda_{\text{co-target}} < \lambda_{\text{target}}$). It can be observed that the information disclosed by the target herself compromises her privacy more than the information disclosed by her co-target, *e.g.*, the cell $(0.6,0)$ is lighter (which means that the target's privacy is lower) than the cell $(0,0.6)$.

By comparing the columns "$\lambda_{\text{co-target}} = 1$" and "no co-target" (two right-most columns in Figure 5a), we can observe the privacy loss stemming from the use, through the co-location information, of the co-target's mobility profile alone (as the co-target never discloses her location). This is substantial.

Finally, in the extreme case where the target never discloses location information and her co-target always does (top-left cell of the heat-maps in Figures 5b and 5c), the privacy loss for the target is 330m, which corresponds to a decrease of 16%. This case (and in general the cases where the target never discloses location information, *i.e.*, the top row of the heat-maps) highlights the fact that, as reported co-locations involve two users, users lose some control over their privacy: Without revealing any information about herself, a user can still have her privacy decreased by other users, due to co-location information.

For the rest of the evaluation, we focus on the case where all users have the same LPPM settings (*i.e.*, same values of λ).

Comparison of the Proposed Heuristics. Here, we compare, through experimentation (we leave the analytical comparison to future work), the proposed inference algorithms for the localization attack, by taking into account different scenarios, as depicted in Figure 6. In scenario (a), we consider, in turn, all target users in our set and perform an individual localization attack on each of them, using only their own reported locations and no co-locations. This corresponds to the baseline case $\omega = 0\%$, which was presented in detail in Figure 4b. We then consider the case of an adversary that exploits co-locations. We assume the adversary observes a limited proportion, $\omega = 50\%$, of the existing co-locations. Scenario (b) corresponds to the case of an adversary that, in order to attack a target user, performs an optimal joint inference attack on the target and her co-target, as described in Section 3. This scenario corresponds to the case $\omega = 50\%$ in Figure 4b. Scenarios (c) and (d) correspond to the case of an adversary that performs an optimal joint attack on the target and her **two co-targets**. We distinguish two cases, (c) – in which the co-locations between the co-targets are ignored and (d) – in which all co-locations between any of the three users are considered. We make this distinction solely to quantify the privacy loss stemming from the use of co-locations that do not directly involve the target. In practice, an adversary would always consider scenario (d) as it takes into account more information at no extra cost. Finally we consider scenario (e), that corresponds to an adversary that uses reported all co-locations but solves an individual inference problem for each user, as described in 4.2.

Figure 7 shows the results of our comparison. The graph on the left shows a box-plot representation of users' privacy, for each of scenarios (a)-(e). To quantify the different effects on the users' privacy of the set of considered co-locations and of the heuristic used, we show (right) the absolute and relative privacy loss, with respect to scenario (a), for each of the scenarios (b)-(e). It can be observed by comparing scenarios (a)-(d) that, unsurprisingly, the users' privacy decreases with the amount of considered co-locations. However, the comparison between scenarios (c) and (d) shows that co-locations between the target's co-targets does not significantly improve the performance of the localization attack. Finally, we observe that the second heuristic, which takes into account all co-locations outperforms the first heuristic ($N \leq 3$), at a lower computational cost.

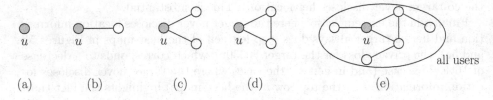

(a)   (b)   (c)   (d)   (e)

Fig. 6. Co-locations considered in the evaluation: (a) no co-locations, (b) only co-locations between the target and co-target$_1$ (Heuristic 1, $N = 2$), (c) only co-locations between the target and co-target$_1$ and between the target and co-target$_2$ (Heuristic 1, $N = 3$), (d) all co-locations between the target, co-target$_1$ and co-target$_2$ (Heuristic 1, $N = 3$), (e) all co-locations (Heuristic 2). In scenarios (b)-(e), we consider that $\omega = 50\%$ of the co-locations are reported.

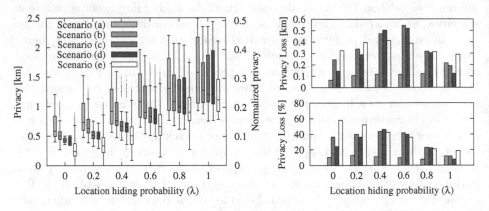

Fig. 7. Comparison of the different localization attacks for the scenarios (a)-(e) depicted in Figure 6. The privacy loss (right) is evaluated wrt scenario (a).

6   Related Work

Location is identity. Even if the set of locations shared by a user is anonymized, and her true identity is hidden from the location-based service provider, the observed trajectories can be re-identified [5, 9, 12, 15]. This attack is made by linking available information about users' mobility in the past with their observed traces. To protect against such attacks, many location obfuscation mechanisms have been proposed in the literature; they suggest users hide their locations at certain locations, or reduce the accuracy or granularity of their reported locations [4, 8, 13]. These techniques increase users' privacy by making it more difficult for an adversary to de-anonymize users and localize or track them over time. The location privacy of users in such settings can be computed using the expected error of an adversary in estimating their true locations [20]. In such an inference framework, an adversary has a background knowledge on users' mobility models; this is used to reconstruct the full trajectories of the users, given the anonymized and obfuscated observed traces.

The adversary's information, however, is not limited to mobility models. With most users being members of social networks, an adversary can de-anonymize location traces by matching the graph of co-traveler users with their social network graph [21]. Co-travelers are those who have been in each others' physical proximity for a considerable number of times. Researchers have extensively studied the problem of inferring social ties between users based on their physical proximity [3,7]. Recent revelations about NSA surveillance programs also show that this type of information is of great use for tracking and identifying individuals [2].

The correlation between different users' information also opens the door to a new type of privacy threat. Even if a user does not reveal much information about herself, her privacy can be compromised by others. In [11], the authors study how information revealed, from pictures, by a user's friends in social networks can be used to infer private information about her location. Private information about, for example, user profile and her age can also be inferred from shared information on online social networks [6,17]. Mobile users, connecting to location-based services from a same IP address, can also compromise the privacy of those who want to keep their location private [23]. The loss in privacy, due to other users, has also been shown in other contexts such as genomics [10,14].

Extracting co-location information about users, i.e., who is with whom, is becoming increasingly easier. More specifically, with the proliferation of mobile social networks, where users can check-in themselves and others to different locations, the threat of available co-location information on users' location privacy is clear (as pointed out in [22]). Despite the mentioned works on quantifying the location privacy and the privacy of users in social networks, as well as the extensive research on privacy loss due to others, there has not been a study on evaluating location privacy considering co-location information. We bridge the gap between studies on location privacy and social networks, and we propose the first analytical framework to quantify the effects of co-location information on location privacy, where users can also make use of obfuscation mechanisms.

7   Conclusion

In this paper, we have studied the effect on users' location privacy when co-location information is available, in addition to individual (obfuscated) location information. To the best of our knowledge, this is the first paper to quantify the effects of co-location information, that stems from social relationships between users, on location privacy; as such it constitutes a first step towards bridging the gap between studies on location privacy and social networks. We have shown that, by considering the users' locations jointly, an adversary can exploit co-location information to better localize users, hence decreasing their individual privacy. Although the optimal joint localization attack has a prohibitively high computational complexity, the polynomial-time approximate inference algorithms that we propose in the paper provide good localization performance. An important observation from our work is that a user's location privacy is no longer entirely in her control, as the co-locations and the individual location information disclosed by other users significantly affect her own location privacy.

The message of this work is that protection mechanisms must not ignore the social aspects of location information. Because it is not desirable to report dummy lists of co-located users (as this information is displayed on the users' profiles on social networks), a location-privacy preserving mechanism needs instead to generalize information about co-located users (*i.e.*, replace the names of the co-located users by the type of social tie, *e.g.*, "with two friends") or to generalize the time (*i.e.*, replace the exact time of the co-location with the period of the day, *e.g.*, replacing 11am with "morning", when the co-location is declared *a posteriori*) of a social gathering as well as the locations of users at other locations, in order to reduce the effectiveness of the attacks we suggested in this paper. We intend to tackle the design of social-aware location-privacy protection mechanisms (running on the users' mobile devices) to help the users assess and protect their location privacy when co-location information is available.

Acknowledgments. The authors are thankful to Stefan Mihaila for his help in collecting useful statistics about the use of co-location on Foursquare. This work was partially funded by the Swiss National Science Foundation with grant 200021-138089.

References

1. Baum, L.E., Petrie, T.: Statistical inference for probabilistic functions of finite state markov chains. The Annals of Mathematical Statistics 37(6), 1554–1563 (1966)
2. How the NSA is tracking people right now (2013),
   http://apps.washingtonpost.com/g/page/national/how-the-nsa-is-tracking-people-right-now/634/ (last visited: February 2014)
3. Crandall, D.J., Backstrom, L., Cosley, D., Suri, S., Huttenlocher, D., Kleinberg, J.: Inferring social ties from geographic coincidences. Proc. of the National Academy of Sciences (PNAS), 1–6 (2010)
4. Damiani, M.L., Bertino, E., Silvestri, C.: The PROBE framework for the personalized cloaking of private locations. Transactions on Data Privacy 3, 123–148 (2010)
5. De Mulder, Y., Danezis, G., Batina, L., Preneel, B.: Identification via location-profiling in GSM networks. In: WPES 2008: Proc. of the 7th ACM Workshop on Privacy in the Electronic Society, pp. 23–32 (2008)
6. Dey, R., Tang, C., Ross, K., Saxena, N.: Estimating age privacy leakage in online social networks. In: INFOCOM 2012: Proc. of the 31st Annual IEEE Int'l Conf. on Computer Communications, pp. 2836–2840 (2012)
7. Eagle, N., Pentland, A., Lazer, D.: Inferring Friendship Network Structure by Using Mobile Phone Data. Proc. of the National Academy of Sciences (PNAS) 106, 15274–15278 (2009)
8. Ghinita, G., Damiani, M.L., Silvestri, C., Bertino, E.: Preventing velocity-based linkage attacks in location-aware applications. In: GIS 2009: Proc. of the 17th ACM Int'l Symp. on Advances in Geographic Information Systems, pp. 246–255 (2009)

9. Golle, P., Partridge, K.: On the anonymity of home/work location pairs. In: Tokuda, H., Beigl, M., Friday, A., Brush, A.J.B., Tobe, Y. (eds.) Pervasive 2009. LNCS, vol. 5538, pp. 390–397. Springer, Heidelberg (2009)

10. Gymrek, M., McGuire, A.L., Golan, D., Halperin, E., Erlich, Y.: Identifying personal genomes by surname inference. Science 339(6117), 321–324 (2013)

11. Henne, B., Szongott, C., Smith, M.: Snapme if you can: Privacy threats of other peoples' geo-tagged media and what we can do about it. In: WiSec 2013: Proc. of the 6th ACM Conf. on Security and Privacy in Wireless and Mobile Networks, pp. 95–106 (2013)

12. Hoh, B., Gruteser, M., Xiong, H., Alrabady, A.: Enhancing security and privacy in trac-monitoring systems. IEEE Pervasive Computing 5(4), 38–46 (2006)

13. Huang, L., Yamane, H., Matsuura, K., Sezaki, K.: Silent cascade: Enhancing location privacy without communication QoS degradation. In: Clark, J.A., Paige, R.F., Polack, F.A.C., Brooke, P.J. (eds.) SPC 2006. LNCS, vol. 3934, pp. 165–180. Springer, Heidelberg (2006)

14. Humbert, M., Ayday, E., Hubaux, J.P., Telenti, A.: Addressing the concerns of the lacks family: Quantification of kin genomic privacy. In: CCS 2013: Proc. of the 20th ACM Conf. on Computer and Communications Security, pp. 1141–1152 (2013)

15. Krumm, J.: Inference attacks on location tracks. In: LaMarca, A., Langheinrich, M., Truong, K.N. (eds.) Pervasive 2007. LNCS, vol. 4480, pp. 127–143. Springer, Heidelberg (2007)

16. Krumm, J.: A survey of computational location privacy. Personal Ubiquitous Computing 13(6), 391–399 (2009)

17. Mislove, A., Viswanath, B., Gummadi, K.P., Druschel, P.: You are who you know: Inferring user profiles in online social networks. In: WSDM 2010: Proc. of the 3rd ACM Int'l Conf. on Web Search and Data Mining, pp. 251–260 (2010)

18. Narayanan, A., Shmatikov, V.: De-anonymizing social networks. In: S&P 2009: Proc. of the 30th IEEE Symp. on Security and Privacy, pp. 173–187 (2009)

19. Shokri, R., Theodorakopoulos, G., Danezis, G., Hubaux, J.-P., Le Boudec, J.-Y.: Quantifying location privacy: The case of sporadic location exposure. In: Fischer-Hübner, S., Hopper, N. (eds.) PETS 2011. LNCS, vol. 6794, pp. 57–76. Springer, Heidelberg (2011)

20. Shokri, R., Theodorakopoulos, G., Le Boudec, J.Y., Hubaux, J.P.: Quantifying location privacy. In: S&P 2011: Proc. of the 32nd IEEE Symp. on Security and Privacy, pp. 247–262 (2011)

21. Srivatsa, M., Hicks, M.: Deanonymizing mobility traces: Using social network as a side-channel. In: CCS 2012: Proc. of the 19th ACM Conf. on Computer and Communications Security, pp. 628–637 (2012)

22. Vicente, C., Freni, D., Bettini, C., Jensen, C.S.: Location-related privacy in geosocial networks. IEEE Internet Computing 15(3), 20–27 (2011)

23. Vratonjic, N., Huguenin, K., Bindschaedler, V., Hubaux, J.P.: How others compromise your location privacy: The case of shared public IPs at hotspots. In: De Cristofaro, E., Wright, M. (eds.) PETS 2013. LNCS, vol. 7981, pp. 123–142. Springer, Heidelberg (2013)

24. Zheng, Y., Liu, L., Wang, L., Xie, X.: Learning transportation mode from raw GPS data for geographic applications on the web. In: WWW 2008: Proc. of the 17th ACM Int'l Conf. on World Wide Web, pp. 247–256 (2008)

Do Dummies Pay Off? Limits of Dummy Traffic Protection in Anonymous Communications

Simon Oya[1], Carmela Troncoso[2], and Fernando Pérez-González[1,2]

[1] Signal Theory and Communications Dept., University of Vigo, Spain
{simonoya,fperez}@gts.uvigo.es
[2] Gradiant (Galician R&D Center in Advanced Telecommunications), Spain
ctroncoso@gradiant.org

Abstract. Anonymous communication systems ensure that correspondence between senders and receivers cannot be inferred with certainty. However, when patterns are persistent, observations from anonymous communication systems enable the reconstruction of user behavioral profiles. Protection against profiling can be enhanced by adding dummy messages, generated by users or by the anonymity provider, to the communication. In this paper we study the limits of the protection provided by this countermeasure. We propose an analysis methodology based on solving a least squares problem that permits to characterize the adversary's profiling error with respect to the user behavior, the anonymity provider behavior, and the dummy strategy. Focusing on the particular case of a timed pool mix we show how, given a privacy target, the performance analysis can be used to design optimal dummy strategies to protect this objective.

Keywords: anonymous communications, disclosure attacks, dummies.

1 Introduction

Anonymization is a popular mechanism to provide private communications. Anonymous communication [1] ensures that relationships between senders and receivers of messages cannot be inferred with certainty by the adversary. These schemes hide communication patterns by delaying and changing the appearance of messages [2] in such a way that sent messages can be ascribed to a set of potential receivers, often denoted as anonymity set. In practice, user behavior and latency constrain the composition of anonymity sets, which in turn enables an adversary observing the anonymous communication system to reconstruct persistent behavioral user profiles [3–6].

A common approach to improve users' protection against profiling is to introduce dummy traffic, either generated by users [7] or by the anonymity provider [8]. The effectiveness of this countermeasure has been studied theoretically from the perspective of individual messages in [9]. With respect to profiling, dummy traffic has been tackled in [5, 10], where the authors empirically compute the number of rounds that the attacker takes to correctly identify some or all recipients of

E. De Cristofaro and S.J. Murdoch (Eds.): PETS 2014, LNCS 8555, pp. 204–223, 2014.

a sender. The analyses in [5, 10] are limited in two aspects. On the one hand, the results strongly depend on the specific cases considered in the experiments, and it is difficult to get insight on their applicability to other scenarios. On the other hand, the analyses only consider the ability of the adversary in identifying communication partners, but not her accuracy at estimating the intensity of the communication; i.e., the users' profiles.

In this paper we propose an analysis methodology based on the least squares approach introduced in [6] that permits system designers to characterize the adversary's profiling error with respect to the user behavior, the anonymity provider behavior, and the dummy strategy. Our estimator can be used to characterize the error for bilateral relationships, individual user profiles, or the population as a whole. Our approach can accommodate a wide range of high-latency anonymous communication schemes providing the analyst with a bound on the protection achievable through the use of dummy traffic.

Another shortcoming of previous works [5, 9, 10] is that the proposed evaluation strategies cannot be used to guide the design of effective dummy generation strategies, which is recognized to be a hard problem [11]. This has lead the deployed high latency anonymous communication systems to either implement arbitrary dummy strategies [12] or no dummy traffic at all [11]. Our methodology can be used to support the design of dummy strategies by approaching strategy selection as an optimization problem in which the error of the adversary is maximized. The optimization criteria can be chosen by the designer to satisfy different privacy objectives, e.g., balancing the protection among users, or favoring individual users or relationships.

We illustrate the operation of our methodology using a timed binomial pool mix. We provide a performance analysis of this mixing strategy in presence of both static sender-based and mix-based dummy traffic, showing that their contribution to the adversary's error can be decoupled and analyzed independently. Departing from this analysis we design dummy traffic strategies according to two privacy criteria: increasing the estimation error for all relationships by a constant factor, and guaranteeing a minimum estimation error for any relationship. By hiding relationships, both criteria hinder the inference of user profiles.

Next section describes an abstract model of an anonymous communication system with dummies, and Section 3 introduces a least squares-based profile estimator. We analyze in Sect. 4 the performance of this estimator when the anonymous channel is a timed binomial pool mix. The result of this analysis is used in Sect. 5 to design optimal dummy strategies, evaluated in Sect. 6. We discuss practical aspects of our method in Sect. 7 and finally conclude in Sect. 8.

2   System and Adversary Model

In this section we introduce the system and adversary model considered in the paper, as well as the general notation of the paper (summarized in Table 1). Throughout the document we use capital letters to denote random variables and lower-case letters to denote their realizations. Vectors and matrices are denoted by boldface characters. Vectors of random variables are upper-cased, while their realizations are lower cased. Matrices are always denoted by upper-case boldface characters; whether they are random matrices or realizations will be clear from the context. Furthermore, we use $\mathbf{1}_n$ to denote the all-ones column vector of size n, $\mathbf{1}_{n \times m}$ to denote the all-ones $n \times m$ matrix and $\mathbf{I}_n$ for the $n \times n$ identity matrix.

System Model. Our system consists of a population of N senders, designated by index $i \in \{1, 2, \cdots, N\}$, which exchange messages with a set of M receivers, designated by index $j \in \{1, 2, \cdots, M\}$, through a high-latency mix-based anonymous communication channel. Messages in the system may be real or dummy messages: decoy messages indistinguishable from real traffic. We consider two types of *dummy traffic*:

- **Sender-based dummies:** senders may send *dummy* messages to the mix along with their *real* messages. Sender-based dummies are recognized and discarded by the mix.
- **Mix-based dummies:** the mix-based system may send *dummy* messages to the receivers along with the *real* messages from the senders. Receivers are able to identify dummy messages and discard them.

Mix-based anonymous communication channels protect profiles by delaying messages and outputting them in batch in what are called *rounds* of mixing. We consider that the total number of messages generated by user i in round r is modeled by the random variable X_i^r. User messages can be real, modeled by random variable $X_{\lambda,i}^r$, or dummy, modeled by $X_{\delta,i}^r$. These messages are sent to an anonymous communication channel in which a round of mixing consists of the following sequence of four stages, shown in Fig. 1. In the first stage, dummy messages are identified and discarded (Stage 1), while the real messages go inside the pool (Stage 2). Messages inside the pool are delayed until a specific *firing condition* is fullfilled, and then a number of them, chosen according to a *batching strategy*, exit the pool. Messages leaving the pool (modeled by $X_{s,i}^r$) traverse a mixing block (Stage 3), which changes their appearance cryptographically to avoid bit-wise linkability. Messages staying in the pool are mixed with incoming real messages from subsequent rounds until they are fired. Finally, mix-based dummies are added the output traffic and messages are delivered to their recipients (Stage 4). The number of mix-based dummies sent in round r is modeled by X_{MIX}^r, and random variables $Y_{\lambda,j}^r$, $Y_{\delta,j}^r$ and Y_j^r model the number of real, dummy, and total messages received by receiver j in round r, respectively.

We also define the following vectors and matrices, which shall come handy later: matrix $\mathbf{U}$ is an $\rho \times N$ matrix which contains all the input observations, i.e., its (r, i)-th element is X_i^r. Similarly, matrix $\mathbf{U}_s$ contains in its (r, i)-th position the random variable $X_{s,i}^r$. Moreover, $\mathbf{H} \doteq \mathbf{I}_M \otimes \mathbf{U}$ and $\mathbf{H}_s \doteq \mathbf{I}_M \otimes \mathbf{U}_s$, where $\otimes$ denotes the Kronecker product. Vectors $\mathbf{Y}_j \doteq [Y_j^1, \cdots, Y_j^\rho]^T$ and $\hat{\mathbf{Y}}_{\delta,j} \doteq [Y_{\delta,j}^1, \cdots, Y_{\delta,j}^\rho]^T$ contain the random variables modeling the total (or just dummy) number of messages received by j in each round. Finally, $\mathbf{Y} \doteq [\mathbf{Y}_1^T, \cdots, \mathbf{Y}_M^T]^T$ and $\hat{\mathbf{Y}}_\delta \doteq [\hat{\mathbf{Y}}_{\delta,1}^T, \cdots, \hat{\mathbf{Y}}_{\delta,M}^T]^T$.

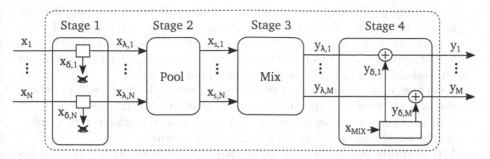

Fig. 1. Abstract model of a round in a mix-based anonymous communications channel (we omit the subscript r for the sake of clarity.)

We model the sending behavior of users in our population with two parameters:

- **Probability of real message:** the probability of real messages models how frequently users send real messages, and is denoted by $P_{\lambda_i}, i = 1, \cdots, N$. In other words, a message sent by i is real with probability P_{λ_i}, dummy otherwise. We make no assumptions on the values of P_{λ_i} other than $0 \leq P_{\lambda_i} \leq 1$, and that the probabilities of real messages are static during the observation period. Note that P_{λ_i} does not constrain the distributions that model the number of messages sent by users (X_i^r, $X_{\lambda,i}^r$ and $X_{\delta,i}^r$).
- **Sender profile:** the sender profile of user i models this sender's choice of recipients for her messages. It is defined as the vector $\mathbf{q}_i \doteq [p_{1,i}, p_{2,i}, \cdots, p_{M,i}]^T$, where $p_{j,i}$ denotes the probability that sender i sends a real message to receiver j. We also define the unnormalized receiver profile $\mathbf{p}_j \doteq [p_{j,1}, \cdots, p_{j,N}]^T$ and the vector containing all transition probabilities $\mathbf{p} \doteq [\mathbf{p}_1^T, \cdots, \mathbf{p}_M^T]^T$. We make no assumptions on the shape of the sender profiles other than $\mathbf{q}_i$ is in $\mathcal{P}$, the probability simplex in $\mathbb{R}^M$, i.e., $\mathcal{P} \doteq \left\{ \mathbf{r} \in \mathbb{R}^M : r_i \geq 0, \sum_{i=1}^M r_i = 1 \right\}$. We assume, nevertheless, that users' behavior is stationary during the observation period (the transition probabilities $p_{j,i}$ do not change between rounds), independent (the behavior of a user does not affect the behavior of the others) and memoryless (the messages sent by a user in a round do not affect the behavior of that user in subsequent rounds). We discuss the implications of the hypotheses above being false in Sect. 7.

The behavior of the mix-based anonymous communication channel is modeled by four parameters:

- **Firing condition:** the firing condition is an event, e.g., the arrival of a message (theshold mix) or the expiration of a timeout (timed mix), that causes the mix to forward some of the messages it has stored in its pool to their recipients.
- **Batching strategy:** the batching strategy models how messages are chosen to leave the pool. This strategy is determined by the function $F_{r,k}$, which

models the probability that a message arriving in round k leaves the mix in round r $(r \geq k)$. We do not make any assumption on the values of these parameters, other than $\sum_{r=k}^{\infty} F_{r,k} = 1$, i.e., every message will eventually leave the pool and get to its recipient. This function can for instance model a threshold mix ($F_{k,k} = 1$), or a binomial pool mix [10, 5].

- **Average mix-based dummies:** this parameter, denoted as δ_{MIX}, defines the average number of dummy messages generated by the mix each round. Note that our model does not assume any specific distribution for the number of mix-based dummies that are generated each round.
- **Mix dummy profile:** we denote by $\mathbf{q}_{\text{MIX}}$ the vector modeling the distribution of mix-based dummies among the receivers, $\mathbf{q}_{\text{MIX}} \doteq \{p_{1,\text{MIX}}, \cdots, p_{M,\text{MIX}}\}$ where $p_{j,\text{MIX}}$ is the probability that a dummy message generated by the mix is sent to receiver j ($\mathbf{q}_{\text{MIX}} \in \mathcal{P}$).

Adversary Model. We consider a global passive adversary that observes the system during ρ rounds. The adversary is able to see the identity of each sender and receiver communicating through the mix, but she is not able to link any two messages by their content nor distinguish between real and dummy messages. We assume that the adversary knows all the parameters of the system (e.g., the batching strategy determined by $F_{r,k}$, the parameters modeling the generation of dummy messages P_{λ_i} and δ_{MIX}, the mix dummy profile $\mathbf{q}_{\text{MIX}}$). The goal of the adversary is to infer the sending profiles of the users in the system from the observations, i.e., to obtain an estimator $\hat{p}_{j,i}$ of the probabilities $p_{j,i}$ given the input and output observations x_i^r and y_j^r, for every $i \in \{1, 2, \cdots, N\}$, $j \in \{1, 2, \cdots, M\}$ and $r \in \{1, 2, \cdots, \rho\}$.

3   A Least Square Profile Estimator for Dummy-Based Anonymization Systems

We aim here at deriving a least squares estimator for the probabilities $p_{j,i}$ for every $i = 1, 2, \cdots, N$ and $j = 1, 2, \cdots, M$, given the observation of ρ rounds of mixing, x_i^r and y_j^r for $r = 1, \cdots, \rho$ and $\forall i, j$. Following the methodology in [13], we derive the estimator of $p_{j,i}$ by looking for the vector of probabilities $\mathbf{p}$ which minimizes the Mean Squared Error (MSE) between the random vector $\mathbf{Y}$ and the observed realization $\mathbf{y}$:

$$\hat{\mathbf{p}} = \underset{\mathbf{q}_i \in \mathcal{P},\, i=1,\cdots,N}{\arg\min} \; \mathrm{E}\left\{\|\mathbf{y} - \mathbf{Y}(\mathbf{p})\|^2\right\} \tag{1}$$

where we have written $\mathbf{Y}(\mathbf{p})$ to stress the fact that the output distribution depends on all the transition probabilities $\mathbf{p}$. Note that, for notational simplicity, we are dropping the conditioning on $\mathbf{U}$ here. Even though the estimator in (1) minimizes the average error in the outputs, this does not mean it necessarily minimizes the error in the estimation of the probabilities $\mathbf{p}$. As shown in the derivations in [13], one can set the alternative problem

$$\hat{\mathbf{p}} = \underset{\mathbf{q}_i \in \mathcal{P},\, i=1,\cdots,N}{\arg\min} \; \left\{\|\mathbf{y} - \mathrm{E}\{\mathbf{Y}(\mathbf{p})\}\|^2\right\} \tag{2}$$

Table 1. Summary of notation

Symbol	Meaning
N	Number of senders in the population, denoted by $i \in \{1, 2, \cdots, N\}$
M	Number of receivers in the population, denoted by $j \in \{1, 2, \cdots, M\}$
$F_{r,k}$	Probability that a message arriving in round k leaves in round r
$p_{j,i}$	Probability that user i sends a real message to receiver j
$p_{j,\mathrm{MIX}}$	Probability that the mix sends a mix-based dummy message to receiver j
$\mathbf{q}_i$	Sender profile of sender i, $\mathbf{q}_i \doteq [p_{1,i}, p_{2,i}, \cdots, p_{M,i}]^T$
$\mathbf{q}_{\mathrm{MIX}}$	Mix dummy profile, $\mathbf{q}_{\mathrm{MIX}} \doteq [p_{1,\mathrm{MIX}}, p_{2,\mathrm{MIX}}, \cdots, p_{M,\mathrm{MIX}}]^T$
$\mathbf{p}_j$	Unnormalized receiver profile for receiver j, $\mathbf{p}_j \doteq [p_{j,1}, p_{j,2}, \cdots, p_{j,N}]^T$
$\mathbf{p}$	Vector of transition probabilities, $\mathbf{p} \doteq [\mathbf{p}_1^T, \mathbf{p}_2^T, \cdots, \mathbf{p}_M^T]^T$
P_{λ_i}	Probability that user i sends a real message instead of a dummy
δ_{MIX}	Average number of mix-based dummies generated by the mix each round
ρ	Number of rounds observed by the adversary
$x_{\lambda,i}^r(x_{\delta,i}^r)$	Number of real (dummy) messages sent by user i in round r
x_i^r	Total number of messages sent by user i in round r, $x_i^r \doteq x_{\lambda,i}^r + x_{\delta,i}^r$
$x_{s,i}^r$	Number of real messages sent by user i that leave the pool in round r
$y_{\lambda,j}^r(y_{\delta,j}^r)$	Number of real (dummy) messages received by j in round r
y_j^r	Total number of messages received by j in round r, $y_j^r \doteq y_{\lambda,j}^r + y_{\delta,j}^r$
x_{MIX}^r	Number of mix-based dummies generated by the mix in round r
$\mathbf{U}\ (\mathbf{U}_s)$	$\rho \times N$ matrix with all input observations $(\mathbf{U})_{r,i} = x_i^r\ ((\mathbf{U}_s)_{r,i} = x_{s,i}^r)$
$\mathbf{H}\ (\mathbf{H}_s)$	$\mathbf{I}_M \otimes \mathbf{U}\ (\mathbf{I}_M \otimes \mathbf{U}_s)$
$\mathbf{y}_j$	Column vector containing the values y_j^r for $r = 1, \cdots, \rho$
$\mathbf{y}_{\delta,j}$	Column vector containing the values $y_{\lambda,j}^r$ for $r = 1, \cdots, \rho$
$\mathbf{y}$	Column vector containing all the output messages $\mathbf{y} \doteq [\mathbf{y}_1^T, \mathbf{y}_2^T, \cdots, \mathbf{y}_M^T]^T$
$\mathbf{y}_\delta$	Vector of output dummies $\mathbf{y}_\delta \doteq [\mathbf{y}_{\delta,1}^T, \mathbf{y}_{\delta,2}^T, \cdots, \mathbf{y}_{\delta,M}^T]^T$
$\hat{p}_{j,i}, \hat{\mathbf{p}}_j, \hat{\mathbf{p}},$	Adversary's estimation of $p_{j,i}$, $\mathbf{p}_j$ and $\mathbf{p}$, respectively.
$\hat{\mathbf{y}}_\delta, \hat{\mathbf{y}}_{\delta,j}.$	Adversary's estimation of $\mathbf{y}_{\delta,j}$ and $\mathbf{y}_\delta$.
$\hat{\mathbf{U}}_s, \hat{\mathbf{H}}_s.$	Adversary's estimation of $\mathbf{U}_s$ and $\mathbf{H}_s$.

in order to get an estimator $\hat{\mathbf{p}}$ that is not only unbiased, but also *asymptotically efficient*, i.e., the vector of estimated probabilities $\hat{\mathbf{p}}$ converges to the true value as the number of observations increases $\rho \to \infty$.

From the relations among the variables in Fig. 1, we can compute the expected value of the output $\mathbf{Y}(\mathbf{p})$ given the input observations $\mathbf{U}$ obtaining $E\{\mathbf{Y}(\mathbf{p})\} = \hat{\mathbf{H}}_s \cdot \mathbf{p} + \hat{\mathbf{y}}_\delta$ (see Appendix), where

- $\hat{\mathbf{H}}_s \doteq \mathbf{I}_M \otimes \hat{\mathbf{U}}_s$, and $\hat{\mathbf{U}}_s$ (see (31)) is the matrix containing the attacker's estimation of the hidden random variables $X_{s,i}^r$, which model the number of messages from user i that leave the mix in round r (cf. Fig. 1).
- $\hat{\mathbf{y}}_\delta$ is the adversary's estimation of the number of mix-based dummies that are sent to each receiver in each round, and is given by $\hat{\mathbf{y}}_\delta = (\mathbf{I}_M \otimes \delta_{\mathrm{MIX}} \mathbf{1}_\rho) \cdot \mathbf{q}_{\mathrm{MIX}}$.

Interestingly, removing the constraints from (2) leads to an estimator which is still unbiased and asymptotically efficient, as proven in [13], and also makes a

detailed performance analysis manageable as we show in Sect. 4. In the rest of
this section we focus on the unconstrained estimator and refer to [13] for further
information about the constrained variant. The solution to the unconstrained
problem

$$\hat{\mathbf{p}} = \underset{\mathbf{q}_i \ i=1,\cdots,N}{\arg\min} \left\{ \|\mathbf{y} - \hat{\mathbf{H}}_s \cdot \mathbf{p} - \hat{\mathbf{y}}_\delta\|^2 \right\} \tag{3}$$

is given by the Moore-Penrose pseudo-inverse, i.e., $\hat{\mathbf{p}} = (\hat{\mathbf{H}}_s^T \hat{\mathbf{H}}_s)^{-1} \hat{\mathbf{H}}_s^T (\mathbf{y} - \hat{\mathbf{y}}_\delta)$.
This solution can be decoupled [13] resulting in a more tractable and efficient
equation, where $\hat{\mathbf{y}}_{\delta,j} \doteq \delta_{\text{MIX}} p_{j,\text{MIX}} \mathbf{1}_\rho$ contains the expected number of mix-based
dummies sent to receiver j in each round,

$$\hat{\mathbf{p}}_j = (\hat{\mathbf{U}}_s^T \hat{\mathbf{U}}_s)^{-1} \hat{\mathbf{U}}_s^T (\mathbf{y}_j - \hat{\mathbf{y}}_{\delta,j}) \qquad j = 1, \cdots, M \tag{4}$$

Given the system parameters as well as the input and output observations $\mathbf{U}$ and
$\mathbf{y}$, the adversary can use (4) to get an estimation of the users' sending profiles.

4   Performance Analysis of the Least Squares Estimator in a Timed Pool Mix Anonymous Communication System with Dummies

In this section, we assess the performance of the least-squares estimator in (4)
with respect to its profiling accuracy, measured as the Mean Squared Error of the
estimated transition probabilities $p_{j,i}$ ($\text{MSE}_{j,i} = |\hat{p}_{j,i} - p_{j,i}|^2$) representing users'
behavior. We have chosen to analyze the performance of this estimator because
it is, to the best of our knowledge, the best estimator of the users' profiles that
accounts for dummy traffic. The only attack in the literature extended to cover
dummy traffic is the Statistical Disclosure Attack (SDA) [10, 11] and it is already
shown in [13, 14] that the least squares-based approach performs asymptotically
better than SDA. It must be noted that the Bayesian inference estimator (Vida)
in [4] may return a better estimation than our least squares estimator. However,
its computational cost is huge even for a threshold mix [13] and it would become
prohibitive in a pool mix with dummies.

For the performance analysis in this section, we consider the particular case
when the anonymous communication channel is a *binomial timed pool mix* [15],
and the number of messages sent by the users, as well as the dummies generated
by the mix, are Poisson-distributed. In a binomial timed pool mix, the firing
condition is a timeout and the batching strategy mandates that individual mes-
sages leave the pool with probability α every round, i.e., $F_{r,k} = \alpha(1 - \alpha)^{r-k}$.
The behavior of this mix is stationary, since the value of $F_{r,k}$ only depends on
the difference $r - k$. Using λ_i as the *sending rate*, and δ_i as the *dummy rate*,
representing the average number of real messages, respectively dummies, sent by
user i, this scenario can be summarized as

$$X_{\lambda,i}^r \sim \text{Poiss}(\lambda_i), \quad X_{\delta,i}^r \sim \text{Poiss}(\delta_i), \quad X_{\text{MIX}}^r \sim \text{Poiss}(\delta_{\text{MIX}})$$

$$P_{\lambda_i} = \lambda_i/(\lambda_i + \delta_i), \quad F_{r,k} = \alpha(1 - \alpha)^{r-k} \tag{5}$$

Even though the results we provide correspond to the above case we must stress that the reasoning followed in the derivation is applicable to any other system that can be represented by the model in Sect. 2.

4.1 Profiling Error of the Least Squares Estimator

Under the hypotheses stated in (5), the least squares estimator is unbiased and, defining $\alpha_q \doteq \alpha/(2-\alpha)$ and $\alpha_r \doteq \alpha(2-\alpha)/(2-\alpha(2-\alpha))$, the $\text{MSE}_{j,i}$ of a single transition probability estimated is given by [16]:

$$\text{MSE}_{j,i} \approx \frac{1}{\rho} \cdot \frac{1}{\alpha_q} \cdot \frac{1}{\lambda_i} \cdot \left(1 + \frac{\delta_i}{\lambda_i}\right) \cdot \left(1 - \frac{\lambda_i + \delta_i}{\sum_{k=1}^{N}(\lambda_k + \delta_k)}\right) \cdot$$

$$\left(\sum_{k=1}^{N} \lambda_k p_{j,k} + \delta_{\text{MIX}} p_{j,\text{MIX}} - \frac{\alpha_q}{\alpha_r} \sum_{k=1}^{N} \lambda_k P_{\lambda_k} p_{j,k}^2\right)$$

(6)

This result holds when: i) the probability that each sender sends a message to receiver j is negligible when compared to the rate at which receiver j receives messages from all users ($p_{j,i} \ll \sum_k \lambda_k p_{j,k}$), ii) the number of rounds observed is large enough ($\rho \to \infty$), and iii) $\lambda_i + \delta_i \ll (\sum_k(\lambda_k + \delta_k))^2$.

Interestingly, the terms in (6) that depend on i and j in can be decoupled,

$$\text{MSE}_{j,i} \approx \frac{1}{\rho} \cdot \frac{1}{\alpha_q} \cdot \epsilon_s(i) \cdot \epsilon_r(j) \tag{7}$$

where $\epsilon_s(i)$ and $\epsilon_r(j)$ denote functions that only depend on the sender i and the receiver j respectively. This property proves to be very useful when designing strategies to distribute the dummy traffic as we later see in Sect. 5.

The latter expression allows to extract qualitative conclusions on the protection dummy traffic offers to senders and receivers. As it was already shown in [13], the MSE decreases with the number of rounds observed as $1/\rho$, and delaying messages in the pool increases the $\text{MSE}_{j,i}$ by a factor $(2-\alpha)/\alpha$ with respect to a scenario with no delay (i.e., $\alpha = 1$).

We now analyze the contribution to the MSE of the users' behavior. The sender-side contribution $\epsilon_s(i)$ consists of three terms:

$$\epsilon_s(i) = \frac{1}{\lambda_i} \cdot \left(1 + \frac{\delta_i}{\lambda_i}\right) \cdot \left(1 - \frac{\lambda_i + \delta_i}{\sum_{k=1}^{N}(\lambda_k + \delta_k)}\right) \tag{8}$$

1. The term $1/\lambda_i$ implies that the error when estimating the profile $\mathbf{q}_i = [p_{1,i}, \cdots, p_{M,i}]^T$ decreases as that user participates in the system more often. Naturally, when more information about the user becomes available to the adversary, it becomes easier to accurately estimate her behavior.
2. The second term, $1 + \delta_i/\lambda_i$, is always larger or equal than one, meaning that sender-based dummies always hinder the attacker's estimation. The weight

of this component depends on the ratio between the dummy rate and the sending rate. Hence, a user who sends real messages very often would need to send many more dummies to get the same level of protection than a user who rarely participates in the system.

3. The last term is in general negligible since, in a normal scenario, the participation of a single user is negigible when compared to the total traffic, i.e., $\lambda_i + \delta_i \ll \sum_{k=1}^{N}(\lambda_k + \delta_k)$. However, when user i's traffic is clearly dominant among the others, this term decreases the overall gain i gets from dummies. Therefore, although sender-based dummies always increase the protection of a user, they offer diminishing returns when only one user is trying to protect herself by sending dummies.

On the other hand, receiver-side contribution, $\epsilon_r(j)$, consists of three summands:

$$\epsilon_r(j) = \sum_{k=1}^{N} \lambda_k p_{j,k} + \delta_{\text{MIX}} p_{j,\text{MIX}} - \frac{\alpha_q}{\alpha_r} \sum_{k=1}^{N} \lambda_k P_{\lambda_k} p_{j,k}^2 \qquad (9)$$

1. The first summand is the rate at which j receives real messages from the senders. We call this term *receiver rate* and denote it by λ'_j. It is interesting to note that, contrary to the sending rates where large values of λ_i compromise the anonymity of the senders; large values of receiver rates increase the protection of the receivers. In other words, it is harder for the attacker to estimate probabilities related to a receiver which is contacted by a large number of senders than related to one receiving few messages.

2. The second summand is the rate at which j receives dummy messages from the mix. The interesting part about this summand is that it can be adjusted by the mix, to give more protection to a specific receiver j by increasing the number of dummies addressed to that recipient, i.e., increasing $p_{j,\text{MIX}}$.

3. The last summand depends on the mix parameters and the users' behavior. Since $\alpha_q/\alpha_r \leq 1$ and $P_{\lambda_k} \leq 1$, when users do not focus their messages in few others, i.e., $p_{j,i} \ll 1$, this summand becomes negligible. However, if there is no dummy traffic ($P_{\lambda_k} = 1$ and $\delta_{\text{MIX}} = 0$) and no pool is implemented ($\alpha_q/\alpha_r = 1$), this term must be taken into account. In this case $\epsilon_r(j)$ depends on the variance of the outputs, i.e. $\sum_{k=1}^{N} \lambda_k p_{j,k}(1 - p_{j,k})$, meaning that it would easier for the attacker to estimate probabilities $p_{j,k}$ of receivers that get messages from senders whose behavior has low variance (i.e., senders that always choose the same receiver, $p_{j,k} = 1$, or users that never send to a receiver, $p_{j,k} = 0$). Adding delay or introducing dummy traffic increases the variance of the output, thus reducing the dependency of the error on the sending profiles.

The fact that we can differentiate the contribution of i and j in (6) also allows for a graphic interpretation of the adversary's estimation error. Figure 2a represents the values of $\text{MSE}_{j,i}$ as a function of i and j, in a scenario without dummies where for simplicity we have assumed that the sending rates are distributed in ascending order according to the senders' index i, and the receiving rates are

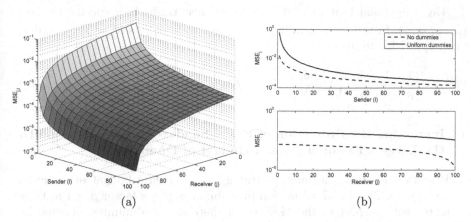

Fig. 2. (a) $\text{MSE}_{j,i}$ as a function of i and j in a scenario where λ_i are sorted in ascending order and λ'_j in descending order. (b) Comparison of the average $\text{MSE}_{j,i}$ along j and i with and without dummies. ($N = 100$, $M = 100$, $\rho = 10\,000$, $\alpha = 0.5$, $\sum \lambda_k = 500$. In (b), $\delta_{\text{SEND}} = \delta_{\text{MIX}} = 250$).

distributed in descending order according to the receivers' index j. Fig. 2b shows the average $\text{MSE}_{j,i}$ over j and i, offering a comparison with a system where the distribution of the dummies is uniform in both the input and output flows: $\epsilon_s(i)$ determines the evolution of $\text{MSE}_{j,i}$ with i (top) and $\epsilon_r(j)$ the evolution with j (bottom). This means that by distributing dummies among sender-based and mix-based dummies, which in turn modify the value of $\epsilon_s(i)$ and $\epsilon_r(j)$, we can shape the $\text{MSE}_{j,i}$. We use this idea in the next section to design dummy strategies that satisfy different privacy criteria.

5   Designing Dummy Traffic Strategies

In this section, we study how to distribute dummy traffic in order to guarantee different privacy criteria. In other words, we aim at finding the values of the parameters δ_i for $i \in \{1, \cdots, N\}$ and $p_{j,\text{MIX}}$ for $j \in \{1, \cdots, M\}$ that maximize a certain cost function representing some privacy objective. We consider that the mix performs this optimization and informs each user i of the amount of dummies δ_i she must send on average. The implementation of the return channel is left out of the scope of this paper. We assume that the *total number of dummies* δ_{TOT} that can be sent *on average* per round is constrained. We denote the average number of sender-based dummies on each round as $\delta_{\text{SEND}} \doteq \sum_{i=1}^{N} \delta_i$, and the average number of mix-based dummies as δ_{MIX}. We put no restriction on the distribution of dummies among senders and mix other than $\delta_{\text{SEND}} + \delta_{\text{MIX}} \leq \delta_{\text{TOT}}$. For notational simplicity, in the remainder of the section we omit the constraints $0 \leq p_{j,\text{MIX}} \leq 1$, $\sum_{j=1}^{M} p_{j,\text{MIX}}$, $\delta_i \geq 0$ and $\sum_{i=1}^{N} \delta_i = \delta_{\text{SEND}}$ in the equations.

In order to keep the optimization problems tractable, we assume that the contribution of a single user to the total input traffic is negligible (i.e., $\lambda_i + \delta_i \ll$

$\sum_{k=1}^{N}(\lambda_k + \delta_k))$ and that users do not focus their traffic in a specific receiver (i.e., $p_{j,i} \ll 1$). In this case, defining the receiver rate of j as $\lambda'_j \doteq \sum_{k=1}^{N} \lambda_k p_{j,k}$, we can approximate (6) as:

$$\widetilde{\text{MSE}}_{j,i} = \frac{1}{\rho} \cdot \frac{1}{\alpha_q} \cdot \frac{1}{\lambda_i} \cdot \left(1 + \frac{\delta_i}{\lambda_i}\right) \cdot (\lambda'_j + \delta_{\text{MIX}} p_{j,\text{MIX}}) = \frac{1}{\rho} \cdot \frac{1}{\alpha_q} \cdot \tilde{\epsilon}_s(i) \cdot \tilde{\epsilon}_r(j) \quad (10)$$

5.1   Increasing the Protection of Every Sender-Receiver Relation by the Largest Factor β given a Budget of Dummies δ_{TOT}

In this section we design a dummy strategy that, given a budget of dummies δ_{TOT}, increases $\text{MSE}_{j,i}$ of each transition probability $p_{j,i}$ by a factor $\beta \geq 1$ as large as possible with respect to the MSE when there are no dummies, denoted by $\text{MSE}^0_{j,i}$. Departing from (10) we can formalize this problem as:

$$\begin{array}{ll}
\underset{\delta_1, \cdots, \delta_N, q_{\text{MIX}}}{\text{maximize}} & \widetilde{\text{MSE}}_{j,i}, \qquad \forall i, j \\[2mm]
\text{subject to} & \widetilde{\text{MSE}}_{j,i} = \beta \cdot \widetilde{\text{MSE}}^0_{j,i}, \qquad \forall i, j \\[2mm]
& \delta_{\text{SEND}} + \delta_{\text{MIX}} = \delta_{\text{TOT}}
\end{array} \qquad (11)$$

Since the effects of the sender-based and mix-based dummies can be decoupled, we can split the optimization into three subproblems:

1. Find the distribution of δ_i that increases $\tilde{\epsilon}_s(i)$ by a factor β_{SEND} for all i.
2. Find the distribution of $p_{j,\text{MIX}}$ that increases $\tilde{\epsilon}_r(j)$ by a factor β_{MIX} for all j.
3. Find the distribution of δ_{TOT} between δ_{SEND} and δ_{MIX} that maximizes the overall increase $\beta = \beta_{\text{SEND}} \cdot \beta_{\text{MIX}}$.

Optimal Distribution of Sender-Based Dummies. We want to find the distribution of δ_i among senders that increases $\tilde{\epsilon}_s(i)$ by a factor β_{SEND} compared to the dummy-free case. Since $\tilde{\epsilon}_s(i) = 1/\lambda_i \left(1 + \frac{\delta_i}{\lambda_i}\right)$, sending δ_i dummies increases the MSE in a factor $\beta_{\text{SEND}} = 1 + \delta_i/\lambda_i$. We can now obtain the sender based dummy distribution, ensuring the that $\sum_{i=1}^{N} \delta_i = \delta_{\text{SEND}}$, as follows:

$$\beta_{\text{SEND}} = 1 + \frac{\delta_{\text{SEND}}}{\sum_{k=1}^{N} \lambda_k} \implies \delta_i = \frac{\lambda_i}{\sum_{k=1}^{N} \lambda_k} \cdot \delta_{\text{SEND}}, \qquad \forall i \qquad (12)$$

This confirms the intuition given in Sect. 4, that the number of dummies a user should send to achieve a certain level of protection is proportional to her sending rate of real messages.

Optimal Distribution of Mix-Based Dummies. Similarly, we want to find the distribution of $p_{j,\text{MIX}}$ among receivers that increases $\tilde{\epsilon}_r(j)$ by a factor β_{MIX} compared to the dummy-free case. Since $\tilde{\epsilon}_r(j) = \lambda'_j + \delta_{\text{MIX}} p_{j,\text{MIX}}$, assigning sending dummies with probability $p_{j,\text{MIX}}$ to receiver j increases the MSE by a factor

$\beta_{\text{MIX}} = 1 + \delta_{\text{MIX}} p_{j,\text{MIX}} / \lambda'_j$. We can now obtain the sender-based dummy distribution, ensuring that $\sum_{j=1}^{M} p_{j,\text{MIX}} = 1$, as follows:

$$\beta_{\text{MIX}} = 1 + \frac{\delta_{\text{MIX}}}{\sum_{m=1}^{M} \lambda'_m} \Longrightarrow p_{j,\text{MIX}} = \frac{\lambda'_j}{\sum_{m=1}^{M} \lambda'_m}, \qquad \forall j \qquad (13)$$

As said in Sect. 4, the protection that receivers enjoy is proportional to their receiving rate. Therefore, to increase all $\text{MSE}_{j,i}$s by the same factor, more mix-based dummies have to be given to those receivers that receive more real messages.

Optimal Distribution of the Overall Amount of Dummies. Using the distributions obtained, and since $\sum_{k=1}^{N} \lambda_k = \sum_{m=1}^{M} \lambda'_m$, we can write $\widetilde{\text{MSE}}_{j,i}$ as

$$\widetilde{\text{MSE}}_{j,i} = \widetilde{\text{MSE}}_{j,i}^{0} \cdot \beta_{\text{SEND}} \cdot \beta_{\text{MIX}} = \widetilde{\text{MSE}}_{j,i}^{0} \left(1 + \frac{\delta_{\text{SEND}}}{\sum_{k=1}^{N} \lambda_k} \right) \left(1 + \frac{\delta_{\text{MIX}}}{\sum_{k=1}^{N} \lambda_k} \right) \qquad (14)$$

The distribution of the total amount of dummies that maximizes the increase in $\widetilde{\text{MSE}}_{j,i}$ is therefore $\delta_{\text{SEND}} = \delta_{\text{MIX}} = \delta_{\text{TOT}}/2$. This result is particularly interesting: if we are to increase the relative protection of each user equally, the protection we get from sender-based and mix-based dummies is the same regardless of the system parameters. That is, assigning all our available dummies to the senders or to the mix is equivalent in terms of MSE, and distributing the dummies evenly between the input and output flow is optimal, being the maximum achievable gain $\beta \approx \left(1 + \frac{\delta_{\text{TOT}}}{2 \sum_k \lambda_k} \right)^2$.

5.2   Increasing the Minimum Protection to Every Sender-Receiver Relation given a Budget of Dummies δ_{TOT}

Our second design strategy consists in ensuring that, given a budget of dummies δ_{TOT}, the distribution maximizes the minimum level of protection for all relationships in the system. This implies that dummies are assigned to senders i and receivers j in relationships whose estimation error $\text{MSE}_{j,i}$ is low, in order to increase the minimum $\text{MSE}_{j,i}$ in the system. From a graphical point of view, we can see this as a two-dimensional waterfilling problem: we need to increase the lower $\text{MSE}_{j,i}$ in Fig. 2a up to a minimum, which can be larger as more dummies δ_{TOT} are available. More formally, we want to solve:

$$\begin{array}{cc} \underset{\delta_1, \cdots, \delta_N, \mathbf{q}_{\text{MIX}}}{\text{maximize}} & \underset{i,j}{\min} \widetilde{\text{MSE}}_{j,i} \\ \text{subject to} & \delta_{\text{SEND}} + \delta_{\text{MIX}} = \delta_{\text{TOT}} \end{array} \qquad (15)$$

As in the previous problem, we can separate the problem in three steps:

1. Find the distribution of δ_i that maximizes $\min_i \tilde{\epsilon}_s(i)$.
2. Find the distribution of $p_{j,\text{MIX}}$ that maximizes $\min_j \tilde{\epsilon}_r(j)$.
3. Find the distribution of δ_{TOT} among δ_{SEND} and δ_{MIX} that maximizes the minimum $\text{MSE}_{j,i}$ in the system.

Optimal Distribution for Sender-Based Dummies. We aim at finding the distribution of $\{\delta_i\}$ that increases the minimum value of $\tilde{\epsilon}_s(i) = \frac{1}{\lambda_i}\left(1 + \frac{\delta_i}{\lambda_i}\right)$ over i, making it as large as possible given the budget of dummies. Formally,

$$\underset{\delta_1,\cdots,\delta_N}{\text{maximize}} \quad \underset{i}{\min}\ \tilde{\epsilon}_s(i)$$

$$\text{subject to} \quad \sum_{i=1}^{N}\delta_i = \delta_{\text{SEND}} \tag{16}$$

Let $\mathcal{A}$ be the set containing the indices of those senders to whom we assign dummies, i.e., $\mathcal{A} \doteq \{i : \delta_i > 0\}$. Let $\tilde{\epsilon}_{s,\text{MIN}}$ be the minimum value of $\tilde{\epsilon}_s(i)$ we achieve with this strategy. Then, the following statements are true:

- We do not assign sender-based dummies to those users k whose $\tilde{\epsilon}_s(k) \geq \tilde{\epsilon}_{s,\text{MIN}}$ without dummies; i.e., we only use sender-based dummies to help users achieve that minimum.
- There is no gain in assigning dummies to a user k if by doing so we are increasing $\tilde{\epsilon}_s(k)$ above any other $\tilde{\epsilon}_s(i)$; every user $k \in \mathcal{A}$ fullfills $\tilde{\epsilon}_s(k) = \tilde{\epsilon}_{s,\text{MIN}}$.

Given $\tilde{\epsilon}_s(k) = \tilde{\epsilon}_{s,\text{MIN}}$, and to ensure $\sum_{k=1}^{N}\delta_k = \sum_{k\in\mathcal{A}}\delta_k = \delta_{\text{SEND}}$ we can get an expression for $\tilde{\epsilon}_{s,\text{MIN}}$:

$$\tilde{\epsilon}_{s,\text{MIN}} = \frac{1}{\lambda_k}\left(1 + \frac{\delta_k}{\lambda_k}\right) \implies \tilde{\epsilon}_{s,\text{MIN}} = \frac{\delta_{\text{SEND}} + \sum_{k\in\mathcal{A}}\lambda_k}{\sum_{k\in\mathcal{A}}\lambda_k^2} \tag{17}$$

In order to compute $\mathcal{A}$, we assume w.l.o.g. that the indices are given to users such that their sending frequencies are sorted in *descending* order, $\lambda_1 \geq \cdots \geq \lambda_N$ and we let $\mathcal{A}_i \doteq \{1,\cdots,i\}$. Then, $\mathcal{A} = \mathcal{A}_n$ where n is the minimum value that meets[1]

$$\frac{1}{\lambda_n} \leq \frac{\delta_{\text{SEND}} + \sum_{k\in\mathcal{A}_n}\lambda_k}{\sum_{k\in\mathcal{A}_n}\lambda_k^2} \leq \frac{1}{\lambda_{n+1}} \tag{18}$$

Finally, we assign

$$\delta_i = \begin{cases} \lambda_i\left(\lambda_i\tilde{\epsilon}_{s,\text{MIN}} - 1\right), & \text{if } i \in \mathcal{A}_n \\ 0, & \text{otherwise.} \end{cases} \tag{19}$$

Optimal Distribution for Mix-Based Dummies. Similarly, we aim at finding the distribution of $p_{j,\text{MIX}}$ among receivers that increases the minimum value of $\tilde{\epsilon}_r(j)$, making it as large as possible given the budget of dummies. Using $\tilde{\epsilon}_r(j) = \lambda'_j + \delta_{\text{MIX}}p_{j,\text{MIX}}$, the problem can be formulated as:

$$\underset{p_{1,\text{MIX}},\cdots,p_{M,\text{MIX}}}{\text{maximize}} \quad \underset{j}{\min}\ \tilde{\epsilon}_r(j)$$

$$\text{subject to} \quad \sum_{j=1}^{M}p_{j,\text{MIX}} = 1 \tag{20}$$

---

[1] If the condition is not met because all $1/\lambda_n \leq \tilde{\epsilon}_{s,\text{MIN}}(\mathcal{A}_n)$, then we can assume that $n = N$, i.e., all users will send dummies.

We define the set $\mathcal{B}$ as the send of receivers that get mix-based dummies, $\mathcal{B} \doteq \{j : p_{j,\text{MIX}} > 0\}$ and the minimum value of our optimization function we achieve with this strategy as $\tilde{\epsilon}_{r,\text{MIN}}$. Then, following the procedure described above, we get

$$\tilde{\epsilon}_{r,\text{MIN}} = \frac{\delta_{\text{MIX}} + \sum_{j \in \mathcal{B}} \lambda'_j}{|\mathcal{B}|} \tag{21}$$

where $|\mathcal{B}|$ denotes the number of elements of $\mathcal{B}$. If the receiver rates are sorted in *ascending* order, $\lambda'_1 \leq \lambda'_2 \leq \cdots \leq \lambda'_M$ and $\mathcal{B}_j \doteq \{1, 2, \cdots, j\}$, then the set of receivers that receive dummy messages is $\mathcal{B} = \mathcal{B}_n$ where the value of n is the smallest that meets

$$\lambda'_n \leq \frac{\delta_{\text{MIX}} + \sum_{j \in \mathcal{B}_n} \lambda'_j}{|\mathcal{B}_n|} \leq \lambda'_{n+1} \tag{22}$$

Finally, we assign

$$p_{j,\text{MIX}} = \begin{cases} \dfrac{1}{\delta_{\text{MIX}}} \left(\tilde{\epsilon}_{r,\text{MIN}} - \lambda'_j \right), & \text{if } j \in \mathcal{B}_n \\ 0, & \text{otherwise.} \end{cases} \tag{23}$$

Optimal Distribution of the Overall Amount of Dummies. In this case we cannot get a closed-form expression for the optimal distribution of δ_{TOT} among δ_{SEND} and δ_{MIX}, since it depends on the sizes of the sets $\mathcal{A}$ and $\mathcal{B}$. The minimum $\widetilde{\text{MSE}}_{j,i}$ we achieve is for relationships where both sender and receiver are allocated dummies. Plugging the distributions (19) and (23) into (10), we obtain

$$\min_{j,i} \widetilde{\text{MSE}} = \frac{1}{\rho} \cdot \frac{1}{\alpha_q} \cdot \frac{\delta_{\text{SEND}} + \sum_{k \in \mathcal{A}} \lambda_k}{\sum_{k \in \mathcal{A}} \lambda_k^2} \cdot \frac{\delta_{\text{MIX}} + \sum_{m \in \mathcal{B}} \lambda'_m}{|\mathcal{B}|} \tag{24}$$

Optimal values for δ_{SEND} and δ_{MIX} can be computed by performing an exhaustive search along $\delta_{\text{SEND}} + \delta_{\text{MIX}} = \delta_{\text{TOT}}$, computing each time the sets $\mathcal{A}$ and $\mathcal{B}$ as explained above. It is interesting to note that, if the number of dummies available is large enough, i.e., $\delta_{\text{TOT}} \to \infty$, every sender and receiver is assigned dummies. In this case, since $\sum_{k=1}^{N} \lambda_k = \sum_{m=1}^{M} \lambda'_m$, the optimal strategy would be to distribute the total amount of dummies evenly between the input and the output traffics, i.e., $\delta_{\text{SEND}} = \delta_{\text{MIX}} = \delta_{\text{TOT}}/2$.

6   Evaluation

In this section we evaluate the performance of the dummy traffic design strategies designed in Sect. 5, and validate them against the theoretical bound for the adversary's error in (6) through a simulator written in the Matlab language.[2] The scope of this analysis is focused on supporting our theoretical findings rather than comparing our estimator with existing attacks.

---

[2] The code will be available upon request.

Experimental Setup. We simulate a system with $N = 100$ senders and $M = 100$ receivers. The sending frequencies of the users are sorted in ascending order, in such a way that λ_i is proportional to i, and the average total number of real messages sent by all users is $\sum \lambda_i = 500$. The sending profiles $\mathbf{q}_i$ are set such that user i sends messages to herself and all other users $k < i$ with the same probability, i.e., $p_{j,i} = 1/i$ if $j \leq i$ and $p_{j,i} = 0$. This ensures that receiving rates λ_j' are sorted in descending order. The probability that a message is fired after each round is set to $\alpha = 0.5$, and the number of rounds observed by the attacker is $\rho = 10\,000$. The theoretical $\text{MSE}_{j,i}$ for this scenario without dummies is shown in Fig. 2a. Though not realistic, this experiment is sufficient to illustrate the operation of the strategies in Sect. 5. The amount of dummies that users and mix send and their distribution change between experiments. We run four experiments, two for each dummy strategy in Sect. 5. We repeat each experiment 200 times and plot the average results.

6.1 Increasing the Protection of Every Sender-Receiver Relation by the Largest Factor β Given a Budget of Dummies δ_{TOT}

First, we study the influence of the distribution of dummies among senders and mix in the factor β that can be achieved with this strategy, when on average $\delta_{\text{TOT}} = 500$ dummies per round are available. Figure 3a shows the evolution of β for different distributions of dummy messages between senders (δ_{SEND}) and mix (δ_{MIX}). We see that the maximum increase is achieved when dummies are divided equally between the senders and the mix, as predicted in Sect. 5.1. We note that the maximum β in the figure is slightly higher than $\beta = 2.25$ that would be obtained using the approximation (10) used to design the dummy traffic strategy, meaning that the adversary estimation is worse than predicted by the theory.

For the particular case where $\delta_{\text{SEND}} = \delta_{\text{MIX}} = \delta_{\text{TOT}}/2$, we plot in Fig. 3b the average $\text{MSE}_{j,i}$ over i (top) and j (bottom) with and without dummies (note the vertical axis logarithmic scale). We see that indeed all $\text{MSE}_{j,i}$ increase by a constant factor, $\beta = 2.261$. The figure also shows that (6) accurately models the profiling error.

6.2 Maximizing the Minimum Protection to Every Sender-Receiver Relation Given a Budget of Dummies δ_{TOT}

First, we study the influence of the distribution of dummies among senders and mix on the maximum minimum $\text{MSE}_{j,i}$ that can be achieved with this strategy, when on average $\delta_{\text{TOT}} = 500$ dummies per round are available. Fig. 4a shows the evolution of the average minimum $\text{MSE}_{j,i}$ depending on the distribution of dummies between the senders and the mix. In the scenario considered in our experiment, the maximum minimum $\text{MSE}_{j,i}$ achievable is obtained when approximately 40% of the dummies are assigned to the senders and the remaining 60% to the mix. This is because, in this strategy, the rate of sender-based dummies depends quadratically on the real sending rate (c.f. (19)), while the number of

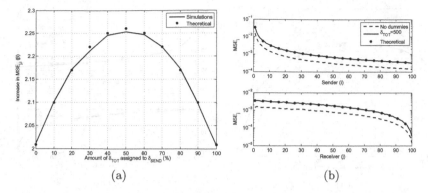

Fig. 3. (a) Evolution of β with the fraction of dummies distributed among senders and mix. (b) Average $\text{MSE}_{j,i}$ evolution over i (top) and j (bottom) when dummies are distributed uniformly among senders and mix. ($N = 100$, $M = 100$, $\rho = 10\,000$, $\alpha = 0.5$, $\delta_{\text{TOT}} = 500$).

mix-based dummies depends linearly on the real receiving rate (c.f. (23)). Hence, mix-based dummies can be distributed more efficiently and it is preferable to assign the mix a larger budget than to the senders. We note that this result depends strongly on the users behavior. In fact, if the real traffic is distributed uniformly among receivers but few senders generate the majority of the traffic, allocating a large fraction of dummy traffic to the senders becomes the best option.

This is better shown in Fig. 4b. The top plot shows the $\text{MSE}_{j,i}$ along i when there are no dummies, and when only sender-based dummies are available ($\delta_{\text{SEND}} = \delta_{\text{TOT}}$; $\delta_{\text{MIX}} = 0$). As expected, more dummies increase the minimum $\text{MSE}_{j,i}$, but, since the average number of sender-based dummies depends quadratically on the real sending rate, few senders with high rates exhaust the budget, which constrains the maximum minimum error achievable in the system. On the other hand, allocating all the dummies to the mix (Fig. 4b, bottom) allows to spread the distribution of dummies among more relationships, which in turn provides better overall protection than the previous case.

7 Discussion

In this section we discuss how to adapt the derivation of the least squares estimator in Sect. 3 to scenarios where pool and users' behavior are outside of the model considered throughout the document.

Non-static Sending Profiles. In practice users' behavior is expected to change over time. Our estimator can be adapted to account for dynamic profiles by implementing the Recursive Least Squares algorithm [17]. This algorithm includes a *forgetting factor*, which determines how fast the algorithm "forgets" past observations. Tuning this parameter, one can choose between getting a high-variance

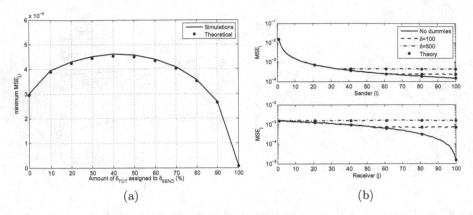

Fig. 4. (a) Evolution of the minimum $\mathrm{MSE}_{j,i}$ with the fraction of dummies distributed among senders and mix. (b) Average $\mathrm{MSE}_{j,i}$ evolution over i when only sender-based dummies are available (top), and j when only mix-based dummies are available (bottom). ($N = 100$, $M = 100$, $\rho = 10\,000$, $\alpha = 0.5$, $\delta_{\mathrm{TOT}} = 100, 500$).

estimator of the recent users' sending profile or obtaining a more stable long-term sending profile.

Non-independent Users with Memory. Although our model considers disjoint sets of senders and receivers, it can easily accommodate the case where users both send and receive messages. In this scenario, users' sending behavior may be dependent on messages sent or received in the past (e.g., email replies). Given a model of these interactions between users one can compute the expected value of the output observations given the inputs, and then proceed with the derivation of the estimator as in Sect. 3.

Non-static Dummy Strategies. If the probability of sending a real message (P_{λ_i}) changes over time, a per-round probability $P_{\lambda_i}^r$ could be defined. This dynamic probability can be used in the derivations in the Appendix (c.f. (30)) to account for the effect of this variation on the attacker's estimation of the hidden variables $X_{s,i}^r$. When the average mix-based dummies (δ_{MIX}) or the mix profile ($\mathbf{q}_{\mathrm{MIX}}$) vary over time, an aware attacker can include this behavior in (26), modifying the expected value of the outputs. Designing adaptive dummy strategies is left as subject for future work.

Complex Batching Strategies. Our anonymous channel model does not cover pool mixes whose batching strategy depends on the number of messages in the pool, such as that used by Mixmaster [12]. However, extending our model to this scenario is straightforward: the adversary can estimate the average number of messages in the pool by discarding a percentage of the incoming messages that are expected to be dummy, and therefore she can get an estimate of the average number of messages from each user that leave in each round, $X_{s,i}^r$. The estimator would still be formulated as (4).

8   Conclusions

In this paper, we have proposed a methodology to analyze mix-based anonymous communication systems with dummy traffic. Following a least squares approach, we derive an estimator of the probability that a user sends messages to a receiver. This estimator allows us to characterize the error of the adversary when recovering user profiles, or individual probabilities, with respect to the system parameters. Furthermore, it can be used to design dummy strategies that satisfy a wide range of privacy criteria.

As an example, we have studied the performance of the least squares estimator on a timed binomial pool mix, which enables us to derive qualitative conclusions about the effects of static dummy traffic on the adversary's error. We have used this estimator to design dummy strategies that, given a budget of dummies, achieve two privacy targets: increase the protection of each sender and receiver relationship equally, and maximize the minimum protection provided to any relationship between users. The empirical evaluation of these strategies validates our theoretical results and confirms the qualitative intuitions drawn in the performance analysis.

Our methodology improves our understanding on the effect of dummy traffic on privacy in anonymous communication systems. It can be seen as a step forward towards the development of a systematic method to design dummy traffic, especially important to evaluate and improve privacy protection in deployed mix-based systems such as [11, 12].

Appendix A: Derivation of the Expected Value of the Output Messages Given the Inputs

We aim here at deriving an expression for the expected value of the random vector of the output observations $\mathbf{Y}(\mathbf{p})$ given the input observations $\mathbf{U}$, i.e., $E\{\mathbf{Y}(\mathbf{p})|\mathbf{U}\}$. For simplicity, we assume that by the time the adversary starts observing the system the pool is empty. In practice, the initial messages in the pool would appear as noise in the initial output observations and its effect can be disregarded when the number of observations in large, as explained in [13]. For notational simplicity, we also omit writing the conditioning on $\mathbf{U}$ explicitly.

In order to relate in a statistical way the input and output flows of the mix, we follow the abstract model for the timed pool mix in Fig. 1. The different variables in this model can be *related backwards* in the following way:

- The number of output messages for receiver j in round r is $Y_j^r \doteq Y_{\lambda,j}^r + Y_{\delta,j}^r$. We can model the components refering to the real and dummy messages as:
  - Given the messages exiting the pool block $x_{s,i}^r$ for every sender i, the number of real messages leaving the mix $Y_{\lambda,j}^r$ for each receiver j is the sum of N multinomials, where $\mathbf{q}_i \doteq [p_{1,i}, \cdots, p_{M,i}]^T$:

$$\left\{ Y_{\lambda,1}^r, \cdots, Y_{\lambda,M}^r \,\middle|\, x_{s,1}^r, \cdots, x_{s,N}^r \right\} \sim \sum_{i=1}^{N} \text{Multi}\left(x_{s,i}^r, \mathbf{q}_i \right) \qquad (25)$$

- Likewise, given the number of mix-based dummies generated in round r, x_{MIX}^r, and $\mathbf{q}_{\text{MIX}} \doteq [p_{1,\text{MIX}}, \cdots, p_{M,\text{MIX}}]^T$; $Y_{\delta,j}^r$ can be modeled as:

$$\left\{ Y_{\delta,1}^r, \cdots, Y_{\delta,M}^r \,\middle|\, x_{\text{MIX}}^r \right\} \sim \text{Multi}\left(x_{\text{MIX}}^r, \mathbf{q}_{\text{MIX}}\right) \tag{26}$$

Later, we use: $\text{E}\left\{Y_{\delta,j}^r\right\} = \text{E}\left\{X_{\text{MIX}}^r\right\} \cdot p_{j,\text{MIX}} = \delta_{\text{MIX}} \cdot p_{j,\text{MIX}}$.

- The messages leaving the pool from user i in round r, $X_{s,i}^r$, may come from any of the real messages sent by that user in the current and previous rounds. We can write $X_{s,i}^r = \sum_{k=1}^r X_{s,i}^{r,k}$, where $X_{s,i}^{r,k}$ is the random variable modeling the number of messages from user i that were sent in round k and leave the mix in round r $(r \geq k)$. These random variables can be modeled, given the number of real messages sent by i in round r, $x_{\lambda,i}^r$, as:

$$\left\{ X_{s,i}^{k,k}, X_{s,i}^{k+1,k}, \cdots, X_{s,i}^{k+l,k}, \cdots \,\middle|\, x_{\lambda,i}^k \right\} \sim \text{Multi}\left(x_{\lambda,i}^k, \{F_{k,k}, F_{k+1,k}, \cdots, F_{k+l,k}, \cdots\}\right) \tag{27}$$

- Finally, given the total number of messages from user i that were sent in round r, x_i^r, the number of real messages sent in that round $X_{\lambda,i}^r$ follows

$$\left\{ X_{\lambda,i}^r \,\middle|\, x_i^r \right\} \sim \text{Bin}\left(x_i^r, P_{\lambda_i}\right) \tag{28}$$

We now compute $\text{E}\{\mathbf{Y}(\mathbf{p})\}$. From (25) and (26), we get $\text{E}\{\mathbf{Y}_j(\mathbf{p}_j)|\mathbf{U}_s\} = \mathbf{U}_s \cdot \mathbf{p}_j + \delta_{\text{MIX}} \mathbf{1}_\rho \cdot p_{j,\text{MIX}}$ and thus $\text{E}\{\mathbf{Y}(\mathbf{p})|\mathbf{U}_s\} = (\mathbf{I}_M \otimes \mathbf{U}_s) \cdot \mathbf{p} + (\mathbf{I}_M \otimes \delta_{\text{MIX}} \mathbf{1}_\rho) \cdot \mathbf{q}_{\text{MIX}}$. Using this last equality together with the law of total expectation, we can write

$$\text{E}\{\mathbf{Y}(\mathbf{p})\} = \text{E}\{\text{E}\{\mathbf{Y}(\mathbf{p})|\mathbf{U}_s\}\} = (\mathbf{I}_M \otimes \text{E}\{\mathbf{U}_s\}) \cdot \mathbf{p} + (\mathbf{I}_M \otimes \delta_{\text{MIX}} \mathbf{1}_\rho) \cdot \mathbf{q}_{\text{MIX}} \tag{29}$$

For notational simplicity, let $\hat{\mathbf{y}}_\delta \doteq \text{E}\{\mathbf{Y}_\delta\} = (\mathbf{I}_M \otimes \delta_{\text{MIX}} \mathbf{1}_\rho) \cdot \mathbf{q}_{\text{MIX}}$ be the attacker's estimation of the number of mix-based dummies sent each round. Likewise, let $\hat{\mathbf{U}}_s \doteq \text{E}\{\mathbf{U}_s\}$ be the estimation the attacker makes of the non-observable random matrix $\mathbf{U}_s$ and $\hat{\mathbf{H}}_s \doteq \mathbf{I}_M \otimes \text{E}\{\mathbf{U}_s\}$. In order to compute an element of $\hat{\mathbf{U}}_s$, i.e., $\hat{x}_{s,i}^r$, we use the law of total expectation repeatedly

$$\hat{x}_{s,i}^r \doteq \text{E}\left\{ X_{s,i}^r \,\middle|\, \mathbf{U} \right\} = \sum_{k=1}^r \text{E}\left\{ X_{s,i}^{r,k} \,\middle|\, X_k^i \right\} = \sum_{k=1}^r \text{E}\left\{ \text{E}\left\{ X_{s,i}^{r,k} \,\middle|\, X_{\lambda,i}^k \right\} \,\middle|\, X_k^i \right\}$$
$$= \sum_{k=1}^r \text{E}\left\{ X_{\lambda,i}^k \,\middle|\, X_k^i \right\} \cdot F_{r,k} = \sum_{k=1}^r x_i^k P_{\lambda_i} F_{r,k} \tag{30}$$

For compactness, we define the $\rho \times \rho$ matrix $\mathbf{B}$, which contains in its (r,k)-th position the value $F_{r,k}$ if $r \geq 0$ and 0 otherwise; and the diagonal matrix $\mathbf{P}_\lambda \doteq \text{diag}\{P_{\lambda_1}, P_{\lambda_2}, \cdots, P_{\lambda_N}\}$. Then, we can write

$$\hat{\mathbf{U}}_s = \mathbf{B} \cdot \mathbf{U} \cdot \mathbf{P}_\lambda \tag{31}$$

Plugging (31) into (29), we get $\text{E}\{\mathbf{Y}(\mathbf{p})\} = (\mathbf{I}_M \otimes \hat{\mathbf{U}}_s) \cdot \mathbf{p} + \hat{\mathbf{y}}_\delta$; with $\hat{\mathbf{y}}_\delta = (\mathbf{I}_M \otimes \delta_{\text{MIX}} \mathbf{1}_\rho) \cdot \mathbf{q}_{\text{MIX}}$ and $\hat{\mathbf{U}}_s$ in (31), which concludes the proof.

Acknowledgments. This work was partially supported by the Spanish Government and the European Regional Development Fund under project TACTICA, by the Galician Regional Government under project Consolidation of Research Units GRC2013/009, and by the EU 7th Framework Programme (FP7/2007-2013) under grant agreements 610613 (PRIPARE) and 285901 (LIFTGATE).

References

1. Danezis, G., Diaz, C., Syverson, P.: Systems for anonymous communication. In: Rosenberg, B. (ed.) Handbook of Financial Cryptography and Security. Cryptography and Network Security Series, pp. 341–389. Chapman & Hall/CRC (2009)
2. Chaum, D.: Untraceable electronic mail, return addresses, and digital pseudonyms. Communications of the ACM 24(2), 84–90 (1981)
3. Agrawal, D., Kesdogan, D.: Measuring anonymity: The disclosure attack. IEEE Security and Privacy 1(6), 27–34 (2003)
4. Danezis, G., Troncoso, C.: Vida: How to use bayesian inference to de-anonymize persistent communications. In: Goldberg, I., Atallah, M.J. (eds.) PETS 2009. LNCS, vol. 5672, pp. 56–72. Springer, Heidelberg (2009)
5. Mathewson, N., Dingledine, R.: Practical traffic analysis: Extending and resisting statistical disclosure. In: Martin, D., Serjantov, A. (eds.) PET 2004. LNCS, vol. 3424, pp. 17–34. Springer, Heidelberg (2005)
6. Pérez-González, F., Troncoso, C.: Understanding statistical disclosure: A least squares approach. In: Fischer-Hübner, S., Wright, M. (eds.) PETS 2012. LNCS, vol. 7384, pp. 38–57. Springer, Heidelberg (2012)
7. Berthold, O., Langos, H.: Dummy traffic against long term intersection attacks. In: Dingledine, R., Syverson, P.F. (eds.) PET 2002. LNCS, vol. 2482, pp. 110–128. Springer, Heidelberg (2003)
8. Diaz, C., Preneel, B.: Taxonomy of mixes and dummy traffic. In: Working Conference on Privacy and Anonymity in Networked and Distributed Systems, pp. 215–230. Kluwer Academic Publishers (2004)
9. Díaz, C., Preneel, B.: Reasoning about the anonymity provided by pool mixes that generate dummy traffic. In: Fridrich, J. (ed.) IH 2004. LNCS, vol. 3200, pp. 309–325. Springer, Heidelberg (2004)
10. Mallesh, N., Wright, M.: Countering statistical disclosure with receiver-bound cover traffic. In: Biskup, J., López, J. (eds.) ESORICS 2007. LNCS, vol. 4734, pp. 547–562. Springer, Heidelberg (2007)
11. Danezis, G., Dingledine, R., Mathewson, N.: Mixminion: Design of a type iii anonymous remailer protocol. In: IEEE Symposium on Security and Privacy, pp. 2–15. IEEE Computer Society (2003)
12. Möller, U., Cottrell, L., Palfrader, P., Sassaman, L.: Mixmaster Protocol — Version 2. IETF Internet Draft (July 2003)
13. Pérez-González, F., Troncoso, C., Oya, S.: A least squares approach to the traffic analysis of high-latency anonymous communication systems, http://webs.uvigo.es/gpscuvigo/sites/default/files/publications/lsda2013.pdf
14. Oya, S., Troncoso, C., Pérez-González, F.: Meet the family of statistical disclosure attacks. In: IEEE Global Conference on Signal and Information Processing, 4p. (2013)
15. Díaz, C., Serjantov, A.: Generalising mixes. In: Dingledine, R. (ed.) PET 2003. LNCS, vol. 2760, pp. 18–31. Springer, Heidelberg (2003)
16. Oya, S., Troncoso, C., Pérez-González, F.: Technical report tsc/so/02052014: Derivation of the mean squared error of the least squares estimator in a timed pool mix with dummy traffic, http://webs.uvigo.es/gpscuvigo/sites/default/files/publications/trpets14.pdf
17. Haykin, S.: Adaptive Filter Theory, 4th edn. Prentice Hall (2002)

Exploiting Delay Patterns for User IPs Identification in Cellular Networks

Vasile Claudiu Perta, Marco Valerio Barbera, and Alessandro Mei

Sapienza University, Rome, Italy
{perta,barbera,mei}@di.uniroma1.it

Abstract. A surprisingly high number of mobile carriers worldwide do not block unsolicited traffic from reaching their mobile devices from the open Internet or from within the cellular network. This exposes mobile users to a class of low-resource attacks that could compromise their privacy and security. In this work we describe a methodology that allows an adversary to identify a victim device in the cellular network by just sending messages to its user through one or more messaging apps available today on the mobile market. By leveraging network delays produced by mobile devices in different radio states and the timeliness of push notifications, we experimentally show how our methodology is able to quickly identify the target device within 20 messages in the worst case through measurements on a large mobile network.

Keywords: Cellular Networks, Security, Privacy.

1 Introduction

The shift from a peer-to-peer to a cloud-based, centralized communication model has made todays mobile devices less exposed to many of the network security threats that characterise desktop computers, such as intrusions through vulnerable listening services. This might be one of the reasons why an unexpectedly high number of cellular network carriers do not block unsolicited traffic from reaching their devices either from the open Internet, or from within the cellular network itself [18]. Unsurprisingly, this configuration is far from secure, and could be exploited to provide harm to the network [18], or, most importantly, to compromise the privacy and security of the end users. For instance, by monitoring the characteristics of the Internet path towards a mobile device, the user location may be tracked in a fine-grained way [21]. Using a "stealth-spam" attack like that described by Peng *et al.* [14], instead, an adversary may quickly drain the user device battery or data plan with a simple stream of UDP packets. Finally, an accurate characterization of RRC radio states of the device [17] could be leveraged to monitor the Internet traffic patterns of the user. Interestingly, these attacks do not necessarily require a powerful adversary, but can be launched by virtually anyone who either knows the IP of the victim user device in the cellular network, or, at least, can individuate a small set of candidate IPs. Given the wide range of IPs that may be assigned to a device, this may sound like a very strong requirement at first. Actually, in many cases it is not. In this paper, we describe a methodology that allows to leverage push-notification services to detect the user IP address in a cellular network.

Our main contributions are the following.

E. De Cristofaro and S.J. Murdoch (Eds.): PETS 2014, LNCS 8555, pp. 224–243, 2014.

- We define a lightweight methodology for matching users with their IPs in cellular networks. The methodology leverages the delay patterns produced at different radio states together with the near-real-time characteristics of push-based services. To the best of our knowledge, we are the first to show how network delays on cellular networks constitute an effective side-channel that can be used to undermine user privacy.
- We show how our methodology works with the most popular instant messaging apps and is robust with respect to various network and signal-strength conditions.
- We give a precise evaluation of the amount of resources the methodology requires, both in terms of bandwidth and number of instant messages.
- We experimentally validate our methodology through measurements on over 260K IPs of a large cellular network and show that it is able to correctly individuate the user device IP with less than 20 messages.

The rest of this paper is organised as follows. Section 2 introduces the attacker model. In Section 3 we show how network delays can be used as a side channel to infer the recent network activity on a remote mobile device. In Section 4, we describe our IP detection methodology, and present the experimental results in Section 5. Section 6 discusses the feasibility of our methodology. Related work and future research directions are presented in Section 7 and Section 8.

2   Attacker Model

We are interested in knowing whether an adversary can detect, in a cellular network, the IP address of the mobile device of a given user. Note that the IP could be either private or public, depending on whether the operator deployed NAT or not. In the case NAT is used, the attack has to be carried out from within the cellular network. If the adversary owns a popular website, mobile app, or cloud-based service, obtaining the user IP may be trivial. In fact, such an adversary has a larger number of options to violate end-users privacy and security, and falls outside the scope of this paper. In our scenario, instead, the adversary is a malicious small entity, or even a single person that is not necessarily trusted by the user, but that, at the same time, the user does not perceive as a particular privacy or security threat because of its apparently limited power. This model, which is similar to that assumed by Le Blond et al. [11], includes people in the user social circle (e.g., friends, coworkers) or entities such as the user employer. These are weak adversaries potentially interested in knowing the whereabouts or habits of the user, or in provoking the user some kind of damage, such as depleting her monthly data plan or systematically consuming the smartphone battery for the rest of the day. Adversaries of this kind may have strong personal reasons to attack the user and, at the same time, may already have some information about their target that they could use, such as the user cellular network operator, phone number, e-mail address, phone model (e.g., Android, iPhone, BlackBerry), or coarse-grained geographical location (e.g., a city, or a state).

Assumptions. Given the above adversarial model, we assume the adversary is someone socially close enough to the victim user that they share a connection through a social app or service that includes a near real-time messaging facility, such as Facebook Messenger, Google Hangouts, Skype, WhatsApp, Viber, and SnapChat. Our concept of social strength is therefore not necessarily measured in terms of real-life friendship but is much more relaxed. In fact, it is not uncommon for users to have several hundreds of online friends [1]. Considering how easy it is to establish relationships in some online services [3], an adversary may even create one or more fake identities to use for the attack, depending on the case. Another assumption is that the cellular network operator of the user is known, and that it allows unsolicited traffic to reach the mobile devices from the Internet or from the cellular network itself. According to recent statistics on over 180 UTMS carriers worldwide [18], this is true in more than 50% of the cases. Given that the popularity of cellular network operators in various countries is typically very skewed, knowing the cellular network operator of the victim user does not represent an issue. Moreover, getting this type of information from an online friend may not be hard, considering that, for instance, Facebook has a mobile phone number field in the contact description. Finally, we do not make strong assumptions about the amount of bandwidth resources available to the adversary, although there is a relation between bandwidth and detection time, as we discuss in Section 4.3.

3   Delay-Based Network Activity Detection in Cellular Networks

The cornerstone of our user IP detection methodology in cellular networks is a method that leverages network delays to accurately infer the transmission patterns of a mobile device, such as a smartphone. In this section we describe the characteristics of cellular network radio resource assignment that enable it.

3.1   Radio Resource Assignment in Cellular Networks

Radio resources in cellular networks are allocated to mobile devices in relation to the volume of data they are sending or receiving from the network. This process is regulated by means of transitions in a Radio Resource Control (RRC) state machine that is associated to each device [20]. In 3G networks, these states are typically three: IDLE, CELL_FACH, and CELL_DCH, corresponding to no, low, or full radio resources allocated, respectively. Transitions from lower to higher resources states are triggered by some network activity, and are referred to as a promotions. The opposite transitions are instead referred to as a demotions. Although state transitions parameters can be independently defined by each mobile network operator [17,18], two general rules always apply. First, a promotion from IDLE is triggered when *any* amount of data has to be transferred, whereas a CELL_FACH to CELL_DCH promotion is triggered when the data rate exceeds a given threshold defined by the operator (*e.g.,* 2Kbit/s). Second, state demotions are triggered from the CELL_FACH and CELL_DCH state after a period of no network activity referred to as *tail time*. Tail times relative to the CELL_FACH and CELL_DCH states are operator-defined, although the former is typically longer than the latter as it consumes less radio and energy resources. As an example, we show the state machine configuration of a popular network carrier in Figure 1. We can notice how in this configuration a transition to the CELL_FACH state is first required in order to get the full-resources available in the CELL_DCH state. Other operators may use a more aggressive configuration, allowing a direct promotion from the IDLE directly to the CELL_DCH state.

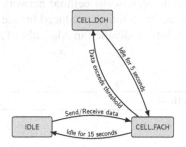

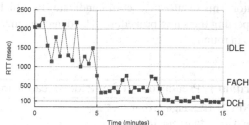

Fig. 1. Example of RRC state machine

Fig. 2. Example of effect of network usage on observed RTT (round-trip time) towards the device

3.2   Inferring RRC States from Network Delay Measurements

The device current RRC state and its responsiveness to network events are tightly related. This comes for two reasons. First, state promotions, especially those from the IDLE state, are time expensive, as they require a number of control messages to be exchanged between the device and the Radio Network Controller (RNC). Second, a device in the CELL_FACH state typically observes higher delays due to the lower amount of allocated radio resources and to its lower transmission power. A key observation is that the extra delays caused by promotions from the IDLE state and by the low resources of the CELL_FACH state are significantly higher than typical network delays, and can be easily distinguished from each other. To give an example, in Figure 2 we show a sequence of round-trip time (RTT) measurements performed every 17 seconds towards a device using the RRC machine state configuration shown in Figure 1. When the device is idle, the RTTs fall in the $[1s, 2.5s)$ range. Such high delays are not produced at the network level, but are caused by promotions from the IDLE to the CELL_FACH state. Indeed, RTT measurements are spaced by an amount of time larger than the CELL_FACH tail time, which is large enough to make the state machine transit back to the IDLE state between measurements. After 5 minutes, a concurrent traffic on the device is generated with a rate of 0.5 kbit/s, enough to keep its RRC state machine in the CELL_FACH state. In this state, the RTTs drop into the $[250ms, 1s)$ range, although they are still higher than expected, due to the low resources associated to the device. Finally, when the device is allocated full radio resources in the CELL_DCH state, the RTTs fall in the $[0ms, 250ms)$, which is the actual network round-trip time between the measuring host and the mobile device. Overall, the strong difference between delays imposed at the various states makes a single round-trip time measurement a surprisingly robust and effective way to remotely infer the recent network activity of any given device in a cellular network.

4   User IPs Identification in Cellular Networks

In this section we present a novel methodology that leverages the delay-based RRC state inference to spot the IP of a target user in the cellular network. With this method, an adversary who has some *indirect* way to produce traffic on the target device can ensure it to be in a high-power state (*i.e.,* CELL_FACH, CELL_DCH) at specific moments, producing a distinctive network delay pattern on the mobile device. At the same time, the adversary looks for similar patterns across all the devices of the cellular network operator. This results in a set of candidate IPs which can be iteratively reduced in size by repeating the same procedure. The detection methodology, detailed in Algorithm 1, works in rounds.

Algorithm 1. Pseudocode of the IP identification method

---

1. **INPUT**: IP_Range, nrounds, T_{wait}
2. **for** i := 1 **to** nrounds **do**
3.   RTTs := new map()
4.   generate_traffic_start()
5.   **for all** IP ∈ IP_Range **do**
6.   RTTs[IP] := measure_RTT()
7.   **end for**
8.   generate_traffic_stop()
9.   **for all** IP ∈ IP_Range **do**
10.   **if** is_match(RTTs[IP]) = **False then**
11.   IP_Range := IP_Range \ {IP}
12.   **end if**
13.   **end for**
14.   sleep(T_{wait})
15. **end for**
16. return IP_range

At each round, the generate_traffic function is used to generate traffic on the target device by sending messages to the its user through an instant messaging app. In the meanwhile, the current RRC state of all the devices in the IP_Range set is identified by measuring their round-trip times, as explained in Section 3. Round-trip times can be performed through ICMP echo requests (pings), or by sending SYN packets to a closed port and waiting for the relative RST packet. At the end of the measurements, traffic generation is paused and the is_match function is used to filter-out the set of all the devices whose radio was not at a high power state. Aside from the target device, this includes all the other devices in the network that were using the radio during the measurement. What enables this methodology to filter them out is the fact that mobile devices, as opposite to laptops or mobile hotspots, are not likely to constantly use the network resources for long periods of time, whereas the target device can be forced to transmit at will.

Methodology Parameters. Our detection methodology takes three parameters, namely IP_Range, nrounds, and T_{wait}. The first one, IP_Range, is the initial candidate set of IPs assigned to the target user device. In case the operator assigns public IPs to its devices, a simple whois query with the operator AS name or number(s) reveals the initial IP set[1]. In case private IPs are used, the set of potential IPs may be very large, such as the private 10.0.0.0/8 subnet which is approximately 16M IPs wide. Starting from the whole subnet does not constitute an obstacle, but it still may slow down the detection procedure, requiring more rounds to shrink the candidate set of IPs to reasonable values. The initial IP_Range set can be considerably restricted if the user's coarse-grained geographical location is known. In fact, although the correspondence between IP address and location in cellular networks is not as strong as in wired networks [25], several other network features can be found (e.g., the minimum round-trip time, and the RRC state machine configuration parameters) to effectively map IP addresses of mobile devices to a geographic area, like a big city or a state [18]. This would not require a large amount of bandwidth, and would not violate our attacker model.

The nrounds parameter determines the number of refinements the procedure can perform. A larger number of rounds helps reducing the candidate set, but, at the same time, requires a higher number of messages to be sent to the target user. Ideally, the adversary should use the smallest possible number of rounds, depending on his objective. For instance, to perform a DoS to the user device, the adversary may be satisfied to save the bandwidth needed for the attack by reducing the IP_Range to a few thousand devices, in line with our weak attacker model. For other tasks, the final IP_Range should be smaller. In any case, in Section 5 we show how just 10 rounds are sufficient to reduce the final IP_Range set to a handful of devices.

Lastly, the T_{wait} parameter determines the frequency with which instant messages are sent to the target user. In general, the higher the frequency, the less time it takes for the adversary to individuate the user IP. However, a very high message frequency may make the user suspicious about the adversary's intent, and may actually require more rounds (messages) to detect the target device IP (more on this in Section 5). In this case, a stronger social relationship with the user may help disguising the instant messages as a regular chat.

4.1 Indirectly Generating Traffic on the Target User Device

Our IP identification method requires the adversary to ensure that, in the time span the round-trip time to all the mobile devices is measured, the target user device radio is in a high power state (e.g., CELL_FACH or CELL_DCH), yielding a distinctive sequence of low round-trip times. According to our attacker model (cf., Section 2), the adversary is able to send the victim an instant message through one or more social messaging apps. These apps typically include a push-notification facility to notify users of incoming messages in a timely fashion, representing an ideal way to indirectly generate traffic on the victim user device at specific moments. To confirm this intuition, we experimentally tested the responsiveness of the push notification systems used by the most popular messaging apps available on the market today, namely, WhatsApp, Viber, Google Hangouts, Skype, Facebook Messenger and SnapChat. More specifically, we measured the time span between the instant the adversary sends a message to the victim and the instant the victim device actually receives it, forcing the RRC state to be either CELL_FACH or CELL_DCH, depending on the configuration (cf., Section 3). According

---

[1] https://www.team-cymru.org/Services/ip-to-asn.html

to our measurements, push notifications of all the aforementioned apps alert the user always within a timespan of at most 5 seconds after the message has been sent, depending also on the initial RRC state of the device. Push notifications delays are therefore low enough for the adversary to control the observed delays towards the victim device in a relatively fine-grained way and with good accuracy. It is worth noticing that we did not observe any difference in responsiveness between messages sent when the device is active (*i.e.*, the screen is on and unlocked) or in sleep mode (*i.e.*, the device has not been recently used, and the screen is off). This allows an adversary to generate traffic on the device even without the user being immediately aware of it (*e.g.*, when the phone is muted, or at night). As an example, we show in Figure 3 the sequence of

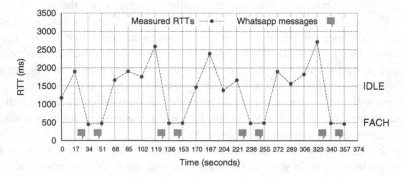

Fig. 3. Example of traffic generation on the target device by means of WhatsApp messages. To detect the CELL_FACH state, round-trip times are measured every 17 seconds.

radio states inferred while generating traffic towards a test device through WhatsApp messages. Round-trip time measurements are spaced by 17 seconds, which are slightly higher than the tail time of the CELL_FACH state in Figure 1. The figure shows how the state inferred 5 seconds after a message was sent is always CELL_FACH (*i.e.*, RTT $\in [300ms, 1s)$). We can also observe how the state machine does not transit back to the IDLE state when another instant message is sent before the CELL_FACH tail time expires. This is an important detail, as it enables an adversary to extend the time the target device radio is at a high power at will, if needed. Finally, observe how the traffic generated by the push notifications may not be high enough to trigger a transition to the CELL_DCH state. The adversary should therefore conservatively assume that the target device is in the CELL_FACH state after a message is received, even though concurrent traffic on the user device may actually make the radio transit at a CELL_DCH state. This does not represent a limitation though, as the difference between round-trip times at CELL_FACH and at IDLE is high enough to reliably tell the two states apart.

Overall, this experiment shows that a single round-trip time measurement can easily detect the network activity triggered by an instant message. We argue that, aside from those we experimentally tested, most of the instant messaging apps available on the market today can be leveraged, given their real-time nature. In fact, according to our experience, any messaging app using the Google Cloud Messaging (GCM) push notifications is a good candidate. This is, for instance, the case of not just Google Hangouts, but also of Skype and Facebook Messenger. In principle, other apps may be used too, such as Facebook, Twitter, or GMail. However, having no strict real time requirements, their notifications may be delayed by several seconds, or even minutes, making it harder to detect the user IP.

Setting Up the Attack. As a preliminary step, the adversary should compare the time it takes to perform a single round-trip time measurement towards the devices in the IP_Range set with the amount of time the traffic generated by the push notifications can keep the target user device radio at a high power state. Depending on the RRC state machine configuration, the latter may be the CELL_FACH tail time only, or the sum of CELL_FACH and CELL_DCH tail times. If this time is too short, the adversary may need to extend it by sending a sequence of well-spaced instant messages, as we have shown in Figure 3. To learn the RRC state machine configuration, the adversary can use the technique described by Qian *et al.* [17] either remotely or from a device under his control in the cellular network, as we did for our experiments. If the approximate geographical area where the victim device resides (*i.e.,* a city, or a state) is not known, the adversary may need to account for different possible CELL_FACH and CELL_DCH tail times. To avoid false negatives, the adversary should conservatively assume that the shortest tail times are used on the target device. This makes our detection methodology adaptive to any RRC state machine configuration an operator might use in his network.

4.2   Factors Affecting the Detection Accuracy

For our detection methodology to succeed in real-life scenarios, packet loss and delay variations caused by cross traffic or wireless signal interferences have to be taken into account. In this section, we quantify the impact these factors have on the IP detection accuracy.

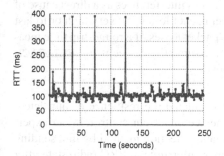

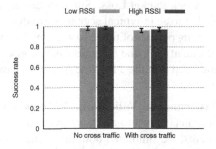

Fig. 4. Round-trip time measurements in presence of cross-traffic produced by a Youtube video streaming

Fig. 5. Probability of measuring a low RTT ($\leq$ 1s) after a push notification under different signal strength and cross traffic conditions

Cross-Traffic. Cross traffic represents a potential issue, as it is well known that, due to the use of large buffers, it might introduce extra network delay variations. However, the relative increase in round-trip time produced by cross traffic is still small with respect to the much higher delays observed when the device is in the IDLE state (*i.e.,* 500ms against more than 1 second). Only when cross traffic is close to the bottleneck link capacity for long time, the extra delay can reach the order of seconds [9] and the adversary could mistakenly infer that the RRC state was IDLE. Given the bursty nature of traffic in mobile networks [19] we deem this as an extreme scenario. In fact, mobile devices are typically used for short periods of time, and non-user generated traffic is produced by background apps and services regularly downloading short updates from the network (*e.g.,* social network status updates, emails, and so on). Moreover, even streaming apps, which are considered to be resource-hungry services, use temporary buffers to store up to several seconds of pre-fetched media content. To experimentally confirm the low impact of cross traffic on our detection procedure, we measured the round-trip time towards a device under our control that was downloading a Youtube video. This well represents one of the most intensive network activities that can be triggered by a user. Results, presented in Figure 4, show that, despite the video being downloaded, for most of the time the measured round-trip times match very closely those typical of the CELL_DCH state, like those shown in Figure 2. As expected, only a few measurements show the effect of some queueing delay (*e.g.,* 400ms), but never reach values close to those typical of the IDLE state.

Wireless Signal Interferences. Due to the loss-recovery mechanisms typically used in cellular networks, wireless signal interferences can introduce extra delays too. Garcia *et al.* [4] have experimentally shown that, in exceptional cases, this can introduce spikes of delay of up to 400 milliseconds in UTMS networks. These delays are still lower than the round-trip times generated at the IDLE state, thus not producing false negatives.

Network Packet Loss. Since we can exclude wireless interferences as a direct cause of packet loss, in typical scenarios we do not expect packet loss to be very high or to last for long periods of time. To account for sporadic packet losses, if a round-trip time measurement fails, the adversary may conservatively assume the device is in CELL_FACH and keep it in the IP_Range set for an extra round.

Experimental Validation. We experimentally evaluated the resilience of our detection mechanism to all the above factors with a device under our control. In our experiments, we simulated both the traffic generation and detection method by first sending a WhatsApp message to the target device, and then inferring the RRC radio state after 5 seconds the message was sent in order to account for the time it may take for the push notification to reach the device. During each test, the device was put under different cross-traffic and signal strength conditions. More specifically, cross traffic was produced by downloading a Youtube video, as in Figure 4. For what concerns the signal strength, we tested two different scenarios: One with poor and one with good signal, corresponding to RSSI ~ -95dBm and RSSI ~ -79dBm, respectively. Each combination of cross-traffic and signal strength was tested 300 times. According to our results, shown in Figure 5, measured round-trip times are within the expected threshold in both cross traffic and poor signal strength conditions for more than 99% of the cases. Given these results, allowing a small percentage of round-trip times measurement to fail would make our detection mechanism resistant to a wide range of conditions.

4.3 Scanning the Mobile Operator's Network

To reduce the number of messages required to be sent at each round, the adversary should minimize the time needed to measure the round-trip times towards the devices in the IP_Range. For this task, a tool like ZMap could be used. ZMap is a network scanner by Durumeric *et al.* [6] that is specifically tailored for performing fast, large-scale network scans with commodity hardware. As a proof-of-concept we developed an ICMP echo request (ping) scanner module for ZMap and tested it against the 1.7M IPs wide address space of a popular cellular network that assigns public, reachable IPs to its devices. Taking as a reference the 15 seconds CELL_FACH tail time in Figure 1, and the 5 second to be waited before the messages arrive to the device, to perform a single round-trip time measurement on all the IP space in time would require 46Mbit/s using ICMP echo packets of 36 bytes. In practice, we observed that the number of IPs that are active at any given time in the address space is much smaller, that is, around 500K (30% of the total), which is consistent to what observed by Qian *et al.* in a U.S. mobile network carrier public address space [18]. This allows to restrict the initial IP_Range and reduce the bandwidth needed to just 14Mbit/s.

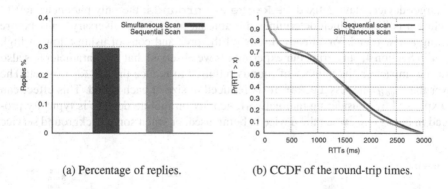

(a) Percentage of replies.   (b) CCDF of the round-trip times.

Fig. 6. Results with different scan strategies

We experimentally verified whether large network scans produce some bottleneck in the cellular network infrastructure, which could have an impact on the detection accuracy. To do so, we compared the results obtained by scanning the whole public IP space of the operator in two different ways. First, with a simultaneous scan over the whole address space range. Then, by dividing the address space in smaller chunks (*i.e.*, 65K devices) and scanning each of them separately, waiting for 30 seconds between subsequent scans. The results obtained are shown in Figure 6. In Figure 6a, we can observe how the number of replies received is in both cases very close to 30%, showing that no extra packets loss was introduced during the simultaneous scan. Figure 6b, comparing the two round-trip time distributions obtained, shows that no relevant extra queueing delay is produced either.

In Figure 7 we study the relation between size of the IP_Range set to be scanned, the bandwidth available to the adversary, and the number of messages to be sent at each round to keep the radio of the target device at a high power state for enough time, according to the state machine configuration of our test operator (shown in Figure 1). We can observe how, even with lower bandwidths (i.e., 5Mbit/s), just one message buys the adversary enough time to scan a whole /16 subnet ($\sim$ 65K IPs). As we are going to show next, the exponential drop in size of IP_Range allows to use just one message per round in the majority of the cases.

5   Experimental Results

We experimentally evaluated our IP detection methodology on a popular cellular network operator which assigns public, reachable IPs to its devices. As the target device, we used a Samsung Galaxy S Plus. As initial IP_Range set, we used four /16 subnets (i.e., 262K IPs) from which IP addresses are typically assigned to the devices in our geographical region. The RRC state machine configuration used by the operator in the area is the one shown in Figure 1. Consistently with our experiments in Section 4.1, we conservatively instrumented the is_match function to keep in the IP_Range set all the devices that are either in CELL_FACH or CELL_DCH state (i.e., RTT $\leq$ 1s), as our push notifications were not necessarily able to trigger a transition to CELL_DCH on the target device. Having fixed IP_Range and nrounds, the only parameter left to be chosen is T_{wait}, which determines the amount of time the adversary waits before starting a new round. We already discussed the pros and cons of using a low or high T_{wait} in Section 4, but during our experiments we observed that this parameter has also a strong impact on the number of rounds required to reduce the IP_Range set: The lower the T_{wait}, the less IP_Range is reduced in size at each round. This effect can be explained by considering that network activity on mobile devices is typically produced in bursts (e.g., when the device is being used, or when some background service

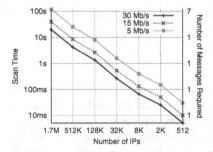

Fig. 7. Time required to send ICMP echo requests to all the IPs in IP_Range from our probing host

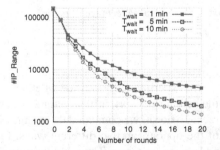

Fig. 8. Number of IPs left after each round of Algorithm 1 using different T_{wait} values

downloads an update). Thus, the closer two rounds are in time, the higher is the probability that the devices that were transmitting (*i.e.*, not in IDLE) at the previous round will be still transmitting during the following one, and will not be removed from the IP_Range set. Using a larger T_{wait}, instead, increases the probability that the devices in IP_Range go back to the IDLE state between rounds. Starting from this observation, to test our detection methodology we used three different values of T_{wait}, namely 1, 5, and 10 minutes. We want to stress here that these values are just representative of what an adversary could use, and that the T_{wait} parameter does not necessarily need to be fixed. For instance, the adversary may very well disguise the messages sent to the victim user as a regular chat. In this case, the timings between messages (*i.e.*, rounds) to the victim could vary according to the conversation.

We performed 5 independent tests for each of the T_{wait} parameters in the timespan of three days, between 10am to 8pm. The measurement machine was hosted in our university's network, and we used the custom ping-probe module for ZMap. Our machine, an Intel Core2Duo with a 100Mbit network interface, takes around 10 seconds to perform round-trip time measurement when the IP_Range size is maximum (*i.e.*, 262K IPs), which corresponds to a rate of around 27 Mbit/s. For the instant messages we used WhatsApp, as it provides a handy API through which automated tests can be performed. A number of other apps may be used as well, as discussed in Section 4.1. In order to account for packet losses, if a device stops replying for at most two rounds, we assume it was in CELL_FACH and we don't remove it from the IP_Range set. Finally, we used 1 second as a round-trip time threshold to detect the IDLE state, consistently with the experiments presented in Section 4.1.

Results in Figure 8 show the number of remaining candidates in IP_Range after each round, averaged across all the tests. First of all, we can observe how, during the first round, the size of IP_Range suddenly drops from 262K to just around 80K. This is caused by IPs not always being active, as we already observed in Section 4.3. As we anticipated, when the T_{wait} parameter is too low (*i.e.*, 1 minute), the size of the IP_Range decreases very slowly with respect to the other two cases, which, instead, show similar performances. Using wait time larger than 10 minutes may further improve the results, but would also be more time expensive for the adversary. Surprisingly, with T_{wait} set to 5 minutes and 10 minutes, in just 10 rounds the IP_Range gets reduced to between 2K and 3K IPs, that is, 7% and 3% of the initial size of the IP_Range set. This result may be good enough if the objective of the adversary is to save the resources needed to perform a DoS attack against the victim user. For other type of attacks, the adversary may want to get an even smaller set of candidate IPs of the victim device. As we show next, this can be achieved with just a slightly more accurate model of the Internet usage pattern of the victim.

5.1 Monitoring the Network Usage

One characteristic we observed about the set of devices that stay in the IP_Range for more than 10 rounds across all our experiments, is that they are mostly characterised by periods of network activity that are exceptionally long with respect to those typical of mobile devices [10,18]. To get a more clear view of this phenomenon, we randomly selected 10K IP addresses that resulted to be online and measured their round-trip time

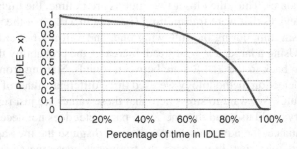

Fig. 9. CCDF of the percentage of time the devices were found in the IDLE state

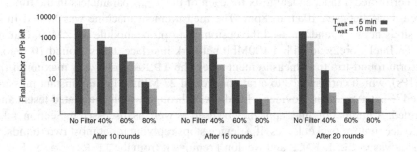

Fig. 10. Filtering IPs based on the percentage of idle time

every minute for one hour. Figure 9 shows that around 80% of the devices were found to be in IDLE for more than 60% of the time. This idle time should be consistent to the typical traffic patterns of mobile devices [10,18], who are also very limited in terms of energy autonomy [16]. Following this intuition, we believe that typical mobile devices, such as smartphones or tablets, are unlikely to exhibit traffic patterns with very long periods of network activity. In fact, it is reasonable to expect that the cellular network operator uses its IP address space for other type of services too (*e.g.,* 3G hotspots, publicly accessible WiFis, 3G USB sticks, and so on). For this reason, the adversary may safely assume that, in the long run, the target IP will be found to be idle for at least a P_{idle} percentage of time, and remove from the IP_Range set the devices with a higher percentage of transmission time. This could computed by keep measuring the round-trip time of the devices even in the time period between consecutive rounds, that is, when no message is sent to the user with generate_traffic(). After a sufficient number of rounds, an accurate profile of the network usage over time of the devices in IP_Range can be built and used to filter out devices with an unexpectedly high network activity. We tested the effectiveness of this profiling technique in our experiments by monitoring the state of the devices in IP_Range every minute and using different values of P_{idle}. The results, presented in Figure 10, show that, after 10 rounds, even conservatively assuming an at most 40% of idle time, we can remove up to 87% of the devices when T_{wait} set to both 5 and 10 minutes, corresponding to 50 minutes and 1 hour and 40 minutes, respectively. If the adversary can make a stronger assumption on the idle time of the target device, such as by setting P_{idle} to be 80%, then the final IP_Range set gets reduced to just 6 and 3 devices respectively. Using a larger number of rounds helps further decreasing the possible number of user IPs with a less restrictive assumption on their idle time. For instance, with 15 rounds, corresponding to 1 hour and 15 minutes and 2 hours and 30 minutes, assuming P_{idle} to be 60%, the number of final IPs is less than 10. We exactly identified the target device IP using 15 rounds and $P_{idle} = 80\%$ or with 20 rounds and $P_{idle} \geq 60\%$. Although we leave a thorough analysis of the typical activity patterns of smartphones as a future work, our results show that this filtering technique can achieve a very high accuracy with just 10 or 15 instant messages to the victim user. Moreover, our results show that using a T_{wait} time of 10 minutes does not provide a significant advantage. So, if only a limited amount of time is available for the adversary to restrict the user IP, T_{wait} may be set to 5 minutes.

In general, depending on what additional information is available about the victim, the adversary will always choose a time window that maximizes P_{idle} of the target device during the attack. In fact, there are several scenarios in which the interaction between a user and the mobile device may be minimum: while driving (maybe during commute), during lectures (if the target is a student or professor), during trials (if the target is a judge or lawyer), at night, *etc.*.

5.2   Fingerprinting the Mobile OS

Perhaps surprisingly, the operating system is another information that can be inferred while measuring the round-trip times towards the devices in IP_Range, and that the adversary can exploit for an easier individuation of the target user IP. This is made possible by the choice that different operating systems make of the initial time-to-live (TTL) values to the ICMP echo reply they generate. For instance, the TTL distribution obtained during a sample scan, reported in Figure 11, is characterised by three steps in the vicinity of 64, 128 and 255, which correspond to the initial TTLs used by Linux (including Android) and Apple OSes (TTL 64), Windows (TTL 128), and BlackBerry

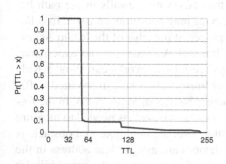

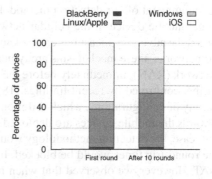

Fig. 11. ICMP echo reply TTL distribution during a sample scan

Fig. 12. OSes inferred before (left) and after (right) Algorithm 1 is run (nrounds = 10, $T_{wait} = 5m$)

(TTL 255) devices.[2] A similar TTL-based fingerprinting technique has been described by Vanaubel *et al.* [24]. Interestingly, although they use the same initial TTL, iOS devices can be told apart from Linux and OSX ones by observing that iOS listens for external connections on the TCP port 62078, which is reported as `iphone-sync` by nmap. Thus, using ZMap to perform a parallel SYN scan on this port the adversary can identify Apple mobile devices with just the same amount of effort and time required by a round-trip time measurement towards the devices in the `IP_Range` set. Overall, if the operating system of the victim user's device is known to the adversary, this mix of TTL-based and port-based OS detection methods allows to easily restrict the initial `IP_Range` set, reducing the number of rounds required to find the IP of the target device. As an example, in Figure 12 (left column) we show the distribution of the inferred OSes on the initial `IP_Range` we used for our experiments. We can observe how the low percentage of Windows and BlackBerry devices makes their users particularly vulnerable to our detection method. For instance, the IP of a BlackBerry user can be identified with just 15 rounds and P_{idle} of just 40%. To conclude, notice that, as the number of rounds increases, the OSes distribution changes considerably (compare left and right column of Figure 12). In particular, the percentage of Windows devices after 10 rounds increases more than 4 times, whereas the percentage of iOS devices decreases. Considering that devices that stay in the `IP_Range` set for several rounds are those with the lowest idle time (*cf.*, Section 5.1), we deem this as a confirmation of the intuition that these devices may not be actual smartphones, but, rather, other devices getting connectivity from the cellular network.

6   Discussion

In this section we investigate the feasibility of our detection methodology, and discuss alternatives and possible countermeasures.

6.1   Firewalls and NATs

A requirement of our detection methodology is the possibility of directly reaching the target mobile device in the cellular network. Thus, NATs or firewalls in the path between the adversary measurement host and the device may constitute an issue. In cellular networks, these mechanisms are typically deployed at the edge of the Radio Access Network (RAN), immediately before the public Internet. According to our experience, further confirmed by recent findings [18], todays' cellular networks can show a wide variety of configurations, which differ on whether firewalls blocking unsolicited traffic towards the mobile devices are deployed, or whether NAT is used (or both). In the former case, the detection methodology would not work, as the packets needed to measure the round-trip times would be blocked. In the latter case, the only potential obstacle is NAT. However, we observed that when mobile devices are assigned an address in the private IP space, they are still freely reachable by other devices in the same cellular network, allowing NAT to be circumvented by an adversary that has access to a device

---

[2] We could only use a limited number of BlackBerry phones to confirm their initial TTL value.

Table 1. Number of mobile network carriers whose mobile devices are assigned public, reachable IP addresses. Subscribers percentage is a coarse estimation based on publicly available data.

	Africa	Asia	Europe	Oceania	N. America	S. America
# Carriers	5	33	35	3	9	14
Subscribers %	7	56	27	40	54	73

in the target cellular network. Considering that subscribing to a mobile data plan is relatively cheap, we believe this is not a strong requirement, even for reasonably weak adversaries.

Finding Public IP Operators. To get a more complete view of the cellular network operators worldwide that allow their devices to be directly reached from the open Internet, we independently collected a list of mobile network operators that assign public, reachable IP addresses to their devices. As opposed to previous approaches [18], we used a centralised approach. As in Section 5.2, we leveraged the fact that iOS devices listen for external connections on iphone-sync port. This allowed us to spot all the publicly reachable iOS devices by scanning the entire Internet IP space for hosts listening on this port using ZMap. The scan took 10 hours, and yielded $\sim$ 9.4M IPs in 6315 unique Autonomous Systems (AS) distributed across 189 countries. We were able to associate $\sim$ 7.5M of these devices ($\sim$ 83% of all the hosts we detected) to 103 among the main network operators in each country [3], by looking at the name of their originating ASes. Table 1 gives, the number of operators found in each continent, and their total estimated share of customers. Given the strong market penetration of iOS devices, we believe this is a fairly accurate preliminary list of mobile operators that provide unrestricted access to their devices from the open Internet. Our results show that the potential number of users that can be identified with our methodology is far from negligible. In fact, in all the continents, the mobile carriers allowing a direct access to their devices own a substantial part of the market share (in terms of number of subscribers). Overall, our evaluation provides a much broader view of this phenomenon with respect to previous studies, with a significantly smaller effort. This comes at a price of a lower accuracy. For instance, associating an AS to its corresponding mobile carrier is not always trivial, and may require a manual examination of the AS names.

6.2   IP Duration

The amount of time a mobile device is assigned a given IP address in the cellular network is another aspect that may affect our detection methodology. The longer the time, the easier will be for the adversary to spot the device IP, and greater it will be the possibility to harm the end-user. Typically, the IP address assigned to a mobile device never changes as long as the device gets not disconnected from the network. This holds for both cellular networks that assign addresses in the public IP space, and for operators that, instead, use NAT. In the latter case, the public IP assigned to connections originating from the device may change in an unpredictable fashion, depending on how the

---
[3] http://en.wikipedia.org/wiki/List_of_mobile_network_operators

network is configured, as also reported by Balakrishnan *et al.* [2]. This does not constitute an issue, though, because, when NAT is used, the adversary would need to get access to the private side of the cellular network, where IP typically change only when a disconnection occurs. For these reasons, the habits of mobile users play an important role in our attack scenario. For instance, if the user switches to a WiFi network, or turns the device off, then the device IP will almost surely change the next time a data connection to the cellular network is established. However, even for users that have access to WiFi during the day, there are still large time windows across the day in which their mobile devices are connected to the mobile network, such as when the user is on the move, or in some public place (*e.g.,* a pub), and so on. This is confirmed by a mobile app dataset used by Qian *et al.* [18], according to which for more than 80% of the times, a mobile device is continuously connected to the mobile network for more than 4 hours. This is a time frame that leaves more than enough time for the adversary to both identify the user device with good accuracy and to perform a focused attack, like a resource drain attack [14].

6.3   Alternative Approaches

An alternative to our attack could be that of tricking the user to visit a malicious website under the adversary's control that keeps a record of the connecting IPs. While this would require less resources on the adversary's side, there are two main reasons to prefer our detection methodology. First, it does not assume the active participation of the victim user, which allows the adversary to detect the device IP even when the device is left unattended, as mentioned in Section 5.1. This would reduce the chances that the user takes any countermeasure on time, assuming that the push notifications triggered by the adversary raise any suspicion at all. This highlights the second advantage of our methodology, that is, the fact that it is harder to be detected as it leverages the (misleading?) perception that push notifications represent a safe channel that cannot be exploited by external adversaries. On the other hand, we believe that being repeatedly asked to follow a certain link is more likely to raise some suspicion. For this reason, our methodology is more suitable in cases where the adversary is interested in attacking the user multiple times, like in the location tracking scenario mentioned in Section 1.

6.4   Countermeasures

The most obvious countermeasure the operator can implement to block our IP detection methodology is to deploy a firewall that does not allow incoming unsolicited traffic towards the devices inside the network. From the user's perspective, this may come at the cost of limiting the possibility of using P2P applications or of hosting publicly accessible services in the cellular network. However, this does not constitute a real issue as it is very uncommon to have such services hosted on mobile devices. From the operator's perspective, instead, completely blocking all incoming traffic makes it very difficult to troubleshoot faults or misconfigurations inside the network. For this reason, a very common practice is to allow at least ICMP messages in echo-reply mode. We believe that the most effective way would be to implement a firewall directly on the mobile devices themselves, without relying on the intervention of the operator. This way, all outgoing

ICMP traffic and unsolicited TCP connections it could be safely blocked, preventing an adversary to remotely probe the device. A less obvious but more effective way for the operator to countermeasure this attack would be to deploy IPv6, with an addressing scheme robust to network scanning (*e.g.*, DHCPv6 with non sequential addresses). Given the huge address space of typical IPv6 subnets, this would make the scanning unfeasible even if we consider a much stronger adversarial model.

7 Related Work

Our mechanism for inferring RRC states from network delay measurements builds upon recent findings about the characteristics of cellular network resource allocation. Qian *et al.* [17] propose a way to fully characterise the RRC state machine by just externally probing a device. In [16] they improve on their previous characterisation methodology. Perala *et al.* [15] introduce a 3G Transition Triggering Tool (3G3T), to determine RRC state transition parameters used in 4 target cellular networks across 3 different countries.

A number of attacks on cellular networks have been presented so far. Traynor *et al.* [23] study how even relatively small botnets of mobile phones can degrade the network service in large-sized regions. Peng *et al.* [14] provide a detailed security evaluation of the mobile data accounting architecture. They also describe a stealth-spam attack that drains the mobile data plan of a target user. Lee *et al.* [12], show that it is possible to overload the radio network controller in a UMTS network by means of control messages. Qian *et al.* [18] present a way to create a map of IPs in a geographical area that can be used in a focused signaling DoS attack to the network.

Several attacks have been proposed that use network delay as a side-channel. Hopper *et al.* [8] show how round-trip times allow malicious web servers to link client requests traversing the same circuit in Tor. Ling *et al.* [13] investigate a network-delay based side-channel attack to infer web sites accessed by a user trough a VPN/SOCKS proxy. Gong *et al.* [7] show how the same information can be inferred from the round-trip time between a probing host and a home DSL router.

Stober *et al.* [22] show that an UMTS eavesdropper can identify a smartphones by means of the network traffic it generates. Le Blond *et al.* [11] show how inconspicuous Skype calls can be used to get coarse-grained users mobility over time. Their method allows to identify the public IP address of a mobile device, which does not correspond to the actual IP address if the user is behind NAT. On the opposite, our technique works also from within the private cellular network address space, exposing mobile also users behind NAT. Moreover, our method is more general, as it can leverage any instant message application, Skype included.

8 Conclusions and Future Work

In this work, we presented a novel method that leverages the delay-based radio state inference in combination with real-time push notification subsystems to identify the IP of a target user in the cellular network. The information obtained in this way represents a potential threat to mobile users, as it permits even weak adversaries to perform focused attacks on users using a small amount of resources, such as inferring the user location, depleting the user data plan, or inferring the user Internet activity. Our results, performed on over 260K IPs of a large cellular network, show that, with just 10 messages, the potential set of IP addresses gets reduced to just 3%. With a more accurate model of the victim user Internet usage pattern, the target user device can be correctly identified with just 15 messages. A further improvement can be achieved assuming the OS running on the target device (*e.g.*, Android, iOS, Windows, or BlackBerry) is known. As a future work, we are investigating the possibility of using the radio state identification technique to deanonymize Tor [5] users in the cellular network. In addition, we plan to evaluate whether remotely monitoring the sequence radio states of a mobile device can be used to build an accurate fingerprint of the Internet traffic of its user. We believe our work may introduce a new, more general research direction on delay-based user fingerprinting on cellular networks, which we intend to explore in the near future.

References

1. Backstrom, L., Boldi, P., Rosa, M., Ugander, J., Vigna, S.: Four degrees of separation. In: WebSci. ACM (2012)
2. Balakrishnan, M., Mohomed, I., Ramasubramanian, V.: Where's that phone?: Geolocating IP addresses on 3G networks. In: IMC. ACM (2009)
3. Bilge, L., Strufe, T., Balzarotti, D., Kirda, E.: All your contacts are belong to us: automated identity theft attacks on social networks. In: WWW. ACM (2009)
4. Cano-Garcia, J.M., Gonzalez-Parada, E., Casilari, E.: Experimental analysis and characterization of packet delay in UMTS networks. In: Koucheryavy, Y., Harju, J., Iversen, V.B. (eds.) NEW2AN 2006. LNCS, vol. 4003, pp. 396–407. Springer, Heidelberg (2006)
5. Dingledine, R., Mathewson, N., Syverson, P.: Tor: The second-generation onion router. Tech. rep., DTIC Document (2004)
6. Durumeric, Z., Wustrow, E., Halderman, J.A.: ZMap: Fast Internet-wide scanning and its security applications. In: USENIX Security (2013)
7. Gong, X., Borisov, N., Kiyavash, N., Schear, N.: Website detection using remote traffic analysis. In: Fischer-Hübner, S., Wright, M. (eds.) PETS 2012. LNCS, vol. 7384, pp. 58–78. Springer, Heidelberg (2012)
8. Hopper, N., Vasserman, E.Y., Chan-Tin, E.: How much anonymity does network latency leak? TISSEC 13(2), 13 (2010)
9. Jiang, H., Liu, Z., Wang, Y., Lee, K., Rhee, I.: Understanding bufferbloat in cellular networks. In: CellNet SIGCOMM Workshop. ACM (2012)
10. Jo, H.H., Karsai, M., Kertész, J., Kaski, K.: Circadian pattern and burstiness in mobile phone communication. New Journal of Physics 14(1), 013055 (2012)
11. Le Blond, S., Zhang, C., Legout, A., Ross, K., Dabbous, W.: I know where you are and what you are sharing: exploiting P2P communications to invade users' privacy. In: IMC. ACM (2011)
12. Lee, P.P., Bu, T., Woo, T.: On the detection of signaling DoS attacks on 3G wireless networks. In: INFOCOM. IEEE (2007)
13. Ling, Z., Luo, J., Zhang, Y., Yang, M., Fu, X., Yu, W.: A novel network delay based side-channel attack: Modeling and defense. In: INFOCOM. IEEE (2012)
14. Peng, C., Li, C.Y., Tu, G.H., Lu, S., Zhang, L.: Mobile data charging: new attacks and countermeasures. In: CCS. ACM (2012)
15. Perala, P.H., Barbuzzi, A., Boggia, G., Pentikousis, K.: Theory and practice of RRC state transitions in UMTS networks. In: GLOBECOM Workshops. IEEE (2009)

16. Qian, F., Wang, Z., Gerber, A., Mao, Z., Sen, S., Spatscheck, O.: Profiling resource usage for mobile applications: a cross-layer approach. In: MobiSys. ACM (2011)
17. Qian, F., Wang, Z., Gerber, A., Mao, Z.M., Sen, S., Spatscheck, O.: Characterizing radio resource allocation for 3G networks. In: IMC. ACM (2010)
18. Qian, Z., Wang, Z., Xu, Q., Mao, Z.M., Zhang, M., Wang, Y.M.: You can run, but you cant hide: Exposing network location for targeted DoS attacks in cellular networks. In: NDSS (2012)
19. Ricciato, F., Hasenleithner, E., Romirer-Maierhofer, P.: Traffic analysis at short time-scales: an empirical case study from a 3G cellular network. Transactions on Network and Service Management 5(1), 11–21 (2008)
20. Romero, J.P., Sallent, O., Agusti, R., Diaz-Guerra, M.A.: Radio resource management strategies in UMTS. John Wiley & Sons (2005)
21. Soroush, H., Sung, K., Learned-Miller, E., Levine, B.N., Liberatore, M.: Turning Off GPS Is Not Enough: Cellular location leaks over the internet. In: De Cristofaro, E., Wright, M. (eds.) PETS 2013. LNCS, vol. 7981, pp. 103–122. Springer, Heidelberg (2013)
22. Stöber, T., Frank, M., Schmitt, J., Martinovic, I.: Who do you sync you are?: smartphone fingerprinting via application behaviour. In: WiSec. ACM (2013)
23. Traynor, P., Lin, M., Ongtang, M., Rao, V., Jaeger, T., McDaniel, P., La Porta, T.: On cellular botnets: measuring the impact of malicious devices on a cellular network core. In: CCS. ACM (2009)
24. Vanaubel, Y., Pansiot, J.J., Mérindol, P., Donnet, B.: Network fingerprinting: TTL-based router signatures. In: IMC. ACM (2013)
25. Xu, Q., Huang, J., Wang, Z., Qian, F., Gerber, A., Mao, Z.M.: Cellular data network infrastructure characterization and implication on mobile content placement. In: SIGMETRICS. ACM (2011)

Why Doesn't Jane Protect Her Privacy?

Karen Renaud[1], Melanie Volkamer[2], and Arne Renkema-Padmos[2]

[1] School of Computing Science, University of Glasgow, Glasgow, UK
karen.renaud@glasgow.ac.uk
[2] CASED / TU Darmstadt, Hochschulstraße 10, 64289, Darmstadt, Germany
name.surname@cased.de

Abstract. End-to-end encryption has been heralded by privacy and security researchers as an effective defence against dragnet surveillance, but there is no evidence of widespread end-user uptake. We argue that the non-adoption of end-to-end encryption might not be entirely due to usability issues identified by Whitten and Tygar in their seminal paper "Why Johnny Can't Encrypt". Our investigation revealed a number of fundamental issues such as incomplete threat models, misaligned incentives, and a general absence of understanding of the email architecture. From our data and related research literature we found evidence of a number of potential explanations for the low uptake of end-to-end encryption. This suggests that merely increasing the availability and usability of encryption functionality in email clients will not automatically encourage increased deployment by email users. We shall have to focus, first, on building comprehensive end-user mental models related to email, and email security. We conclude by suggesting directions for future research.

Keywords: email, end-to-end encryption, privacy, security, mental model.

1 Introduction

Email was introduced in MIT's CTSS MAIL around 1965 [46]. At this point privacy was not a primary concern. Subsequently, STARTTLS [36,25] led to the deployment of opportunistic transport layer encryption for email transmission. Recently, more email providers have started applying it by default, effectively protecting email privacy in transit. However, email providers themselves, and those who might be able to hack into the email servers, have full access to our email communication. *End-to-end* (E2E) encryption by end-users would protect emails from access by email providers and hackers too. Facilitating tools are readily available, including PGP/OpenPGP [4,10,9], PEM [30,31,32,33], MOSS [13], PKCS#7 [26], and S/MIME [39,40,41] according to Davis [14]. However, they generally have minimal real-world application outside of specific use cases.

The "Summer of Snowden" [23] has put digital security back in the limelight, and there has been a slew of new proposals for facilitating E2E encrypted secure messaging (e.g. DarkMail, LEAP, Pond, Mailpile, Brair), but there is, as yet, little evidence of mass uptake of E2E email encryption. The question that remains is *"Why is the use of end-to-end email security so limited?"* Previously, the poor usability of E2E encryption tools was advanced as the most likely explanation [50,44]. However, usability has improved

E. De Cristofaro and S.J. Murdoch (Eds.): PETS 2014, LNCS 8555, pp. 244–262, 2014.

in the interim and this might no longer be the primary obstacle it used to be. Other papers cite interoperability difficulties between different tools and technical problems as contributing factors [34]. The research question we want to answer is: *"which other explanations, besides the previously highlighted problems, could explain the low uptake of E2E encryption?"* If other reasons exist, they will need to be addressed before we can hope to increase the uptake of E2E encryption.

To explore other potential explanations, we need to consider more human related than purely usability aspects because E2E email encryption is undeniably effortful. Hence the user has to be convinced of the need for E2E encryption, and the rewards that will accrue as a result [7]. Consequently, it makes sense to study end-user mental models of email and email security; i.e. do users actually understand the threats to their emails and do they know which particular threats could be ameliorated by means of E2E encryption? Note that if users don't have the correct mental models, or don't have any mental model of email architecture and potential threats at all, they are unlikely to encrypt their emails. If this is so, then in addition to addressing the technical and usability issues of email encryption, we will have to work on developing the correct mental models, so that these can eventually lead to a desire to encrypt and subsequent adoption. Some researchers have reported issues with respect to flawed end-user mental models in other security related contexts: with respect to anonymous credentials [49], wrt. firewalls [38,15], wrt. warnings [6], and wrt. mobile security [29]. Thus it is very likely, that similar issues wrt. mental models related to email, and email security, exist.

We conducted semi-structured interviews with lay people and a survey (containing the same questions) with a class of computer science students because we chose to focus on these two different groups to explore their respective end-user mental models. We anticipated that their mental models would differ given their very different backgrounds.

In order to answer our research question, we proposed seven possible explanations why people do not generally use E2E email encryption deduced from a natural progression from awareness, to understanding, to acting (Section 2). These seven possible explanations were evaluated based on an analysis of the interviews and survey responses as well as by examining related research literature in the context of usable security and mental models (Sections 3 and 4). We confirmed six of the seven explanations. Obviously, in order to change the situation in the future towards more privacy protection in email communication, all of these need to be addressed. We thus conclude the paper by suggesting that future work focus on finding ways to address these different themes (Section 5). Due to the general nature of our findings and proposals, we expect that amelioration will apply equally to email communication and to other privacy-critical applications.

2   Proposed Explanations

Here we provide a list of possible explanations for non-uptake of E2E encryption. To generate these explanations we formulated a developmental pathway to adoption of E2E email encryption. We identified seven different states starting with general, then usability-related and then states related to interoperability and technology (see Fig. 1):

1. They do not have any *awareness* of privacy as a concern.

2. They are aware of the possibility of privacy violation of their emails but do not take any action for a variety of different reasons, perhaps because it does not *concern* them.
3. They know that the privacy of their emails can be violated but are not aware that this can happen in transit or at the mail server side. They may subsequently attempt to protect themselves against client-based threats, but *do not use E2E encryption.*
4. They know that the privacy of their emails can be violated in transit or at the mail server side but they *do not take any action* because they fail to see the need to act.
5. They know that the privacy of their emails can be violated (transit/server) and they want to prevent this but they *do not know how* to protect their emails against these types of threats, i.e. that they should use E2E encryption. They lack the knowledge, or have only partial knowledge.
6. They are concerned that the privacy of their emails can be violated (transit/server) and they understand that they can use E2E encryption to prevent this, but they *can't* do it.
7. They are concerned that the privacy of their emails can be violated and they understand that they can use E2E encryption to prevent this, and they are able to do it, but still they have reasons not to — *they get side-tracked for some or other reason.*

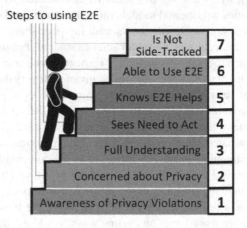

Fig. 1. Progression Towards E2E Encryption Deployment

For each of these explanations we will examine the relevant research literature and statements made by the participants in our study to see whether each is supported or challenged.

3   The Study

We performed an exploratory study consisting of semi-structured interviews, and subsequent qualitative analysis in order to identify users' mental models of email security and thereby to answer the question *"Which of the Proposed Explanations for the Non-Uptake of E2E Encryption Can be Validated?"*. The research philosophy of this study is interpretivistic [51]. This is typical for research carried out where explanations are sought for activities in natural settings where we hope to make cautious generalisations based on a study of a limited number of participants. The research approach is inductive, seeking to construct theories by means of identification of patterns in the data [5].

From 2 to 6 December 2013[1], we performed 21 interviews in Glasgow, of whom 18 participants consented to having their interview recorded and transcribed. The participants were a convenience sample of students and staff at The University of Glasgow, and were recruited through personal and social networks.

The questions in the study were based on several discussion sessions among the authors. As there is no 'one' widely-accepted method for identifying mental models, we decided to use both drawings with think-aloud and semi-structured interviews in order to gather both types of data.

Both parts were tested in a pre-study. For the test run, the survey was given to six people to fill in on paper, and the drawing tasks were also tried in-person with two individuals, as well as generally asking around to get an impression of people's frame of mind. From the pre-study we became aware of unclear question framing. For the study design we removed stickers with concrete threats (e.g. NSA, anonymous, viruses), created a custom diagram to be used in the debrief, added think-aloud, updated the way that questions were asked (e.g. specifically asking about security problems), and reworked the stickers based on icons from Microsoft Outlook 2013.

For the interviews, first the participant received a warm-up exercise for think-aloud, was handed the questionnaire, and then the questions were asked while the responses were recorded over audio. They were debriefed afterwards. These question categories were included in the study:

Free-hand drawing. Participants were asked to draw the transmission infrastructure and process that allows an email from a friend to arrive in their inbox. They were asked if they would change the drawing if they were sending the email, or if the email was sent by a bank.

Template drawing. In the second stage, a sheet of stickers was given to the participants, and they were asked to make another drawing of the transmission infrastructure. They were told they did not have to use all stickers and that they could draw additional items.

Security problems. Participants were asked what security problems they were aware of regarding email, who causes these problems, and where they are caused. They were asked to mark the location where the problem takes place on the diagram made from the stickers.

Security concerns. They were also asked about their general level of concern around the security problems of email that they mentioned, which problems they were most and least concerned about (as well as the reason), and what coping mechanisms they put in place to deal with the concerns they had.

---

[1] We obtained ethical approval from the College of Science and Engineering at Glasgow University (#CSE01327).

Demographics. Participants were asked whether they used webmail and/or a desktop client, which email client they use, their occupation, sex, and age group.

Debriefing and Closing Remarks. At the end of the study the interviewed partici-pants were debriefed about the true goal of the study.

Permission was requested for a transcript of the recording to be made and used in a publication. They were also asked whether they were willing to take part in future studies, and whether they would like to receive a copy of the paper resulting from this research.

Participants were informed about the topic of the study (transmission of email), but were not briefed about the precise goal of the study (determining understanding of email security). Note that we did not mention the concept of end-to-end encryption to the participants, nor did we suggest that they ought to encrypt their emails. They were told that they could stop at any time, and that they would not be penalised in any way for doing so when participating in any courses taught by the researchers.

The interview group consisted of 9 females and 12 males, with 7 individuals in age group 18-24 and 14 individuals in age group 25-34. Of the participants, 8 used webmail, 11 used webmail and desktop email clients, and 2 weren't sure.

In addition to the data collected from lay persons, we also wanted to collect data from computer science students as they ought to have a better understanding of the email infrastructure and the potential threats. However, due to resource limitations, it was not possible to conduct and transcribe another twenty interviews, so we administered a survey containing the same questions to a classroom context. We acknowledge that this stoppes us from collecting individual think-aloud transcripts or speaking to the students personally but we did gain valuable insights despite these limitations.

Both the survey and interview groups stepped through the same survey: the same materials were used for both. The interviewer walked through all questions with the interview participants. The classroom group completed the survey individually without assistance.

The survey group consisted of 8 females and 16 males (1 blank answer), with 12 individuals in age group 18-24, 11 individuals in age group 25-34, and 1 individual in age group 35-44 (1 blank answer). Of the participants, 13 used webmail, 8 used webmail and desktop email clients, 3 used desktop clients, and one was not sure.

4   Results and Reflection

We performed a qualitative analysis of the results, based on an inductive approach, to determine which of the explanations could be supported. We independently analysed our participants' responses, then conferred in order to agree.

Since this was a qualitative study we, like Wash [48], do not report how many users alluded to each of the explanations in their statements. We do attempt to give a flavour of our findings, in order to allow the reader to understand the different mental models that are revealed by our study.

In the following subsections we report on whether any statements made by the partic-ipants support or challenge the explanations we advanced in Section 2. We also discuss the results in relation to existing findings from the literature. As described in the study section, we performed the study with two groups: lay people and experts. We did not detect any differences between the two groups, however, so the rest of this section is an analysis of both the interviews and the surveys.

4.1 Explanation 1: No Privacy Awareness

A possible reason why E2E encryption is not widely used might be that people do not have any *awareness* of privacy as a concern.

Analysis from interviews/survey. We did not find any general evidence for this explanation from the interviews and surveys — the participants were indeed aware of the fact that their privacy could be violated when using email. Quotes that support the case that people are aware of privacy are:

> ".. it kind of gets more into the privacy of people's life, somehow"
> "it's just like a virtual ... loss ... of privacy"
> "it's about privacy concern and he is collecting data, and based on that data
>   maybe he is profiling"
> "mitigate by not sending emails containing sensitive information.

In particular, general privacy-related violations were mentioned far more frequently than specific concerns such as the integrity, authenticity and availability of email. There is also some evidence that the NSA's activities have had some influence as shown by quotes like

> "... NSA, a group of intelligence; they are just monitoring normal people"

Findings from literature. In the literature there are similar findings that people are more aware of privacy violations than of any other type of violations [47]. Few people mentioned specific aspects such as integrity and availability in a study into online security understanding [19]. In a study on connection security, people only considered confidentiality and encryption in their definitions [18]. For smartphones the issue of theft and loss made availability salient in a study on smartphone security [35].

Summary. While the majority appeared aware of privacy concerns related to email, there was at least one who did not mention privacy, sensitive data, private data or anything related to this.

4.2 Explanation 2: Privacy Aware, But Not Concerned

Another explanation that can be advanced is that they are not concerned about the problems even though they are aware of the potential privacy violations that can occur.

Analysis from interviews/survey. From the interviews and surveys, different reasons have been identified that may help to explain why people may not see the need to protect their privacy in the email context even though they are aware of potential privacy issues. Relevant statements and corresponding quotes from the study are:

Theme 1: Nothing to hide: "And I don't feel that I have something to [laughs] to hide, though I don't like people, uh, getting in my stuff"; "[I'm least concerned about] [s]nooping. I think that unless I have something to hide it doesn't bother me."; "But in general, I don't know if that is that, uh, important or is it that interesting. I don't know. It, it's not very sensitive, so the risk is not that high,"; "Given for me as a private person because I don't have, you know, so private data which I'm concerned about that no one ever should read that and I—like 99% of my emails are just formal stuff".

Theme 2: No harm "But they are not affected directly."; "Not to do any harm to me, rather he is actually collecting data."; "I think, umm, that would always happen, the monitoring thing. So, I would say that yeah ... the, the hacking thing is more, more of a concern."

Theme 3: They don't feel important enough "Emails of some high officials, high-position officials in government so ... they may ... cause problems."; "I think it just, um, depends on your personality if you have someone famous."

Theme 4: Private emails are not critical "I would be more concerned if it was my official Inbox, of my company, but this I'm, I'm since I am a student and I am right now only talking about my personal email box"; "I'm talking about personal emails there."; "So I think there are possibly two main cyber threats for me as a private person, and then if you're an institution or a business company, then there might be more"

Theme 5: Someone else's responsibility "There has to be the clients, or the, the, the person providing the client services is responsible for making sure that it's secure. So if you have a decent email service provider they should be able to ensure that you can only see emails that are on your account and you only see emails after you've logged on, and things like that"; "You-the whole thing about not just email security but the whole cyber security in general, you have to ... we're most of the time at the mercy of the people providing the service."

Theme 6: Assuming that security is already taken care of "I'm not, I'm not aware of any, sort of, like, when I'm sending just a general email, umm, I assume [laughs] that it's quite safe and it hasn't been commandeered by an external source, or anything like that."; "That's why it's personal computer and personal email. That's-I think that's the, the, the worst case scenario if every time I send an email or had a conversation online, someone else can see it. It's not good."; "It works, but I suppose that the securities during the, during that path we draw before, it should be really h-hard to break, first of all."

Findings from literature. Other researchers studying privacy issues in other contexts such as social networks also concluded that there was often a mismatch between being aware of privacy issues and taking action. Acquisti and Grossklags found that "even if individuals have access to complete information about their privacy risks and modes of protection, they might not be able to process vast amounts of data to formulate a rational privacy-sensitive decision" [2]. Users might also be driven by immediate gratification over rational decision-making [1]. Gross and Rosson [24] confirm the attitude of generally feeling that security was the IT department's job, not that of their study's participants.

Summary. There is plenty of evidence, both from our study and from the literature, that if people are generally aware of privacy issues with email communication this does not mean that they will expend the effort to protect their privacy. Thus, we can conclude that this second explanation is indeed a feasible reason why E2E encryption is not widely used.

4.3 Explanation 3: Privacy Concerned with Misconceptions

A third possible explanation is that users know that the privacy of their emails can be violated but do not know that this can happen both in transit and at the mail server. They may subsequently attempt to protect themselves against other types of threats and might not use E2E encryption.

Analysis from interviews/survey. Analysing the interviews and the surveys reveals that neither threats at the email server side in terms of either hacking the server or internals having access, nor threats on the network, are those that are most often mentioned. The threats that are most often mentioned are related to password security and malicious attachments.

Theme 1: Password Issues: Quotes which clearly provide evidence that most people have password problems in mind when thinking about how to secure email communication are: "I think this is the main thing, related... basically, if your password is secure with you, then I think your mailbox is secure."; "If your password is... you know, falls into the wrong hands... most concerned obviously is someone getting access into my mailbox, obviously, by logging in";

The responses to the question on countermeasures show that people mentioning password-related threats also mention corresponding countermeasures such as: "Trying to use as many different passwords as possible without keeping, uh, keep forgetting them."; "Good password, change password regulary."; "Set a very good password, including numericals and alphabets, lowercase, uppercase, special characters.";

Theme 2: Malicious Attachment: Quotes indicating that people have malicious attachments in mind when thinking about email related threat are: "files you don't really want to . you might receive viruses"; "if you open an attachment which includes viruses or something like that"; "you can receive any virus".

Similarly, responses to the question on countermeasures show again that people mentioning malicious attachments also mention anti-virus software (e.g."From the sending side, well, you might actually, ahh, send something you're not aware to send somehow, ahh, or you might actually end up sending emails even though you don't know it") or advocating careful usage as a corresponding countermeasure. Examples for careful usage are: "Don't open any emails from an unknown."; "I do my own mental virus scan in my limited abilities, in my head.".

Theme 3: Further Mentioned Threats: Other mentioned threats not related to the server or transit threats are:

– *Concerned about security of end-point devices*
  "I'm not an expert at all but, ahh, got a virus, and for that reason it kept on sending automatic emails from his ... his email address", "But for some reason these random emails pop up and ... on my Hotmail before. I had to cancel it because all these people were getting emails from me that I had ... um, when I was in the military. And they were all getting emails, and I hadn't sent any emails.".

– *Concerned about someone having physical access to their device*
  "[A]t the university, sometimes I open my mailbox and I just forget to, ahh, sign out.";
  "I work with my laptop, and sometimes I leave my laptop alone."

Findings from literature. People in our study were most likely to mention password security and virus as malicious attachments which is related to Wash's [48] findings on "names for viruses models about viruses, spyware, adware, and other forms of malware [were] which referred to [by everyone] under the umbrella term virus'" [48]. Also related to Wash's and others' findings is that one of the issues with security is that people's s are incomplete i.e. they try to apply countermeasures against those threats they are aware of and they think these will address all threats.

Finally with respect to encryption in particular, Garfinkel suggests that the trust model of PGP (Web of Trust) is too hard for many users to grasp [21]. Keller *et al.* [27] report that the detailed properties of the cryptographic primitives that are used in public-key cryptography can be hard to grasp. Additionally the public-key infrastructures, on which many E2E encrypted email programmes are built, might be difficult to comprehend: "[T]he usability problems uncovered in the Johnny user study were not driven by the PGP 5.0 program itself, nor by the lack of training offered within the program, but by the underlying key certification model used by PGP." [21].

Summary. While this shows that when people are aware of a concrete threat, in this case passwords being hacked and malicious attachments, they take or try to take remedial actions. However, our analysis also provides evidence that some people are not aware of any other threats and in particular are not aware of threats related to the server and the transit. Correspondingly there is evidence for explanation 3, that many participants have various (mis)understandings that direct them towards specific countermeasures that are not relevant for adoption of E2E encryption.

4.4 Explanation 4: Privacy Concerned, with Sound Understanding, But Does Not See Need to Act

The fourth possible explanation is that users know that the privacy of their emails can be violated, and have a sound understanding that this can happen during transit or at the mail server side, and also know that they can use E2E encryption. However, they do not take any action for different reasons.

First, we validated whether there were actually people who were aware of threats related to the server and transmission. There is strong evidence that at least some people

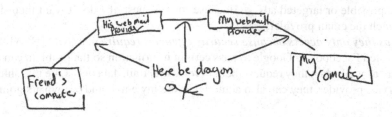

Fig. 2. Understanding of the email architecture of participant B-24: "here be dragons"

are aware of these threats as the following quotes show (as well as Figure 2): "I don't like my personal emails to be accessible by the email provider", "it's always that they have control on everything"; "It's a bit strange that Google can read what I am, uh, sending or, uh, receiving from-from friends, or-or-or partners or businessmen.; "The data transmission in general, from server to Internet, should... could be, could be a problem."; "I would imagine it would be somewhere from leaving her computer to being out here, and then before coming then in my computer."

Analysis from interviews/survey. In order to validate this explanation from the interviews and surveys, we checked whether people who mentioned threats related to the server or the transit necessarily saw the need to protect against these threats. We identified reasons why it might be worthwhile for people to take action themselves to protect against hackers gaining access to the mail servers, against email service providers having access, or even against anyone listening on the network. For each of the three themes we provide quotes:

   Theme 1: No need to protect against hackers gaining access "... or to the server, but I don't know how, ... how easy it is to ... have access in the whole server for a company"; "With the cyber security in place, I think Gmail would not allow someone to get into its stuff like that. So probably, I might be a little less concerned about that."; "I'm the least concerned about hackers. Okay. That's mainly because I use two-step verifica-verification on my email, and I will see if it works."; "I think the server is most sensitive one, but for me it's less concern because, um, I care about the money I have to pay and if I want it very secure I have to invest money."

   Theme 2: No need to protect against email providers having access in general... "You can say that for security reason it might be useful" [having access to the e-mails]; "But sometimes it looks at patterns and words in the email. Most of them, they will actually read the email. Maybe then scan through the message and they see things that sound fishy, they, they can highlight to you that the message looks like it's not very genuine"

   – *... as they only scan to enable targeted advertisements ...* "Who can scan your email and know the content. And then based an advertising"; "They you need to be able to parse it, right, for targeted ads"; "Possibly least concerned is if something, uh, if my email provider is reading or like scripting my emails and therefore showing me possible or targeted ads. ... Because to be honest, if I don't want them I'll just switch the email provider."

- *... as they only access because security agencies require access:* "[NSA] they requested Facebook or Google to pass certain information so the problem can appear here as well when they request them to release certain data or maybe my, ahh, email service provider, they can also actually access my email and see what's going on"

Theme 3: No Need to Protect against network related attacks "And there's always the chance that it could be intercepted and read, and maybe even duplicated and stuff like that. [..] So I really don't see that as a big problem."

Findings from literature. There is an interesting aspect regarding paying for security and how much people are willing to pay. Will they accept insecure or less secure services as long as these are free? This has also been studied and presented in the literature. "[I]ndividuals are willing to trade privacy for convenience or bargain the release of personal information in exchange fore relatively small rewards." [2], and "Many perverse aspects of information security that had been long known to practitioners but just dismissed as 'bad weather' turn out to be quite explicable in terms of the incentives facing individuals and organisations, and in terms of different kinds of market failure." [3]. Finally, the "nothing to hide" fallacy [45] comes across strongly. Conti and Sobiesk [12] found that many of the respondents in their study also exhibited this perception.

Summary Our data provides evidence that this fourth explanation (that is, that users know that the privacy of their emails can be violated, and have a sound understanding that this can happen during transit or at the mail server side, but do not take any action) is a viable explanation for the poor uptake of E2E encryption.

4.5 Explanation 5: Privacy Concerned, with Sound Understanding, But Does Not Know How to Act

Another possible explanation is that while people are aware that their privacy can be violated, are concerned about privacy problems, and see the need to prevent these, they may not be aware of the efficacy of E2E encryption to protect their communications. They may believe that other measures are efficacious. Because they do not know, or are only partially aware, that they can use E2E encryption as a precaution, they do not use/consider it but may consider other options.

Findings from interviews/surveys. The analysis of the surveys, in particular, revealed a number of themes why people do not use E2E encryption although they see a need to protect themselves (against server side privacy violations ans against network attacks). The identified themes are 'think there is nothing they can do', 'unclear about countermeasures', and 'wrong understanding of encryption'. In the following we explain these themes and provide quotes for each of the themes:

Theme 1: Think there is nothing they can do: Due to the lack of knowledge about encryption and, in particular, about E2E encryption, some people believe that they cannot prevent email providers from gaining access to their emails. Quotes providing evidence for this theme are: "Is never gonna change."; "There's no solution for that."; "It's always that they have control on everything."

Theme 2: Other types of (more or less effective) countermeasures: "So whenever, uh, I have to send some very, like, uh, highly, uh, you know, secret information, I do not prefer mail. I prefer talking on phone; "Like to split up into different things, and I would say that send some of them by Facebook, but some of them by emails; "I am definitely not sending my credit card information or stuff like that or very-very personal data within, um, an email. I try to do that personally or within different steps."

Theme 3: Wrong understanding of encryption: Overall, only very few participants mentioned the term 'encryption' at all. Most of those who mentioned it seem to have a wrong understanding of encryption and in particular E2E encryption as the following quotes show: "Definitely encrypt the email, make sure I knew it wasn't a fake."; "[I'm aware of problems related to] firewall and cryptography, public and private passwords" Of particular interest is this statement from one of the participants using https: "The only thing that I use is I actually enable https for my Facebook, Gmail, etcetera. So I use secured connection to login, so that like I use SSL and there... it's a secure.". This is only a first step however, and only secures the connection between the device and the mail provider but does not mitigate against the amail provider or any connection afterwards as https might not be enabled.

Findings from literature. Wash [48] postulates that people had some idea of some kinds of threats and tried to use countermeasures that they believed would address the threats they were aware of. If their threat models are incorrect these countermeasures will probably not help, but the invisibility of breaches will keep them blissfully unaware of this. Gross and Rosson [24] reported that the participants in their study had an incorrect and dated understanding of the actual threats they were subject to. They seemed to conflate security with functionality in many cases.

Summary. Based on the findings from the interviews and surveys, and the findings in the literature, we can confirm the explanation that some people do not use E2E encrypted email because they are not aware, or do not understand, the protection techniques that are available.

4.6   Explanation 6: Privacy Concerned, Wants to Act, But Cannot

In this subsection we analyse whether the theoretical explanation of "They know that the privacy of their emails can be violated (transit/server) and they understand that they can use E2E encryption to prevent this, but they are not able to use it".

Findings from interviews/surveys. The analysis of the interviews and the surveys does not provide much evidence that this is actually a reason, i.e. not being *able* to encrypt was not something our participants complained about. The only related quote is:

"[Encrypting email is] less effective because not everyone knows to to user this / decrypt / etc.)"

The fact that participants did not mention more related issues might be because we did not use the term "E2E encryption" in our questions and, in particular, we did not ask our participants whether they ever tried to use E2E encryption or to relate their experiences with using it. This omission was deliberate: we wanted to gauge *their* mental models, not prompt them by mentioning E2E encryption.

Findings from literature.   One of the mantras of the field of usable security is that security systems are not used because they are too complicated, because people *cannot* use them. Whitten & Tygar published their seminal "Johnny" paper in 1999 [50]. They suggest that security software is intrinsically harder to use than "normal" software [50].

Many of the papers published about email encryption and the difficulties users experience with it make a basic assumption that the problem is that they *can't* encrypt [50,11,44,20,52,34,43]. This suggests that the user wants to do something but is prevented from doing so by the complexity of the system and the poor design of the interface. Some researchers have worked on creating better interfaces to address this problem [17].

Summary.   While the Whitten and Tygar paper states that poor usability is discouraging adoption, many people do not even reach this stage, and are stuck in different mindsets. Thus, while users with good understanding and motivation may be foiled by poor user interface design or a lack of technological support, many have different reasons for non-adoption that will need to be resolved before contributions to the usability challenge become meaningful.

4.7   Explanation 7: Privacy Concerned, Knows How to Act, Can Act But Does Not

In this subsection we analyse whether the theoretical explanation of "They know that the privacy of their emails can be violated (transit/server), and they understand that they can use E2E encryption to prevent this, and they are able to use the tools, but they get side-tracked for some reason.' was mentioned by our participants or by other researchers.

Findings from interviews/surveys.   From the data we collected there is no evidence to confirm this explanation.

Findings from literature.   Users appear to have an over-optimistic bias in their risk perceptions, especially with respect to information security. This self-serving bias is also related to a perception of controllability with respect to information security threats, i.e. what we control we consider less risky than that which we do not control [42,37]. Furthermore, interoperability and availability of keys on different devices are issues mentioned by [34]. Another possibility is that users are simply mimimising effort, and encryption, being effortful, seems too much trouble.

Dingledine and Mathewson [16] studied the tendency of users to not use security features. In general, in case of high effort and only a nebulous nature of the consequences, it was not used. Unfortunately, it is difficult to compute the cost of security, or even the lack thereof [28]. Furthermore, Gaw *et al.* [22] offers another potential reason. In the analysed organisation where employees did have the knowledge and ability, email was not universally encrypted. As reasons they identified that employees considered it paranoid to encrypt all emails, suggesting a social element to their decision making.

Summary. While there is not much evidence from our interviews and surveys to support this explanation there is some evidence from the literature supporting this explanation. It is possible that we would also have identified similar themes from interviews if we had included people who either do use, or have discontinued using, E2E encryption.

4.8   Summary and Discussion

Table 1 summarises our findings, in terms of whether our explanations were confirmed by our studies and literature review, or not.

Table 1. Support for the Seven Explanations

Proposed Explanation	Literature	Participant Statements
1. No Awareness		(✓)
2. No Concern	✓	✓
3. Misconceptions of How to Protect	✓	✓
4. No Perceived Need to Take Action	✓	✓
5. Needs to Take Action But Does Not Know How to Act	✓	✓
6. Inability to use E2E Encryption	✓	
7. Becoming Side-Tracked	✓	

We were not able to find strong evidence for a non-awareness of privacy as an explanation for non-adoption of E2E encryption. However, the gap between theoretical and practical privacy awareness pointed out by Burghardt *et al.* [8] could be confirmed in the context of email from our studies as increased awareness does not have converted into widespread adoption of E2E email encryption. Their lack of understanding, misconceptions and incomplete mental models of email security (refering to explanation 2-5) meant they did not even think about using E2E encryption. Correspondingly, it is not too surprising that from the qualitative studies was that not being able or willing to encrypt (poor usability - explanation number 6 and becoming side-tracked - explanation number 7) was rarely mentioned by the participants. These misconceptions also explain why people taking action to protect themselves mainly deploy (traditional) mechanisms such as secure passwords, anti-virus software, and careful usage. From our data, we identified three cross-cutting factors that could contribute towards the explanations we cited in Section 2. *The first contributory factor could be their lack of understanding, misconceptions and incomplete mental models of email security* might be that there was, in general, very little understanding of how email was transmitted and stored and how the email architecture works. We could observe this from their drawings - e.g. in Figure 3 (computers directly connecting and email floating across to the recipient) and Figure 4 (here the lock and key may indicate that users think that more technologies are in place than HTTPS, and possibly have an expectation of end-to-end encryption) - as well as from their statements:

Fig. 3. Examples from first set of drawings

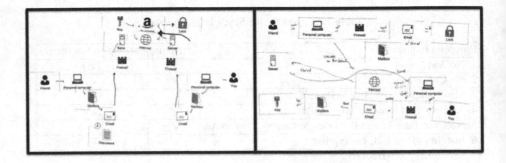

Fig. 4. Examples from second set of drawings

"[I]t'll go into the sky somewhere, and then it will [go] down to my computer"
"[I]t's all an invisible process to me. The way that I understand is that you liter-
    ally just click send' then a second later it appears in their inbox [laughs]."
"Umm, well, yeah, this type of thing is actually, ahh, quite a ... a mysterious
    thing for me."

A *second contributory factor* might be that they lack understanding of the possible consequences of not protecting themselves. For instance, most of those who *were* aware of email providers having full access to their emails rationalised this instead of being concerned. They advanced several reasons for why this was acceptable, e.g. that it facilitated scanning of emails which they considered needed to occur for security purposes or to allow targeted advertisements (the price they pay for a free email service). Others, with more understanding and a greater level of concern, often did not act to protect their privacy because they considered it futile in the face of surveillance actions by powerful governments. Interestingly, there did not seem to be significant differences between mental models held by lay persons and computer science students taking part in our study.

A *third contributory factor* that emerged from our data was that problems might be attributable to the information sources that inform people generally. Our study provided evidence for the fact that people gain knowledge primarily via stories told by others or based on personal experience:

> "I have friends that, uh, their per-their personal accounts w-was hacked."
> "And also I think I've heard from my friend that they could catch everything from here [laughs] somehow."
> "[A friend] got a virus, and for that reason it kept on sending automatic emails from his ... his email address."

This would explain why many people seem to have an awareness of "good password practice", but not about privacy protection using E2E encryption, which has enjoyed much less attention in the media.

5   Conclusion and Future Work

The Snowden revelations have highlighted the importance of end-to-end encryption as a privacy preserving tool. We posed the question *"Why is the use of end-to-end email security so limited?"*. In order to answer this question, we set out by proposing a developmental pathway, a progression to E2E encryption, comprising of seven explanatory states.

We carried out a qualitative study (both semi-structured interviews and a survey) in order to identify mental models from both lay persons and computer science students. We considered that this study would serve to confirm or challenge our proposed explanations. We also carried out a literature review to determine whether the explanations could be verified from the established research literature. We did confirm four of the seven explanations from our study, and an extra two from the research literature.

As future work it would be beneficial to come up with ways of ameliorating the situation, finding ways of advancing users along the pathway to awareness, concern, knowledge, understanding, usage, and eventual adoption. Since we identified flawed or incomplete mental models in states two to five, specific questions that can be investigated in future to address these mental model related issues could include:

- How can we help users to understand the threats to their emails?
- How can we elicit a sense of concern in end-users with respect to privacy violations such that they make an attempt to explore privacy preservation tools?
- How can we communicate countermeasures and desirable precautionary behaviours effectively?
- How can we dispel the "nothing to hide" myth, so that end users do indeed see the need to act to preserve their privacy once they know how, i.w. better understand the consequences at least in the long run?
- In general, how can we nurture and foster comprehensive and complete mental models of E2E to ensure that users want to encrypt, know how to encrypt and, most importantly, do encrypt.

Acknowledgement. This paper has been developed within the project usable secure email communication' - which is funded by the CASED (Center for Advanced Security Research Darmstadt) and the Horst Görtz Foundation and the EC SPRIDE project - funded by the German Federal Ministry of Education and Research.

References

1. Acquisti, A.: Privacy in electronic commerce and the economics of immediate gratification. In: Proceedings of the 5th ACM Conference on Electronic Commerce EC 2004, pp. 21–29. ACM, New York (2004)
2. Acquisti, A., Grossklags, J.: Privacy and rationality in individual decision making. IEEE Security & Privacy 2, 24–30 (2005)
3. Anderson, R., Moore, T.: The economics of information security. Science 314(5799), 610–613 (2006)
4. Atkins, D., Stallings, W., Zimmermann, P.: PGP Message Exchange Formats. RFC 1991 (Informational), obsoleted by RFC 4880 (August 1996), http://www.ietf.org/rfc/rfc1991.txt
5. Bhattacherjee, A.: Social science research: principles, methods, and practices (2012)
6. Bravo-Lillo, C., Cranor, L.F., Downs, J.S., Komanduri, S.: Bridging the gap in computer security warnings: A mental model approach. Security & Privacy 9(2), 18–26 (2011)
7. Bright, P., Goodin, D.: Encrypted e-mail: How much annoyance will you tolerate to keep the NSA away?, aRS Technica (June 2013), http://arstechnica.com/security/2013/06/encrypted-e-mail-how-much-annoyance-will-you-tolerate-to-keep-the-nsa-away/
8. Burghardt, T., Buchmann, E., Böhm, K.: Why do privacy-enhancement mechanisms fail, after all? a survey of both, the user and the provider perspective. In: Workshop W2Trust, in Conjunction with IFIPTM, vol. 8 (2008)
9. Callas, J., Donnerhacke, L., Finney, H., Shaw, D., Thayer, R.: OpenPGP Message Format. RFC 4880 (Proposed Standard), updated by RFC 5581 (November 2007), http://www.ietf.org/rfc/rfc4880.txt
10. Callas, J., Donnerhacke, L., Finney, H., Thayer, R.: OpenPGP Message Format. RFC 2440 (Proposed Standard), obsoleted by RFC 4880 (November 1998), http://www.ietf.org/rfc/rfc2440.txt
11. Clark, S., Goodspeed, T., Metzger, P., Wasserman, Z., Xu, K., Blaze, M.: Why (special agent) Johnny (still) can't encrypt: a security analysis of the APCO project 25 two-way radio system. In: Proceedings of the 20th USENIX Conference on Security, p. 4. USENIX Association (2011)
12. Conti, G., Sobiesk, E.: An honest man has nothing to fear: User perceptions on web-based information disclosure. In: Proceedings of the 3rd Symposium on Usable Privacy and Security, SOUPS 2007, pp. 112–121. ACM, New York (2007), http://doi.acm.org/10.1145/1280680.1280695
13. Crocker, S., Freed, N., Galvin, J., Murphy, S.: MIME Object Security Services. RFC 1848 (Historic) (October 1995), http://www.ietf.org/rfc/rfc1848.txt
14. Davis, D.: Defective sign & encrypt in S/MIME, PKCS# 7, MOSS, PEM, PGP, and XML. In: USENIX Annual Technical Conference, General Track, pp. 65–78 (2001)
15. Diesner, J., Kumaraguru, P., Carley, K.M.: Mental models of data privacy and security extracted from interviews with Indians. In: 55th Annual Conference of the International Communication Association (ICA), New York, May 26-30 (2005)

16. Dingledine, R., Mathewson, N.: Anonymity Loves Company: Usability and the Network Effect. In: The Fifth Workshop on the Economics of Information Security (WEIS 2006), June 26-28 (2006)
17. Fahl, S., Harbach, M., Muders, T., Smith, M., Sander, U.: Helping Johnny 2.0 to Encrypt His Facebook Conversations. In: Proceedings of the Eighth Symposium on Usable Privacy and Security, SOUPS 2012, pp. 11:1–11:17 (2012)
18. Friedman, B., Hurley, D., Howe, D.C., Felten, E., Nissenbaum, H.: Users' conceptions of web security: A comparative study. In: CHI 2002 Extended Abstracts on Human Factors in Computing Systems, pp. 746–747. ACM (2002)
19. Furman, S.M., Theofanos, M.F., Choong, Y.Y., Stanton, B.: Basing cybersecurity training on user perceptions. IEEE Security & Privacy 10(2), 40–49 (2012)
20. Furnell, S.: Why users cannot use security. Computers & Security 24(4), 274–279 (2005)
21. Garfinkel, S.L., Miller, R.C.: Johnny 2: A user test of key continuity management with s/mime and outlook express. In: Proceedings of the 2005 Symposium on Usable Privacy and Security, pp. 13–24. ACM (2005)
22. Gaw, S., Felten, E.W., Fernandez-Kelly, P.: Secrecy, flagging, and paranoia: adoption criteria in encrypted email. In: Proceedings of the SIGCHI Conference on Human Factors in Computing Systems, pp. 591–600. ACM (2006)
23. Greenwald, G., MacAskill, E., Poitras, L.: Edward Snowden: the whistleblower behind the NSA surveillance revelations. The Guardian 9 (2013)
24. Gross, J.B., Rosson, M.B.: Looking for trouble: understanding end-user security management. In: Proceedings of the 2007 Symposium on Computer Human Interaction for the Management of information Technology, p. 10. ACM (2007)
25. Hoffman, P.: SMTP Service Extension for Secure SMTP over Transport Layer Security. RFC 3207 (Proposed Standard) (February 2002), http://www.ietf.org/rfc/rfc3207.txt
26. Kaliski, B.: PKCS #7: Cryptographic Message Syntax Version 1.5. RFC 2315 (Informational) (March 1998), http://www.ietf.org/rfc/rfc2315.txt
27. Keller, L., Komm, D., Serafini, G., Sprock, A., Steffen, B.: Teaching public-key cryptography in school. In: Hromkovič, J., Královič, R., Vahrenhold, J. (eds.) ISSEP 2010. LNCS, vol. 5941, pp. 112–123. Springer, Heidelberg (2010)
28. Lampson, B.: Privacy and security: Usable security: How to get it. Commun. ACM 52(11), 25–27 (2009)
29. Lin, J., Amini, S., Hong, J.I., Sadeh, N., Lindqvist, J., Zhang, J.: Expectation and purpose: understanding users' mental models of mobile app privacy through crowdsourcing. In: Proceedings of the 2012 ACM Conference on Ubiquitous Computing, UbiComp 2012, pp. 501–510. ACM, New York (2012)
30. Linn, J.: Privacy enhancement for Internet electronic mail: Part I: Message encipherment and authentication procedures. RFC 989, obsoleted by RFCs 1040, 1113 (February 1987), http://www.ietf.org/rfc/rfc989.txt
31. Linn, J.: Privacy enhancement for Internet electronic mail: Part I: Message encipherment and authentication procedures. RFC 1040, obsoleted by RFC 1113 (1988), http://www.ietf.org/rfc/rfc1040.txt
32. Linn, J.: Privacy enhancement for Internet electronic mail: Part I - message encipherment and authentication procedures. RFC 1113 (Historic), obsoleted by RFC 1421 (August 1989), http://www.ietf.org/rfc/rfc1113.txt
33. Linn, J.: Privacy Enhancement for Internet Electronic Mail: Part I: Message Encryption and Authentication Procedures. RFC 1421 (Historic) (February 1993), http://www.ietf.org/rfc/rfc1421.txt
34. Moecke, C.T., Volkamer, M.: Usable secure email communications: criteria and evaluation of existing approaches. Information Management & Computer Security 21(1), 41–52 (2013)

35. Muslukhov, I., Boshmaf, Y., Kuo, C., Lester, J., Beznosov, K.: Understanding users' requirements for data protection in smartphones. In: 2012 IEEE 28th International Conference on Data Engineering Workshops (ICDEW), pp. 228–235. IEEE (2012)
36. Newman, C.: Using TLS with IMAP, POP3 and ACAP. RFC 2595 (Proposed Standard), updated by RFC 4616 (June 1999), http://www.ietf.org/rfc/rfc2595.txt
37. Nordgren, L.F., Van Der Pligt, J., Van Harreveld, F.: Unpacking perceived control in risk perception: The mediating role of anticipated regret. Journal of Behavioral Decision Making 20(5), 533–544 (2007)
38. Raja, F., Hawkey, K., Hsu, S., Wang, K., Beznosov, K.: Promoting a physical security mental model for personal firewall warnings. In: CHI 2011 Extended Abstracts on Human Factors in Computing Systems, CHI EA 2011, pp. 1585–1590. ACM, New York (2011)
39. Ramsdell, B.: S/MIME Version 3 Message Specification. RFC 2633 (Proposed Standard), obsoleted by RFC 3851 (June 1999), http://www.ietf.org/rfc/rfc2633.txt
40. Ramsdell, B.: Secure/Multipurpose Internet Mail Extensions (S/MIME) Version 3.1 Message Specification. RFC 3851 (Proposed Standard), obsoleted by RFC 5751 (July 2004), http://www.ietf.org/rfc/rfc3851.txt
41. Ramsdell, B., Turner, S.: Secure/Multipurpose Internet Mail Extensions (S/MIME) Version 3.2 Message Specification. RFC 5751 (Proposed Standard) (January 2010), http://www.ietf.org/rfc/rfc5751.txt
42. Rhee, H.S., Ryu, Y.U., Kim, C.T.: I am fine but you are not: Optimistic bias and illusion of control on information security. In: Avison, D.E., Galletta, D.F. (eds.) ICIS. Association for Information Systems (2005), http://dblp.uni-trier.de/db/conf/icis/icis2005.html#RheeRK05
43. Ruoti, S., Kim, N., Burgon, B., van der Horst, T., Seamons, K.: Confused Johnny: When Automatic Encryption Leads to Confusion and Mistakes. In: Proceedings of the Ninth Symposium on Usable Privacy and Security, SOUPS 2013, pp. 5:1–5:12. ACM, New York (2013)
44. Sheng, S., Broderick, L., Koranda, C.A., Hyland, J.J.: Why Johnny still can't encrypt: Evaluating the usability of email encryption software. In: Symposium On Usable Privacy and Security (2006)
45. Solove, D.J.: I've got nothing to hide and other misunderstandings of privacy. San Diego L. Rev. 44, 745 (2007)
46. Van Vleck, T.: Electronic mail and text messaging in CTSS, 1965-1973. IEEE Annals of the History of Computing 34(1), 4–6 (2012)
47. Volkamer, M., Renaud, K.: Mental models – general introduction and review of their application to human-centred security. In: Fischlin, M., Katzenbeisser, S. (eds.) Buchmann Festschrift. LNCS, vol. 8260, pp. 255–280. Springer, Heidelberg (2013)
48. Wash, R.: Folk Models of Home Computer Security. In: Proceedings of the Sixth Symposium on Usable Privacy and Security, SOUPS 2010, pp. 11:1–11:16. ACM, New York (2010)
49. Wästlund, E., Angulo, J., Fischer-Hübner, S.: Evoking comprehensive mental models of anonymous credentials. In: Camenisch, J., Kesdogan, D. (eds.) iNetSec 2011. LNCS, vol. 7039, pp. 1–14. Springer, Heidelberg (2012)
50. Whitten, A., Tygar, J.D.: Why Johnny cant encrypt: A usability evaluation of PGP 5.0. In: Proceedings of the 8th USENIX Security Symposium, vol. 99, McGraw-Hill (1999)
51. Williams, M.: Interpretivism and generalisation. Sociology 34(2), 209–224 (2000)
52. Woo, W.K.: How to Exchange Email Securely with Johnny who Still Can't Encrypt. Master's thesis, University of British Columbia (2006)

Measuring Freenet in the Wild: Censorship-Resilience under Observation

Stefanie Roos[1], Benjamin Schiller[2], Stefan Hacker[2], and Thorsten Strufe[1]

[1] Technische Universität Dresden, Germany
`firstname.lastname@tu-dresden.de`
[2] Technische Universität Darmstadt, Germany
`lastname@cs.tu-darmstadt.de`

Abstract. Freenet, a fully decentralized publication system designed for censorship-resistant communication, exhibits long delays and low success rates for finding and retrieving content. In order to improve its performance, an in-depth understanding of the deployed system is required. Therefore, we performed an extensive measurement study accompanied by a code analysis to identify bottlenecks of the existing algorithms and obtained a realistic user model for the improvement and evaluation of new algorithms.

Our results show that 1) the current topology control mechanisms are suboptimal for routing and 2) Freenet is used by several tens of thousands of users who exhibit uncharacteristically long online times in comparison to other P2P systems.

1 Introduction

Systems that allow users to communicate anonymously, and to publish data without fear of retribution, have become ever more popular in the light of recent events[1]. Freenet [1–3] is a widely deployed completely decentralized system focusing on anonymity and censorship-resilience. In its basic version, the Opennet mode, it provides sender and receiver anonymity but establishes connections between the devices of untrusted users. In the Darknet mode, nodes only connect to nodes of trusted parties. Freenet aims to achieve fast message delivery over short routes by arranging nodes in routable small-world network. However, Freenet's performance has been found to be insufficient, exhibiting long delays and frequent routing failures [4].

In this paper, we investigate the reasons for the unsatisfactory performance of the deployed Freenet. The evaluation of Freenet so far has mainly been based on theoretical analyses and simulations, relying on vague assumptions about the user behavior. Such analytical or simulative user models, however, often differ significantly from reality. We consequently measured the deployed system to shed light on two critical points. First, we analyzed the topology of Freenet and its impact on the routing performance. In particular, we considered the neighbor

---

[1] `http://www.theguardian.com/world/the-nsa-files`

E. De Cristofaro and S.J. Murdoch (Eds.): PETS 2014, LNCS 8555, pp. 263–282, 2014.

selection in the Opennet and the interaction between Opennet and Darknet. Secondly, we measured the user behavior in Freenet with regard to number of users, churn behavior, and file popularity.

Our results indicate that the real-world topology differs largely from the assumptions made in the design, thus identifying a potential reason for the lack of performance. Over a period of 8 weeks, we discovered close 60,000 unique Freenet installations. With respect to their online behavior, the Freenet users exhibit a medium session length of more than 90 minutes, which is slightly longer than in other Peer-to-Peer systems. The session length distribution can be well modeled by a lognormal distribution and a Weibull distribution.

The results were obtained using both passive and active large-scale monitoring adapted to deal with the specific constraints of the Freenet protocol. They provide new insights into the actual workings of Freenet and can be used to design improved algorithms.

2 Background

In this Section, we introduce Freenet and present related work on measurements in P2P systems in general.

2.1 Freenet

Freenet was originally advertised as a censorship-resilient publication system [1, 2], referred to as Opennet. During the last years, the system has been extended to include a membership-concealing Darknet [3], where connections are only established to trusted users. Furthermore, the functionalities of Freenet have been extended beyond simple publication of content: Freesites, complete websites hosted in Freenet, offer the possibility to store and retrieve vast amounts of information[2]. An instant messaging system[3] and an email system[4] have been built on top of Freenet as well. All of these components use the same application-independent algorithms and protocols for storing, finding, and retrieving content, which are discussed in the following. First, we explain how users and files are identified in Freenet. Afterwards, we discuss how data is stored and retrieved, before detailing how the topology of Opennet and Darknet is created. Our descriptions are based upon [1,2] for the Opennet, and [3] for the Darknet, as well as on the source code at the time of the respective measurement.

In Freenet, users and files are identified and verified using cryptographic keys. A user's public and private key are created upon initialization of her node and used to sign published files. In addition, each node has a location, i.e., a key from the key space that files are mapped to. In analogy to a peer's identifier in a distributed hash table, Freenet nodes are responsible for storing files whose key is close to their location. For files, various keys exist that all share the

---

[2] https://wiki.freenetproject.org/Freesite
[3] https://freenetproject.org/frost.html
[4] https://freenetproject.org/freemail.html

same key space derived from the SHA-1 hash function: The content hash key (*CHK*) is the hash of the file itself and can be used for checking its integrity. Keyword signed keys (*KSK*s) are the hash of a descriptive human-readable string enabling keyword searches. The signed subspace key (*SSK*) contains the author's signature for validating a file's origin. Recently, *SSK*s are often replaced by updateable subspace keys (*USK*s), which allow versioning of files. Public keys, required for the validation of signatures, can be obtained directly from the owner or from Freenet indexes, i.e., Freesites that provide lists of publicly available files, their descriptions, and keys.

File storage, discovery, and retrieval is based on a deterministic routing scheme, a distance-directed depth-first search. Unless a node can answer a request, it forwards the message to its neighbor whose location is closest to the target key. Each request is identified by a random message ID enabling nodes to detect and prevent loops. In case a node cannot forward the message to another neighbor, backtracking is applied (see [1]).

During a storage request, the file is stored by any node on the path whose location is closer to the file key than any of its neighbors, by the last node on the path, and by any node that was online for at least 20 hours during the last two days. When a file is found, it is sent back to the requesting node on the inverse path. The contact information of the responding node is added but probabilistically changed by any node on the path to conceal the origin's address. This should provide plausible deniablility, i.e., uncertainty which node actually provided the file.

In Opennet and Darknet, the overlay topology is established differently. Opennet nodes send join requests to publicly known seed nodes that forward the request based on the joining node's location. The endpoints of such requests can be added as neighbors. The maximum number of neighbors depends on a node's bandwidth. Binding the degree of a node to the bandwidth provides an incentive to contribute more bandwidth because high-degree nodes receive a better performance on average.[5]. Based on their performance in answering requests, neighbors can also be dropped to make room for new ones. In the Darknet mode, nodes only connect to trusted contacts, which have to be added manually. Instead of accepting new neighbors with close locations, Darknet nodes adapt their location to establish a better embedding into the key space [5]. Both the neighbor selection in Opennet and the location adaption in Darknet are supposed to structure the network such that the probability to have a neighbor at distance d scales with $1/d$ for $d \geq c > 0$ for some constant c. The design is motivated by Kleinberg's model: Nodes are arranged in a m-dimensional lattice with *short-range links* to those closest on the lattice. Furthermore, nodes at distance x are chosen as *long-range contacts* with a probability proportional to $1/d^r$. Kleinberg showed that the routing is of polylog complexity if and only if $r = m$ equals the number of dimensions [6]. Consequently, a distance distribution between neighbors that asymptotically scales with $1/d$ would be optimal for the 1-dimensional namespace of Freenet.

---

[5] https://wiki.freenetproject.org/Configuring_Freenet#Connecting_to_the
_Opennet

2.2   Related Work

Most scientific publications on Freenet focus on the performance [5, 7] and attack resilience [8–10] of the routing algorithm. Their evaluations are based on theoretical analysis, simulations, and small-sized testbeds. The simulations in the original paper are based upon rather unrealistic assumptions such as no or uniform node churn, uniform content popularity, and uniform storage capacities [1, 3]. So far, only two measurement studies have been performed in the real system, both with a rather small scope: The first, conducted in 2004, was an 18 days passive monitoring of the connection duration between neighbors. The average observed connection time was 34 seconds, indicating that Freenet nodes frequently change neighbors [11]. The second study, aiming at an estimation of Freenet's network size, was performed in 2009. For measurement purposes, 80 Freenet nodes were inserted into the network. These nodes were then manipulated to drop and establish new connections at a higher rate to increase the number of discovered nodes. During 80 hours of measurements, 11, 000 unique node location were found. The number of concurrently online nodes was measured to be between 2, 000 and 3, 000 [4]. Hence, measurements on Freent so far are outdated and focus on single aspects of the protocol or user behavior only. The results are too general to suggest improvements and provide an accurate churn model for evaluating them. Alternative designs to Freenet for anonymous or membership-concealing P2P systems have been discussed in [4, 12–14]. However, they have not been widely deployed or rely on unstructured systems, which do not allow efficient resource discovery.

In contrast, there is vast related work on measurements in P2P systems in general. We briefly summarize their results regarding the user behavior in order to compare Freenet users to users of large-scale file-sharing networks without enhanced security protocols. The most frequently studied aspects of such systems are network size and churn. For the latter, the session length, i.e., the time a node stays online at a time, is of particular interest. The network size is usually determined by counting all nodes encountered during a certain time period. A subset of these nodes is then regularly contacted to track their online time and then derive a churn model from the observed data. How such a concept can be realized highly depends on the system under observation. In Freenet, contacting arbitrary nodes other than a node's direct neighbors is not possible. Hence, existing approaches can not be applied directly and are thus not discussed here in detail. The churn behavior of users has been measured in most large-scale P2P systems, in particular Napster [15], Gnutella [15], FastTrack [16], Overnet [17], Bittorrent [18, 19], and KAD [20, 21]. The observed median session length lies between 1 minute and 1 hour [22]. Measurements indicate that the shape of the session length distribution resembles a power-law: Exponential [18], Pareto [23], Weibull [21], and lognormal [21] distributions have been fitted. Our results show that the Freenet session length can be fitted reasonably well to a lognormal distribution, but the median online time is slightly higher than in all existing measurements of P2P-based systems.

3   Methodology

The data required for addressing most questions could be obtained using passive monitoring, i.e., using nodes that only observe the system and output additional log information. The analysis of users' churn behavior required us to perform active monitoring, i.e., running instrumented nodes that periodically request information.

We used Freenet version *1407* for all measurements prior to August 2012, version *1410* for measurements in September and October 2012, version *1442* for measurements in Spring 2013 and version *1457* for all later measurements[6].

In the remainder of this Section, we detail the two different monitoring approaches and describe how we extracted the desired information from the collected logs.

Locations of monitoring nodes were chosen uniformly at random unless stated otherwise. More sophisticated placement strategies would require additional knowledge of the global topology, which is not straightforward to obtain. The number of monitoring nodes varies over the experiments, depending both on the type of the measurement (e.g. local samples vs. global information needed) and the available resources at the time.

3.1   Passive Monitoring

We applied passive monitoring by inserting a set M of monitoring nodes in the network. They executed the normal code and followed the protocol like any regular node. We extended the Freenet logging mechanism to store all messages sent to and received from other nodes. The logged data allowed us to observe all changes in the neighborhood as well as all requests and the corresponding replies passing through these monitoring nodes.

Passive monitoring was used to collect data for the analysis of the neighbor selection, for determining the network size and the origin of users, for investigating file popularity and user activity, and for analyzing the impact of parallel Darknets.

Distance and Degree Distribution : The goal was to find out if the distances between neighbors in the overlay actually follow the distribution from Kleinberg's model [6]. In addition, we measured the degree distribution, which influences the routing success observed in the system.

Upon establishing a connection, nodes provide each other with their own location and the locations of their neighbors. Whenever the neighborhood changes, all neighbors are informed of the change. Hence, by logging all such messages, we obtained the degree of all neighbors of monitoring nodes and the distances between them and their neighbors. Denote the measurement duration by T. We took snapshots of the neighborhood of our monitoring nodes each t time units.

Let $G_k = (V_k, E_k)$ be a snapshot after $t \cdot k$ minutes for $k = 0 \ldots K$ with $K = \lfloor T/t \rfloor$. The node set V_k consisted of our monitoring nodes M, the neighbors

---

[6] https://github.com/freenet/fred-staging/releases

of nodes in M, and their neighbors. The subgraph G_k was induced, i.e., the edge set E_k consisted of all edges between nodes in V_k. We determined the empirical distance distribution of neighbors as the weighted average over all snapshots. Let $l(e)$ be the distance between the endpoints of edge e. Recall that for any set A, the indicator function $\mathbf{1}_A(x)$ is 1 if $x \in A$ and 0 otherwise. Then the empirical distance distribution $\hat{L}$ was computed by

$$P(\hat{L} \leq x) = \sum_{k=0}^{K} \sum_{e \in E_k} \frac{\mathbf{1}_{[-\infty,x)}(l(e))}{\sum_{k=0}^{K} |E_k|}. \tag{1}$$

When obtaining the degree distribution, our own nodes might not represent a good sample for the average user with regard to bandwidth and uptime. Since both influence the degree of a node, we only considered the sets $N_k(m) \setminus M$ of neighbors of $m \in M$ at time $t \cdot k$. Let $deg(v)$ denote the degree of a node v. Analogously to the distance distribution, the empirical degree distribution of neighbors $\hat{D}'$ was then obtained as [7]

$$P(\hat{D}' = x) = \sum_{k=0}^{K} \sum_{m \in M} \sum_{v \in N_k(m) \setminus M} \frac{\mathbf{1}_x(deg(v))}{\sum_{k=0}^{K} \sum_{m \in M} |N_k(m)|}. \tag{2}$$

Then, note the probability of being a neighbor of a node is proportional to the degree of a node. If the degree distribution of the network is D, the degree distribution D' of randomly chosen neighbors is given by

$$P(D' = x) = \frac{xP(D = x)}{\mathbb{E}(D)}. \tag{3}$$

Our measurements provided the empirical degree distribution of neighbors $\hat{D}'$. So an empirical degree distribution $\hat{D}$ was obtained by solving a system of linear equations based on Eq. 3. Let d_m denote the maximal observed degree. The system of linear equations consisted of $d_m + 1$ equations with $d_m + 1$ variables $P(\hat{D} = x)$ for $x = 1 \dots d_m$ and $\mathbb{E}(\hat{D})$. The first d_m equations were derived from transforming Eq. 3 to $xP(D = x) - P(D' = x)\mathbb{E}(D) = 0$. The last equation used that $\hat{D}$ is a probability distribution, so that $\sum_{x=1}^{d_m} P(\hat{D} = x) = 1$. The system of equations thus could be solved using Gaussian elimination.

Darknet : In order to evaluate the impact of small Darknets with few links into the Opennet, we manually created a Darknet topology consisting of 10 nodes. These nodes were connected in a ring topology of which 4 nodes established a connection to a monitoring node m that participated in the Opennet. The node m logs all file requests and the corresponding responses that pass through it. Based on the logs, we then distinguish between requests forwarded into the Opennet by m and requests forwarded into the Darknet. The difference of the success rate between forwarding to Opennet and to Darknet nodes then indicates the impact of such small Darknets.

---

[7] It is intended that nodes in the intersection of two neighborhoods are counted multiple times in order to obtain $\hat{D}$ from $\hat{D}'$.

Network Size and User Origin : We logged Freenet locations, IP addresses and ports of the Opennet neighbors of monitoring nodes. Each Opennet node is uniquely characterized by a persistent location, in contrast to Darknet nodes, which change location in order to adapt to the topology. For the Opennet, we hence uniquely identify Freenet instances by their location. Note that a user participating with multiple instances is counted several times. In contrast to the location, the IP address of a user changes over time. Furthermore, a Freenet node might advertise several IP port combinations. We logged the IP address only for obtaining the geolocation of users, not as an identifying feature.

Popularity Analysis : All requests for files seen by a monitoring node were logged, in particular the routing key of each file. We then obtained a popularity score for a key k by dividing the number of requests for k by the total number of requests.

3.2   Active Monitoring

We used active monitoring for tracking the online times of nodes. In the active mode, monitoring nodes periodically sent messages into the network to determine if a certain node is online. This approach allowed us to determine to what extend it is possible to track a user's online time in Freenet. Also, we established a churn model for Freenet users including session length, intersession length, and connectivity factor.

Up to September 2012, using messages of type *FNPRoutedPing* allowed us to query for nodes by their location. The message is routed through the network like any normal request. If a node with the specified location is found, a reply is sent back to the requester. From September 2012, information about nodes outside of the second neighborhood could only be obtained by using the *FN-PRHProbeRequest*. As a reply to this message, one specified information, e.g. the location or the uptime, about a random node from the network is returned. The node is chosen by executing an random walk with Metropolis-Hastings correction for 18 hops, so that every node should be selected close to uniformly at random [8]. Note that the message type *FNPRoutedPing* clearly allowed tracking of nodes, whereas *FNPRHProbeRequest* abolishes the possibility to query for a specific node. Hence, we also show that tracking is possible with *FNPRHProbeRequest*, a message that is still supported by the current Freenet version (*1459*).

In both approaches, we estimated the session starts $S(u)$ and endpoints $E(u)$ of a node u based on our measurements. From these sets, we characterized churn behavior as follows: Let $s_j(u)$ and $e_j(u)$ denote the j-th smallest element in $S(u)$ and $E(u)$, respectively. The total time of the measurement was T. The length of the j-th session of node u was then computed as $sess_j(u) = e_j(u) - s_j(u)$ given that u is online for at least j sessions. Similarly, the j-th intersession length was computed as $inter_j(u) = s_{j+1}(u) - e_j(u)$. Session and intersession length provide information on the reliability of nodes and the amount of maintenance required

---

[8] https://wiki.freenetproject.org/index.php?title=FCPv2/ProbeRequest

to keep the structure of the network intact. The connectivity factor of a node u is then defined as the fraction of time u was online, i.e., $conn(u) = \frac{\sum_{j=1}^{|S(u)|} sess_j(u)}{T}$. The connectivity factor is decisive for determining how often a file is available at a node. Moreover, we analyzed the number of nodes in the network to see if there are diurnal patterns. The fraction of online nodes for each point in time t and set of observed nodes Q are given by $f(t) = \frac{|\{u \in Q : \exists j : s_j(u) \leq t, e_j(u) \geq t\}|}{|Q|}$.

Using *FNPRoutedPing*. The methodology using *FNPRoutedPing* was to first collect locations of nodes and then ping each of those locations every X time-units. However, pings are routed within the Freenet network and are thus not guaranteed to find a node even if it is online. We solved this problem by pinging a node multiple times from different monitoring nodes. The maximal number of pings per node was chosen empirically such that the probability that a node would answer at least one of our pings was found to be sufficiently high.

We hence conducted the measurement as follows: First, we distributed our monitoring M equally in the key space, i.e., at locations $i/|M|$ for $i = 0 \ldots |M| - 1$. We divided n nodes to ping in sets of size $n/|M|$. Every X timeunits, each monitoring node pinged $n/|M|$ nodes and reported to a central server, which nodes had answered the requests. Nodes that had not been found were rescheduled to be pinged by a different monitoring node. After a node had been unsuccessfully pinged by k monitors, it was considered to be offline. k was chosen empirical by pinging our own monitoring and choosing k such that an online node would be detected with probability at least p[9]. We obtained the session starts and ends from the logged data as follows: The total time of our measurement was divided into K intervals $I_1, \ldots, I_K$ of length X. For any node u, we determined a sequence of boolean values $on_0(u), on_1(u), \ldots, on_K(u), on_{K+1}(u)$, so that $on_i(u)$ is true if u has been detected in interval $i = 1 \ldots K$ and $on_i(u) = false$ for $i = 0, K + 1$. Then $S(u)$ consisted of the start times of all intervals in which u was discovered but has not been discovered in the proceeding interval, i.e., $S(u) = \{(i - 1)X : i \in \{1, \ldots K\}, on_i(u) = true, on_{i-1} = false\}$. Analogously, $E(u) = \{iX : i \in \{1, \ldots K\}, on_i(u) = true, on_{i+1} = false\}$.

Using *FNPRHProbeRequest*. The methodology using *FNPRHProbeRequest* was to send a large number of requests for node locations into the network from different locations and gather all replies together with a timestamp. A node was considered offline if no reply from it had been received for at least time τ.

More precisely, we obtained an ordered set $R(u) = \{r_1(u), \ldots, r_{|R(u)|}(u)\}$ with $r_i(u) \in [0, T]$ of reply dates for each user/location u. The start of a session was assumed to be the first time a node had replied after not replying for τ timeunits, i.e., $S(u) = \{r_i(u) \in R(u) : i = 1 \text{ or } r_i(u) - r_{i-1}(u) \geq \tau\}$. Analogously, the end of a session was defined as the point in time of the last received reply $E(u) = \{r_i(u) \in R(u) : i = |R(u)| \text{ or } r_{i+1}(u) - r_i(u) \geq \tau\}$. For choosing

---

[9] We are aware that the estimation is only valid under the assumption that our monitoring nodes are representative for all nodes.

a suitable value for τ, let req be the number of answered requests per time unit. Assuming that indeed all nodes are selected with equal probability, the probability that a node does not respond to any of the $req \cdot \tau(p)$ requests is given by

$$1 - p = (1 - 1/n)^{req \cdot \tau(p)} \tag{4}$$

for a network of n nodes. $p \in \{0.9, 0.925, 0.95, 0.975, 0.99, 0.999\}$ was used. A low p indicates that the probability to accidentally cut one session into multiple session is high, in particular for long sessions. With increasing p, the probability to merge multiple sessions into one increases as well.

3.3 Data Set and Privacy

Our research was conducted in agreement with the German Federal Data Protection Act (in particular §28 and §40). In order to protect the privacy of Freenet's users, we carefully made sure to erase all identifying information from our collected data after computing the necessary statistics. The collected IP addresses were the potential link between Freenet users and their real-world identity. Note that the IP addresses were only required for obtaining the geolocation and the count of diverse IPs, and were deleted afterwards. We did not record the IP address in our database for all remaining measurements, in particular the tracking of users was done solely based on their Freenet location, which is unrelated to the real-world identity. The recorded data is available upon request.

4 Topology Characteristics

In this Section, we present the results regarding the distance and degree distribution of the Opennet. Using simulations, we then show that Freenet's current ID selection fails to provide the desired routing performance. Finally, we discuss the impact that separate Darknets attached to the main Opennet topology have on the routing quality of the overall system.

4.1 Distance and Degree Distribution

The number of hops, also called the routing length, needed to discover a file is essential for the performance of a P2P system. It is mainly influenced by the number of neighbors a node has and the locations of these neighbors in the key space.

The distance distribution between neighbors is supposed to be close to Kleinberg's model. However, nodes connect to those answering requests independently of their location, so that we would rather expect the distance between neighbors to be distributed uniformly at random. The degree distribution is directly related to the bandwidth of the nodes, i.e., a higher degree should correspond to a high bandwidth. The degree distribution of neighbors is expected to show nodes with a degree above average, since they are more likely to be selected as neighbors.

Setup: The data for this analysis was obtained from a two week measurement in May 2013 using 12 instrumented Freenet clients.

Results: Figure 1a shows the cumulative distance distribution observed in our measurements in comparison to the function $1/d$ for $d > 0.01$. Indeed, each node had a high number of close neighbors. However, contacts at distance exceeding 0.05 seemed to be chosen uniformly at random, as indicated by the linear increase of the distribution function.

With regard to the degree distribution, there are several peaks in the degree distribution around 13, 50, 75 and 100 (cf. Figure 1b). Indeed, these seem to correspond to typical bandwidth, e.g. for 2 Mbit/s 100 neighbors are allowed. Note that we observed nodes with a degree of up to 800, but nodes with a degree of more than 100 make up less than 1 %. Nodes with a degree of less than 10 are likely to be in the start-up phase since by default a node is allowed at least 14 neighbors.

Discussion: We have seen that nodes have a high number of close neighbors. These are probably found by announcements sent via the seed nodes and routed towards a node's own location. However, the long-range contacts are chosen uniformly at random, i.e., with a probability proportional to $\frac{1}{d^0}$ rather than with probability of $\frac{1}{d^1}$. The routing cost when nodes are connected independently of their locations is of order $n^{2/3}$ [6].

4.2   Simulation Study of Freenet's Routing Performance

To illustrate the impact of our previous derivation, we performed a simulation study of the Freenet routing algorithm.

Setup: We generated a ring topology with 15,000 nodes corresponding to the network size estimated in Section 5.1. Each node was assigned a random location in $[0, 1)$, corresponding to Freenet's key space. Each node was connected to the k closest nodes on the ring. In addition, for each node a random integer l was chosen according to the empirical degree distribution we observed in the Freenet network. The node was then given $d = max\{l - 2k, 0\}$ long-range contacts chosen proportional to $1/d^r$ for $r = 0$ (independent of the distance as in Freenet) and $r = 1$ (anti-proportional to the distance suggested by Kleinberg).

Reults: The average routing length was less than 13 hops for an optimal distance distribution ($r = 1$), but 37.17 hops for $r = 0$, i.e., the distance distribution we found in Freenet. When connecting each node to the 3 closest nodes on the ring, i.e., $k = 3$, the average routing length for $r = 0$ decreased to 28 because progress was made using the additional short-range links, but the average routing length for $r = 1$ increased by 30% to 17 hops. These results show that Freenet's performance can be drastically improved by, e.g., dropping and adding connections based on the distance of node identifiers. A Kademlia-like bucket system [24] could be used to achieve the desired distance distribution while still allowing a

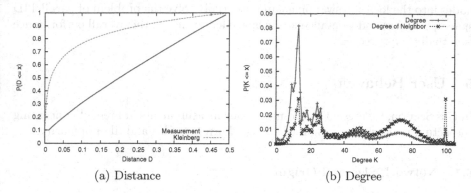

(a) Distance   (b) Degree

Fig. 1. Distance Distribution of neighbors, Degree Distribution, and the Degree Distribution of neighbors

wide choice of neighbors. So, the decision of dropping a neighbor can be made both on its performance and its location. The number of buckets of the number of contacts per bucket and hence the degree can be chosen dependent on the bandwidth a node contributes to the system, in order to retain this incentive of the current neighbor selection scheme. An alternative approach can be to include Opennet in the location swapping algorithm used by Darknet nodes, which has been shown to achieve a Kleinberg-like distance distribution in [5] for a static network. An in-depth simulation study is required to give concrete guidelines.

4.3   Darknet

We expected that requests forwarded into the Darknet would fail more frequently because the Opennet node responsible for the requested key is not topologically close to Darknet nodes with similar locations.

Setup: The measurement was conducted for a duration of 140 hours in April 2014. We manually set up a small Darknet consisting of 10 nodes and connected two of these nodes to one monitoring node in the Opennet.

Results: In total, the monitoring node received $3{,}540{,}000$ requests and forwarded 47.94% into the Darknetnet. While 8.46% of the requests forwarded into the Opennet were successful, only 0.08% of the Darknet requests returned the requested resource. Overall, only 4.4% of the requests forwarded by the monitor were successful.

Discussion: The performance decrease only considers requests forwarded via our monitoring node, and thus the impact of one small Darknet on the overall performance is low. However, we have seen that forwarding messages into the Darknet can clearly decrease the success rates if Darknet and Opennet are only connected by one link. If such Darknets exist in large numbers, they might be partly responsible for low success rate of Freenet routing. Including Opennet nodes into the location swapping can potentially solve the problem of parallel ID spaces, but as stated a detailed study is needed to show if the overall performance is actually improved.

5   User Behavior

In this Section, we present the results of our measurements in Freenet concerning the actual network size, origin of nodes, churn behavior and file popularity.

5.1   Network Size and Origin

We expected to discover a few thousand of concurrently online nodes, as observed in earlier measurements [4]. As the main goal of Freenet is to provide censorship-resilience, we also expected to find users from countries where either Internet censorship is applied or at least heavily discussed. While in the first case, services such as Tor [25] or Freenet are needed to retrieve the desired content, the use of anonymous and censorship-resilient communication might be increased due to a heightened awareness of potential privacy breaches in the second case.

Setup: Our measurements were conducted for 8 weeks in June to August 2012 using 55 instrumented Freenet clients.

Results: During the eight week measurement period, we observed a total of 58, 571 unique locations. The number of distinct IP addresses was 102, 376. Most locations were discovered during the first two weeks, afterwards only one or two new locations were found most days. On some days, however, several tens of new locations were discovered within one hour. The sudden increase was probably due to measurement activities by other institutions. Excluding these bursts, we see a convergence in the number of discovered locations, indicating that we were aware of most active Freenet clients. The observed difference between the number of locations and IPs is explained by the frequent use of non-static IPs. While the increase in discovered IPs is largest in the first days, the numbers grow constantly throughout the measurement, as can be expected if active users regularly change their IP. In addition, nodes can advertise more than one IP address at a time. Whereas the majority of nodes (84.4%) had only a single IP address over the whole period, about 10% advertised 2 and 3.6% 3 different IPs. On a closer look, nodes with more than 10 IP addresses were commonly located at universities, but also at the Tor proxy network *TKTOR-NET*, indicating that some users aim to hide their IP address in the Opennet by using Tor. At the time of the measurement, TKTOR-NET provided three exit nodes that participated in Freenet. IPs from various anonymous VPN were discovered as well. The discovered nodes were mainly traced back to Europe and North America, as can be seen in Figure 2. Nearly a quarter of the discovered installations were located in the USA, an eighth in Germany. Together with France and Great Britain, these countries made up more than half of all encountered nodes.

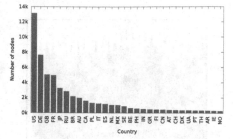

p	$\tau(p)$	$\theta(q_i(p))$: mean,min,max
0.900	3:27	0.993,0.989,0.996
0.925	3:53	0.993,0.989,0.996
0.950	4:29	0.992,0.989,0.995
0.975	5:31	0.991,0.987,0.994
0.990	6:54	0.989,0.983,0.993
0.999	10:22	0.984,0.979,0.989

Fig. 3. FNProbeRequest Statistics: Time $\tau(p)$ without reply until a node is declared offline, and the estimation $q_i(p)$ of detecting an online node

Fig. 2. Distribution of Freenet nodes over countries

Discussion: Our results show that Freenet is widely used. We discovered close to 60,000 active Freenet installations. So there clearly is demand for privacy-preserving communication and publication. Nevertheless, the typical Opennet user does not seem to be located in countries typically associated with Internet censorship. However, our study does not shed light on Darknet and Tor users.

5.2 Churn

In this Section, we discuss and compare the results for the two methods to measure churn behavior in Freenet introduced in Section 3.2. In all measurement studies of file-sharing systems, very short medium session length of less than 1 hour were observed. We expected to see such short sessions as well, corresponding to down- or uploads of one specific data item, especially if the content is sensitive and online times are short to minimize the risk of capture. However, Freenet users are advised to leave their clients running for at least 24 hours, so that we expected a comparable high fraction of long session as well. For both measurements, we first state the set-up and the results, but leave the discussion until the end of this subsection. In addition, we shortly discuss both the accuracy of our measurement as well as the additional load on the network created by the measurement.

Setup: The first measurement study was used to analyze the long-term behavior of a large set of nodes over more than a month, identifying daily and weekly patterns. The second measurement was needed because nodes were not contacted frequently enough to provide an accurate description of the session length distribution. The differences in the methodology were due to a change in the Freenet code between the first and the second measurement, which abolished the *FN-PRoutedPing* message used for locating specific nodes.

Using *FNPRoutedPing*. We performed the measurements querying every node at most $k = 5$ times. In order to observe the long-term behavior of nodes, the measurement period was chosen to be $X = 1h$. The value of k was chosen, such that our own nodes replied with a probability of 99.9%. The measurements were executed over a period of 28 days in August and September 2012 using 55 instrumented Freenet clients.

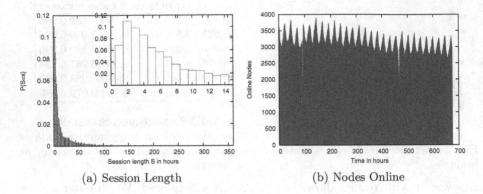

(a) Session Length   (b) Nodes Online

Fig. 4. Churn characteristics using *FNPRoutedPing* for node discovery

Results: The session length distribution is shown in Figure 4a, using bins of 1 hours in agreement with our measurement period. The majority of session lasted less than two hours, only 1.7% of the sessions lasted longer than 100 hours. The longest observed session was 357 hours. Note that there was a drop in the session length at about 8 and 17 hours, most probably because some nodes are only online during certain parts of the day.

The inter-session time follows a similar distribution: Roughly 10% of the inter-sessions are between 1 and 2 hours. Potential reasons are the missed probing due to the probabilistic nature of the measurements, crashes, and short-time connectivity breaks, e.g., when moving a laptop from home to work. Furthermore, there is a peak at the about 8 hours, in agreement with the corresponding peak of session length of roughly 16-17 hours. The results indicate that some users only run their clients during the day. The average connectivity factor of all nodes was rather high, namely 0.19.

The average number of discovered nodes was $3,207$ of the $15,503$ pinged nodes. The number of discovered nodes over time can be seen in Figure 4b. Diurnal patterns can be clearly identified. There was a maximum in the number of users at 10 PM CEST and a minimum at 10 AM CEST. In general, the number of online nodes in our sample varied between $2,500$ and $3,600$. So the network size changed periodically, but not drastically.

Accuracy and Load: The session length is only estimated within an accuracy of $2X = 2$ hours, hence we only considered the long term behavior in this measurement. Note that the results represent a lower bound on the fraction of long session because nodes can be accidentally declared offline during a session. As for the measurement cost, we found that without an measurement, a Freenet node forwarded on average around $13,000$ file requests and replies per hour, not considering maintenance costs. The average maintenance traffic produced by our measurement was less than 500 messages per node per hour.

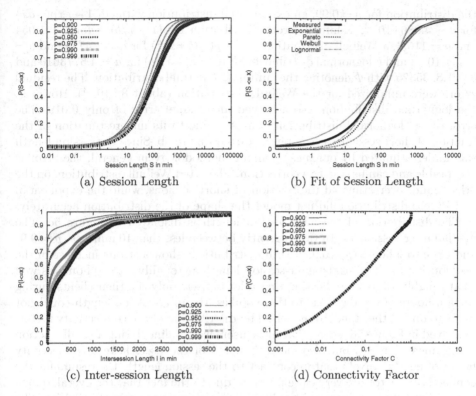

(a) Session Length   (b) Fit of Session Length

(c) Inter-session Length   (d) Connectivity Factor

Fig. 5. Session length for a) all considered p, and b) $p = 0.99$ fitted to common session length models, c) inter-session length, and d) connectivity factor

Using *FNPProbeRequest*. The measurement was conducted in November 2013 over a period of 9 days using 150 instrumented clients. We varied p, the lower bound on the probability that an online node replies within a time $\tau(p)$, between 0.9, 0.925, 0.95, 0.975, 0.99, and 0.999 as described in Section 3.2. Our monitoring nodes received at least $req = 10,000$ replies per minute. Choosing $\tau(p)$ according to Eq. 4 with an estimate of $n = 15,000$ resulted in intervals of roughly 3 ($p = 0.9$) to 10 ($p = 0.99$) minutes as can be seen in Table 3. Note that p is a lower bound on the probability to discover a node since we consider a lower bound on req and an upper bound on n.

Results: The median session length of the second measurement was between 49 to 110 minutes, depending on p. In particular, the median session lengths for $p = 0.975$ and $p = 0.99$ were 95 and 99 minutes, respectively. The distribution of the session length is shown in Figure 5a. We fitted the distribution to the most commonly used models for the session length (e.g., [21]), in order to see if they provide adequate accuracy to be used as models of Freenet user behavior in simulations. The non-linear least square fit function in R^{10} was used to fit

---

[10] http://stat.ethz.ch/R-manual/R-patched/library/stats/html/nls.html

the distribution for $p = 0.99$: an exponential distribution with cdf $1 - exp(-ax)$ for $a = 4.086 \cdot 10^{-3}$, a shifted Pareto distribution $1 - (1 + x/b)^{-a}$ for $a = 1.054$ and $b = 116.3$, a Weibull distribution $1 - exp(-(b * x)^a)$ for $a = 0.4788$ and $b = 5.355 \cdot 10^{-3}$, and a lognormal distribution $\Phi((log(x) - a)/b)$ for $a = 4.5773610$ and $b = 1.8235325$ with Φ denoting the cumulative normal distribution. The residual errors were minimized for the Weibull distribution (about $8 \cdot 10^{-3}$). However, the lognormal distribution also achieved an residual error of only 0.019. The error of the lognormal distribution is mostly due to its underestimation of the fraction of short sessions, as can be seen from Figure 5b. Since the session length was underestimated by our measurement methodology in general, the error is acceptable and can be seen as a correction. The fitted Weibull distribution, on the other hand, overestimated the fraction of short sessions, while the exponential and Pareto distribution did not model the shape of the distribution accurately.

The distribution of the inter-session length is displayed in Figure 5c. The median inter-session length varied greatly between less than 10 minutes ($p = 0.9$) and close to 6 hours ($p = 0.999$). All distributions show a strong increase in the distribution function of the inter-session length at roughly 8 to 10 hours as well as at roughly 16 to 17, indicating that a lot of users only run their clients during certain hours of the day. Due to these spikes, the inter-session length could not be fit to any of the standard models. The distribution of the connectivity factor, displayed in Figure 5d, shows that most users were online during a small fraction of the measurement, but also more than 5% of the users have a connectivity factor of nearly 1. Note that in contrast to the session length, the results for the connectivity factor are very close for all p, due to the fact that the overall online time is not largely influenced by splitting one session into multiple sessions. The average connectivity factor is around 0.22.

Accuracy and Load: We show that indeed our method selected nodes uniformly at random, and captured more than 98% of all online nodes. As stated in Section 3, assuming that the *htl* counter is set high enough, all nodes should reply with roughly equal probability. In particular, the number of requests answered by our monitoring nodes should be approximately normal distributed. We performed a Kolmogorov-Smirnoff test, which indicates a normal distribution (p-value of roughly 0.06). So nodes seem to be selected uniformly at random, which allowed us to obtain a lower bound on the probability of detecting an online node as follows. The size of a static network can be estimated by performing two samples and considering the size of their intersection [26]. Note that in a dynamic network only a lower bound is obtained since the population changes in consecutive intervals and the intersection consists of at most all nodes online in both intervals. We split the measurement period into intervals of length $\tau(p)$, and determined the sample A_i of all nodes responding to a probe in interval i. We then computed the fraction of the intersection $f_i = \frac{|A_i \cap A_{i+1}|}{|A_i \cup A_{i+1}|}$. For the probability q_i to sample a node during interval i. The probability that a node is sampled in interval i and $i + 1$ is $q_i q_{i+1}$, and the probability that it is sampled in at least one interval is $1 - (1 - q_i)(1 - q_i q_{i+1})$. For a static network and constant q_i, the expected value of f_i would be $\mathbb{E}(f_i) = \frac{q_i^2}{1-(1-q_i)^2}$. We hence obtained an unbiased estimate $\theta(q_i) = \frac{2f_i}{1+f_i}$ by transforming $f_i = \frac{q_i^2}{1-(1-q_i)^2}$. The values computed for mean, minimal, and maximum $\theta(q_i)$ over all intervals exceed 0.98 (but for the minimum in case of $p = 0.999$ as displayed in Table 3), so that indeed we captured the majority of online nodes per interval. For long intervals $\tau(p)$, the estimate on the accuracy decreases below p since the changes in the population outweighed the improved accuracy of an increased number of probes. However, the probability to be detected in every interval decreases exponentially with the session length and the reciprocal of interval length $\tau(p)$. For a probability of 0.98 to detect a node, the chance to be accidentally declared offline during 1 hour (more than 15 times $\tau(p)$) is still close to 30 % for $p = 0.9$ and $p = 0.95$, explaining the short median session length for low values of p and the high number of short intersessions of less than 10 minutes. Hence, the higher values

The overhead produced by FNPRoutedPing is about 2000 messages per hour, which makes up a noticeable but not large fraction of the roughly 13,000 requests and replies that need to be processed normally.

Discussion: We conducted two measurements. The first one was a long-term measurement over more than 4 weeks, in order to find diurnal and weekly pattern. We found that the fraction of long sessions was considerably higher in Freenet than in BitTorrent. Pouwelse [19] found that at most 3.8% of BitTorrent users stay longer than 10 hours and only 0.34% longer than 100 hours. In comparison, we observed close to 2% of sessions lasting longer than 100 hours. We clearly observed diurnal patterns, though they are not as distinct as in other applications, such as in Facebook [27]. The second measurement study was conducted to obtain more fine-grained results on the session and inter-session length, in order to evaluate the applicability of common churn models used in simulators. We discovered that the session length is reasonably well modeled by lognormal or Pareto distributions, but not by a Weibull or exponential distribution. In contrast, Stutzbach's results from 2006 indicate that churn in structured P2P systems is well modeled by lognormal and Weibull distributions [21]. The median session length was 4 hours in the first measurement, but less than 2 hours in the second measurement. Potential reasons are the high inaccuracy of the first measurement. For example, a session length of slightly more than 2 hours can accidentally be declared as 3 hours. Furthermore, nodes are only pinged every hour, so that short inter-sessions can be missed. However, both measurements indicate a longer median session length than the 1 to 60 minutes observed in Napster [15], Gnutella [15], FastTrack [16], Overnet [17], Bittorrent [19], and KAD [20, 21]. The inter-session length could not be modeled by commonly used distributions such as Pareto, because both measurements exhibited local maxima at about 8 and 16 hours. Such behavior has not been remarked in the related work, to the best of our knowledge. In summary, our results indicate that Freenet users are online longer than users of common file-sharing applications. Furthermore, clear diurnal patterns can be observed by considering the number of online nodes and the inter-session length.

An ulterior result of the churn analysis is that the online time of nodes can be reliably tracked, even without the possibility to ping a specific node. In this measurement, we only tracked the nodes by their location. However, locations of Opennet nodes can be mapped to IP addresses by inserting monitoring nodes in the system and tracking the location and IP of neighbors as presented in Section 5.1. The knowledge of online time now enables intersection attacks on the anonymity [28]. As a consequence, the seemingly harmless *FNPProbeRequest*, which returns information of a random node in the network, can potentially be abused for harming the anonymity. Because the focus of our study was the efficiency rather than the security of the system, we did not perform a detailed study on the potential damage. However, the reliability in tracking our own nodes indicates that *FNPProbeRequest* should be removed from the set of Freenet's functionalities. It mainly seems to be used by Freenet developers to obtain statistics about the network, but as seen above, the data is poorly anonymized and can be potentially abused.

5.3   File Popularity, User Activity, and Content

The popularity of files in file-sharing systems is assumed to be Zipf-distributed, i.e., the majority of requests address a small number of files. In contrast to P2P-based content distribution systems, Freenet provides the storage and retrieval of Freesites and blogs, which are clearly different from regular popular media. Hence, it is unclear if the aforementioned properties also hold for Freenet.

Setup: The measurement was conducted in Autumn 2012 using 11 instrumented Freenet clients. Their locations were chosen uniformly at random.

Results: During the measurement, we logged several hundred thousands of file requests. The 1,000 most popular files all received more than 21,000 requests, indicating that the majority of regular Freenet users requested those files. Our results indicate a Zipf-distribution for file popularity in agreement with the results on BitTorrent [20,29]. The most popular file accounts for 0.73% of seen requests, the second most popular file only for 0.45%. The 30-th popular file only accounts for 0.25% of the requests. Hence, after the fast decrease in popularity for the first files, the decrease is then slower and steadier.

Discussion: Our analysis of file popularity and user activity mostly agrees with the common assumptions. There are few very popular files, and the majority of the files is not requested frequently. Similarly, most files are published by a small set of users. We did not fit the popularity distribution, since local caching of popular files is bound to reduce the number of actually observed requests for popular files in comparison to less popular files. Consequently, our measurements underestimate the popularity of popular files, and the actual numbers are not reliable. However, the existence of a Zipf-like distribution can be assumed from the results, even if the actual shape of the distribution is skewed. Hence, the Least-Recently-Seen caching used in Freenet and designed for such popularity distributions should be very effective.

6   Conclusion

We showed how to conduct measurements in Freenet despite its obfuscation protocols. The results verify that the routing in Freenet is insufficient with regard to the neighbor selection and the interaction between Opennet and Darknet. Furthermore, we obtained a realistic churn model of Freenet users. In the future, we aim to evaluate our proposed neighbor selection and routing algorithms in a trace-driven simulation model based on the user behavior measurements and integrate them into the Freenet client code.

Acknowledgments. We thank Jan-Michael Heller and Christina Heider for their help in conducting the measurements, and Rob Jansen and the anonymous reviewers for their valuable comments.

References

1. Clarke, I., Sandberg, O., Wiley, B., Hong, T.W.: Freenet: A distributed anonymous information storage and retrieval system. In: Federrath, H. (ed.) Anonymity 2000. LNCS, vol. 2009, pp. 46–66. Springer, Heidelberg (2000)
2. Clarke, I., Hong, T.W., Miller, S.G., Sandberg, O., Wiley, B.: Protecting free expression online with freenet. IEEE Internet Computing (2002)
3. Clarke, I., Sandberg, O., Toseland, M., Verendel, V.: Private communication through a network of trusted connections: The dark freenet (2010)
4. Vasserman, E.Y., Jansen, R., Tyra, J., Hopper, N., Kim, Y.: Membership-concealing overlay networks. In: CCS (2009)
5. Sandberg, O.: Distributed routing in small-world networks. In: Workshop on Algorithm Engineering and Experiments, ALENEX 2006 (2006)
6. Kleinberg, J.: The small-world phenomenon: An algorithmic perspective. In: Symposium on Theory of Computing (2000)
7. Roos, S., Strufe, T.: A contribution to darknet routing. In: INFOCOM (2013)
8. Evans, N.S., GauthierDickey, C., Grothoff, C.: Routing in the dark: Pitch black. In: ACSAC (2007)
9. Schiller, B., Roos, S., Hoefer, A., Strufe, T.: Attack resistant network embeddings for darknets. In: SRDSW (2011)
10. Tian, G., Duan, Z., Baumeister, T., Dong, Y.: A traceback attack on freenet. In: INFOCOM (2013)
11. Cramer, C., Kutzner, K., Fuhrmann, T.: Bootstrapping locality-aware p2p networks. In: ICON (2004)
12. Mittal, P., Borisov, N.: Shadowwalker: peer-to-peer anonymous communication using redundant structured topologies. In: Proceedings of the 16th ACM Conference on Computer and Communications Security, pp. 161–172. ACM (2009)
13. Isdal, T., Piatek, M., Krishnamurthy, A., Anderson, T.E.: Privacy-preserving p2p data sharing with oneswarm. In: SIGCOMM (2010)
14. Mittal, P., Caesar, M., Borisov, N.: X-vine: Secure and pseudonymous routing using social networks. arXiv preprint arXiv:1109.0971 (2011)
15. Krishna Gummadi, P., Saroiu, S., Gribble, S.D.: A measurement study of napster and gnutella as examples of peer-to-peer file sharing systems. Computer Communication Review (2002)

16. Sen, S., Wang, J.: Analyzing peer-to-peer traffic across large networks. IEEE/ACM Transactions on Networking (2004)
17. Bhagwan, R., Savage, S., Voelker, G.M.: Understanding availability. In: Kaashoek, M.F., Stoica, I. (eds.) IPTPS 2003. LNCS, vol. 2735, pp. 256–267. Springer, Heidelberg (2003)
18. Guo, L., Chen, S., Xiao, Z., Tan, E., Ding, X., Zhang, X.: Measurements, analysis, and modeling of bittorrent-like systems. In: IMC (2005)
19. Pouwelse, J., Garbacki, P., Epema, D.H.J., Sips, H.J.: The bittorrent P2P file-sharing system: Measurements and analysis. In: van Renesse, R. (ed.) IPTPS 2005. LNCS, vol. 3640, pp. 205–216. Springer, Heidelberg (2005)
20. Krishna Gummadi, P., Dunn, R.J., Saroiu, S., Gribble, S.D., Levy, H.M., Zahorjan, J.: Measurement, modeling, and analysis of a peer-to-peer file-sharing workload. In: SOSP (2003)
21. Stutzbach, D., Rejaie, R.: Understanding churn in peer-to-peer networks. In: IMC (2006)
22. Rhea, S., Geels, D., Roscoe, T., Kubiatowicz, J.: Handling churn in a dht. Computer Science (2003)
23. Bustamante, F., Qiao, Y.: Friendships that last: Peer lifespan and its role in p2p protocols. In: Web Content Caching and Distribution, pp. 233–246 (2004)
24. Maymounkov, P., Mazières, D.: Kademlia: A peer-to-peer information system based on the XOR metric. In: Druschel, P., Kaashoek, M.F., Rowstron, A. (eds.) IPTPS 2002. LNCS, vol. 2429, pp. 53–65. Springer, Heidelberg (2002)
25. Dingledine, R., Mathewson, N., Syverson, P.F.: Tor: The second-generation onion router. In: USENIX Security Symposium (2004)
26. Mane, S., Mopuru, S., Mehra, K., Srivastava, J.: Network size estimation in a peer-to-peer network. University of Minnesota, MN, Tech. Rep. (2005)
27. Schneider, F., Feldmann, A., Krishnamurthy, B., Willinger, W.: Understanding online social network usage from a network perspective. In: IMC (2009)
28. Wolinsky, D.I., Syta, E., Ford, B.: Hang with your buddies to resist intersection attacks. In: CCS (2013)
29. Hefeeda, M., Saleh, O.: Traffic modeling and proportional partial caching for peer-to-peer systems. IEEE/ACM Trans. Netw. (2008)

Dovetail: Stronger Anonymity
in Next-Generation Internet Routing

Jody Sankey and Matthew Wright

University of Texas at Arlington, USA
jody@jsankey.com, mwright@uta.edu

Abstract. Given current research initiatives advocating "clean slate" Internet designs, researchers have the opportunity to design an internetwork layer routing protocol that provides efficient anonymity by decoupling identity from network location. Prior work in anonymity for the next-generation Internet fully trusts the user's ISP. We propose Dovetail, which provides anonymity against an active attacker located at any single point within the network, including the user's ISP. A major design challenge is to provide this protection without including an application-layer proxy in data transmission. We address this in path construction by using a *matchmaker* node (an end host) to overlap two path segments at a *dovetail* node (a router). The dovetail then trims away part of the path so that data transmission bypasses the matchmaker. We develop a systematic mechanism to measure the topological anonymity of our designs, and we demonstrate their privacy and efficiency by Internet-scale simulations at the AS-level.

1 Introduction

When we use the Internet, a wide range of identifying information is commonly revealed, but one of the hardest forms of identity to remove is that defined by the network routing protocol (*layer 3*), since this identity is used to deliver data. In today's Internet, IP is the primary layer 3 protocol and IP addresses are in every data packet. Recording a user's IP address can allow an adversary to uniquely identify her, link that identity with her online activity, correlate connections to different services, and partially reveal her geographical and network locations. Previous work has proposed *low-latency anonymity systems* to conceal a user's identity [1, 2], including her IP address. Tor in particular has been adopted by hundreds of thousands of privacy-concious users worldwide [3]. Current anonymity systems, however, work by creating an overlay network on top of the layer 3 protocol, requiring a sequence of IP transmissions to disguise the original sender. This sequential forwarding and the queueing and processing required in intermediary nodes create substantial delay and overhead.

We prefer an alternative formulation for this problem: Rather than attempting to conceal a global layer 3 identifier by adding complexity in application protocols, we believe that the layer 3 protocol should not reveal a global identity.

E. De Cristofaro and S.J. Murdoch (Eds.): PETS 2014, LNCS 8555, pp. 283–303, 2014.

Instead, we leave identity management to higher layers in the protocol stack, in only those applications where it provides mutual benefit.

While privacy by itself is unlikely to motivate a change away from IP routing, a range of additional concerns have emerged within the networking field [4], including scalability, security, mobility, challenged environments, and network management, leading to major research initiatives investigating "clean slate" Internet designs [5–7] that could be used to build the *next-generation Internet (NGI)*. A wide range of different NGI routing concepts have already been proposed as a result of these activities [8–14]. Network virtualization research, showcased in testbeds such as GENI [15], offers hope for a progressive transition to a future routing protocol. These initiatives in NGI provide an opportunity to imagine anonymous communications that do not rely on an overlay network.

We thus propose *Dovetail*, an NGI routing protocol that prevents association of source and destination by an attacker located at any fixed point within the network. Recently, Hsiao et al. proposed LAP, a lightweight NGI anonymity protocol [16]. Unlike LAP, however, Dovetail provides protection against observation by local eavesdroppers and by an untrusted ISP, which is a critical requirement for many privacy-conscious users.

A major design challenge is to provide this protection without including a proxy in data transmission, which would be much slower than only traversing routers. We address this challenge in path construction by asking a *matchmaker* node (an end host) to put together two path segments so that they overlap at a *dovetail* node (a router), and enabling the dovetail to trim away the part of the path with the matchmaker. This technique is implemented using public-key operations only at the source and the matchmaker, while routers use only symmetric encryption and decryption of short header fields and a simple hash chain. The protocol enables the choice of many different paths through the network and does not require a trusted third party.

In brief, our key contributions are: (1) a novel privacy-preserving NGI routing protocol, (2) a systematic mechanism for measuring anonymity in terms of topological identity, and (3) evaluation of our protocol in terms of topological anonymity using an Internet-scale simulation.

2   Objectives

In this section, we describe the goals of the system we intend to deliver and the attacker we design against.

2.1   Anonymity Objectives

We refer to the party who initiates a connection as the *source* and the opposite party as the *destination*, although data is able to pass in both directions once the connection is established. Using the terminology of Pfitzmann and Hansen [17], we aim to provide *unlinkability* between the source and destination, such that no network location is able to sufficiently distinguish whether the source and destination are related, except for the source itself. This implies that network locations with good information on the source identity have little information on the destination identity, and vice versa. Throughout our work, we constrain ourselves to the identifying properties defined at the network layer: network identity and network location, or *topographical anonymity* [16].

We do not protect the packet contents, which reside in higher network layers and are thus out of scope for this paper. Content should be protected end-to-end using a protocol such as IKEv2, which protects sender and receiver identities [18]. Such protection is effectively mandatory for strong anonymity protections, as many other forms of Internet identification exist, such as device fingerprinting [19] and persistent cookies [20]. Additionally, higher-level protocols like IKEv2 should be used with restricted options and implementations to limit the possibility of finger-printing.

2.2   Performance and Practicality Objectives

Any anonymity system must route traffic fast enough to gain widespread adoption and thus provide a large set of potential message sources [21]. Performance problems with Tor have been widely discussed, and they are considered an important factor limiting its adoption [22,23]. We aim to provide a lightweight system where all communication for an established connection remains within the core networking infrastructure and occurs at layer 3. This avoids the frequently slow *last mile* connections [24] in overlay anonymity systems and also the queuing required to move between layers in the protocol stack. Finally, we require that our system provides mechanisms to trade anonymity for performance.

Another key to widespread adoption is recruiting service providers. Our work targets a future Internet, so Dovetail need only compete with other future routing protocols rather than motivate service providers to switch away from IP. Today's ISP business models may not apply, but it is unlikely that service providers are willing to spend substantial time and infrastructure for privacy. Our goal is to ensure that costs for service providers are limited, such that benefits for privacy-aware consumers are enough incentive to participate in the protocol. To this end, we recognize that Internet routers have high throughput and low computing resources per flow, so we limit cryptographic operations and avoid maintenance of any per-connection routing state. Additionally, our design does not require significant extra traffic and does not violate basic notions of consumer-provider relationships that exist in today's Internet.

2.3   Attack Model

Selecting an attack model for anonymity systems is a challenging task in its own right, as the adversary may be different for different users and its capabilities are not known in advance. A few key points guide our choices. First, protecting a low-latency connection from an adversary who can observe traffic at multiple points of the network is very difficult. Tor uses layered encryption and fixed packet sizes to prevent trivial linkability, but this comes with significant expense and does not hide traffic patterns, which are linkable with a small chance of error [25]. Adding sufficient delays and cover traffic to mask traffic patterns is expensive and can be undermined by manipulating the patterns [26, 27]. Second, users may be suspicious of any service provider that can link them with their Internet activities. This applies to anonymity service providers, such as Anonymizer.com, and also to Internet service providers. ISPs have proved to not be fully trustworthy with private browsing data [28, 29]. We therefore aim to prevent any element of our system from being able to deanonymize users. Third, a user's local communication may be subject to eavesdropping, e.g. at a wireless hotspot or by an employer. Unlike LAP, we aim to protect against such adversaries. Fourth, many of the adversaries that we aim to protect against would be capable of various active attacks, such as replay or packet header manipulation, so we also aim to limit the exposure that such attacks might cause.

We thus consider an adversary who is *active* but *local*. Active means the adversary is able to initiate connections and to violate the rules of the protocol for the connections in which she is involved, in addition to passively monitoring these connections. We define local as confined to a single *Autonomous System* (AS) within the Internet. ASes are the level at which routing information and policies are commonly shared, so a compromise in security at one router may affect multiple routers controlled by the same AS. In contrast, in order to span multiple ASes, an attack must either compromise multiple organizations or involve collusion between these organizations. We note that if a particular set of ASes were suspected of collusion, our client logic could easily be modified to include no more than one member of the set in each connection. Our adversary is assumed to have local knowledge of traffic, but global knowledge of the network topology and routing data.

More concretely, the possible attackers we aim to protect against include: a local eavesdropper, the source ISP, the destination ISP, any single AS in between, any node facilitating our protocol operations, and the destination itself. Thus, we aim for significantly greater protection than LAP or a centralized proxy server like Anonymizer.com.

Given that we only protect against a single observation point, we offer no protection against attacks that require multiple observation points, even though such attacks may be practical for state-level adversaries [30] or Internet exchange points [31]. In common with LAP, but not Tor, we do not try to prevent trivial linkability based on packet contents and sizes. This means that linking attacks with multiple observation points need lower computational and storage resources and succeed with fewer observations than against Tor. Additionally, if both the source and destination are customers of the same ISP, it is simple for the ISP to correlate traffic. Again, Tor provides basic protection that makes this attack slightly harder, while both LAP and Dovetail provide no protection.

3   Background

In this section, we cover two research areas of direct relevance to our problem: source-controlled routing protocols and low-latency anonymity systems. Within each area, we describe a proposal that our design builds upon.

3.1   Source-Controlled Routing

One theme spanning a number of next-generation Internet routing proposals is that of source-controlled routing, in which the originator of a data packet has some control over the route it takes, usually using routing control information carried in the data packet. In some protocols, the source has influence over the route but not complete control [12, 14]; in others, the source explicitly declares the route that should be taken [10, 13]. As we explain in Sect. 4.1, this ability to express a route at the source has benefits for anonymity in addition to the robustness and flexibility considerations that initially motivated the research.

Pathlet Routing. Pathlet routing [10] is one example of a source-controlled routing system. Each entity within a network defines a number of virtual nodes (or *vnodes*) and advertises path segments (or *pathlets*) that pass between these vnodes. Vnodes are a virtual construct, so a single physical router may process packets for multiple vnodes, or a single vnode may be distributed across multiple physical routers. Each vnode is defined by a forwarding table containing the set of allowed outgoing pathlets. All packets arriving from a particular communication peer are processed by one vnode whose forwarding table defines the set of allowed routes for that peer. The pathlet protocol provides an expressive system that is able to represent many different types of routing policy.

To send a packet, the source assembles a list of adjacent pathlets defining the intended route and includes this list in the packet header. Each pathlet is represented by a variable length Forwarding ID (*FID*), an index into the forwarding table of the vnode that defined the pathlet. When a vnode receives a packet, it removes the first FID and uses this as an index into its forwarding table to determine which link the packet should be sent over. Only legal routes are defined in the forwarding tables. Therefore, it is impossible to violate the routing policy by invoking unannounced routes, since no such routes exist. Pathlet routing moves the responsibility for network route creation from the network infrastructure to the end hosts originating traffic. This provides two features that are helpful for the design of Dovetail: First, the large routing information base embodying network topology need only be consulted each time a new route is constructed, and not each time a packet is forwarded. Second, it provides flexibility for an end host to control how its packets will traverse the network.

3.2   Low-Latency Anonymity Systems

A number of low-latency anonymity systems have been proposed with response times that are sufficient for general-purpose interactive use, such as Web browsing. Some of these have been fielded [1, 2, 32]. Current low-latency anonymity systems may be categorized as either centralized or distributed. Centralized systems pass all traffic though an anonymizing proxy, which must be trusted. Distributed systems overlay an additional network on top of the current layer 3 protocol and therefore require multiple IP transmissions to deliver each packet from source to destination. These multiple transmissions, together with processing inside the intermediate hosts, contribute to latencies that are substantially higher than Internet usage without anonymization [33].

Lightweight Anonymity and Privacy. In Lightweight Anonymity and Privacy (LAP) [16], Hsiao et al. propose the anonymity scheme that inspires our work. Their protocol relies upon *packet-carried forwarding state*, where the information required to deliver a packet is stored within the packet itself. To establish a connection, the source constructs a packet containing a sequence of *autonomous domains* (ADs) describing the route. As each AD receives the packet, it encrypts its own routing instruction using a private symmetric key and forwards the packet to the next AD. Once a connection has been constructed in this manner, data may be exchanged between the endpoints using the resulting encrypted header. Each path construction request contains a nonce that influences the encryption process, allowing a source to construct multiple unlinkable connections over the same route by using different nonces. Header padding may be included to partially obfuscate the path length. During construction, each AD on the path learns the identity of all ADs that follow it but not the identity of the ADs before it. Some information on predecessor identity may be inferred based on knowledge of the preceding AD, network topology, routing policy, observed header length, and observed response time, but these are not quantified. LAP assumes the user's own ISP is trustworthy, and it provides no protection of source-destination unlinkability against a local eavesdropper or an observer at the source ISP. Given previous well-publicized ISP indiscretions [28, 29] and the possibility of a hacker infiltrating this single point of failure, it seems unlikely that privacy-conscious users will share this assumption.

Other than LAP, ANDãNA is the only other next-generation Internet anonymity protocol that we know of [34]. It is only designed for named-data networks and it is built using onion routing, both of which are very different from Dovetail.

4   Design

In this section, we first provide context for our design point and then describe the protocol from four different perspectives in increasing detail.

4.1   Layer 3 Anonymity Design Space

To provide a broadly applicable anonymity system, we assert that any layer 3 solution should provide two features:

Deviation from Shortest Path. An eavesdropper can measure information on the length of the network path before and after her vantage point. If a routing protocol always selects the shortest possible route, then when the shortest route between participants is significantly shorter or longer than the Internet average, the protocol will reveal this information and limit their anonymity.

Partitioned Routing Information. When the routing information is stored as a single field, such as an IP address, any entity with access to the field may calculate the destination identity. When routing information is divided across multiple fields, then an entity must access multiple fields to learn the destination identity. Fields may be protected independently to prevent this access.

Source-controlled routing is useful since it accommodates both of these features: when the source of a message can dictate a path, she is free to pick one that is not the shortest, and she may express the path as a separate instruction for each entity along the route. Dovetail builds upon the pathlet source routing protocol presented by Godfrey et al. [10]. Pathlet routing works well for our system, but we are not reliant on any unique feature of this protocol. The principles we describe could be applied to any protocol that provides complete control over the selected route and a wide range of allowable routes.

4.2 Network Model

We propose a clear distinction in routing at the AS boundary; each AS should expose the minimum number of vnodes and pathlets necessary to satisfy its routing policies. This distinction provides two practical benefits: First, minimizing the number of externally visible vnodes reduces the size of the routing information base that must be held in end hosts. Second, distinguishing between internal and external connectivity allows an AS to retain a flexible and dynamic internal routing policy. Adjacent ASes share routing information to establish the network topology. This communication should be secured against MITM attacks that could selectively filter the topology. We assume that hosts know the numeric identity of the vnodes they wish to contact. An equivalent to DNS would be required to translate human-readable identities into vnode identities. The translation service itself could be accessible using Dovetail to protect privacy, but is outside the scope of our current work.

The most common form of routing policy used in the Internet today is *valley-free routing* [35], which reflects the contractual relationships between ASes. A *customer* AS is one who pays a *provider* AS to forward its traffic, while two ASes with a *peer* relationship will each forward each other's traffic without payment. In valley-free routing, each AS will only forward traffic when there is a financial incentive to do so, i.e. when the traffic originates from or is destined for a paying customer. As illustrated in Figure 1a, two vnodes are required per AS to enforce this strict definition of a valley-free routing policy: one to receive traffic from customer ASes and one to receive traffic from peer and provider ASes. Although valley-free routing is common, Internet routing allows for arbitrarily complex policies, and valley-free routing is not ubiquitous [36]. In particular, there are a growing number of Internet exchange points (IXPs), which offer ASes the ability to peer with each other and thereby save money [37]. Most transit and

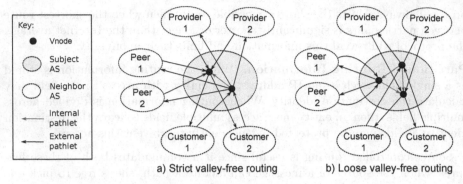

Fig. 1. AS vnode and pathlet structure by routing policy

access provider ASes will peer with any non-customer AS [38]. This suggests that peering is compatible with ASes' incentives and is likely to continue to be common.

We thus consider a slightly relaxed routing policy, which we refer to as *loose valley-free*. In this scheme, an AS will allow traffic to pass between its peers. The AS would not receive payment from a customer for performing this service, but also is not required to make a payment and could avoid payments at other times if peers provide a reciprocal service. As shown in Figure 1b, three vnodes are required per AS to enforce a loose valley-free routing policy: one to receive traffic from customer ASes, one to receive traffic from provider ASes, and the third to send and receive peer traffic.

For good anonymity properties as described in Section 4.4, Dovetail relies on a modest fraction of ASes using the loose valley-free policy or other policies that are less strict than valley-free routing. If all ASes use strict valley-free routing, Dovetail still provides anonymity, but with smaller anonymity sets.

4.3   Path Construction

Figure 2 illustrates the Dovetail path creation process. A Dovetail path comprises multiple *path segments*. As with LAP, an AS that is present on a path segment may learn the identity of subsequent ASes and its direct predecessor, but not earlier ASes.

The path cannot be constructed directly from the source to the destination, since the source's ISP would be able to link source and destination. Instead, we make use of a randomly selected, untrusted third-party vnode called the *match-maker*. This matchmaker may either be an end host or functionality exposed by a service provider. Providing matchmaker services should cost little relative to enabling our protocol in routers. The identities of vnodes willing to act as match-makers could be distributed as a part of routing information maintenance.

The source encrypts the identity of the final destination using a public key for the matchmaker and builds a *head* path segment to the matchmaker, who then extends the path to the destination with a *tail* path segment. Here, the source

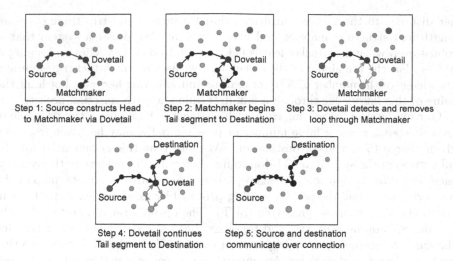

Fig. 2. Construction of a Dovetail connection

ISP no longer learns the identity of the destination, only of the matchmaker. The matchmaker learns the identity of the destination, but cannot identify the source through the intervening ASes. The source may learn the matchmaker's public key without compromising anonymity by requesting a signed certificate over the same path used to establish the connection. To improve performance and minimize the trust we must place in the matchmaker, we prefer that the matchmaker not be involved in the exchange of data. Therefore, we require that the head and tail segments cross at some vnode, referred to as the *dovetail*[1]. The source encrypts the identity of the dovetail and provides it to the matchmaker for inclusion on the tail segment. The dovetail detects the crossing condition and joins the two segments, removing the loop in the path along with the matchmaker.

The tail path segment would ideally be selected by the source, but the source does not have complete knowledge of distant Internet topology. The matchmaker has sufficient knowledge to construct a path to the destination, but the user's anonymity can be degraded if an AS appears on both the head and tail segments, and therefore we prefer that the tail segment avoids ASes already used on the head segment. Providing a list of head ASes to the matchmaker would reveal substantial information on the source identity, so instead we ask the matchmaker to return a set of potential tail routes that the source selects from. The source then sends its choice to the matchmaker to complete the route.

4.4 Segment Route Selection

A source-controlled routing system may attempt to obfuscate path length, but an attacker located on the path will be able to infer some information about

---

[1] We use the term to reflect a dovetail joint in carpentry, where two elements are joined securely and compactly.

her distance to the source and destination through round trip timing, packet length and structure analysis, and active probing. We prefer a system that is robust even when an attacker learns path length to one that relies on keeping it hidden. For the remainder of the discussion, we assume the attacker has perfect knowledge of the number of ASes preceding and following her own, but limit the value of this knowledge through a non-deterministic path selection process.

Our mechanism for routing each path segment is based upon the principle of *path diversity*, where a large number of possible paths may be taken from any given source to any given destination. We note that this is beneficial for the robustness of the system in addition to its anonymity. To achieve path diversity, each host must have a comprehensive, but not necessarily complete, map of the network. We extend the pathlet routing protocol by exporting extra pathlets in addition to the shortest path tree (SPT). The optimal set of additional pathlets depends on network size and topology, but our experiments show that for the current Internet, is it appropriate to export 50% of the SPT size, selecting pathlets closest to the sender. An important consequence is that routing knowledge varies across the network, and so any assessment of available path options can only be made in the context of the vnode (in our case, the source or the matchmaker) selecting the path. Maintenance of routing information in response to network changes could be performed using path vector distribution methods similar to BGP [39], but this is not relevant to the anonymity properties of the system and so is not discussed further.

When a host constructs a path segment, it will normally have a wide range of options available with different *costs*, where we define cost as the number of times the route changes AS. Other cost metrics such as latency or bandwidth could also be integrated into the protocol. The distribution of options across cost reflects the network topology between the source and destination. Selecting a random path uniformly from among the complete set of options would reveal information about this distribution, such as picking the most common path cost most frequently, and thus leak information about the topology. Instead, we use a *cost window approach*: we select a path by first selecting a path cost and then randomly selecting one of the paths at this cost.

4.5   Data Packet Structure

Dovetail extends the basic packet format used in pathlet routing, providing a set of different packet types composed of variable-length segments. Each dovetail path is constructed using a path construction packet and a construction return packet. Data is then exchanged over the path using a sequence of encrypted data and encrypted response packets. The data formats and processing algorithms for these packets are provided in our technical report [40]. In summary, these algorithms provide the following security properties:

1. An AS does not learn the identity of ASes before its immediate predecessor.
2. AS routing information is protected by a key known only to the AS.
3. Different connections travelling over the same route do not produce the same ciphertext.

4. The final ciphertext for each AS depends on the entire path.
5. An AS may only create a removable loop in the path when given access to privileged information. This information is only given to the matchmaker.

5 Security Analysis

In this section, we assess the security of the Dovetail protocol. We consider a range of anonymity attacks that might be applied against the protocol and then analyze the information available to a passive attacker at each point in the network. We end with brief discussions of timing attacks and attacks on availability and integrity.

5.1 Attacks on Anonymity

As Dovetail is lightweight, it does not protect against attacks that succeed against an overlay system like Tor. In particular, an entity who can observe traffic at multiple points in the connection can link both of those points, which can link a source to her destinations. In Dovetail, this is trivial, as the packet contents are not encrypted differently at different points in the network. In Tor, however, timing analysis can enable this linking with high accuracy [26,27]. Other attacks that rely on multiple points of observation, such as selective denial of service [41] and predecessor [42] attacks will be just as effective in Dovetail. Additionally, Dovetail is vulnerable to the same types of side-channel attacks that impact Tor [43–47].

The primary information available to a passive attacker in the network is the cost to the source and destination and the preceding and following ASes in the path, and we examine the affect of these on anonymity in Section 5.2. Beyond this, however, we need to examine additional attacks that could leverage the unique aspects of the Dovetail protocol. These attacks include:

Observe or Correlate Packet Content. Dovetail is a layer 3 protocol and does not provide any protections for the data it carries. In cases where packet content would reveal identity, or where confidentiality is important, a higher layer protocol such as IKEv2 should be used to provide encryption [18].

Correlate Connections from a Source. Each connection includes a source-defined nonce. When the source changes this nonce, a different ciphertext will be produced, preventing an observer from associating multiple connections over the same path from their header content. When connections between a source-destination pair are distinctive, and may hence be correlated by some other property, the source could reuse the same matchmaker and path to prevent intersection and predecessor attacks.

Replay Packets. A replayed packet will take the same path as its original transmission and therefore not provide an attacker with new information. An adversary might try to probe for the source by prepending an unencrypted path to a recorded packet, but each AS empties the unencrypted segment on receipt to prevent this attack.

Probe for a Later AS. To determine the destination of an observed connection, an attacker on the head segment may try to construct many new connections through the same dovetail and search for matches in the header ciphertext. Dovetail protects against this attack by including a hash of the entire path in the IV for encrypted transit segments. Any change in the selected path will therefore perturb the ciphertext for all segments.

Probe for an Earlier AS. The joining of a Dovetail path provides confirmation that the joining AS appeared on the path twice, and an attacker may wish use this feature to probe for suspected predecessors. During connection construction, an attacker may attempt to extend the path to a suspect and then back to herself, where she could observe whether a join occurred. Our use of hash chaining prevents this attack, since the attacker cannot replicate the nonce initially presented to the suspect. The matchmaker is provided with an earlier nonce to create a legal join and may perform some probing, but this is heavily constrained by the dovetail-matchmaker cost limit.

Matchmaker Intersection. The matchmaker provides the source with a set of possible tail segments from which the source picks one. Since the source will not select an AS already on the head segment, including it's own ISP, the matchmaker could try to offer tail segments that help it isolate possible source ASes. In particular, if there is a source AS of interest A, then the matchmaker could pick tail segments that include likely ASes between itself and A. If the source avoids these tail segments, it adds to the likelihood that the source is in A. However, fully unmasking the source AS with this type of intersection attack would require a large number of requests. As matchmakers are selected randomly from a large set, an attacker located at any particular matchmaker is unlikely to receive many connection requests from the same source.

Modify the Requested Path. An AS along the path could modify the unencrypted header segment to alter the route taken for the remainder of the path segment, but gains little from doing so. All vnodes along a path segment can identify the destination, and earlier vnodes have a better knowledge of the source. Thus, an attacker that places herself later in the same path segment does not learn any additional information regarding source or destination.

Modify the Tail Path. The matchmaker could use a different tail option than that selected by the source. However, the matchmaker does not learn whether unselected paths were acceptable and cannot identify the source and so cannot predict whether a particular path will be bad for that source. A matchmaker could speculatively route all connections through a particular ISP to allow identification of any sources within that ISP. This attack may be effective given a sufficient number of matchmakers, but widespread collusion falls outside our attack model.

5.2 Anonymity Analysis

A passive adversary who observes a dovetail path segment during construction learns the destination of the segment, the preceding AS, and may measure the cost to the source. In our technical report [40], we show how these properties may be used by an eavesdropper to calculate an anonymity set for the source of a path segment. The size of this set increases as the attacker moves further from the source, but also depends upon the algorithm used to select the segment path. We consider two different algorithms, showing that our *cost window* approach is superior or equal to shortest path selection in all cases. In addition, we present an entropy based assessment of *effective anonymity set size*, utilizing differences between the routing tables of potential sources.

We now discuss the complete set of source and destination identity information available to a passive adversary at each location on a Dovetail path, using both the path construction packet and the construction return packet. Whenever a measurable cost is discussed, this infers that a set of possible identities can be constructed.

Source Identity. The source identity is known to the source ISP. An attacker at each subsequent AS towards the matchmaker (which includes the dovetail node) can use its knowledge of the preceding AS identity, cost from the source, and all subsequent pathlets up to the matchmaker to limit the possible source identities. At the matchmaker itself, for paths of more than three or four hops, the number of possible sources should be quite large. After the matchmaker, the amount of information about the source will be even less.

Destination Identity. The destination identity is known to every AS from the matchmaker to the destination ISP due to the construction request. Any AS on the head segment between the dovetail and the matchmaker, but that does not appear on the data path, has no knowledge of the destination. Between the source and the dovetail, an attacker can measure the cost from the destination to her own AS using the data return path. If the attacker is able to guess which AS on the head segment serves as the dovetail, she can infer cost from the destination to the dovetail.

As intended, locations where the source is easily identified have little information about the destination and vice versa. The dovetail is the closest AS to the source that learns destination identity; it is typically the strongest location for a passive attacker. To avoid elevating the capability of an attacker located at the dovetail AS, we require that this AS only appear on the head segment once. Any other AS that appears twice in a given segment gains no additional information from its second inclusion.

Each segment of the dovetail path serves a purpose in maintaining a particular anonymity property; this should be considered when setting the segment length. The head segment must be long enough to conceal source identity from the dovetail, and the tail segment must be long enough to conceal destination identity from the source ISP. Finally, we note that uniform random selection of the matchmaker, uncorrelated with either the source or destination, is effective in isolating the anonymity properties of our system. An AS on the head segment can identify the matchmaker, but this does not help to identify the destination; an AS on the tail segment may be able to identify the matchmaker, but this does not help to identify the source.

5.3   Response Timing Attacks

The path diversity used to select each segment should hinder an attacker's ability to identify participants from response timing data. Each potential source could have used one of many thousand possible routes to reach the destination, and each of these routes has its own latency distribution. The superposition of these distributions blurs the range of possible response times for a source significantly when compared to shortest path routing and thus makes distinguishing between different sources harder.

5.4   Availability and Integrity Attacks

Violate routing policy. As with pathlets, all forwarding tables entries are valid expressions of the routing policy, and hence it is not possible to construct a path that violates this policy.

Construct Arbitrarily Long Paths. Our packet design constrains the maximum length of both encrypted and unencrypted packet header segments and thus limits the longest path an adversary intending to waste resources can construct.

Overload a Matchmaker. A matchmaker could be overloaded by sending a large number of continuation requests, but matchmakers are distributed throughout the network and the effect on clients is minor if the first matchmaker they contact is unavailable.

Overload a Routing vnode. Our forwarding operations are simple and intended to operate at the full data rate of a router. Connection construction requires more operations, but a maximum connection rate could be enforced to constrain this resource utilization.

Modify Packet Contents. Dovetail is a layer 3 protocol and does not provide any protections for the data it is used to carry. In cases where integrity is important, a higher layer protocol should be used to provide authentication.

Discard Packet Data. If the quality of service provided by a connection drops below some threshold, this would be observed as a failure, for which the recommended remedy is to reconnect over a different path. Paths are constructed by random selection from the available routes, and so this reconnection is likely to remove any intermediate AS discarding data.

6   Evaluation

Our proposal is evaluated primarily by simulation, using a model of the complete Internet at the AS level. In this section, we first introduce our simulation and input data, then discuss the anonymity and cost results for path segments and for complete paths, and conclude by estimating a variety of resource requirements for our system.

6.1 Simulation Scope

Our simulation models a network of ASes, each containing up to three routing vnodes plus host vnodes to represent its end users and matchmaking capability. ASes are connected by pathlets that codify their contractual arrangement; customer, provider, or peer. All pathlets within an AS have a cost of zero and all pathlets between different ASes have a cost of one. We simulate the exchange of routing information at initialization, leading to a unique routing perspective for each AS that contains all routing vnodes but not all pathlets. Separately, we simulate packets at a bit level during a connection, allowing us to test header design to ensure that routers and the matchmaker could correctly run the protocol.

Our Internet topology is derived from the CAIDA *inferred AS relationship dataset* [48]. The dataset contains *sibling* relations, which permitted infinitely long valley-free routes in some circumstances. To avoid optimistic bias, we replaced all sibling relationships with the more restrictive *peer* relationship. This reclassification causes 5.5% of the network to lose complete reachability, so we disallow traffic originating from or terminating at these ASes. We consider each AS without customer ASes to be a service provider for end users and add a host vnode to represent these users. Ideally, we would model the number of users, but accurate ISP customer size data are not available. Rather than risk skewing our conclusions, we restrict ourselves to measuring anonymity based on the number of possible source or destination ISPs, recognizing that some ISPs are far larger than others. We consider a mixture of ASes following the strict and loose valley-free routing policies defined in Section 4.2. Experimentation shows that when all ASes follow a strict valley-free routing policy, the number of routing options is limited, but introducing even a small proportion of loose valley-free ASes leads to far greater diversity. 10% loose valley-free ASes gives a median of 91,000 options for each path, and we use this topology for the remainder of our evaluation. Studies show that strict valley-free routing is not universal today [36], but we acknowledge that our selection of 10% is arbitrary.

6.2 Single Segment Performance

To select a path segment, the source compiles a set of available routes using a modified depth first search. Our implementation limits this set to a maximum cost of 13, based on the longest distance present in the network, and also a maximum of 20,000 routes at each path cost to limit computation. We first select a cost from the set of *available costs* (i.e. costs with at least one route) and then select a random route of this cost. In our technical report [40] we evaluate four selection algorithms that differ in their probability of selecting a given cost. Based on this evaluation we use the *Exponential4* algorithm, which selects longer paths less frequently but never selects a path with a cost under four. The Exponential4 algorithm results in an average cost approximately 25% greater than shortest path routing, and yet it achieves an anonymity set containing over half the network in 98% of the tests.

6.3   Complete Path Performance

We now evaluate the anonymity and cost properties of complete paths. Dovetail includes parameters that users can configure to trade performance against anonymity. Our objective here is to demonstrate the anonymity limit of this sliding scale, but many users will prefer a lower setting. The parameter settings we use are:

Dovetail to Matchmaker Cost = Two. Provides strong limits on matchmaker capability without requiring that dovetail and matchmaker are adjacent.

Source to Matchmaker Algorithm = Exponential6. Effectively delivers Exponential4 at the dovetail.

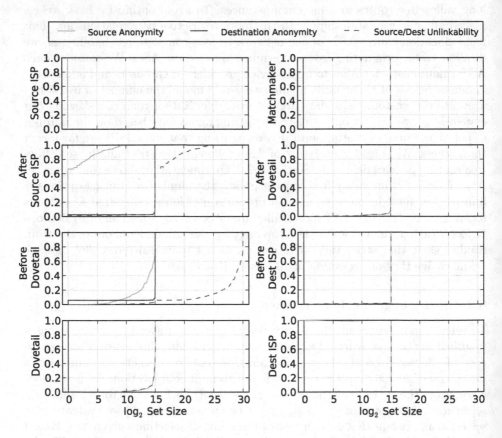

Fig. 3. Source and destination anonymity set size along the complete path

Dovetail to Destination Algorithm = Exponential4. Shown to provide near maximum anonymity [40].

In our experiment, we select source and destination hosts at random and construct a dovetail path between them. The matchmaker generates eight tail path options and the source selects one from this set. Where possible, the source selects an option that does not reuse a head AS, but in 23% of paths constructed all options required such reuse.[2] We measure the source and destination anonymity set size observable by an attacker at each location in the path. Random selection of a matchmaker decouples the source and destination anonymity sets, and therefore we can also consider the *source-destination unlinkability*, i.e. the number of potential source-destination pairs associated with an observed connection, to be the product of the source and destination anonymity set sizes. Figure 3 presents the distribution of these three properties at a series of key locations along the path, and Figure 4 presents the cost distribution, with the cost of shortest path routing included for comparison with IP and LAP.

Each successive step adds ambiguity to the source identity. At the dovetail AS, source anonymity is approximately equal to network size in 80% of cases. Destination identity is known at the dovetail and all subsequent locations, but locations prior to the dovetail are unable to calculate a meaningful destination identity. No location except the source is able to clearly link source and destination. The AS immediately preceding the dovetail is most likely to be duplicated in head and tail segments, being adjacent to an AS that is always present in both. As illustrated by the destination anonymity for "Before Dovetail", this occurred in 5% of our experiments. The dovetail may partially calculate source identity in around 20% of cases, but this is limited to around one thousand possible source ISPs, each containing many users.

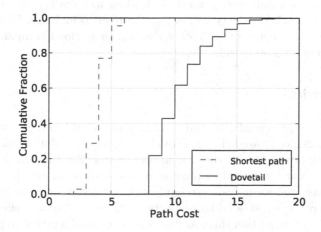

Fig. 4. Cost distribution for complete path

---

[2] We plan in future work to develop a heuristic to select dovetail vnodes with a lower probability of reuse.

Figure 4 shows that a Dovetail path passes through approximately 2.5 times more ASes than the shortest path routing used in the current Internet. This is a modest penalty when compared to the prevailing option for anonymity today; an anonymous circuit in Tor typically passes through three relays for a total of four IP paths, including six more last-mile connections than a direct path, and incurs additional processing and queuing delays at each relay.

6.4   Resource Utilization

Rather than proposing a near-term solution, we aim to show that privacy is a feasible feature to include in future routing protocol designs. Nevertheless, we now briefly consider a variety of resource requirements to demonstrate that implementation would be feasible.

Host Memory Utilization. Each Dovetail host must maintain a model of the Internet to generate routes. In the 2012 dataset we use there are 252,666 visible pathlets, of which an average of 22% are known, requiring 680kB.

Router Memory Utilization. A Dovetail forwarding table scales with the number of local peers and not the total number of Internet prefixes as with BGP. All forwarding information is carried by the packet itself, and so a router need not store any information per connection.

Router Latency. The only cryptographic operation required to forward a data packet is a symmetric decryption of one word. This is the same task performed by LAP; Hsiao et al. measure an additional latency of under one microsecond in a software-based implementation of their system [16].

Transmission Efficiency. A Dovetail packet must specify a complete path rather than only an endpoint, potentially leading to large headers and low efficiency. The average header length in our experiments is 92 bytes. Given an MTU of 1500 bytes, this represents a 3.5% reduction in payload compared to IPv6. LAP would require a 60 byte header.

7   Conclusion

In this paper we presented Dovetail, a next-generation Internet routing protocol, and have demonstrated that it provides a workable solution for anonymity at the network layer. The overhead is approximately 2.5 times that of shortest path routing when configured to provide near complete anonymity against our chosen attacker, and we include mechanisms to exchange anonymity for performance. We have demonstrated key aspects of the feasibility and effectiveness of this direction and hope this this motivates serious consideration of privacy as a requirement in the development of other next-generation routing protocols.

Acknowledgements. We thank our shepherd, Amir Houmansadr, and numerous anonymous reviewers for their help in improving the paper. This material is based upon work supported by the National Science Foundation under CAREER Grant No. CNS-0954133.

References

1. Reiter, M., Rubin, A.: Crowds: Anonymity for web transactions. ACM ToISS (1998)
2. Dingledine, R., Mathewson, N., Syverson, P.: Tor: The second-generation onion router. In: USENIX Security (2004)
3. The Tor Project, Inc.: Tor metrics portal: Users, `https://metrics.torproject.org/users.html` (accessed: February 11, 2014)
4. Paul, S., Pan, J., Jain, R.: Architectures for the future networks and the next generation internet: A survey. Computer Communications (2011)
5. The National Science Foundation: NSF NeTS FIND initiative, `http://www.nets-find.net/index.php` (accessed: February 11, 2014)
6. CORDIS: FIRE home page, `http://cordis.europa.eu/fp7/ict/fire/home_en.html` (accessed: February 11, 2014)
7. National Institute of Information and Communications Technology: "AKARI" architecture design project for new generation network, `http://www.nict.go.jp/en/photonic_nw/archi/akari/akari-top_e.html` (accessed: February 11, 2014)
8. Papadopoulos, F., Krioukov, D., Bogua, M., Vahdat, A.: Greedy forwarding in dynamic scale-free networks embedded in hyperbolic metric spaces. In: IEEE INFOCOM (2010)
9. Bhattacharjee, B., Calvert, K., Griffioen, J., Spring, N., Sterbenz, J.P.: Postmodern internetwork architecture. NSF Nets FIND Initiative (2006)
10. Godfrey, P.B., Ganichev, I., Shenker, S., Stoica, I.: Pathlet routing. In: ACM SIGCOMM (2009)
11. Farinacci, D., Lewis, D., Meyer, D., Fuller, V.: The locator/ID separation protocol (LISP). RFC 6830 (2013)
12. Yang, X., Wetherall, D.: Source selectable path diversity via routing deflections. ACM SIGCOMM Computer Communication Review (2006)
13. Yang, X.: NIRA: A new internet routing architecture. In: ACM SIGCOMM FDNA (2003)
14. Zhang, X., Hsiao, H.C., Hasker, G., Chan, H., Perrig, A., Andersen, D.G.: SCION: Scalability, control, and isolation on next-generation networks. In: IEEE S&P (2011)
15. Falk, A.: GENI at a glance (2011), `http://www.geni.net/wp-content/uploads/2011/06/GENI-at-a-Glance-1Jun2011.pdf`
16. Hsiao, H.C., Kim, T.J., Perrig, A., Yamada, A., Nelson, S.C., Gruteser, M., Meng, W.: LAP: Lightweight anonymity and privacy. In: IEEE S&P (2012)
17. Pfitzmann, A., Hansen, M.: A terminology for talking about privacy by data minimization, v0.34 (2010), `http://dud.inf.tu-dresden.de/literatur/Anon_Terminology_v0.34.pdf`
18. Kaufman, C., Hoffman, P., Nir, Y., Eronen, P.: Internet Key Exchange Protocol Version 2 (IKEv2). RFC 5996 (Proposed Standard), Updated by RFCs 5998, 6989 (September 2010)
19. Eckersley, P.: How unique is your web browser? In: Atallah, M.J., Hopper, N.J. (eds.) PETS 2010. LNCS, vol. 6205, pp. 1–18. Springer, Heidelberg (2010)

20. Soltani, A., Canty, S., Mayo, Q., Thomas, L., Hoofnagle, C.J.: Flash cookies and privacy. In: SSRN eLibrary (2009)
21. Acquisti, A., Dingledine, R., Syverson, P.: On the economics of anonymity. In: Wright, R.N. (ed.) FC 2003. LNCS, vol. 2742, pp. 84–102. Springer, Heidelberg (2003)
22. Dingledine, R., Murdoch, S.J.: Performance improvements on Tor or, why Tor is slow and what we're going to do about it (2009), http://www.torproject.org/press/presskit/2009-03-11-performance.pdf
23. Jansen, R., Johnson, A., Syverson, P.: LIRA: Lightweight Incentivized Routing for Anonymity. In: NDSS (2013)
24. Dischinger, M., Haeberlen, A., Gummadi, K.P., Saroiu, S.: Characterizing residential broadband networks. In: ACM SIGCOMM IMC (2007)
25. Levine, B.N., Reiter, M.K., Wang, C.-X., Wright, M.: Timing attacks in low-latency mix systems. In: Juels, A. (ed.) FC 2004. LNCS, vol. 3110, pp. 251–265. Springer, Heidelberg (2004)
26. Houmansadr, A., Kiyavash, N., Borisov, N.: RAINBOW: A robust and invisible non-blind watermark for network flows. In: NDSS (2009)
27. Chen, S., Wang, X., Jajodia, S.: On the anonymity and traceability of peer-to-peer voip calls. IEEE Network 20(5), 32–37 (2006)
28. Reimer, J.: Your ISP may be selling your web clicks (2007), http://arstechnica.com/tech-policy/2007/03/your-isp-may-be-selling-your-web-clicks/
29. Dampier, P.: 'Cable ONE spied on customers' alleges federal class action lawsuit (2012), http://stopthecap.com/2010/02/08/cable-one-spied-on-customers-alleges-federal-class-action-lawsuit
30. Syverson, P.: Why I'm not an entropist. In: Christianson, B., Malcolm, J.A., Matyáš, V., Roe, M. (eds.) Security Protocols 2009. LNCS, vol. 7028, pp. 213–230. Springer, Heidelberg (2013)
31. Murdoch, S.J., Zieliński, P.: Sampled traffic analysis by internet-exchange-level adversaries. In: Borisov, N., Golle, P. (eds.) PET 2007. LNCS, vol. 4776, pp. 167–183. Springer, Heidelberg (2007)
32. Boyan, J.: The anonymizer. Computer-Mediated Communication Magazine (1997)
33. Panchenko, A., Pimenidis, L., Renner, J.: Performance analysis of anonymous communication channels provided by Tor. In: ARES (2008)
34. DiBenedetto, S., Gasti, P., Tsudik, G., Uzun, E.: ANDaNA: Anonymous named data networking application. In: NDSS (2013)
35. Gao, L.: On inferring autonomous system relationships in the internet. In: IEEE/ACM ToN (2001)
36. Giotsas, V., Zhou, S.: Valley-free violation in internet routing-analysis based on BGP community data. In: IEEE ICC (2012)
37. Ryan, P.S., Gerson, J.: A primer on Internet exchange points for policymakers and non-engineers (August 2012), http://ssrn.com/abstract=2128103
38. Lodhi, A., Dhamdhere, A., Dovrolis, C.: Open peering by Internet transit providers: Peer preference or peer pressure? In: Proc. IEEE INFOCOM (2014)
39. Rekhter, Y., Li, T., Hares, S.: A border gateway protocol 4 (BGP-4). RFC 4271 (2006)
40. Sankey, J., Wright, M.: Dovetail: Stronger anonymity in next-generation internet routing (April 2014), http://www.jsankey.com/papers/Dovetail.pdf
41. Borisov, N., Danezis, G., Mittal, P., Tabriz, P.: Denial of service or denial of security? In: CCS (2007)

42. Wright, M.K., Adler, M., Levine, B.N., Shields, C.: Passive-logging attacks against anonymous communications systems. ACM Transactions on Information and System Security (TISSEC) 11(2) (2008)
43. Chen, S., Wang, R., Wang, X., Zhang, K.: Side-channel leaks in web applications: A reality today, a challenge tomorrow. In: IEEE S&P (2010)
44. Mittal, P., Khurshid, A., Juen, J., Caesar, M., Borisov, N.: Stealthy traffic analysis of low-latency anonymous communication using throughput fingerprinting. In: ACM CCS (2011)
45. Hopper, N., Vasserman, E.Y., Chan-Tin, E.: How much anonymity does network latency leak? In: ACM CCS (2007)
46. Murdoch, S.J., Danezis, G.: Low-cost traffic analysis of Tor. In: IEEE S&P (2005)
47. Evans, N., Dingledine, R., Grothoff, C.: A practical congestion attack on Tor using long paths. In: USENIX Security (2009)
48. CAIDA: The CAIDA UCSD inferred AS relationships - 20120601 (2012), http://www.caida.org/data/active/as-relationships/index.xml

Spoiled Onions:
Exposing Malicious Tor Exit Relays*

Philipp Winter[1], Richard Köwer[3], Martin Mulazzani[2], Markus Huber[2],
Sebastian Schrittwieser[2], Stefan Lindskog[1], and Edgar Weippl[2]

[1] Karlstad University, Sweden
[2] SBA Research, Austria
[3] FH Campus Wien, Austria

Abstract. Tor exit relays are operated by volunteers and together push
more than 1 GiB/s of network traffic. By design, these volunteers are able
to inspect and modify the anonymized network traffic. In this paper, we
seek to expose such malicious exit relays and document their actions.
First, we monitored the Tor network after developing two fast and modular exit relay scanners—one for credential sniffing and one for active
MitM attacks. We implemented several scanning modules for detecting
common attacks and used them to probe all exit relays over a period of
several months. We discovered numerous malicious exit relays engaging
in a multitude of different attacks. To reduce the attack surface users are
exposed to, we patched Torbutton, an existing browser extension and
part of the Tor Browser Bundle, to fetch and compare suspicious X.509
certificates over independent Tor circuits. Our work makes it possible to
continuously and systematically monitor Tor exit relays. We are able to
detect and thwart many man-in-the-middle attacks, thereby making the
network safer for its users. All our source code is available under a free
license.

1 Introduction

As of January 2014, nearly 1,000 exit relays [30] distributed all around the globe
serve as part of the Tor anonymity network [10]. As illustrated in Fig. 1, the
purpose of these relays is to establish a bridge between the Tor network and the
"open" Internet. A user's Tor circuits—which are basically encrypted tunnels—
are terminated at exit relays and from there, the user's traffic proceeds to travel
over the open Internet to its final destination. Since exit relays can see traffic
as it is sent by clients, Tor users are advised to use end-to-end encryption. By
design, exit relays act as a "man-in-the-middle" (MitM) in between a user and
her destination. This renders it possible for exit relay operators to run various
MitM attacks such as traffic sniffing, DNS poisoning, and SSL-based attacks

---

* This work is the result of merging two PETS submissions. The original titles and
authors were: "Spoiled Onions: Exposing Malicious Tor Exit Relays" by Winter and
Lindskog, and "HoneyConnector: Active Sniffer Baiting on Tor" by Köwer, Mulazzani, Huber, Schrittwieser, and Weippl.

E. De Cristofaro and S.J. Murdoch (Eds.): PETS 2014, LNCS 8555, pp. 304–331, 2014.

such as HTTPS MitM and sslstrip [22]. An additional benefit for attackers is that exit relays can be set up quickly and anonymously, thus making it very difficult to trace attacks back to their origin. While it is possible for relay operators to specify contact information such as an e-mail address,[1] this is optional and as of January 2014, only 56% out of all 4,962 relays publish contact information. Even fewer relays publish *valid* contact information.

To thwart a number of popular attacks, TorBrowser [26]—the Tor Project's modified version of Firefox—ships with the two extensions HTTPS-Everywhere [11] and NoScript [17]. While the former contains rules to rewrite HTTP to HTTPS traffic, NoScript seeks to prevent many script-based attacks. However, there is little clients can do in the face of web sites implementing poor security such as the lack of site-wide TLS, session cookies being sent in the clear, or using weak cipher suites in their web server configuration. Often, such bad practice enables attackers to spy on users' traffic or, even worse, hijack accounts. Besides, TorBrowser

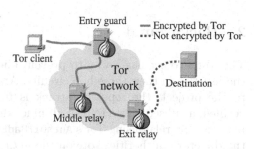

Fig. 1. The structure of a three-hop Tor circuit. Exit relays constitute the bridge between encrypted circuits and the open Internet. As a result, exit relay operators can see—and tamper with—anonymized traffic of users.

cannot protect against attacks targeting non-HTTP(S) protocols such as SSH. All these attacks are not just of theoretical nature. In 2007, a security researcher published 100 POP3 credentials he captured by sniffing traffic on a set of exit relays under his control [25]; supposedly to show the need for end-to-end encryption when using Tor. Section 2.1 discusses additional attacks which were found in the wild.

The main contributions of this paper are:

- We discuss the design and implementation of exitmap, a flexible and fast exit relay scanner which is able to detect several popular MitM attacks.
- We introduce HoneyConnector, a framework to detect sniffing Tor exit relays based on FTP and IMAP bait connections.
- Using exitmap and HoneyConnector, we monitored the Tor network over a period of multiple months in two independent studies. In total, we identified 65 exit relays that conducted MitM attacks or reused sniffed credentials.
- To detect MitM attacks against HTTPS, we propose the design and prototype of a patch for the Torbutton browser extension which fetches and compares X.509 certificates over diverging Tor circuits.

---

[1] Contact information is useful to get in touch with relay operators, e.g., if their relay is not configured correctly.

The remainder of this paper is structured as follows: Section 2 gives a brief background on how misbehaving relays are handled in the Tor network and gives an overview of related work. Section 3 discusses the design and implementation of exitmap and HoneyConnector, our scanners to detect malicious relays. We ran both frameworks for multiple months consecutively and present the attacks we discovered in Section 4 and discuss them in Section 5. Section 6 presents countermeasures to protect against HTTPS MitM attacks. Finally, Section 7 concludes this paper.

2   Background

The Tor Project has a way to prevent clients from selecting bad exit relays as the last hop in their three-hop circuits. After a suspected relay is communicated to the project, the reported attack is first reproduced. If the attack can be verified, a subset of two (out of all nine) directory authority operators manually blacklist the relay using Tor's AuthDirBadExit configuration option. Every hour, the directory authorities vote on the *network consensus* which is a signed list of all relays, the network is comprised of. Among other information, the consensus includes the *BadExit flag*. As long as the majority of the authorities responsible for the BadExit flag—i.e., two out of two—agree on the flag being set for a particular relay, the next network consensus will label the respective relay as BadExit. After the consensus was signed by a sufficient number of directory authorities, it propagates and is eventually used by all Tor clients after 24 hours have passed. From then on, clients will no longer select relays labeled as BadExit as the last hop in their circuits. Note that this does not mean that BadExit relays become effectively useless. They keep getting selected by clients as their entry guards and middle relays. Most of the malicious relays we discovered were assigned the BadExit flag after we reported them to the Tor Project. The relays which escaped the BadExit flag were either merely misconfigured or already offline when we reported them to the Tor Project.

Note that the BadExit flag is not only given to relays which are believed to be malicious. It is also assigned to relays which are misconfigured or are otherwise unable to fulfill their duty of providing unfiltered Internet access. A frequent cause of misconfiguration is the use of third-party DNS resolvers which block certain web site categories such as "pornography" or "proxy/anonymizer". Apart from the BadExit flag, directory authorities can blacklist relays by disabling its *Valid* flag which prevents clients from selecting the relay for *any* hop in its circuit. This option can be useful to disable relays running a broken version of Tor or are suspected to engage in end-to-end correlation attacks.

2.1   Related Work

In 2006, Perry began developing the framework "Snakes on a Tor" (SoaT) [31]. SoaT is a Tor network scanner whose purpose is to detect misbehaving exit relays. Similar to the less advanced torscanner [35], decoy content is first fetched over

Tor, then over a direct Internet connection, and finally compared. Over time, SoaT was extended with support for HTTP, HTTPS, SSH and several other protocols. However, SoaT is no longer maintained and makes use of deprecated libraries. Compared to SoaT, exitmap is more flexible and significantly faster. Similar to SoaT, Marlinspike implemented tortunnel [23] which exposes a local SOCKS interface. Incoming data is then sent over exit relays using one-hop circuits. By default, exitmap does not use one-hop circuits as that could be detected by attackers which could then act honestly.

A first academic attempt to detect malicious exit relays was made in 2008 by McCoy et al. [24]. The authors established decoy connections to servers under their control. They further controlled the authoritative DNS server responsible for the decoy hosts' IP addresses. As long as a malicious exit relay sniffed network traffic with reverse DNS lookups being enabled, the authors were able to map reverse lookups to exit relays by monitoring the authoritative DNS server's traffic. By exploiting that side channel, McCoy et al. were able to find one exit relay sniffing POP3 traffic at port 110. However, attackers can easily avoid that side channel by disabling reverse lookups. The popular tool tcpdump implements the command line switch -n for that exact purpose. In 2011, Chakravarty et al. [5] attempted to detect sniffing exit relays by systematically transmitting decoy credentials over all active exit relays. Over a period of ten months, the authors uncovered ten relays engaging in traffic snooping. Chakravarty et al. could verify that the operators were sniffing exit traffic because they were later found to have logged in using the snooped credentials. While the work of Chakravarty et al. represents an important first step towards monitoring the Tor network, their technique only focused on SMTP and IMAP. At the time of our writing, only 20 out of all ~1,000 exit relays allow connections to port 25. Instead, Honey-Connector focuses on FTP and IMAP. Also, similar to McCoy et al., the authors only discussed traffic snooping attacks which are passive. Active attacks remain entirely unexplored until today.

The Tor Project used to maintain a web page documenting misbehaving relays which were assigned the BadExit flag [18]. As of January 2014, this page lists 35 exit relays which were discovered in between April 2010 and July 2013. Note that not all of these relays engaged in attacks; almost half of them ran misconfigured anti virus scanners or used broken exit policies.[2] Since Chakravarty et al., no systematic study to spot malicious exit relays was conducted. Only some isolated anecdotal evidence emerged [34]. Our work is the first to give a comprehensive overview of *active attacks*. We further publish our code under a free license.[3] By doing so, we enable and encourage continuous and *crowdsourced* measurements rather than one-time scans.

---

[2] An exit relay's *exit policy* determines to which addresses and ports the relay forwards traffic to. Often, relay operators choose to not forward traffic to well-known file sharing ports in order to avoid copyright infringement.

[3] The code is available at http://www.cs.kau.se/philwint/spoiled_onions.

3   Monitoring Tor Exit Relays

We now discuss the design and implementation of exitmap as well as Honey-Connector which are both lightweight Python-based *exit relay scanners*. Their purpose is to systematically create circuits to exit relays which are then probed by modules which establish decoy connections to various destinations. While ex-itmap focuses on active attacks, HoneyConnector seeks to uncover traffic snoop-ing. We aim to provoke exit relays to tamper with or snoop on our connections, thereby revealing their malicious intent. By doing so, we seek to discover and remove all "spoiled onions" in the Tor network. Our adversary model is thus a relay operator who exploits the fact that traffic can be modified or might be unencrypted once it leaves the Tor network. We will also show that our scanners' *modular design* enables quick prototyping of new scanning modules and exitmap's *event-driven architecture* makes it possible to scan all exit relays within a matter of only seconds while at the same time sparing their resources.

3.1   The Design of exitmap

exitmap is an active scanner that is designed to detect MitM attacks of various kinds. The schematic design of exitmap is illustrated in Fig. 2. Our tool is run on a single machine and requires the Python library Stem [32]. Stem implements the Tor control protocol [33] and we use it to initiate and close circuits, attach streams to circuits as well as to parse the network consensus. Upon starting exitmap, it first invokes a local Tor process which proceeds by fetching the newest network consensus in order to know which exit relays are currently online.

Next, our tool is fed with a set of exit relays. This set can consist of a single re-lay, all exit relays in a given country, or the set of all Tor exit relays. Random per-mutation is then performed on the set so that repeated scans do not probe exit re-lays in the same order. This is useful while developing and debugging new scanning modules as it equally dis-tributes the load over all selected exit relays. Once ex-itmap knows which exit relays it has to probe, it initiates cir-cuits which use the respective exit relays as their last hop.

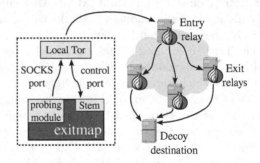

Fig. 2. The design of exitmap. Our scanner invokes a Tor process and uses the library Stem to control it. Using Stem, circuits are created "manually" and attached to decoy connections which are initiated by our probing modules.

All circuits are created asynchronously in the background. Once a circuit to an exit relay is established, Tor informs exitmap about the circuit by sending an asynchronous circuit event over the control connection. Upon receiving the event, exitmap invokes the desired probing module which then proceeds by establishing a connection to a decoy destination (see Section 3.1). Tor creates stream events for new connections to the SOCKS port which are also sent to exitmap. When a stream event is received, we attach the stream of a probing module to the respective circuit. Note that stream-to-circuit attaching is typically done by Tor. In order to have control over this process, our scanner invokes Tor with the configuration option __LeaveStreamsUnattached which instructs Tor to leave streams unattached. For performance reasons, Tor builds circuits preemptively, i.e., a number of circuits are kept ready even if there is no data to be sent yet. Since we want full control over all circuits, we prevent Tor from creating circuits preemptively by using the configuration option __DisablePredictedCircuits. exitmap's probing modules can either be standalone processes or Python modules. Processes are invoked using the torsocks wrapper [36] which hijacks system calls such as socket() and connect() in order to redirect them to Tor's SOCKS port. We used standalone processes for our HTTPS and SSH modules. In addition, probing modules can be implemented in Python. To redirect Python's networking API over Tor's SOCKS port, we extended the SocksiPy module [13]. We used Python for our sslstrip, DNS, XMPP, and IMAPS modules.

Performance Hacks. A naive approach to probing exit relays could be a nontrivial burden to the Tor network; mostly computationally but also in terms of network throughput. We implemented a number of tweaks in order for our scanning to be as fast and cheap as possible.

First, we expose a configuration option for avoiding the default of three-hop circuits. Instead, we only use *two hops* as illustrated in Fig. 3. Tor's motivation for three hops is anonymity but since our scanner has no need for strong anonymity, we only select a static entry relay—ideally operated by exitmap's user—which then directly forwards all traffic to the respective exit relays. We offer no option to use one-hop circuits as that would make it possible for exit relays to isolate scanning connections: A malicious exit relay could decide not to tamper with a circuit if it originates from a non-Tor machine. Since we use a static first hop which is operated by us, we concentrate most of the scan-

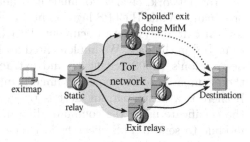

Fig. 3. Instead of establishing a full three-hop circuit, our scanner is able to use a static middle relay; preferably operated by whoever is running our scanner. By doing so, we concentrate the load on one machine while making our scanning activity slightly less stealthy.

ning load on a single machine which is well-suited to deal with the load. Other entry and middle relays do not have to "suffer" from exitmap scans.

However, note that over time malicious exit relays are able to correlate scans with relays, thus determining which relays are used for scans. To avoid this problem, exitmap's first hop should be changed periodically and we hope that by crowdsourcing our scanner, isolating middle relays is no longer a viable option for attackers. Another computational performance tweak can be achieved on Tor's authentication layer. At the moment, there are two ways how a circuit handshake can be conducted; either by using the *traditional TAP* or the *newer NTor* handshake. TAP—short for Tor Authentication Protocol [12]—is based on Diffie-Hellman key agreement in a multiplicative group. NTor, on the other hand, uses the more efficient elliptic curve group Curve25519 [2]. A non-trivial fraction of a relay's computational load can be traced back to computationally expensive circuit handshakes. By favoring NTor over TAP, we slightly reduce the computational load on exit relays. As NTor supersedes TAP and is becoming more and more popular as Tor clients upgrade, we believe that it is not viable for attackers to "whitelist" NTor connections.

Scanning Modules. After discussing exitmap's architecture, we now present several probing modules we developed in order to be able to detect specific attacks. When designing a module, it is important to consider its *indistinguishability* from genuine Tor clients. As mentioned above, malicious relay operators could closely inspect exit traffic (e.g., by examining the user agent string of HTTP requests) and only target connections which appear to be genuine Tor users.

HTTPS. McCoy et al. [24] showed that HTTP is the most popular protocol in the Tor network, clearly dominating other protocols such as instant messaging or e-mail.[4] While HTTPS lags behind, it is still widely used and unsurprisingly, several exit relays were documented to have tampered with HTTPS connections [18] in the past. We implemented an HTTPS module which fetches a decoy destination's X.509 certificate and extracts its fingerprint. This fingerprint is then compared to the expected fingerprint which is hard-coded in the module.[5] If there is a mismatch, an alert is triggered. Originally, we began by fetching the certificate using the command line utility gnutls-cli. We later extended the module to send a TLS client hello packet as it is sent by TorBrowser to make the scan less distinguishable from what a real Tor user would send. Note that an attacker might become suspicious after observing that a Tor user only fetched an X.509 certificate without actually browsing the respective web site. However, at the point in time an attacker would become suspicious, we already have what we need; namely the X.509 certificate.

---

[4] This is particularly true for *connections* but not so much for *bytes transferred*.

[5] Note that it is also possible for modules to fetch the certificate over a direct Internet connection instead of hard-coding the fingerprint.

```
1  function probe( fingerprint, command ) {
2
3      ssh_public_key = "11:22:33:44:55:66:77:88:99:00:aa:bb:cc:dd:ee:ff";
4
5      output = command.execute("ssh -v decoy.host.com");
6
7      if (ssh_public_key not in output) {
8          print("Possible MitM attack by " + fingerprint);
9      }
10 }
```

Fig. 4. Pseudo code illustrating a scanning module which probes SSH. It establishes an SSH connection and verifies if the fingerprint matches the expected value. If the observed fingerprint differs, an alert is raised.

XMPP and IMAPS. Analogous to the HTTPS module, these two modules establish a TLS connection to a decoy destination, extract the server certificate's fingerprint, and compare it to the respective hard-coded fingerprint.

sslstrip. Instead of *interfering* with TLS connections, an attacker can seek to *prevent* TLS connections. This is the purpose of the tool sslstrip [22]. The tool achieves this goal by transparently rewriting HTML documents while on their way from the server to the client. In particular, it rewrites HTTPS links to HTTP links. A secure login form pointing to https://login.example.com is subsequently rewritten to HTTP which causes a user's browser to submit her credentials in the clear. While the HTTP Strict Transport Security policy [15] prevents sslstrip, it is still an effective attack against many large-scale web sites with Yahoo! being only one of them as of January 2014. From an attacker's point of view, the benefit of sslstrip is that it is a comparatively silent attack because browsers will not show certificate warnings. Vigilant users, however, might notice the absence of browser-specific TLS indicators such as lock icons. Our probing module fetches web sites containing HTTPS links over unencrypted HTTP. Afterwards, the module simply verifies whether the fetched HTML document contains the expected HTTPS links or if they were "downgraded" to HTTP.

SSH. The Tor network is also used to transport SSH traffic. This can easily be done with the help of tools such as torsocks [36]. Analogous to HTTPS-based attacks, malicious exit relays could run MitM attacks against SSH. In practice, this is not as easy as targeting HTTPS given SSH's "trust on first use" model. As long as the very first connection to an SSH server was secure, the public key is then stored by the client and kept as reference for subsequent connections. As a result, a MitM attack has to target a client's very first SSH connection. Nevertheless, this practical problem might not stop attackers from attempting to interfere with SSH connections. Our SSH module—conceptually similar to the pseudo code shown in Fig. 4—makes use of OpenSSH's ssh and torsocks to connect to a decoy server. Again, the server's key fingerprint is extracted and compared to the hard-coded fingerprint. However, compared to the HTTPS module, it is difficult to achieve indistinguishability over time. After all, a malicious relay operator could monitor an entire SSH session. If it looks suspicious, e.g., it only fetches the public key, or it lasts only one second, the attacker could decide to whitelist the destination in the future. To work around this problem, we could establish SSH connections to random hosts on the Internet. This, however, is often considered undesired scanning activity and does not constitute good Internet citizenship. Instead, we again seek to solve this problem by publishing our source code and encouraging people to crowdsource exitmap scanning. Every exitmap user is encouraged to use her own SSH server as decoy destination. That way, we hope to achieve destination diversity without bothering arbitrary SSH servers on the Internet.

DNS. While the Tor protocol only transports TCP streams, clients can ask exit relays to resolve DNS records by wrapping domain names in a RELAY_BEGIN cell [9]. Once a circuit is established, this cell is then sent to the exit relay for resolution. In the past, some exit relays were found to inadvertently censor DNS queries, e.g., by using an OpenDNS configuration which blocks certain domain categories such as "pornography" or "proxy/anonymizer" [18]. Our probing module maintains a whitelist of domains together with their corresponding IP addresses and raises an alert if the DNS A record of a domain name is unexpected. This approach works well for sites with a known set of IP addresses but large sites frequently employ a diverse—and sometimes geographically load-balanced—set of IP addresses which is difficult to enumerate. Our module probes domains in the categories finance, social networking, political activism, and pornography.

3.2 The Design of HoneyConnector

HoneyConnector is a framework for establishing bait connections over Tor using unique credentials over FTP and IMAP and detecting their subsequent use to identify sniffing exit relays. The framework can be divided into several components. It consists of the HoneyConnector client which is written in Python, a copy of the Tor client, the Stem [32] library for controlling Tor connections, and a backend database for storing our bait credentials and timestamps, as well as additional exit relay information. The HoneyConnector client is responsible for creating new credentials, establishing the actual bait connection over the respective exit relays, and communicating them to the deployed services over a secure channel for creating the accounts and bait data. Furthermore, HTTPS certificates are fetched by the client and compared with the real certificates to detect MitM attacks against HTTPS. Credentials are checked for duplicates prior to using them, to prevent reusing usernames or passwords. For each protocol—in our current implementation FTP and IMAP—a virtual machine is used for hosting these services, and accessed over the Tor network using bait credentials. This makes it possible to quickly deploy multiple instances for each service. Analogous to exitmap, HoneyConnector uses the library Stem to have control over which exit relay is selected for a circuit and to check if a given exit relay's exit policy allows connections to our bait services. We manually looked for peculiarities in our bait sessions which could have been used to identify them. Afterwards, we changed the status messages sent by pyFTPdlib to match those of vsFTPd. It was not necessary to change the behavior of Dovecot as it is a common mail server found on GNU/Linux systems. Once a scan is started, the network consensus is downloaded and all exit relays are processed sequentially after random permutation.

FTP Scanning. Our HoneyConnector client made use of the Python library ftplib to connect to our bait FTP server. The credentials for the FTP server were generated by the HoneyConnector client, stored in a database, and then forwarded to the FTP server over a secure channel. All FTP usernames are generated by randomly choosing a prefix out of "web", "user", "ftp", "usr", or two random letters followed by a random number between 1 and 999 in combination with a randomly generated password. After sending the credentials, our client waits for 30 seconds in order to assure that the server had enough time to populate the FTP user directory. The client then connects over the Tor network to the FTP server and downloads a random file before closing the connection. After the connection was closed, the client sends a message directly (i.e., not over Tor) to the server, instructing it to delete the user from the server. On the server side we used the pyFTPdlib Python library as it allowed us to modify the source code for logging plaintext credentials; a feature which was hard to find in other FTP server software. The concatenation of username and password allowed us to identify which exit relay sniffed a given pair of credentials.

IMAP Scanning. For implementing our IMAP scan, we used Python's built-in library imaplib. On the server side we used Dovecot due to it being a popular IMAP server and offering the possibility of verbose authentication logging, including writing usernames and passwords to a log file. We believe that for sniffers, IMAP is more interesting than POP3 since messages are kept on the server. As a result, it is stealthier for an attacker to browse the victim's e-mails as they are kept on the server rather than being deleted after downloading them. We reused password lists from the Honeynet Project [27] instead of generating them randomly. These passwords mimic real user passwords, and we manually verified that we do not falsely count regular bruteforce attacks as reconnection (i.e. no other connection attempts within close time vicinity). We further populated all mailboxes with dummy e-mails (the exact amount was randomly chosen from {1..6000}). The e-mails do not need actual content as only the amount of e-mails in the mailbox is transferred but no content. We designed our IMAP setup analogous to the FTP setup discussed above; login credentials are first generated and then sent to the server after their uniqueness was verified. The HoneyConnector client then sleeps for a while to give the server time to populate the newly created mailbox. Subsequently, HoneyConnector simulates an e-mail client checking for new mails. Finally, the client instructs the server to delete the e-mail account and thereby terminates the bait IMAP connection.

4   Experimental Results

The following two sections present the results we obtained by monitoring all Tor exit relays over a period of several months. We begin by presenting active attacks in Section 4.1 which is then followed by sniffing attacks in Section 4.2.

4.1   Detecting MitM Attacks with exitmap

Scanning Performance. On September 19th, we ran our first full scan over all ~950 exit relays which were part of the Tor network at the time. From then on, we scanned all exit relays several times a week. Originally, we began our scans while only armed with our HTTPS module but as time passed, we added additional modules which allowed us to scan for additional attacks. In this section, we will discuss the results we obtained by monitoring the Tor network over a period of seven months.

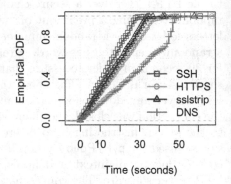

exitmap is also useful to measure the reliability of exit relays. While running our scans, we observed that 84%–88% of circuit creations succeeded. The remaining circuits either timed out or were torn down by the respective exit relay using a DESTROY cell. The performance of our probing modules for all responsive exit relays is illustrated in Fig. 5. The ECDF's x-axis shows the amount of seconds it takes for a module to finish successfully. The y-axis shows the cumulative fraction of all exit relays. The diagram shows that all modules are able to scan at least 98% of all responsive Tor exit relays under 50 seconds. Note that it is possible to artificially slow down exitmap in order to make scans more difficult to detect. At maximum speed, it would be easier for colluding exit relays to correlate decoy connections and mark them as possibly coming from exitmap.

Fig. 5. The performance of some of our probing modules. The DNS module is slower because it resolves several domain names at once. All other modules can scan at least 98% of all responsive Tor exit relays under 40 seconds.

Malicious Relays. Table 1 contains all *40 malicious and misconfigured exit relays* we found. We discovered the first two relays "manually" before we had developed exitmap. All data illustrated in the table was gathered on the day we found the respective attack. It includes the first 4 bytes of the relay's unique 20-byte SHA-1 fingerprint, the IPv4 addresses or netblocks the relay was found to have used over its life time, the advertised bandwidth and the country in which the relay resided according to MaxMind's GeoIP lite database. Furthermore, the relay's configuration problem or the attack it was running, the day the relay was set up and the day we discovered the relay's malicious activity.

Apart from all the conspicuous HTTPS MitM attacks which we will discuss in Section 5.2, we exposed several relays running sslstrip. The relay 5A2A51D4 injected custom HTML code into HTTP traffic (see Appendix B and Section 5.1). The injected HTML code was discovered by our sslstrip module which assures that the returned HTML code is exactly as expected. Besides, relays in Malaysia, Hong Kong, and Turkey were subject to DNS censorship. The relays in Hong Kong seem to have fallen prey to the Great Firewall of China's DNS poisoning; perhaps, the relays made use of a DNS resolver in China. Several domains such as torproject.org, facebook.com and youtube.com returned invalid IP addresses which were also found in previous work [21]. Finally, four relays were misconfigured as they used an OpenDNS policy which censored at least web sites in the category "pornography". The last two relays in the table ran anti virus products which broke into IMAPS sessions; presumably for content inspection. All the remaining relays engaged in HTTPS, SSH, and XMPP MitM attacks. Upon establishing a connection to the decoy destination, these relays exchanged the destination's certificate with their own, self-signed version. Since these certificates were not issued by a trusted authority stored in TorBrowser's certificate store, a user falling prey to such a MitM attack would be redirected to the about:certerror warning page. We will discuss some attacks in greater detail in Section 5.

4.2   Detecting Traffic Sniffing with HoneyConnector

We deployed HoneyConnector on October 13th, 2013, and after an initial testing phase of two weeks on a residential service provider network we deployed it on multiple hosting providers across Europe. The evaluation period lasted until February 10th, 2014, resulting in approximately four months overall deployment. The modified FTP server was deployed in Germany with Hetzner Hosting while the modified IMAP server was deployed with OVH. HoneyConnector can be configured to use multiple server instances of the services, but for the evaluation we decided to go with the baseline minimum of two virtual machines. We cannot ascertain whether the destination's network location was an additional incentive for sniffers, e.g., due to its IP range or hostname. Furthermore, these hosting services might be of particular interest for sniffers since (in the attackers perception) there is no central software update mechanism available to customers, the servers have high availability and high bandwidth, and are prone to misconfiguration due to inexperienced customers. The client establishing the bait connections was run locally on our own machines.

During the four month deployment of HoneyConnector, we registered a total of 255 login attempts with 128 sniffed plaintext credentials, tracing back to 27

Table 1. All 40 malicious and misconfigured exit relays we discovered over a period of seven months. The data was collected right after a relay was discovered. We have reason to believe that all relays whose fingerprint ends with a † were run by the same attacker

Fingerprint	IP addresses	Country	Bandwidth	Problem	First active	Discovery
F8FD29D0†	176.99.12.246	Russia	7.16 MB/s	HTTPS MitM	2013-06-24	2013-07-13
8F9121BF†	64.22.111.168/29	U.S.	7.16 MB/s	HTTPS MitM	2013-06-11	2013-07-13
93213A1F†	176.99.9.114	Russia	290 KB/s	HTTPS MitM (50%)	2013-07-23	2013-09-19
05AD06E2†	92.63.102.68	Russia	5.55 MB/s	HTTPS MitM (33%)	2013-08-01	2013-09-19
45C55E46†	46.254.19.140	Russia	1.54 MB/s	SSH & HTTPS MitM (12%)	2013-08-09	2013-09-23
CA1BA219†	176.99.9.111	Russia	334 KB/s	HTTPS MitM (37.5%)	2013-09-26	2013-10-01
1D70CDED†	46.38.50.54	Russia	929 KB/s	HTTPS MitM (50%)	2013-09-27	2013-10-14
EE215500†	31.41.45.235	Russia	2.96 MB/s	HTTPS MitM (50%)	2013-09-26	2013-10-15
12459837†	195.2.252.117	Russia	3.45 MB/s	HTTPS MitM (26.9%)	2013-09-26	2013-10-16
B5906553†	83.172.8.4	Russia	850.9 KB/s	HTTPS MitM (68%)	2013-08-12	2013-10-16
EFF1D805†	188.120.228.103	Russia	287.6 KB/s	HTTPS MitM (61.2%)	2013-10-23	2013-10-23
229C3722	121.54.175.51	Hong Kong	106.4 KB/s	sslstrip	2013-06-05	2013-10-31
4E8401D7†	176.99.11.182	Russia	1.54 MB/s	HTTPS MitM (79.6%)	2013-11-08	2013-11-09
27FB6BB0†	195.2.253.159	Russia	721 KB/s	HTTPS MitM (43.8%)	2013-11-08	2013-11-09
0ABB31BD†	195.88.208.137	Russia	2.3 MB/s	SSH & HTTPS MitM (85.7%)	2013-10-31	2013-11-21
CADA00B9†	5.63.154.230	Russia	187.62 KB/s	HTTPS MitM	2013-11-26	2013-11-26
C1C0EDAD†	93.170.130.194	Russia	838.54 KB/s	HTTPS MitM	2013-11-26	2013-11-27
5A2A51D4	111.240.0.0/12	Taiwan	192.54 KB/s	HTML Injection	2013-11-23	2013-11-27
EBF7172E†	37.143.11.220	Russia	4.34 MB/s	SSH MitM	2013-11-15	2013-11-27
68E682DF†	46.17.46.108	Russia	60.21 KB/s	SSH & HTTPS MitM	2013-12-02	2013-12-02
533FDE2F†	62.109.22.20	Russia	896.42 KB/s	SSH & HTTPS MitM (42.1%)	2013-12-06	2013-12-08
E455A115	89.128.56.73	Spain	54.27 KB/s	sslstrip	2013-12-17	2013-12-18
02013F48	117.18.118.136	Hong Kong	538.45 KB/s	DNS censorship	2013-12-22	2014-01-01
2F5B07B2	178.211.39	Turkey	204.8 KB/s	DNS censorship	2013-12-28	2014-01-06
4E2692FE	24.84.118.132	Canada	52.22 KB/s	OpenDNS	2013-12-21	2014-01-06
A1AF47E3	207.98.174.40	U.S.	98.3 KB/s	OpenDNS	2013-12-20	2014-01-24
BEB0BF4F†	37.143.14.176	Russia	1.54 MB/s	XMPP MitM	2013-12-16	2014-01-25
C37AFA7F	81.219.51.206	Poland	509.3 KB/s	OpenDNS	2014-02-03	2014-02-06
975ACB99	54.200.151.237	U.S.	2.73 MB/s	sslstrip	2014-01-26	2014-02-08
B40A3DC6	85.23.243.147	Finland	50 KB/s	IMAPS anti virus	2013-11-04	2014-02-10
E5A75EE1	132.248.80.171	Mexico	102.4 KB/s	IMAPS anti virus	2013-04-24	2014-02-10
423BCBCE	54.200.102.199	U.S.	702.66 KB/s	sslstrip	2014-02-13	2014-02-14
F7B4BC6B	54.213.13.21	U.S.	431.78 KB/s	sslstrip	2014-02-14	2014-02-15
DB7C7DDD	37.143.8.242	Russia	267.86 KB/s	sslstrip	2014-02-18	2014-02-18
426E8E2F	54.201.48.216	U.S.	2.25 MB/s	sslstrip	2014-02-09	2014-02-18
D81DAC47	117.18.118.136	Hong Kong	166.31 KB/s	DNS censorship	2014-01-27	2014-02-14
BDBFBBC3	209.162.33.125	U.S.	806.46 KB/s	OpenDNS	2014-03-06	2014-03-06
564E995A	67.222.130.112	U.S.	204.8 KB/s	sslstrip	2013-08-19	2014-03-13
7F2240BF	198.50.244.31	Canada	721.47 KB/s	sslstrip	2014-03-27	2014-04-04
DA7A2EDC	121.121.82.198	Malaysia	82.79 KB/s	DNS censorship	2014-03-07	2014-04-15

sniffing exit relays. Among all 255 login attempts, 136 were targeting FTP and 119 were targeting IMAP. From all 128 sniffed credentials, 97 were for FTP and 31 for IMAP. We observed one of the relays using two different Tor identity fingerprints for different login attempts and sniffed credentials, but since the nickname and IP address stayed the same and Tor's software version changed, we counted it only once. The identity fingerprint can be changed during software updates if no precautions are met by the operator. Overall, 2,611 distinct servers (based on the identity fingerprints) have seen bait connections, but this is considered an upper bound since there was a Tor software update from version 0.2.3 to 0.2.4 in December and there were up to approximately 1,000 exit relays online during the evaluation. Even though the HoneyConnector architecture was initially unstable, a login attempt with sniffed credentials was already registered during the very first night of stability testing (October 13th). In total, we conducted approximately 27,000 bait connection for FTP and IMAP each, resulting in approximately 54,000 plaintext credentials created by the HoneyConnector client software. A total of 0.24% of these credentials were used during reconnects by the sniffing exit relay operators.

Table 2 shows the details of all sniffing exit relays we discovered. Again, it includes the first 4 bytes of the relay's unique 20-byte SHA-1 fingerprint, the relay's bandwidth and country (also resolved using the GeoIP lite database). The triple in angle brackets represents the *1)* unique number of plaintext credentials sent, the *2)* number of different plaintext credentials used by the malicious operator (a subset of the set of unique credentials sent) as well as the *3)* total number of connection attempts conducted with these credentials. If a relay's exit policy permitted it, both IMAP and FTP were used for bait connections. Furthermore, the table shows whether the operator tried to log in using the FTP or the IMAP credentials, or both. The distribution of login attempts over the four month period can be seen in Fig. 6. FTP login attempts are shown as triangles and IMAP as squares. At most, there were ten FTP login attempts a day, whereas IMAP peaked at 33 login attempts a day. On average and across all sniffing nodes, about 60% of the bait credentials sent were used.

Another aspect is the time interval in between the bait connection made by HoneyConnector and the subsequent reconnect by the exit node operator. Fig. 7 shows the time in interval between the transmission of the bait credentials and the reconnection attempts, clustered in (non-linear) time intervals. While the light gray bars only account for the first reconnection attempt, the darker bars account for all reconnection attempts, including repeatedly using the same credentials. About 25% of all login attempts were made within the first eight hours, while half of all reconnection attempts were made within 48 hours. The shortest time period until the first observed reconnection attempt was only three minutes and ten seconds and done by the Estonian exit node "FreedomFighter". The longest observed time interval was related to the reconnection made by "default" located in Hong Kong, with credentials that were sent more than two months before (63 days).

Table 2. All 27 exit relays which were found sniffing login credentials. The triple reads <no. of credentials sent, no. of credentials tried, no of connection attemtps>, *dynamic* refers to multiple IPs from 120.56.0.0/14 and 59.176.0.0/13.

Fingerprint	IP addresses	Country	Bandwidth	Sniffed Protocol	HoneyConnection	Reconnection
08F097F8	58.120.227.83	South Korea	1136.64 KB/s	FTP <36,35,70>	2013-10-17	2013-10-17
0FE41A85	46.246.108.146	Sweden	4326.85 KB/s	FTP <1,1,6>	2014-01-20	2014-01-21
229C3722	121.54.175.51	Hong Kong	168.74 KB/s	FTP <2,1,14>	2013-11-04	2014-01-07
28619F94	dynamic	India	51.94 KB/s	IMAP & FTP <15,4,50>	2013-11-07	2013-11-13
319D548B	91.219.238.139	Hungary	1075.2 KB/s	FTP <2,1,47>	2013-12-24	2013-12-14
3A484AFC	dynamic	India	73.4 KB/s	IMAP & FTP <15,7,55>	2013-10-27	2013-10-30
52E24E09	dynamic	India	57.15 KB/s	IMAP & FTP <7,6,44>	2013-10-17	2013-10-18
5761CB9C	109.87.249.227	Ukraine	2.05 KB/s	FTP <6,2,4>	2013-11-28	2013-11-28
5A2A51D4	111.240.0.0/12	Taiwan	75.47 KB/s	IMAP <1,1,57>	2013-11-02	2014-01-20
5A3B2DEC	66.85.131.84	U.S.	512.0 KB/s	IMAP <6,2,33>	2013-11-30	2013-12-03
6018E567	51.35.183.211	U.K.	312.1 KB/s	FTP <1,1,6>	2014-01-24	2014-01-24
61288460	88.150.227.162	U.K.	353.0 KB/s	IMAP & FTP <31,3,11>	2013-11-14	2013-11-15
6C9AAFEA	dynamic	India	53.95 KB/s	IMAP & FTP <20,12,44>	2013-10-17	2013-10-18
46B3ADE6	85.17.183.69	Netherlands	234.18 KB/s	FTP <2,1,6>	2013-12-27	2014-01-09
8450F3CA	moved once	Germany	2938.88 KB/s	FTP <12,7,16>	2013-12-16	2013-12-16
8A47C9B0	100.42.236.34	U.S.	237.4 KB/s	FTP <3,1,4>	2013-12-03	2013-12-05
9F7DBC53	76.74.178.217	U.S.	133.57 KB/s	FTP <1,1,1>	2013-12-16	2013-12-17
A68412BA	moved once	U.S.	989.67 KB/s	FTP <7,5,13>	2013-12-16	2013-12-17
AA6D6919	85.25.46.189	Germany	59.52 KB/s	FTP <2,1,2>	2013-10-17	2013-10-19
ADE35AA1	dynamic	India	35.53 KB/s	IMAP & FTP <3,3,15>	2013-10-18	2013-10-18
BF74938A	89.79.83.166	Poland	1979.39 KB/s	FTP <7,1,7>	2013-12-23	2013-12-23
C5398CD1	dynamic	India	53.82 KB/s	IMAP & FTP <14,9,43>	2013-10-14	2013-10-15
EBCA226D	46.246.95.193	Sweden	2737.89 KB/s	FTP <1,1,1>	2014-01-21	2014-01-23
F0AAFC6D	dynamic	India	56.65 KB/s	IMAP & FTP <30,16,56>	2013-10-17	2013-10-18
F0DD7385	76.189.8.28	Canada	111.42 KB/s	FTP <1,1,21>	2013-10-14	2013-10-14
F57E0775	151.217.63.51	Germany	537.62 KB/s	IMAP & FTP <24,2,2>	2013-12-29	2013-12-29
FEE8C068	46.22.211.36	Estonia	119.51 KB/s	FTP <5,5,57>	2013-11-21	2013-11-22

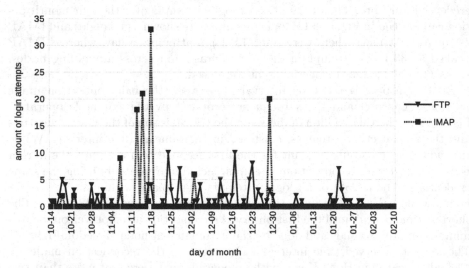

Fig. 6. The diagram illustrates the amount of rogue login attempts over time. While we did not witness any login attempts for most days, some days saw up to 33 login attempts.

5   Discussion

After having presented an overview of our results in Section 4, we now focus on and discuss several interesting aspects of our data sets. In particular, we found several instances of colluding exit relays, destination targeting, and human errors among malicious exit relay operators.

5.1   Data Set Overlap

Only two exit relays were caught by both of our scanners, exitmap as well as HoneyConnector. The first one, 5A2A51D4, was located in Taiwan and was found to sniff IMAP credentials as well as to inject HTML code (see Appendix B). While the HTML code was not malicious at the time we tested the relay, it is possible that the injected code changed over time or that the code changed depending on the HTTP Host header sent by the Tor user. The second relay which was located in Hong Kong, 229C3722, ran sslstrip as well as sniffed FTP credentials.

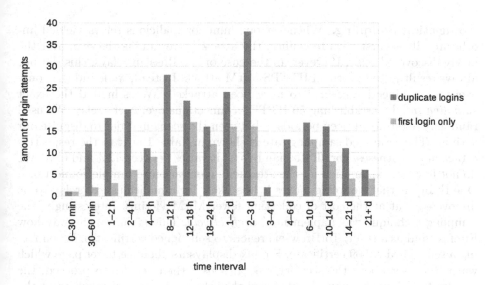

Fig. 7. The time interval between the honey connection and the login attempts

5.2   The "Russian HTTPS Group"

Interestingly, we have reason to believe that all relays in Table 1 whose fingerprint ends with a † were run by *the same person or group of people*. This becomes evident when analyzing the self-signed certificates which were injected for the MitM attacks. In every case, the certificate chain consisted of only two nodes which both belonged to a "Main Authority" and the root certificate of all chains—shown in Appendix A—was *identical*. This means that these attacks can be traced back to a common origin even though it is not clear where or what this origin is as we will discuss later. Apart from the identical root certificate, these relays had other properties in common. First, with the exception of 8F9121BF which was located in the U.S., they were *all located in Russia*. Upon investigating their IP addresses, we discovered that most of the Russian relays were run in the network of a virtual private system (VPS) provider. Several IP addresses were also located in the same netblock, namely 176.99.12.246, 176.99.9.114, 176.99.9.111, and 176.99.11.182. All these IP addresses are part of the netblock GlobaTel-net which spans 176.99.0.0/20. Furthermore, the malicious exit relays all used Tor version 0.2.2.37.[6] Given its age, this is a rather uncommon version number among relays. In fact, we found only two benign exit relays—in Switzerland and the U.S.—which are running the same version. We suspect that the attackers might have a precompiled version of Tor which they simply copy to newly purchased systems to spawn new exit relays. Unfortunately, we have no data which would allow us to verify when this series of attacks began. However, the root certificate shown in Appendix A indicates that it was created on February 12, 2013.

Connection Sampling. Whenever our hunt for malicious relays yielded another result, we first tried to confirm the attack by rerunning the scan over the newly discovered relay. However, in the case of the Russian relays, this did not always result in the expected HTTPS MitM attack. Instead, we found that only every nth connection seemed to have been attacked. We estimated the exact *sampling rate* by establishing 50 HTTPS connections over every relay. We used randomly determined sleep periods in between the scans in order to disguise our activity. The estimated sampling rate is shown in Table 1 next to the respective attack in parentheses. For all Russian relays, it varies between 12% and 68%. We do not have an explanation for the attacker's motivation to sample connections. One theory is that sampling makes it less likely for a malicious exit relay to be discovered; but at the cost of collecting fewer MitM victims. Interestingly, the sampling technique was implemented *ineffectively*. This is due to the way how Firefox (and as a result TorBrowser) reacts to self-signed certificates. When facing a self-signed X.509 certificate, Firefox displays its about:certerror page which warns the user about the security risk. If a user then decides to proceed, the certificate is *fetched again*. We observed that the malicious exit relays treat the certificate re-fetching as a separate connection whose success again depends on the relay's sampling rate. As a result, a sampling rate of n means that a MitM attack will only be successfully with a probability of n^2 rather than n.

Who Is the Attacker?. An important question is where on the path from the exit relay to the destination the attacker is located. At first glance, one might

---

[6] For comparison, as of January 2014, the current stable version is 0.2.4.20. Version 0.2.2.37 was declared stable on June 6th, 2012.

blame the exit relay operator. However, it is also possible that the actual attack happens *after* the exit relay, e.g., in the exit relay's ISP, the network backbone, or the destination's ISP. In fact, such an incident was documented in 2006 for a relay located in China [7]. With respect to our data, we cannot entirely rule out that the HTTPS MitM attacks were actually run by an upstream provider of the Russian exit relays. However, we consider it unlikely for the following reasons: *1)* the relays were located in diverse IP address blocks and there were numerous other relays in Russia which did not exhibit this behavior, *2)* one of the relays was even located in the U.S., *3)* there are no other reported cases on the Internet involving a certification authority called "Main Authority", and *4)* the relays frequently disappeared after they were assigned the BadExit flag. The identity of the attacker is difficult to ascertain. The relays did not publish any contact information, nicknames, or revealed other hints which could enable educated guesses regarding the attacker's origin.

Destination Targeting. While Tor's nature as an anonymity tool renders targeting individuals difficult,[7] an attacker can target classes of users based on their communication *destination*. For example, an attacker could decide to only tamper with connections going to the fictional www.insecure-bank.com. Interestingly, we found evidence for exactly that behavior; at some point the Russian relays began to target at least facebook.com. We tested the HTTPS version of the Alexa top 10 web sites [1] but were unable to trigger MitM attacks despite numerous connection attempts. Popular Russian web sites such as the mail provider mail.ru and the social networking site vk.com also remained unaffected. Note that it is possible that the relays targeted additional web sites we did not test for. Enumerating targeted web sites would mean probing thousands of different web sites. We have no explanation for the targeting of destinations. It might be another attempt to delay discovery by vigilant users. However, according to previous research [16], social networking appears to be just as popular over Tor as it is over the open Internet. As a result, limiting the attack to facebook.com might not delay discovery significantly.

5.3 The "International Sniffer Group"

A group of international exit relays in Table 2 is obviously colluding with the clear intent of sniffing credentials as the credentials that were sent over these nodes were tested in batches. Since the relays are spread over Europe and the U.S., we called it the International group, even though it is possible that they are all operated by the same single person. It consists of the five relays "Chupacabras", "AlleyCAT", "NennoExit", "Aragaun" (Previously "UMBRELLAx-CORP" at the same IP address), and "ShredOwl", located in the U.S., Germany, Netherlands, and Sweden. One of the nodes, "Chupacabras", moved from Germany to the U.S. during our evaluation.

---

[7] We assume of course that Tor users do not deliberately reveal their real identity, e.g., by posting on Internet forums under their real name.

5.4   The "Indian Sniffer Group"

The second group that stuck out during our evaluation is a group of *seven Indian exit relays* in Table 2. These relays were responsible for 104 out of all 255 reconnection attempts (41%) and employed a number of distinguishable reconnect patterns that are unique to this group. All of the seven nodes within this group were operated on dynamic allocated IP addresses belonging to the ISP "Mahanagar Telephone Nigam Ltd.", and had a bandwidth between 50 and 80 KB/s. All relays ran Tor in version 0.2.3.25 on Microsoft Windows; four relays ran Windows 7, while three relays ran Windows Vista. Furthermore, the nodes seemed to change their IP address every six hours, resulting in bad uptime statistics for them. Because of the low bandwidth bundled with the poor uptime statistics, the probability of Tor exit traffic being routed over these nodes is very low.

Most login attempts were made by using the Mail2Web service [28] which obfuscates the real source of the connection. In fact, Mail2Web was solely used by the group of Indian nodes. However, fingerprints of Mozilla Thunderbird version 3.1.20 on Windows Vista was used over Tor on two occasions in November. For reconnecting with FTP, either Microsoft Internet Explorer or Mozilla Firefox was used. All connections made with Internet Explorer originated from one of the nodes which was running at this time which suggests that this browser used the Internet connection directly. All login attempts made with Firefox were conducted through the Tor network but from different exit relays which suggests the use of TorBrowser. The variety of software used and the number of concurrent IP addresses point in the direction that those nodes are operated by more than one individual, although not conclusively.

5.5   Who Reused the Bait Credentials?

For HoneyConnector, the majority of reconnects—145, or 57%—was conducted over the Tor network, i.e., the IP address was part of the Tor network (verified using ExoneraTor [29]) but not the relay which sniffed the credentials. This comes as no surprise since exit relay operators are expected to be familiar with the Tor network. Therefore, it is difficult to conclude who initiated the reconnect. However, 45 reconnections (18%) originated from the same IP address as the exit relay which originally sniffed the credentials. This means that the malicious operator could have used the exit relay for a direct connection (i.e., not over Tor) or Tor was manually configured to use this particular relay as exit. 16% (41) of all reconnections used the service Mail2Web. Since the servers of this service connect directly to a given IMAP server, it is not possible to assess if the user was additionally using Tor, or used this service directly. However, this service was only used by the operator or group of operators from the Indian exit nodes. In 22 cases (9%) of all reconnections, the source IP address was no Tor relay and we were unable to associated the IP address with any VPN service, meaning that the connection was likely originating from a host under the direct control of the relay operator. Within this subset, we found connections from IP addresses that belonged to hosting companies, mobile UMTS Internet services, and private home connections by consumer Internet service providers. One IP address was found to belong to a Japanese university. In two cases, the reverse DNS record of the respective IP address suggests that a VPN service was used.

The software used for the reconnections can also reveal information about the relay operator as its default configuration can be unsuitable for the Tor network [8], and improper usage of client software can lead to deanonymization [3, 4]. This includes default login credentials such as "mozilla@example.com" as password for an anonymous FTP login with Mozilla Firefox, attempts to fetch data over side channels, e.g., Mozilla Thunderbird trying to fetch an XML file containing data for automatic configuration, or simply the IP address of freely available web services such as Mail2Web. The largest amount of reconnections— 117, or 46%—contained no hints or direct information on the software used. Mail2Web was used in 41 (or 16%) reconnections, but since it is a web service connecting to IMAP accounts through a web interface, no additional information could be inferred. All credentials used were sent over Indian relays (see Section 5.4). The connections by Mail2Web were easily recognizable due to the reverse record of the respective IP addresses. The Indian nodes as well as the operator of the British node "AstralNode" used Thunderbird for IMAP reconnections (20% or 51 reconnections) since Thunderbird issues a request for an XML file during account setup containing instructions for automatic configuration. The German exit node "h0rny30c3" is also very likely to have used Thunderbird due to connection patterns, but the request for the auto configuration XML file was not found. As for FTP reconnections, we could identify the use of Firefox and Internet Explorer. The Firefox-based TorBrowser is the browser of choice in the Tor Browser Bundle (TBB), and as such the recommended way of accessing the Tor network. Firefox was used in 25 reconnection (10%), Internet Explorer was used for 21 reconnections (9%).

5.6 Human Errors During Reconnections

Using sniffed credentials is harder than it seems, and we found multiple peculiarities in our logs that we would like to share as well. Out of all 255 reconnection attempts, 31 (or 12%) were made with incorrect credentials, in most cases with apparent copy-paste errors by omitting characters at the beginning or the end of a password; specifically when punctuation or special characters were used. Other instances included multiple pastes of the same password, omitted parts of the IMAP username or typographical errors showing that these passwords were typed manually. We were also able to observe that sniffers monitoring multiple protocols can become confused as to what credentials to use for which service: the node "SuperDuperLative" for example used IMAP bait credentials for FTP reconnections, twice. The operator also tried the password with and without quotation marks in another instance. The operator of the Indian node "atlas" was mixing two different username and password combinations, trying to authenticate for one username with the password of another username. The operator of the relay "pcrrtor1" used a seemingly random password that was not sent as part of any bait connection at all from our side. The operators of "Chupacabras" and "ShredOwl" seem to have pasted the FTP URL into the wrong browser—in both cases they revealed their true IP address by using Google Chrome before switching to Firefox through Tor, clearly visible due to the default anonymous credentials tried by Firefox.

The two biggest spikes of IMAP logins seen in Fig. 6 were made by using the configuration wizard of Mozilla Thunderbird for creating a new connection to an IMAP server, in which the e-mail client uses multiple login attempts to automate setup and to verify if the connection was configured properly. The logs also indicate that further attempts were done afterwards to test and troubleshoot the configuration but since it was not possible to log in with the snooped credentials, Thunderbird would only display error messages. However, most of the recorded logins had either errors in their sequences, certain erratic-appearing client fingerprints with differing reconnection times, pointing us to the conclusion that all reconnections were conducted manually. One exception here could be the reconnections related to the relay "SuperDuperLative": most of these reconnections were made either around a static time or by processing a whole batch of sniffed credentials within a certain timeframe while using Tor.

5.7   Implications for Tor Users

A question which is of interest to Tor users is "what fraction of exit relays is malicious?". To answer this question, it is tempting but insufficient to divide our results by the total number of exit relays, e.g., $\frac{65}{1000} \approx 6\%$. This calculation is biased as it does not consider the *change of exit relays* over time. This metric is captured by the *churn rate*, i.e., the rate at which new exit relays join the network and existing ones leave.

We obtained an idea of the network's churn rate by determining the amount of unique exit relays (based on the relay's identity fingerprint) which were part of the network from September 2013 to March 2014. For every unique relay, we also calculate the amount of hours, it served the net-

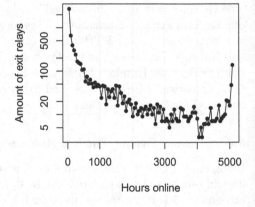

Fig. 8. The amount of hours, all 6,835 unique exit relays spent online in between Sept. 2014 and Mar. 2014. 2,698 exit relays vanished after being part of the network for 50 hours or less.

work. In total, we observed *6,835 unique exit relay identity fingerprints*. The distribution—with intervals of 50 hours—is illustrated in Fig. 8. A total of 2,698 exit relays was online for only 50 hours or less in these seven months. 137 exit relays were online for 5,052 hours or more—which is close to the maximum of 5,088 hours. The diagram clearly shows that given the network's considerable churn rate, our scanners tested many more relays than the overall amount of exit relays at a given point in time. An estimate for the probability of selecting a malicious exit relay in a circuit would also require the consideration of a relay's observed bandwidth.

To protect against sniffing exit relays, end-to-end encryption should be used whenever possible. In particular, HTTPS should be preferred over its unencrypted alternative. The same applies to other protocols which have more secure TLS-based alternatives, e.g., SMTPS or IMAPS. Note that TorBrowser's HTTPS-Everywhere extension automatically redirects the user to many HTTPS-enabled web sites whenever possible. Outside the Tor network, server operators can and should help by enabling ubiquitous encryption for all services they run, e.g., by making use of HTTP Strict Transport Security [14].

5.8 Limitations

For both our frameworks, exitmap and HoneyConnector, performing attribution is problematic, meaning that it is difficult to distinguish if the attacker is the relay operator or any other entity along the path from the exit relay to the destination. This can be for example the relay's ISP, any other ISP along the path, or a nation-state adversary. Even though it is in our opinion unlikely (due to the ease of running a malicious Tor exit relay), it cannot be ruled out entirely. Nevertheless, if such attacks seem to be run by an exit relay whereas they are in fact conducted by the network backbone, it is beneficial to all Tor users that this relay is assigned the BadExit flag.

5.9 Ethical Aspects

Due to exitmap's modular architecture, it can be used for various unintended and even unethical purposes. For example, modules for web site scraping or online voting manipulation come to mind. All sites which naively bind identities to IP addresses might be an attractive target. While we do not endorse such actions, we point out that these activities are hard to stop and will continue to happen and already happen regardless; with or without scanner. If somebody decides to abuse our scanner for such actions, it will at least spare the Tor network's resources more than a naive design. As a result, we believe that by publishing our code, the benefit to the public outweighs the damage caused by unethical usage.

6 Thwarting HTTPS MitM Attacks

The discovery of destination targeting made us reconsider defense mechanisms. Unfortunately, we cannot rule out that there are additional, yet undiscovered exit relays which target low-profile web sites. If we wanted to achieve high coverage, we would have to probe millions of web sites; and considering the connection sampling discussed in Section 5.2, this has to be done repeatedly! After all, an attacker is able to *arbitrarily reduce the scope* of the attack but we are *unable to arbitrarily scale* our scanner. This observation motivated another defense mechanism which is discussed in this section.

6.1   Threat Model

We consider an adversary who is controlling the upstream Internet connection of a small fraction of exit relays.[8] The adversary's goal is to run HTTPS-based MitM attacks against Tor users. We further expect the adversary to make an effort to stay under the radar in order to delay discovery. The actual MitM attack is conducted by injecting self-signed certificates in the hope that users are not scared off by the certificate warning page. Our threat model does not cover adversaries who control certificate authorities which would enable them to issue valid certificates to avoid TorBrowser's warning page. This includes several countries as well as organizations which are part of TorBrowser's root certificate store. Furthermore, we cannot defend against adversaries who control a significant fraction of the Tor network's exit bandwidth.

6.2   Multi Circuit Certificate Verification

As long as an attacker is unable to tamper with all connections to a given destination,[9] MitM attacks can be detected by fetching a public key over *differing paths in the network*. This approach was picked up by several projects including Perspectives [37], Convergence [19] and Crossbear [6]. In this section, we discuss a patch for TorBrowser which achieves the same goal but is adapted to the Tor network. Apart from NoScript and HTTPS-Everywhere, TorBrowser contains another important extension: *Torbutton*. This extension provides the actual interface between TorBrowser and the local Tor process. It directs TorBrowser's traffic to Tor's SOCKS port and exposes a number of features such as the possibility to create a new identity. Torbutton already contains rudimentary code to talk to Tor over the local control port. The control port—typically bound to 127.0.0.1:9151—provides local applications with an interface to control Tor. For example, Torbutton's "New Identity" feature is implemented by sending the NEWNYM signal which instructs Tor to switch to clean circuits so that new application requests do not share circuits with old requests. Torbutton already implements a useful code base for us which made us decide to implement our extension as a patch for Torbutton rather than build an independent extension.

6.3   Extension Design

Our patch hooks into the browser event DOMContentLoaded which is triggered whenever a document (but not necessarily stylesheets and images) is loaded and parsed by the browser. We then check if the URI of the page contains "about:certerror" as TorBrowser displays this page whenever it encounters a self-signed certificate. However, it is not clear whether the certificate is genuinely self-signed or part of an attack. In order to be able to distinguish between these two cases, our patch now attempts to re-fetch the certificate over at least one

---

[8] By "fraction", we mean a relay's bandwidth as it determines how likely a client is to select the relay as part of its circuit.

[9] This would be the case if an attacker controls the destination.

additional and distinct Tor circuit as illustrated in Fig. 9. We create a fresh circuit by sending `SIGNAL NEWNYM` to Tor's control port. Afterwards, we re-fetch the certificate by issuing an `XMLHttpRequest`. If the SHA-1 fingerprints of both certificates match, the certificate is probably genuine.[10] Otherwise, the user might have fallen prey to a MitM attack. False positives are possible, though: large sites could have different certificates for different geographical regions. Note that we are not very likely to witness many false positives as our code is only run upon observing self-signed certificates or certificates which somehow trigger the about:certerror warning page.

Our extension also informs the user about a potential MitM attack. In case of differing certificates, we open a browser dialog which informs the user about the situation. A screenshot of our design prototype is shown in Fig. 10. The dialog points out that this is likely an attack and asks the user for permission to send the data to the Tor Project for further inspection. The submitted data contains the *exit relays* used for certificate fetching as well as the *observed certificates*. We transmit no other data which could be used to identify users; as a result, certificate submission is anonymous. While it is technically possible

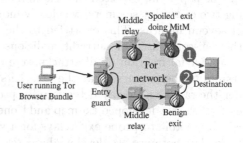

Fig. 9. A user stumbles across a self-signed certificate ❶ which could be an indication for an HTTPS MitM attack ran by a malicious exit relay. To verify if the certificate is genuine, the client re-fetches it over an independent exit relay ❷ and checks if the two certificates match or not.

to transmit the data silently, we believe that users would not appreciate this and consider it as "phoning home". As a result, we seek to obtain informed consent.

6.4 Limitations

Our threat model does not consider adversaries with the ability to issue valid certificates. While our extension could easily be extended to conduct certificate comparison for all observed certificates, it would flood the Tor network with certificate re-fetches. To make matters worse, the overwhelming majority of these re-fetches would not even expose any attacks. There exist other techniques to foil CA-capable adversaries such as certificate

Fig. 10. The popup window in TorBrowser which informs the user about the potential HTTPS MitM attack. The user can agree to submitting the gathered information to the Tor Project for further inspection.

---

[10] Note that powerful adversaries might be able to control multiple exit relays, network backbones, or even the destination.

pinning [20]. By default, our patch re-fetches a self-signed X.509 certificate only once. An attacker who is controlling a significant fraction of exit relays might be able to conduct a MitM attack for the first as well as for the second fetch. Nevertheless, we would eventually expose the attack; it would simply be a matter of time until a client selects two independent exit relays for certificate comparison.

7   Conclusions

In this paper, we revisited the trustworthiness of Tor exit relays. After developing two exit relay scanners, we closely monitored the Tor network over a period of several months. This effort led to the discovery of 65 relays which were either misconfigured or outright malicious. Interestingly, we have evidence that a non-trivial fraction of all attacks were coordinated rather than isolated. Our results further suggest that the attackers made an active effort to remain under the radar and delay detection. To protect the Tor network from malicious exit relays, we developed exitmap and HoneyConnector; easily extensible scanners which are able to probe exit relays for a variety of MitM and traffic sniffing attacks. Furthermore, we developed a patch for TorBrowser's Torbutton extension which is able to fetch self-signed X.509 certificates over different network paths in order to verify their trustworthiness. All our source code is freely available at http://www.cs.kau.se/philwint/spoiled_onions.

Acknowledgments. We want to thank Internetfonden whose research grant funded the authors from Karlstad University. This work has also been supported by COMET K1, FFG – Austrian Research Promotion Agency. Finally, we want to thank Aaron Gibson, Georg Koppen, Harald Lampesberger, and Linus Nordberg for helpful feedback and suggestions.

References

[1] Alexa: The top 500 sites on the web (2013),
     http://www.alexa.com/topsites
[2] Bernstein, D.J.: Curve25519: New Diffie-Hellman speed records. In: Yung, M.,
     Dodis, Y., Kiayias, A., Malkin, T. (eds.) PKC 2006. LNCS, vol. 3958, pp. 207–
     228. Springer, Heidelberg (2006),
     http://cr.yp.to/ecdh/curve25519-20060209.pdf
[3] Le Blond, S., et al.: One Bad Apple Spoils the Bunch: Exploiting P2P Applications
     to Trace and Profile Tor Users. In: LEET. USENIX (2011),
     https://www.usenix.org/legacy/events/leet11/tech/
     full_papers/LeBlond.pdf
[4] Le Blond, S., et al.: Spying the World from Your Laptop: Identifying and Profiling
     Content Providers and Big Downloaders in BitTorrent. In: LEET. USENIX (2010),
     https://www.usenix.org/legacy/event/leet10/tech/
     full_papers/LeBlond.pdf

[5] Chakravarty, S., Portokalidis, G., Polychronakis, M., Keromytis, A.D.: Detecting Traffic Snooping in Tor Using Decoys. In: Sommer, R., Balzarotti, D., Maier, G. (eds.) RAID 2011. LNCS, vol. 6961, pp. 222–241. Springer, Heidelberg (2011), http://www.cs.columbia.edu/~mikepo/papers/tordecoys.raid11.pdf
[6] Crossbear, http://www.crossbear.org
[7] Dingledine, R.: Re: Holy shit I caught 1 (2006), http://archives.seul.org/or/talk/Aug-2006/msg00262.html
[8] Dingledine, R., Mathewson, N.: Anonymity Loves Company: Usability and the Network Effect. In: WEIS (2006), http://freehaven.net/doc/wupss04/usability.pdf
[9] Dingledine, R., Mathewson, N.: Tor Protocol Specification, https://gitweb.torproject.org/torspec.git?a=blob_plain;hb=HEAD;f=torspec.txt
[10] Dingledine, R., Mathewson, N., Syverson, P.: Tor: The Second-Generation Onion Router. In: USENIX Security. USENIX (2004), http://static.usenix.org/event/sec04/tech/full_papers/dingledine/dingledine.pdf
[11] Electronic Frontier Foundation. HTTPS Everywhere (2013), https://www.eff.org/https-everywhere
[12] Goldberg, I.: On the Security of the Tor Authentication Protocol. In: Danezis, G., Golle, P. (eds.) PET 2006. LNCS, vol. 4258, pp. 316–331. Springer, Heidelberg (2006), http://freehaven.net/anonbib/cache/tap:pet2006.pdf
[13] Haim, D.: SocksiPy - A Python SOCKS client module (2006), http://socksipy.sourceforge.net
[14] Hodges, J., Jackson, C., Barth, A.: HTTP Strict Transport Security, HSTS (2012), https://tools.ietf.org/html/rfc6797
[15] Hodges, J., Jackson, C., Barth, A.: RFC 6797: HTTP Strict Transport Security, HSTS (2012), https://tools.ietf.org/html/rfc6797
[16] Huber, M., Mulazzani, M., Weippl, E.: Tor HTTP Usage and Information Leakage. In: De Decker, B., Schaumüller-Bichl, I. (eds.) CMS 2010. LNCS, vol. 6109, pp. 245–255. Springer, Heidelberg (2010), http://freehaven.net/anonbib/cache/huber2010tor.pdf
[17] InformAction. NoScript (2013), http://noscript.net
[18] Known Bad Relays, https://trac.torproject.org/projects/tor/wiki/doc/badRelays
[19] Thoughtcrime Labs. Convergence (2011), http://convergence.io
[20] Langley, A.: Public key pinning (2011), https://www.imperialviolet.org/2011/05/04/pinning.html
[21] Lowe, G., Winters, P., Marcus, M.L.: The Great DNS Wall of China. Tech. rep. New York University (2007), http://cs.nyu.edu/~pcw216/work/nds/final.pdf
[22] Marlinspike, M.: sslstrip, http://www.thoughtcrime.org/software/sslstrip/
[23] Marlinspike, M.: tortunnel, http://www.thoughtcrime.org/software/tortunnel/
[24] McCoy, D., Bauer, K., Grunwald, D., Kohno, T., Sicker, D.C.: Shining Light in Dark Places: Understanding the Tor Network. In: Borisov, N., Goldberg, I. (eds.) PETS 2008. LNCS, vol. 5134, pp. 63–76. Springer, Heidelberg (2008), http://homes.cs.washington.edu/~yoshi/papers/Tor/PETS2008_37.pdf

[25] Paul, R.: Security expert used Tor to collect government e-mail passwords (2007), http://arstechnica.com/security/2007/09/security-expert-used-tor-to-collect-government-e-mail-passwords/

[26] Perry, M., Clark, E., Murdoch, S.: The Design and Implementation of the Tor Browser [DRAFT] (2013), https://www.torproject.org/projects/torbrowser/design/

[27] SkullSecurity. Passwords (2011), https://wiki.skullsecurity.org/Passwords

[28] SoftCom, Inc. Email Hosting Services, http://mail2web.com

[29] The Tor Project. ExoneraTor, https://exonerator.torproject.org

[30] The Tor Project. Relays with Exit, Fast, Guard, Stable, and HSDir flags, https://metrics.torproject.org/network.html#relayflags

[31] The Tor Project. Snakes on a Tor, https://gitweb.torproject.org/torflow.git/tree/HEAD:/NetworkScanners/ExitAuthority

[32] The Tor Project. Stem Docs, https://stem.torproject.org

[33] The Tor Project. TC: A Tor control protocol (Version 1), https://gitweb.torproject.org/torspec.git/blob/HEAD:/control-spec.txt

[34] TOR exit-node doing MITM attacks, http://www.teamfurry.com/wordpress/2007/11/20/tor-exit-node-doing-mitmattacks

[35] Torscanner, https://code.google.com/p/torscanner/

[36] Torsocks: use socks-friendly applications with Tor, https://code.google.com/p/torsocks/

[37] Wendlandt, D., Andersen, D.G., Perrig, A.: Perspectives: Improving SSH-style Host Authentication with Multi-Path Probing. In: ATC. USENIX (2008), http://perspectivessecurity.files.wordpress.com/2011/07/perspectives_usenix08.pdf

A   Malicious X.509 Root Certificate

Below, the root certificate which was shared by all Russian and the single U.S. exit relay is shown. While the domain authority.com does exist as of May 2014, it appears to be unrelated to the CA "Main Authority", the issuer.

```
 1  Certificate:
 2   Data:
 3    Version: 3 (0x2)
 4    Serial Number: 16517615612733694071 (0xe53a5be2bd702077)
 5   Signature Algorithm: sha1WithRSAEncryption
 6    Issuer: C=US, ST=Nevada, L=Newbury, O=Main Authority,
 7     OU=Certificate Management,
 8     CN=main.authority.com/emailAddress=cert@authority.com
 9   Validity
10    Not Before: Feb 12 08:13:07 2013 GMT
11    Not After : Feb 10 08:13:07 2023 GMT
12   Subject: C=US, ST=Nevada, L=Newbury, O=Main Authority,
13     OU=Certificate Management,
14     CN=main.authority.com/emailAddress=cert@authority.com
15   Subject Public Key Info:
16    Public Key Algorithm: rsaEncryption
17     Public-Key: (1024 bit)
18     Modulus:
19      00:da:5d:5f:06:06:dc:8e:f1:8c:70:b1:58:12:0a:
20      41:0e:b9:23:cc:0e:6f:bc:22:5a:05:12:09:cf:ac:
21      85:9d:95:2c:3a:93:5d:c9:04:c9:4e:72:15:6a:10:
22      f1:b6:cd:e4:8e:ad:5a:7f:1e:d2:b5:a7:13:e9:87:
```

```
23      d8:aa:a0:24:15:24:84:37:d1:69:8e:31:8f:5c:2e:
24      92:e3:f4:9c:c3:bc:18:7d:cf:b7:ba:b2:5b:32:61:
25      64:05:cd:1f:c3:b5:28:e1:f5:a5:1c:35:db:0f:e8:
26      c3:1d:e3:e3:33:9c:95:61:6d:b7:a6:ad:de:2b:0d:
27      d2:88:07:5f:63:0d:9c:1e:cf
28    Exponent: 65537 (0x10001)
29  X509v3 extensions:
30    X509v3 Subject Key Identifier:
31    07:42:E0:52:A7:DC:A5:C5:0F:C5:
32    AF:03:56:CD:EB:42:8D:96:00:D6
33    X509v3 Authority Key Identifier:
34    keyid:07:42:E0:52:A7:DC:A5:C5:0F:C5:
35          AF:03:56:CD:EB:42:8D:96:00:D6
36    DirName:/C=US/ST=Nevada/L=Newbury/O=Main Authority
37      /OU=Certificate Management
38      /CN=main.authority.com/emailAddress=cert@authority.com
39    serial:E5:3A:5B:E2:BD:70:20:77
40
41    X509v3 Basic Constraints:
42    CA:TRUE
43  Signature Algorithm: sha1WithRSAEncryption
44    23:55:73:1b:5c:77:e4:4b:14:d7:71:b4:09:11:4c:ed:2d:08:
45    ae:7e:37:21:2e:a7:a0:49:6f:d1:9f:c8:21:77:76:55:71:f9:
46    8c:7b:2c:e8:a9:ea:7f:2f:98:f7:45:44:52:b5:46:a4:09:4b:
47    ce:88:90:bd:28:ed:05:8c:b6:14:79:a0:f3:d3:1f:30:d6:59:
48    5c:dd:e6:e6:cd:3a:a4:69:8f:2d:0c:49:e7:df:01:52:b3:34:
49    38:97:c5:9a:c3:fa:f3:61:b8:89:0f:d2:d9:a5:48:e6:7b:67:
50    48:4a:72:3f:da:28:3e:65:bf:7a:c2:96:27:dd:c0:1a:ea:51:
51    f5:09
```

B   Injected HTML Code

The following HTML code was injected by the relay 5A2A51D4 (see Table 1 and Table 2). It was appended right in front of the closing HTML tag.

```
1 <br>
2 <img src="http://111.251.157.184/pics.cgi"
3  width="1" height="1">
```

When requesting the image link inside the HTML code, the server responds with another HTML document. The full HTTP response is shown below.

```
 1 HTTP/1.1 200 OK
 2 Date: Tue, 14 Jan 2014 17:12:08 GMT
 3 Server: Apache/2.2.22 (Ubuntu)
 4 Vary: Accept-Encoding
 5 Transfer-Encoding: chunked
 6 Content-Type: text/html
 7
 8
 9 <HTML>
10 <HEAD>
11 <TITLE>No Title</TITLE>
12 </HEAD>
13 <BODY>
14
15 </BODY>
16 </HTML>
```

Author Index